PHASER
BY EXAMPLE

**Pello Xabier Altadill
& Richard Davey**

Pello Xabier Altadill

Richard Davey

Disclaimer

This book is self-published by Pello Altadill, and it is not affiliated with Phaser Studio. If you encounter any issues or have questions about the content of this book, please contact me through LinkedIn instead of reaching out to Phaser Studio. I appreciate your understanding.

Authors

How do you do fellow kids?

I've spent some time making games for jams using Phaser. I had to learn by doing and I also learned a lot in those jams, getting feedback and sharing amazing ideas.

Phaser does not require any heavy environment to build games, it's just JavaScript and you can try it on your browser. The source is right there and you will never depend on arbitrary corporate decisions.

I decided to get some of the games I developed to put them together in a book, as a showcase of the well-known game genres. During the struggle to build games you rely heavily on examples and code snippets, and this is precisely the main goal of this text.

Each of these games were created in a weekend and you should not expect them to be optimized. But they explain how to build playable stuff. Along with that, I added some advice that I hope you may find it useful. So, here are the examples, the tools, and some ideas. The rest is up to you!

Pello Xabier Altadill Izura
https://pello.io
https://github.com/pxai

Foreword by Richard Davey, creator of Phaser

I've been working on Phaser for over 11 years now. It's been an incredible journey and I've met so many amazing people along the way. I've seen the framework used in ways I never imagined, and I've seen games created with it that have blown my mind.

When I first started working on Phaser, I had no idea it would become so popular. I just wanted to create a framework that would make it easier for people like Pello to create games for the web. I wanted to make it accessible to everyone, regardless of their skill level.

Like all popular tools, it has evolved over time. It has grown in complexity and features, but at its core, it's still the same framework I started working on all those years ago. In this book you'll find a whole bunch of games that Pello has created using Phaser. They cover a wide range of genres and styles, and they show just how versatile the framework can be. You'll also find lots of content that I've written that dives into the core concepts of Phaser in more details, and hopefully provides a useful starting point for those new to the framework.

I hope you enjoy reading this book as much as I've enjoyed working on Phaser. And I hope it inspires you to create your own games, and to share them with the world.

Richard Davey

https://phaser.io

Contents

0. Introduction — 12
   - Phaser — 12
   - How is the book organized — 13
1. Basic game: runner — 14
   - Init project — 15
   - Player code — 16
   - Generating obstacles, coins and clouds — 16
   - The game! — 21
   - Gameover — 26
   - Other runners or similar games — 29
2. Space Shooter: Starshake — 30
   - Init project — 31
   - Loader — 32
   - Light Particle — 35
   - Generating foes — 36
   - Foes — 42
   - Foes shot — 47
   - Explosion — 50
   - Player — 51
   - Shot — 55
   - Shooting pattern — 56
   - Power Up — 58
   - The game! — 60
   - Scene Effect — 69
   - Splash — 72
   - Transition page — 75
   - Outro — 77
   - Other shooter or similar games — 80
3. Platformer: WallHammer — 81
   - Tiled — 82
   - Init project — 82
   - Loader — 83
   - Bat — 87
   - Zombie — 89
   - Turn — 91

Lunchbox	92
Particle	94
Player code	97
Blow	104
Platform	105
Brick	107
Coin	108
The game!	110
Splash	125
Transition page	128
Outro	131
Other platformers or similar games	133
4. Puzzles: PushPull	134
Init project	135
Loader	136
Block	139
Exit	139
BlockGroup	140
The game!	146
Splash	154
Transition page	158
Outro	160
Other puzzles or similar games	163
5. Roguelike: Bobble Dungeon	164
Init project	165
Loader	166
Bat	170
Bubble	172
Coin	175
Key	177
Dust	178
Fireball	179
Wizard	180
Matter Gravity Fix	183
Dungeon generator	184
See-Saw	192
Player	193
The game!	202

Splash	210
Transition page	214
Outro	216
Other roguelike or similar games	219
Other games using matter physics	219
6. Tell me a story: Marstranded	221
Init project	222
Loader	223
Hole	227
Drone	228
Object	231
Utils	236
Player	238
Braun	243
Game	244
Splash	254
Transition page	257
Outro	262
Other story telling games	265
7. Multiplayer games	266
Blastemup: multiplayer with websockets.	267
Zenbaki: a game for Twitch chat.	276
Other Twitch games	296
8. 3D: Fate	298
Init	299
Bootloader	300
Story	303
Bullet Hell	309
Lightning	311
Utils	312
Splash	314
Game	317
GameOver	330
Outro	332
Reference	334
9. Deep dive into Phaser	335
What is Phaser?	336
The Core Concepts of Phaser	337

10. Detailed look into Game Objects — 359
- Alpha Component — 360
- Blend Mode Component — 362
- Bounds Component — 365
- Crop Component — 367
- Data Manager — 368
- Data Manager Methods — 370
- Depth Component — 382
- Game Object Creator — 384
- Game Object Factory — 391
- Game Objects — 394
- Mask Component — 399
- Origin Component — 402
- Pipeline Component — 404
- Scroll Factor Component — 406
- Sprites and Images — 407
- Transform Component — 408
- Visible Component — 414

11. Cookbook — 416
- Same sound with variants — 417
- Actions on animation events — 417
- Mouse right and left click — 417
- Screen Transitions — 417
- Lightning effect — 418
- Rain or Snow effect — 418
- Lights in the dark — 418
- Underwater swimming effect — 418
- Infinite scrolling background — 418
- Dynamic map — 419
- Adding/Removing tiles from a tiled map — 419
- Map building — 419
- Composed game objects — 419
- Find paths and move foes automatically — 419
- Enemies shooting at player — 420
- Detect screen limit — 420
- Jump simulation on an isometric view — 420
- Parabolic shot — 420
- Bullet hell — 420

Ships in formation	421
Life bar	421
Typing effect	421
Sensors	421
Adding video	422
Valid Words	422
Keep a scoreboard	422
Windows build	422
Index of games	423
12. Assets	**445**
Fonts	446
Graphic assets and Pixel Art	447
Audio assets	449
Converting/Editing your audio assets	450
Maps	451
13. Build & Delivery	**456**
Static HTML	457
NodeJS + Local phaser library	458
NodeJS + Local Phaser with modules	460
Gulp	461
Webpack	465
Parcel	468
Vite	470
Online: phasereditor2d	471
Online: repl.it	471
Online: codesandbox	471
Converting to Windows app	472
Automating itch.io upload	472
Netlify publish	472
14. Juice	**473**
Ideas	474
References	476
15. Jams	**478**
Why you should participate in a jam	479
Jam types	481
Rule of thumb	486
16. 4:44 Rule	**487**
How is it applied?	488

- Just for jams? ... 490
- 17 Level design ... 491
  - Some tips ... 492
  - References ... 503
- 18 Further reading ... 504
  - Other environments ... 505
  - Sites ... 506
  - Youtube ... 506
  - Books ... 507

0. Introduction

You know the story. As a kid, I wanted to understand and learn to make video games. I was young and stupid. Now I'm just stupid but I still want to build games, just for fun. This book explains how to build games using the Phaser framework. We will start from the simplest game and then we will embark on a journey through different genres, where we'll introduce new concepts and Phaser tools for them.

Apart from showing the guts of these games, we'll also dip our toes in other crucial areas like assets management, building and delivery, and a bit of game design. Nothing too fancy just some advice that you may find useful in your journey as a creator; because when it comes to creating games, at least if you want to do it right, it goes far beyond programming. There are many other brainy books about game producing, level design, theory, etc. to go deeper. For now, I'm presuming that you're solo so I will try to put things in your backpack that I wish somebody had told me when I started.

First of all, you must know that there are many people making games. That wonderful idea that you think you have is already implemented in different ways and genres. So, don't get too excited because probably your mastermind plan is not that good. But don't give up because at least you'll learn while building and failing. And there are chances that your worst idea turns out good.

Phaser

Phaser is an open-source framework for building HTML5 games. It uses JavaScript or (TypeScript in the latest version). Phaser allows you to program games just using an editor and a web browser. In addition to that, you can easily create a continuous building system as you would do in any frontend application using Gulp, Webpack, Parcel or other tools as we will see later.

There are other bigger, greater tools and names out for game creators. But as a developer, I like Phaser because the development process is very similar to any other web project. They provide the library but you can set up a building system around it and have total fine-grained control of the whole process. Also, because it's built on a well-known language and a familiar environment: the web. Creating a game and publishing it on the web is pretty straightforward.

To build and run the games, you can just create an HTML file, add a reference to the Phaser library and add JavaScript code. However, in the examples of this book the code is organized in separate files to make it easier to explain and understand. You can see these examples and much more in my repository:

https://github.com/pxai/phasergames

How is the book organized

Games are not just software but also artistic creations. As creations the possibilities are endless and I can't pretend to cover the infinite. Here, I will try to offer a showcase of the most common classic game genres while introducing different aspects of games: scenes, animations, tweens, maps, physics engines, etc.

Then is up to you to get these tools and build your own ideas.

After showing some games, I introduce some aspects of game development that are important to know or at least be aware of.

1. Basic game: runner

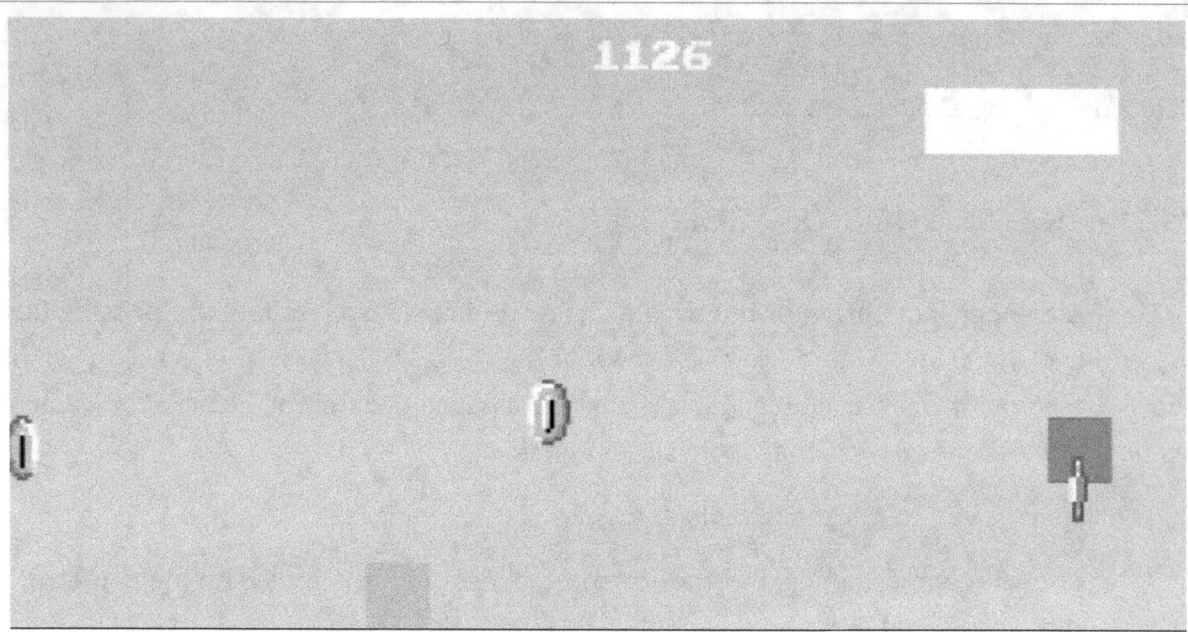

Source code: https://github.com/pxai/phasergames/tree/master/runner

Play it here: https://pello.itch.io/runner

1. Basic game: runner

Let's get started with a very basic game: an infinite runner. Probably you've played the dinosaur game in Chrome every time your Internet connection is lost. This is just the same idea but with rectangles and coins.

Init project

This init file holds the basic configuration of the Phaser game: this is where we define the scenes that take part in the game (like Splash, Game scene, Game Over scene, etc.), and it also configures screen size and position, physics type, etc.

```
import Phaser from "phaser";
import Game from "./game";
import GameOver from "./gameover";
```

This is the main configuration setup for the game:

```
const config = {
  width: 600,
  height: 300,
  scale: {
    mode: Phaser.Scale.FIT,
    autoCenter: Phaser.Scale.CENTER_BOTH,
  },
  autoRound: false,
  parent: "contenedor",
  physics: {
    default: "arcade",
    arcade: {
      gravity: { y: 350 },
      debug: false,
    },
  },
  scene: [Game, GameOver],
};

const game = new Phaser.Game(config);
```

During development phase, it's a good idea to set `debug` to `true`, so we will see outlines around any game object with physical properties.

Player code

This is the class that represents the player. It extends a very basic Phaser game object: a Rectangle. The player is set up in the constructor, where we provide him physics with a body and gravity.

```
class Player extends Phaser.GameObjects.Rectangle {
  constructor(scene, x, y, number) {
    super(scene, x, y, 32, 32, 0x00ff00);
    this.setOrigin(0.5);
    this.scene = scene;
    this.scene.add.existing(this);
    this.scene.physics.add.existing(this);
    this.body.collideWorldBounds = true;
    this.setScale(1);
    this.jumping = false;
    this.invincible = false;
    this.health = 10;
    this.body.mass = 10;
    this.body.setDragY = 10;
  }
}

export default Player;
```

This "player" sucks but don't worry, as we move forward, we will see animated and juicy characters.

Generating obstacles, coins and clouds

Figure 1.1 Red blocks are bad, coins are good.

1. Basic game: runner — Generating obstacles, coins and clouds

The game is a simple infinite runner where the player (the green rectangle) needs to avoid obstacles and pick coins. Those elements are randomly generated.

```
export default class Generator {
  constructor(scene) {
    this.scene = scene;
    this.scene.time.delayedCall(2000, () => this.init(), null, this);
    this.pinos = 0;
  }

  init() {
    this.generateCloud();
    this.generateObstacle();
    this.generateCoin();
  }
```

First is the function that generates the clouds. It creates a new cloud and then calls itself again after a random amount of time. This is done using the Phaser `time.delayedCall` function. Something similar is done for obstacles and coins.

```
  generateCloud() {
    new Cloud(this.scene);
    this.scene.time.delayedCall(
      Phaser.Math.Between(2000, 3000),
      () => this.generateCloud(),
      null,
      this
    );
  }

  generateObstacle() {
    this.scene.obstacles.add(
      new Obstacle(
        this.scene,
        800,
        this.scene.height - Phaser.Math.Between(32, 128)
      )
    );
    this.scene.time.delayedCall(
      Phaser.Math.Between(1500, 2500),
      () => this.generateObstacle(),
      null,
      this
    );
  }

  generateCoin() {
    this.scene.coins.add(
      new Coin(
        this.scene,
```

```
        800,
        this.scene.height - Phaser.Math.Between(32, 128)
      )
    );
    this.scene.time.delayedCall(
      Phaser.Math.Between(500, 1500),
      () => this.generateCoin(1),
      null,
      this
    );
  }
}
```

This is a game object that represents a cloud. It's a simple rectangle with a random size and position. We use a tween to move it from right to left, and then destroy it when it's out of the screen.

```
class Cloud extends Phaser.GameObjects.Rectangle {
  constructor(scene, x, y) {
    const finalY = y || Phaser.Math.Between(0, 100);
    super(scene, x, finalY, 98, 32, 0xffffff);
    scene.add.existing(this);
    const alpha = 1 / Phaser.Math.Between(1, 3);

    this.setScale(alpha);
    this.init();
  }

  init() {
    this.scene.tweens.add({
      targets: this,
      x: { from: 800, to: -100 },
      duration: 2000 / this.scale,
      onComplete: () => {
        this.destroy();
      },
    });
  }
}
```

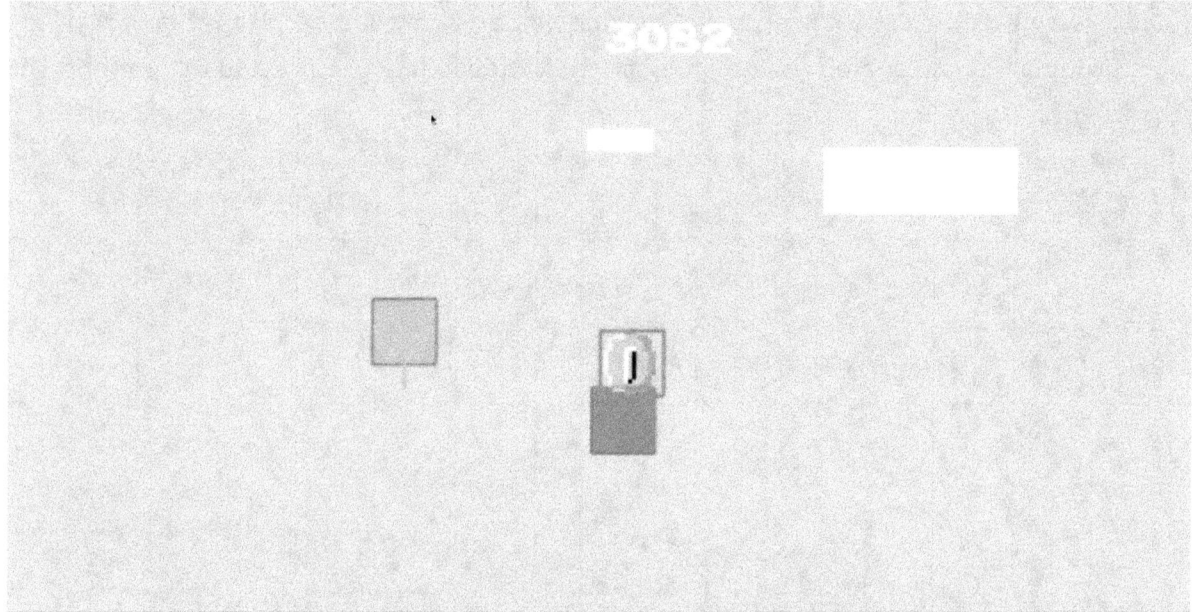

Figure 1.2 Clouds will just move on top without any consequence.

This is a game object that represents an obstacle. It works exactly like the cloud, but it's a red rectangle that is part of the obstacles group that we created in the game scene. It can kill the player if it touches it.

```
class Obstacle extends Phaser.GameObjects.Rectangle {
  constructor(scene, x, y) {
    super(scene, x, y, 32, 32, 0xff0000);
    scene.add.existing(this);
    scene.physics.add.existing(this);
    this.body.setAllowGravity(false);
    const alpha = 1 / Phaser.Math.Between(1, 3);

    this.init();
  }

  init() {
    this.scene.tweens.add({
      targets: this,
      x: { from: 820, to: -100 },
      duration: 2000,
      onComplete: () => {
        this.destroy();
      },
    });
  }
}
```

Next is a game object that represents a coin. It's an animated sprite that is part of the coins group that we created in the game scene. It moves like the previous cloud and the obstacle objects.

Figure 1.3 Coins are floating physical objects.

It can increase the player's score if it touches it.

```
class Coin extends Phaser.GameObjects.Sprite {
  constructor(scene, x, y) {
    super(scene, x, y, "coin");
    scene.add.existing(this);
    scene.physics.add.existing(this);
    this.body.setAllowGravity(false);
    const alpha = 1 / Phaser.Math.Between(1, 3);

    this.init();
  }

  init() {
    this.scene.tweens.add({
      targets: this,
      x: { from: 820, to: -100 },
      duration: 2000,
      onComplete: () => {
        this.destroy();
      },
    });

    const coinAnimation = this.scene.anims.create({
      key: "coin",
      frames: this.scene.anims.generateFrameNumbers("coin", {
        start: 0,
        end: 7,
      }),
      frameRate: 8,
    });
    this.play({ key: "coin", repeat: -1 });
```

```
    }
}
```

We could tweak this generator to increase the difficulty as the game advances.

The game!

This is the game scene itself! As any Phaser `Scene` object it uses three main methods:

- `preload`: where we load game assets: images, sprites, fonts, sounds, maps, etc.

- `create`: where we instantiate and start game elements like player, enemies, or obstacle generators. Also, this is where we define groups for obstacles, coins and clouds and most importantly: we define how these groups behave when they touch the player.

- `update`: the game loop. This method is called repeatedly by Phaser and this is where we can handle player input.

```
import Player from "./player";
import Generator from "./generator";

export default class Game extends Phaser.Scene {
  constructor() {
    super({ key: "game" });
    this.player = null;
    this.score = 0;
    this.scoreText = null;
  }

  init(data) {
    this.name = data.name;
    this.number = data.number;
  }
```

We use the `preload` method to load all the assets that we need for the game. We also set the score to `0` in the registry, so we can access it from other scenes.

```
  preload() {
    this.registry.set("score", "0");
    this.load.audio("coin", "assets/sounds/coin.mp3");
    this.load.audio("jump", "assets/sounds/jump.mp3");
    this.load.audio("dead", "assets/sounds/dead.mp3");
    this.load.audio("theme", "assets/sounds/theme.mp3");
    this.load.spritesheet("coin", "./assets/images/coin.png", {
```

1. Basic game: runner

```
    frameWidth: 32,
    frameHeight: 32,
  });
  this.load.bitmapFont(
    "arcade",
    "assets/fonts/arcade.png",
    "assets/fonts/arcade.xml"
  );
  this.score = 0;
}
```

Here we do several things.

- We use the create method to initialize the game.
- We set some variables to store width and height that we may need later.,
- We set the background color, and create the player, the obstacles, and the coins.
- We also create the keyboard input to listen to the space key.
- Also, we add a collider between the player and the obstacles and an overlap between the player and the coins. The key part there is to set a function that will be called when the player overlaps with a coin or hits an obstacle.

```
create() {
  this.width = this.sys.game.config.width;
  this.height = this.sys.game.config.height;
  this.center_width = this.width / 2;
  this.center_height = this.height / 2;

  this.cameras.main.setBackgroundColor(0x87ceeb);
  this.obstacles = this.add.group();
  this.coins = this.add.group();
  this.generator = new Generator(this);
  this.SPACE = this.input.keyboard.addKey(
    Phaser.Input.Keyboard.KeyCodes.SPACE
  );
  this.player = new Player(this, this.center_width - 100, this.height - 200);
  this.scoreText = this.add.bitmapText(
    this.center_width,
    10,
    "arcade",
    this.score,
    20
  );

  this.physics.add.collider(
    this.player,
    this.obstacles,
    this.hitObstacle,
```

```
      () => {
        return true;
      },
      this
    );

    this.physics.add.overlap(
      this.player,
      this.coins,
      this.hitCoin,
      () => {
        return true;
      },
      this
    );

    this.loadAudios();
    this.playMusic();
```

We use the `pointerdown` event to listen to the mouse click or touch event.

```
    this.input.on("pointerdown", (pointer) => this.jump(), this);
```

We use updateScoreEvent to update the score every 100ms so the player can see the score increasing as long as he survives.

```
    this.updateScoreEvent = this.time.addEvent({
      delay: 100,
      callback: () => this.updateScore(),
      callbackScope: this,
      loop: true,
    });
  }
```

This method is called when the player hits an obstacle. We stop the `updateScoreEvent` so the score doesn't increase anymore. And obviously, we finish the scene.

```
  hitObstacle(player, obstacle) {
    this.updateScoreEvent.destroy();
    this.finishScene();
  }
```

This method is called when the player picks a coin. We play a sound, update the score, and destroy the coin.

```
  hitCoin(player, coin) {
    this.playAudio("coin");
    this.updateScore(1000);
    coin.destroy();
  }
```

We use this `loadAudios` method to load all the audio files that we need for the game.

Then we'll play them using the `playAudio` method.

```
loadAudios() {
  this.audios = {
    jump: this.sound.add("jump"),
    coin: this.sound.add("coin"),
    dead: this.sound.add("dead"),
  };
}

playAudio(key) {
  this.audios[key].play();
}
```

This method is specific to the music. We use it to play the theme music in a loop.

```
playMusic(theme = "theme") {
  this.theme = this.sound.add(theme);
  this.theme.stop();
  this.theme.play({
    mute: false,
    volume: 1,
    rate: 1,
    detune: 0,
    seek: 0,
    loop: true,
    delay: 0,
  });
}
```

This is the game loop. The function is called repeatedly on every frame.

Here is where we can check if a key was pressed or the situation of the player to act accordingly. We use this `update` method to check if the player pressed the space key.

```
update() {
  if (Phaser.Input.Keyboard.JustDown(this.SPACE)) {
    this.jump();
  } else if (this.player.body.blocked.down) {
    this.jumpTween?.stop();
    this.player.rotation = 0;
    // ground
  }
}
```

This is the method that we use to make the player jump. A jump is just a velocity in the Y-axis. Gravity will do the rest.

1. Basic game: runner — The game!

Figure 1.4 When the player jumps, we add a rotation tween.

We also play a jumping sound and we add a tween to rotate the player while jumping.

```
jump() {
  if (!this.player.body.blocked.down) return;
  this.player.body.setVelocityY(-300);

  this.playAudio("jump");
  this.jumpTween = this.tweens.add({
    targets: this.player,
    duration: 1000,
    angle: { from: 0, to: 360 },
    repeat: -1,
  });
}
```

What should we do when we finish the game scene?

- Stop the theme music
- Play the dead sound
- Set the score in the registry to show it in the gameover scene.
- Start the gameover scene.

```
finishScene() {
  this.theme.stop();
  this.playAudio("dead");
  this.registry.set("score", "" + this.score);
  this.scene.start("gameover");
}
```

This method is called every 100ms and it is used to update the score and show it on the screen:

1. Basic game: runner — The game!

```
    updateScore(points = 1) {
      this.score += points;
      this.scoreText.setText(this.score);
    }
}
```

If the player dies, we store the points and we open the scene explained next: GameOver.

Gameover

Figure 1.5 Game over screen.

When the user fails, this is the scene that we show him. It's rather simple: we recover the points to show them and we set up an input listener so when the user just clicks we send him back to the game scene.

```
export default class GameOver extends Phaser.Scene {
  constructor() {
    super({ key: "gameover" });
  }

  create() {
    this.width = this.sys.game.config.width;
    this.height = this.sys.game.config.height;
    this.center_width = this.width / 2;
    this.center_height = this.height / 2;
```

1. Basic game: runner — Gameover

```javascript
    this.cameras.main.setBackgroundColor(0x87ceeb);

    this.add
      .bitmapText(
        this.center_width,
        50,
        "arcade",
        this.registry.get("score"),
        25
      )
      .setOrigin(0.5);
    this.add
      .bitmapText(
        this.center_width,
        this.center_height,
        "arcade",
        "GAME OVER",
        45
      )
      .setOrigin(0.5);
    this.add
      .bitmapText(
        this.center_width,
        250,
        "arcade",
        "Press SPACE or Click to restart!",
        15
      )
      .setOrigin(0.5);
    this.input.keyboard.on("keydown-SPACE", this.startGame, this);
    this.input.on("pointerdown", (pointer) => this.startGame(), this);
  }

  showLine(text, y) {
    let line = this.introLayer.add(
      this.add
        .bitmapText(this.center_width, y, "pixelFont", text, 25)
        .setOrigin(0.5)
        .setAlpha(0)
    );
    this.tweens.add({
      targets: line,
      duration: 2000,
      alpha: 1,
    });
  }

  startGame() {
    this.scene.start("game");
  }
}
```

1. Basic game: runner   Gameover

    Even in simple games like this, it's important to have some kind of challenge, that's why you must show the points on this screen.

Other runners or similar games

Make Way

Source code: https://github.com/pxai/phasergames/tree/master/cars

Play it here: https://pello.itch.io/make-way

Goblin Bakery

Source code: https://github.com/pxai/phasergames/tree/master/goblin

Play it here: https://pello.itch.io/goblin-bakery

Melt Down

Source code: https://github.com/pxai/phasergames/tree/master/penguin

Play it here: https://pello.itch.io/meltdown

Electron

Source code: https://github.com/pxai/phasergames/tree/master/electron

Play it here: https://pello.itch.io/electron

2. Space Shooter: Starshake

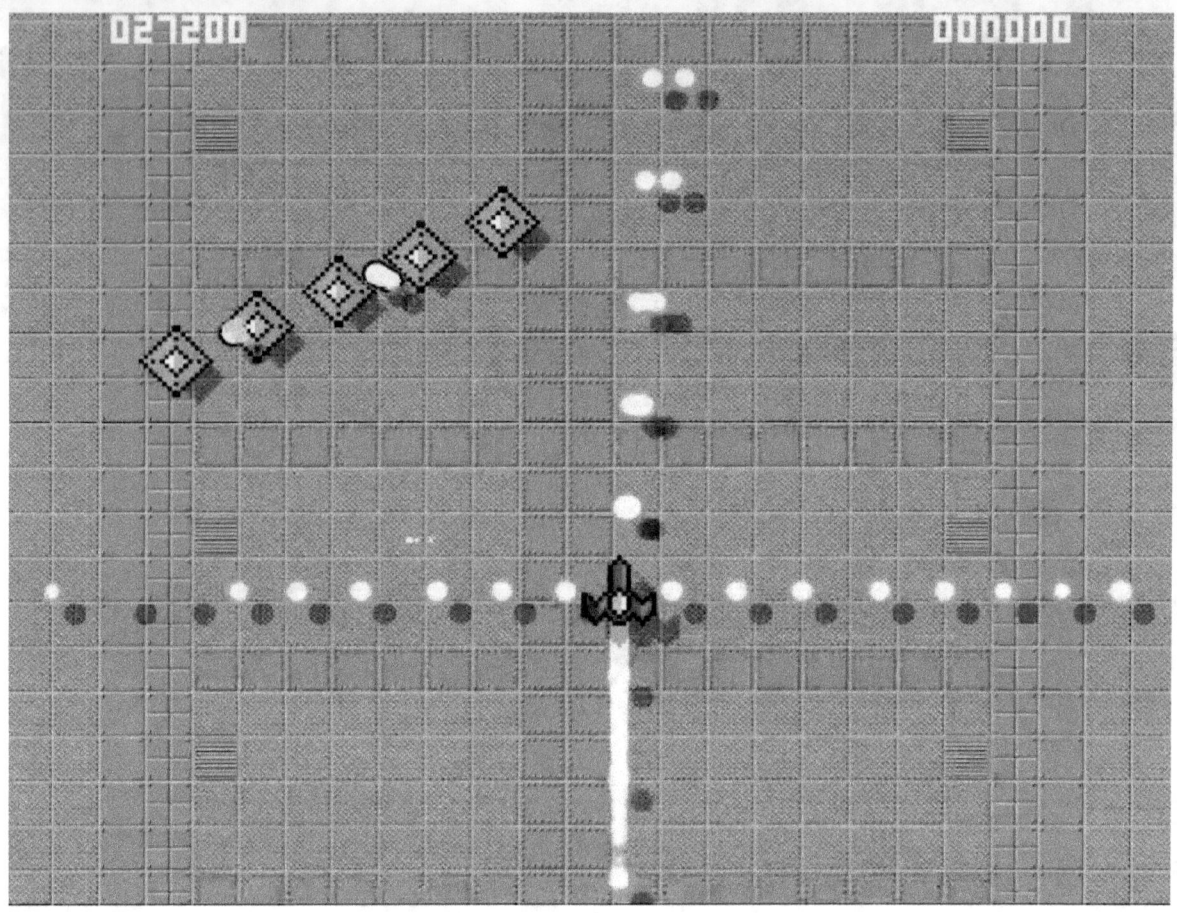

Source code: https://github.com/pxai/phasergames/tree/master/starshake

Play it here: https://pello.itch.io/starshake

2. Space Shooter: Starshake

Space shooters are the reason I got into this: when I was just a kid I saw a Galaga machine and I was in awe, thinking how that thing was even possible. But enough of nostalgia and let's get down to code.

In a shooter, we take control of a space fighter that shoots its way through waves of foe ships. One single hit by the enemy will take us down but with a bit of skill and the help of some power-ups, we can make it to the final boss.

So in this type of game, we'll need to create a player without any gravity, capable of shooting. Every one of those shots is also a `GameObject`. Different types of enemy waves will be generated and in some cases, they will be grouped in formation or following a pattern. The stage is just an infinite background that scrolls down the screen.

Init project

In this case, we'll be adding some more scenes like transitions and most importantly an awesome (well, not that much) Splash scene.

```javascript
import Phaser from "phaser";
import Bootloader from "./bootloader";
import Outro from "./outro";
import Splash from "./splash";
import Transition from "./transition";
import Game from "./game";

const config = {
  width: 1000,
  height: 800,
  scale: {
    mode: Phaser.Scale.FIT,
    autoCenter: Phaser.Scale.CENTER_BOTH,
  },
  autoRound: false,
  parent: "contenedor",
  physics: {
    default: "arcade",
    arcade: {
      gravity: { y: 0 },
      debug: false,
    },
  },
  scene: [Bootloader, Splash, Transition, Game, Outro],
};

const game = new Phaser.Game(config);
```

Loader

Again, this is the first Scene class that we run, just to load all the assets of the game while we show a progress bar.

```
export default class Bootloader extends Phaser.Scene {
  constructor() {
    super({ key: "bootloader" });
  }
}
```

Here we split the loading of the assets into different functions:

```
preload() {
  this.createBars();
  this.setLoadEvents();
  this.loadFonts();
  this.loadImages();
  this.loadAudios();
  this.loadSpritesheets();
  this.setRegistry();
}
```

These are the events we need to control the loading bar and change to splash scene when complete.

```
setLoadEvents() {
  this.load.on(
    "progress",
    function (value) {
      this.progressBar.clear();
      this.progressBar.fillStyle(0x0088aa, 1);
      this.progressBar.fillRect(
        this.cameras.main.width / 4,
        this.cameras.main.height / 2 - 16,
        (this.cameras.main.width / 2) * value,
        16
      );
    },
    this
  );

  this.load.on(
    "complete",
    () => {
      this.scene.start("splash");
    },
    this
  );
}
```

Figure 2.1 This is the loader: a background and the progress bar.

Load the fonts we use in the game:

```
loadFonts() {
  this.load.bitmapFont(
    "wendy",
    "assets/fonts/wendy.png",
    "assets/fonts/wendy.xml"
  );
}
```

Load the images we use in the game:

```
loadImages() {
  this.load.image("logo", "assets/images/logo.png");
  this.load.image("pello_logo", "assets/images/pello_logo.png");
  this.load.image("background", "assets/images/background.png");
  Array(4)
    .fill(0)
    .forEach((_, i) => {
      this.load.image(`stage${i + 1}`, `assets/images/stage${i + 1}.png`);
    });
}
```

Load the audio (sound effects and music) we use in the game:

```
loadAudios() {
  this.load.audio("shot", "assets/sounds/shot.mp3");
  this.load.audio("foeshot", "assets/sounds/foeshot.mp3");
  this.load.audio("foedestroy", "assets/sounds/foedestroy.mp3");
  this.load.audio("foexplosion", "assets/sounds/foexplosion.mp3");
  this.load.audio("explosion", "assets/sounds/explosion.mp3");
  this.load.audio("stageclear1", "assets/sounds/stageclear1.mp3");
  this.load.audio("stageclear2", "assets/sounds/stageclear2.mp3");
  this.load.audio("boss", "assets/sounds/boss.mp3");
  this.load.audio("splash", "assets/sounds/splash.mp3");
  Array(3)
    .fill(0)
    .forEach((_, i) => {
      this.load.audio(`music ${i + 1}`, `assets/sounds/music${i + 1}.mp3`);
    });
}
```

Load the sprite sheets (animated images) we use in the game:

2. Space Shooter: Starshake — Loader

```
loadSpritesheets() {
  this.load.spritesheet("player1", "assets/images/player1.png", {
    frameWidth: 64,
    frameHeight: 64,
  });
  this.load.spritesheet("foe0", "assets/images/foe0.png", {
    frameWidth: 64,
    frameHeight: 64,
  });
  this.load.spritesheet("foe1", "assets/images/foe1.png", {
    frameWidth: 64,
    frameHeight: 64,
  });
  this.load.spritesheet("foe2", "assets/images/foe2.png", {
    frameWidth: 32,
    frameHeight: 32,
  });
  this.load.spritesheet("guinxu", "assets/images/guinxu.png", {
    frameWidth: 128,
    frameHeight: 144,
  });
  this.load.spritesheet("plenny0", "assets/images/plenny0.png", {
    frameWidth: 64,
    frameHeight: 64,
  });
}
```

Set the initial values of the registry. The game was designed to be played by two players, but it can be played by one:

```
setRegistry() {
  this.registry.set("score_player1", 0);
  this.registry.set("power_player1", "water");
  this.registry.set("lives_player1", 0);

  this.registry.set("score_player2", 0);
  this.registry.set("power_player2", "water");
  this.registry.set("lives_player2", 0);
}
```

Create the bars we use to show the loading progress:

```
createBars() {
  this.loadBar = this.add.graphics();
  this.loadBar.fillStyle(0xd40000, 1);
  this.loadBar.fillRect(
    this.cameras.main.width / 4 - 2,
    this.cameras.main.height / 2 - 18,
    this.cameras.main.width / 2 + 4,
    20
  );
```

```
        this.progressBar = this.add.graphics();
    }
}
```

It is not mandatory to split the code into different functions, but when you have several assets of different types and special events, it will be better if you organize it like this.

Light Particle

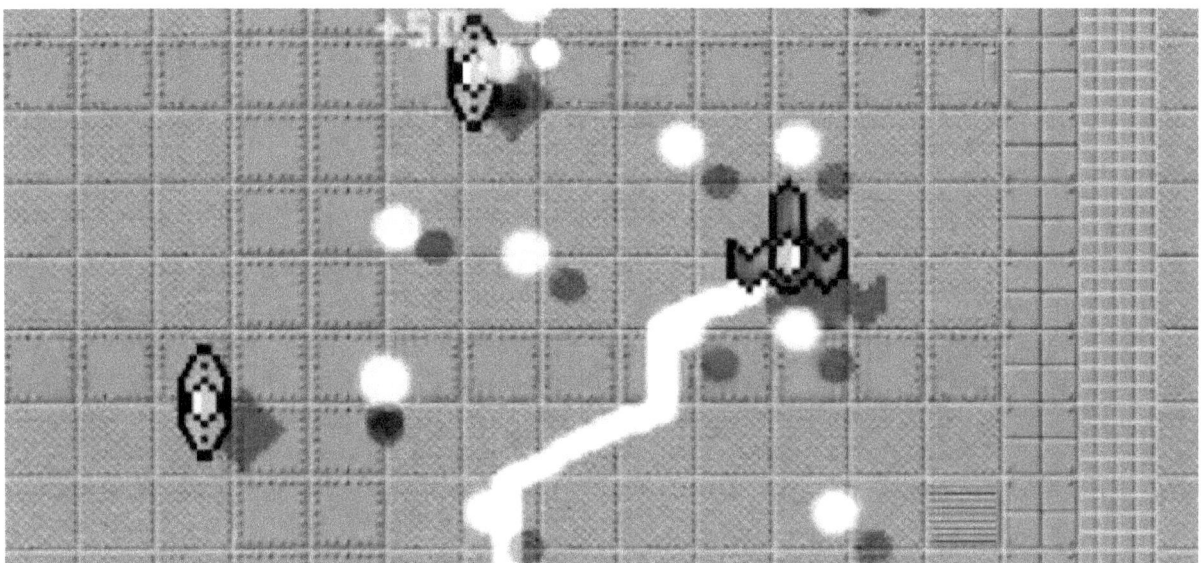

Figure 2.2 Lights are used for shots, in different colors.

We'll be showing particles for trails and other elements that will improve the feedback and the game feel.

```
export class LightParticle extends Phaser.GameObjects.PointLight {
    constructor(scene, x, y, color = 0xffffff, radius = 5, intensity = 0.5) {
        super(scene, x, y, color, radius, intensity);
        this.name = "celtic";
        this.scene = scene;
        scene.add.existing(this);
        scene.physics.add.existing(this);
        this.body.setAllowGravity(false);
        this.body.setVelocityY(300);
        this.init();
    }
```

We add a tween to the particle to make it grow and fade out.

```
    init() {
```

```
      this.scene.tweens.add({
        targets: this,
        duration: Phaser.Math.Between(600, 1000),
        scale: { from: 1, to: 3 },
        alpha: { from: this.alpha, to: 0 },
        onComplete: () => {
          this.destroy();
        },
      });
  }
}
```

Generating foes

The enemies are generated automatically with some frequency. This class takes care of the `Foe` generation at every stage.

```
import Foe from "./foe";

export default class FoeGenerator {
  constructor(scene) {
    this.scene = scene;
    this.waveFoes = [];
    this.generate();
    this.activeWave = false;
    this.waves = 0;
  }
```

This is the main function to generate foes. Depending on the scene number, it will generate different types of foes.

```
  generate() {
    if (this.scene.number === 4) {
      this.scene.time.delayedCall(2000, () => this.releaseGuinxu(), null, this);
    } else {
      this.generateEvent1 = this.scene.time.addEvent({
        delay: 7000,
        callback: () => this.orderedWave(),
        callbackScope: this,
        loop: true,
      });
      this.generateEvent2 = this.scene.time.addEvent({
        delay: 15000,
        callback: () => this.wave(),
        callbackScope: this,
        loop: true,
      });
      if (this.scene.number > 1)
```

```
      this.generateEvent3 = this.scene.time.addEvent({
        delay: 3000,
        callback: () => this.tank(),
        callbackScope: this,
        loop: true,
      });
    if (this.scene.number > 2)
      this.generateEvent4 = this.scene.time.addEvent({
        delay: 5000,
        callback: () => this.slider(),
        callbackScope: this,
        loop: true,
      });
  }
}
```

This is the function that generates the boss.

```
releaseGuinxu() {
  const guinxu = new Foe(
    this.scene,
    Phaser.Math.Between(200, 600),
    200,
    "guinxu",
    0,
    20
  );
  this.scene.playAudio("boss");
  this.laughterEvent = this.scene.time.addEvent({
    delay: 10000,
    callback: () => {
      this.scene.playAudio("boss");
    },
    callbackScope: this,
    loop: true,
  });
  this.scene.tweens.add({
    targets: guinxu,
    alpha: { from: 0.3, to: 1 },
    duration: 200,
    repeat: 10,
  });
  this.scene.foeGroup.add(guinxu);
}
```

This is the function that stops the generation of foes.

```
stop() {
  clearInterval(this.generationIntervalId);
  this.scene.foeGroup.children.entries.forEach((foe) => {
    if (foe === null || !foe.active) return;
    foe.destroy();
```

2. Space Shooter: Starshake — Generating foes

```
  });
}
```

This is called when the scene is finished and it takes care of destroying the generation events.

```
finishScene() {
  this.generateEvent1.destroy();
  this.generateEvent2.destroy();
  if (this.scene.number > 1) this.generateEvent3.destroy();
  if (this.scene.number > 2) this.generateEvent4.destroy();
  this.scene.endScene();
}
```

This is the function that creates the path for the foes to follow in formation.

```
createPath() {
  this.waves++;
  if (this.waves === 3) this.finishScene();
  const start = Phaser.Math.Between(100, 600);
  this.path = new Phaser.Curves.Path(start, 0);

  this.path.lineTo(start, Phaser.Math.Between(20, 50));

  let max = 8;
  let h = 500 / max;

  for (let i = 0; i < max; i++) {
    if (i % 2 === 0) {
      this.path.lineTo(start, 50 + h * (i + 1));
    } else {
      this.path.lineTo(start + 300, 50 + h * (i + 1));
    }
  }

  this.path.lineTo(start, this.scene.height + 50);
  this.graphics = this.scene.add.graphics();
  this.graphics.lineStyle(0, 0xffffff, 0); // for debug
}
```

This is the function that generates a wave of foes in an ordered formation.

```
orderedWave(difficulty = 5) {
  const x = Phaser.Math.Between(64, this.scene.width - 200);
  const y = Phaser.Math.Between(-100, 0);
  const minus = Phaser.Math.Between(-1, 1) > 0 ? 1 : -1;

  Array(difficulty)
    .fill()
    .forEach((_, i) => this.addOrder(i, x, y, minus));
}
```

This function just creates a simple wave of foes.

```
wave(difficulty = 5) {
  this.createPath();
  const x = Phaser.Math.Between(64, this.scene.width - 200);
  const y = Phaser.Math.Between(-100, 0);
  const minus = Phaser.Math.Between(-1, 1) > 0 ? 1 : -1;

  Array(difficulty)
    .fill()
    .forEach((_, i) => this.addToWave(i));
  this.activeWave = true;
}
```

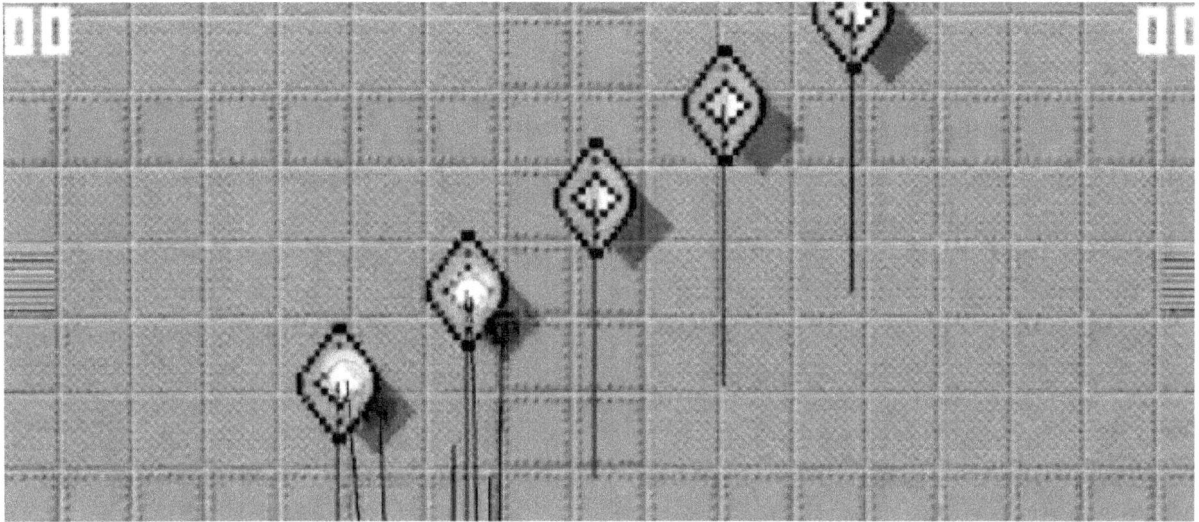

Figure 2.3 A wave of foes.

This function generates a single tank foe:

```
tank() {
  this.scene.foeGroup.add(
    new Foe(this.scene, Phaser.Math.Between(100, 600), -100, "foe2", 0, 620)
  );
}
```

This generates a *slider* foe and adds a rotation tween to it.

```
slider() {
  let velocity = -200;
  let x = 0;
  if (Phaser.Math.Between(-1, 1) > 0) {
    velocity = 200;
    x = -100;
  } else {
    x = this.scene.width + 100;
```

```
    }
    const foe = new Foe(
      this.scene,
      x,
      Phaser.Math.Between(100, 600),
      "foe1",
      velocity,
      0
    );
    this.scene.tweens.add({
      targets: [foe, foe.shadow],
      duration: 500,
      rotation: "+=5",
      repeat: -1,
    });
    this.scene.foeGroup.add(foe);
}
```

This function adds a foe to the scene, in a random position.

```
add() {
    const foe = new Foe(
      this.scene,
      Phaser.Math.Between(32, this.scene.width - 32),
      0
    );
    this.scene.foeGroup.add(foe);
}
```

This function generates and ordered group of foes.

```
addOrder(i, x, y, minus) {
    const offset = minus * 70;

    this.scene.foeGroup.add(
      new Foe(this.scene, x + i * 70, i * y + offset, "foe0", 0, 300)
    );
}
```

This function adds a foe to the wave.

```
addToWave(i) {
    const foe = new Foe(
      this.scene,
      Phaser.Math.Between(32, this.scene.width - 32),
      0,
      "foe0"
    );
    this.scene.tweens.add({
      targets: foe,
      z: 1,
      ease: "Linear",
```

```
      duration: 12000,
      repeat: -1,
      delay: i * 100,
    });
    this;
    this.scene.foeWaveGroup.add(foe);
  }
```

This function updates all foes in the scene. This could be done independently in each foe as we will see in other projects.

```
update() {
  if (this.path) {
    this.path.draw(this.graphics);

    this.scene.foeWaveGroup.children.entries.forEach((foe) => {
      if (foe === null || !foe.active) return;
      let t = foe.z;
      let vec = foe.getData("vector");
      this.path.getPoint(t, vec);
      foe.setPosition(vec.x, vec.y);
      foe.shadow.setPosition(vec.x + 20, vec.y + 20);
      foe.setDepth(foe.y);
    });

    if (this.activeWave && this.checkIfWaveDestroyed()) {
      this.activeWave = false;
      this.scene.spawnShake();
      this.path.destroy();
    }
  }

  this.scene.foeGroup.children.entries.forEach((foe) => {
    if (foe === null || !foe.active || foe.y > this.scene.height + 100)
      foe.destroy();
    foe.update();
  });
}
```

This function checks if the wave of foes has been destroyed so we can generate a power-up.

```
checkIfWaveDestroyed() {
  const foes = this.scene.foeWaveGroup.children.entries;

  return foes.length === foes.filter((foe) => !foe.active).length;
  }
}
```

In this generator, we can tweak the difficulty level and the randomness. As we will see in the platformer example, in games using tiled maps, the enemies can be set on the map configuration.

Foes

Figure 2.4 The basic foe sprite sheet.

There are different types of foes:

- Regular foe fighters: no armor, always in formation.
- Ufos: single armored ships.
- Tanks: ground shooting armored bases.

As we move forward to new stages we'll meet new foes, but all of them are grouped here.

```
import FoeShot from "./foe_shot";
import Explosion from "./explosion";

const TYPES = {
  foe0: { points: 400, lives: 1 },
  foe1: { points: 500, lives: 3 },
  foe2: { points: 800, lives: 2 },
  guinxu: { points: 10000, lives: 20 },
};

class Foe extends Phaser.GameObjects.Sprite {
  constructor(scene, x, y, name = "foe0", velocityX = 0, velocityY = 0) {
    super(scene, x, y, name);
    this.name = name;
    this.points = TYPES[name].points;
    this.lives = TYPES[name].lives;
    this.scene = scene;
    this.id = Math.random();
    if (this.name !== "foe2") {
      this.spawnShadow(x, y);
    }
    scene.add.existing(this);
    scene.physics.add.existing(this);
    this.body.setAllowGravity(false);
    this.body.setCircle(19);
    this.body.setOffset(12, 12);
```

```js
    this.body.setVelocityX(velocityX);
    this.body.setVelocityY(velocityY);
    this.setData("vector", new Phaser.Math.Vector2());
    if (this.name === "guinxu") {
      this.setGuinxuShot();
    }
    this.init();
  }
```

This function sets a tween to the Guinxu foe, so it moves in a zig-zag pattern.

```js
setGuinxuShot() {
  this.patternIndex = 0;
  this.pattern = Phaser.Utils.Array.NumberArrayStep(-300, 300, 50);
  this.pattern = this.pattern.concat(
    Phaser.Utils.Array.NumberArrayStep(300, -300, -50)
  );
  this.scene.tweens.add({
    targets: this,
    duration: 2000,
    y: { from: this.y, to: this.y + Phaser.Math.Between(100, -100) },
    x: { from: this.x, to: this.x + Phaser.Math.Between(100, -100) },
    yoyo: true,
    repeat: -1,
  });
}
```

This function spawns a shadow for each foe. We'll have to update it with the foe itself.

```js
spawnShadow(x, y) {
  this.shadow = this.scene.add
    .image(x + 20, y + 20, this.name)
    .setScale(0.7)
    .setTint(0x000000)
    .setAlpha(0.4);
}

updateShadow() {
  this.shadow.x = this.x + 20;
  this.shadow.y = this.y + 20;
}
```

This function adds an animation to the foe.

```js
init() {
  this.scene.anims.create({
    key: this.name,
    frames: this.scene.anims.generateFrameNumbers(this.name),
    frameRate: 10,
    repeat: -1,
  });
  this.anims.play(this.name, true);
```

```
    this.direction = -1;
  }
```

This function is called from the foe generation. It updates the foe position, checks if it's out of bounds and also updates its shadow.

```
update() {
  if (this.y > this.scene.height + 64) {
    if (this.name !== "foe2") this.shadow.destroy();
    this.destroy();
  }

  if (this.name === "guinxu" && Phaser.Math.Between(1, 6) > 5) {
    this.guinxuShot();
  } else if (Phaser.Math.Between(1, 101) > 100) {
    if (!this.scene || !this.scene.player) return;
    this.scene.playAudio("foeshot");
    let shot = new FoeShot(this.scene, this.x, this.y, "foe", this.name);
    this.scene.foeShots.add(shot);
    this.scene.physics.moveTo(
      shot,
      this.scene.player.x,
      this.scene.player.y,
      300
    );
    this.scene.physics.moveTo(
      shot.shadow,
      this.scene.player.x,
      this.scene.player.y,
      300
    );
  }

  if (this.name !== "foe2") {
    this.updateShadow();
  }
}
```

This takes care of the shots generated by the final boss.

```
guinxuShot() {
  if (!this.scene || !this.scene.player) return;

  this.scene.playAudio("foeshot");
  let shot = new FoeShot(
    this.scene,
    this.x,
    this.y,
    "foe",
    this.name,
    this.pattern[this.patternIndex],
```

```
    300
  );
  this.scene.foeShots.add(shot);
  this.patternIndex =
    this.patternIndex + 1 === this.pattern.length ? 0 : ++this.patternIndex;
}
```

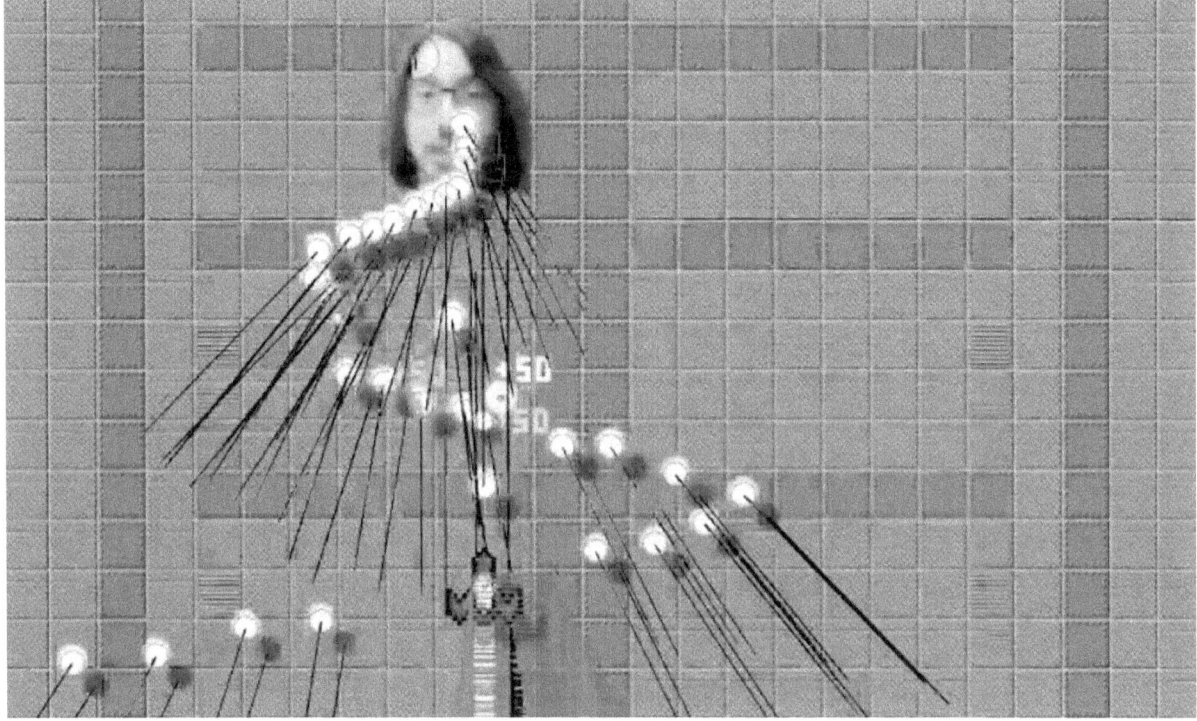

Figure 2.5 The final boss and his special shot pattern.

This function is called when the foe is destroyed, adding an explosion effect along with a tween and showing the points.

```
dead() {
  let radius = 60;
  let explosionRad = 20;
  if (this.name === "guinxu") {
    radius = 220;
    explosionRad = 220;
    this.scene.cameras.main.shake(500);
  }

  const explosion = this.scene.add
    .circle(this.x, this.y, 5)
    .setStrokeStyle(20, 0xffffff);
  this.showPoints(this.points);
  this.scene.tweens.add({
    targets: explosion,
    radius: { from: 10, to: radius },
    alpha: { from: 1, to: 0.3 },
```

2. Space Shooter: Starshake

```
      duration: 250,
      onComplete: () => {
        explosion.destroy();
      },
    });

    new Explosion(this.scene, this.x, this.y, explosionRad);
    if (
      this.name !== "foe2" &&
      this.scene &&
      this.scene.scene.isActive() &&
      this.shadow &&
      this.shadow.active
    )
      this.shadow.destroy();

    if (this.name === "guinxu") {
      this.scene.number = 5;
      this.scene.playAudio("explosion");
      this.scene.endScene();
    }
    this.destroy();
  }
```

As we do when destroying shots, this function shows the points when a foe is destroyed with a simple tween effect.

```
  showPoints(score, color = 0xff0000) {
    let text = this.scene.add
      .bitmapText(this.x + 20, this.y - 30, "wendy", "+" + score, 40, color)
      .setOrigin(0.5);
    this.scene.tweens.add({
      targets: text,
      duration: 800,
      alpha: { from: 1, to: 0 },
      y: { from: this.y - 20, to: this.y - 80 },
      onComplete: () => {
        text.destroy();
      },
    });
  }
}

export default Foe;
```

It could be ok to split this class into different subclasses for each type of enemy.

Foes shot

Each foe shot is a game object controlled by this class.

```
const TYPES = {
  chocolate: { color: 0xaf8057, radius: 16, intensity: 0.4 },
  vanila: { color: 0xfff6d5, radius: 16, intensity: 0.4 },
  fruit: { color: 0x00ff00, radius: 16, intensity: 0.4 },
  water: { color: 0x0000cc, radius: 16, intensity: 0.4 },
  foe: { color: 0xfff01f, radius: 16, intensity: 0.4 },
};

class FoeShot extends Phaser.GameObjects.PointLight {
  constructor(
    scene,
    x,
    y,
    type = "water",
    playerName,
    velocityX = 0,
    velocityY = -300
  ) {
    const { color, radius, intensity } = TYPES[type];
    super(scene, x, y, color, radius, intensity);
    this.name = "foeshot";
    this.scene = scene;
    this.playerName = playerName;
    this.spawnShadow(x, y, velocityX, velocityY);
    scene.add.existing(this);
    scene.physics.add.existing(this);
    if (playerName === "guinxu") this.body.setVelocity(velocityX, velocityY);
    this.body.setAllowGravity(false);
    this.body.setCollideWorldBounds(true);
    this.body.onWorldBounds = true;
    this.body.setCircle(10);
    this.body.setOffset(6, 9);

    this.init();
  }
```

This function spawns a shadow for each shot. We'll have to update it with the shot itself.

```
  spawnShadow(x, y, velocityX, velocityY) {
    this.shadow = this.scene.add
      .circle(x + 20, y + 20, 10, 0x000000)
      .setAlpha(0.4);
    this.scene.add.existing(this.shadow);
    this.scene.physics.add.existing(this.shadow);
    if (this.playerName === "guinxu")
```

```
    this.shadow.body.setVelocity(velocityX, velocityY);
}
```

This function adds a simple effect to the shot to make it flicker.

```
init() {
  this.scene.tweens.add({
    targets: this,
    duration: 200,
    intensity: { from: 0.3, to: 0.7 },
    repeat: -1,
  });
}
```

This function is called when the shot is destroyed, adding an explosion effect along with a tween and showing the points.

```
shot() {
  const explosion = this.scene.add
    .circle(this.x, this.y, 5)
    .setStrokeStyle(10, 0xffffff);
  this.showPoints(50);
  this.scene.tweens.add({
    targets: explosion,
    radius: { from: 5, to: 20 },
    alpha: { from: 1, to: 0 },
    duration: 250,
    onComplete: () => {
      explosion.destroy();
    },
  });
  this.destroy();
}
```

This function shows the points when the shot is destroyed. The points are shown in a bitmap text and they are tweened to make them move up and fade out.

```
showPoints(score, color = 0xff0000) {
  let text = this.scene.add
    .bitmapText(this.x + 20, this.y - 30, "wendy", "+" + score, 40, color)
    .setOrigin(0.5);
  this.scene.tweens.add({
    targets: text,
    duration: 800,
    alpha: { from: 1, to: 0 },
    y: { from: this.y - 20, to: this.y - 80 },
    onComplete: () => {
      text.destroy();
    },
  });
}
```

```
}
export default FoeShot;
```

If you improve this game further, you could have a different type of shot for each type of foe.

Explosion

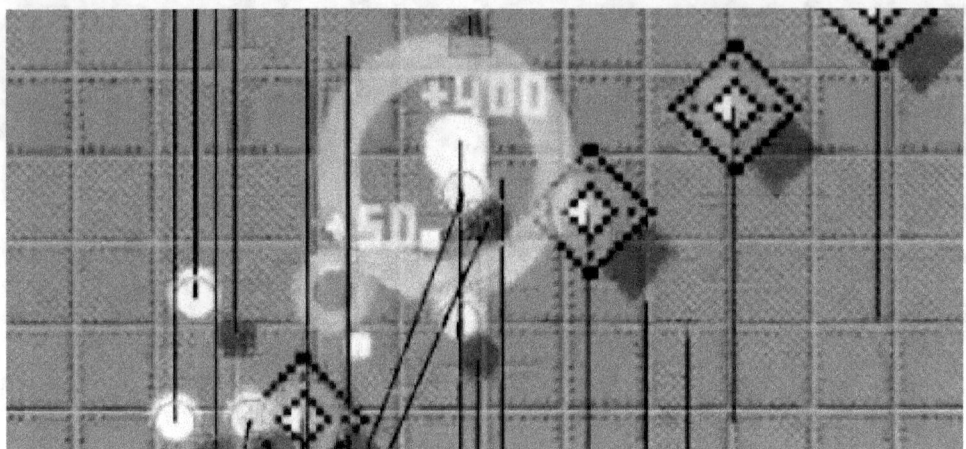
Figure 2.6 Explosions growing on screen.

Explosions are represented by a white ring that grows quickly as it vanishes. There are different sizes but in any case, they are crucial for satisfactory feedback.

```
class Explosion {
  constructor(scene, x, y, radius = 5, min = 5, max = 7) {
    this.scene = scene;
    this.radius = radius;
    this.x = x;
    this.y = y;
    this.lights = Array(Phaser.Math.Between(min, max))
      .fill(0)
      .map((_, i) => {
        const offsetX =
          this.x + Phaser.Math.Between(-this.radius / 2, this.radius / 2);
        const offsetY =
          this.y + Phaser.Math.Between(-this.radius / 2, -this.radius / 2);
        const color = Phaser.Math.Between(0xff0000, 0xffffcc);
        const radius = Phaser.Math.Between(this.radius / 2, this.radius);
        const intensity = Phaser.Math.Between(0.3, 0.8);
        return scene.lights.addPointLight(
          offsetX,
          offsetY,
          color,
          radius,
          intensity
        );
      });
    this.init();
  }
```

This adds a simple effect to the explosion to shrink the lights.

```
    init() {
      this.scene.tweens.add({
        targets: this.lights,
        duration: Phaser.Math.Between(600, 1000),
        scale: { from: 1, to: 0 },
      });
    }
  }
}

export default Explosion;
```

You should also consider having specific explosions or more randomness to the explosion effects.

Player

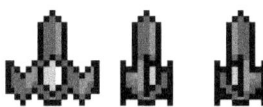

Figure 2.7 The player sprites.

And here is the player. We define the animations for the following: left-right turnings, the controls, we generate a fume trail and of course, we can let him fire and apply shooting power-ups.

```
import Explosion from "./explosion";
import { LightParticle } from "./particle";
import ShootingPatterns from "./shooting_patterns";

class Player extends Phaser.GameObjects.Sprite {
  constructor(scene, x, y, name = "player1", powerUp = "water") {
    super(scene, x, y, name);
    this.name = name;
    this.scene = scene;
    this.spawnShadow(x, y);
    this.powerUp = powerUp;
    this.id = Math.random();
    scene.add.existing(this);
    scene.physics.add.existing(this);
    this.body.setCollideWorldBounds(true);
    this.body.setAllowGravity(false);
    this.body.setCircle(26);
    this.body.setOffset(6, 9);
    this.power = 0;
    this.blinking = false;
    this.shootingPatterns = new ShootingPatterns(this.scene, this.name);
    this.init();
    this.setControls();
```

2. Space Shooter: Starshake — Player

}

We add a shadow to the player, and we'll have to update its position with the player. Alternatively, we could have defined a single `Container` class with the player and the shadow.

```
spawnShadow(x, y) {
  this.shadow = this.scene.add
    .image(x + 20, y + 20, "player1")
    .setTint(0x000000)
    .setAlpha(0.4);
}
```

We set the animations for the player. We'll have 3 animations: one for the idle state, one for moving right, and one for moving left.

```
init() {
  this.scene.anims.create({
    key: this.name,
    frames: this.scene.anims.generateFrameNumbers(this.name, {
      start: 0,
      end: 0,
    }),
    frameRate: 10,
    repeat: -1,
  });
  this.scene.anims.create({
    key: this.name + "right",
    frames: this.scene.anims.generateFrameNumbers(this.name, {
      start: 1,
      end: 1,
    }),
    frameRate: 10,
    repeat: -1,
  });
  this.scene.anims.create({
    key: this.name + "left",
    frames: this.scene.anims.generateFrameNumbers(this.name, {
      start: 2,
      end: 2,
    }),
    frameRate: 10,
    repeat: -1,
  });
  this.anims.play(this.name, true);

  this.upDelta = 0;
}
```

2. Space Shooter: Starshake — Player

We set the controls for the player. We'll use the cursor keys and WASD keys to move the player, and the space bar to shoot.

```
setControls() {
  this.SPACE = this.scene.input.keyboard.addKey(
    Phaser.Input.Keyboard.KeyCodes.SPACE
  );
  this.cursor = this.scene.input.keyboard.createCursorKeys();
  this.W = this.scene.input.keyboard.addKey(Phaser.Input.Keyboard.KeyCodes.W);
  this.A = this.scene.input.keyboard.addKey(Phaser.Input.Keyboard.KeyCodes.A);
  this.S = this.scene.input.keyboard.addKey(Phaser.Input.Keyboard.KeyCodes.S);
  this.D = this.scene.input.keyboard.addKey(Phaser.Input.Keyboard.KeyCodes.D);
}
```

This will be called when the player shoots. We'll play a sound, and then call the shoot method of the current shooting pattern.

```
shoot() {
  this.scene.playAudio("shot");
  this.shootingPatterns.shoot(this.x, this.y, this.powerUp);
}
```

This is the game loop for the player. We'll check if the player is moving, and if so, we'll play the corresponding animation. We'll also check if the player is shooting, and if it is, we'll call the shoot method.

```
update(timestep, delta) {
  if (this.death) return;
  if (this.cursor.left.isDown) {
    this.x -= 5;
    this.anims.play(this.name + "left", true);
    this.shadow.setScale(0.5, 1);
  } else if (this.cursor.right.isDown) {
    this.x += 5;
    this.anims.play(this.name + "right", true);
    this.shadow.setScale(0.5, 1);
  } else {
    this.anims.play(this.name, true);
    this.shadow.setScale(1, 1);
  }

  if (this.cursor.up.isDown) {
    this.y -= 5;
  } else if (this.cursor.down.isDown) {
    this.y += 5;
  }

  if (Phaser.Input.Keyboard.JustDown(this.SPACE)) {
    this.shoot();
  }
```

```
    this.scene.trailLayer.add(
      new LightParticle(this.scene, this.x, this.y, 0xffffff, 10)
    );
    this.updateShadow();
}
```

We update the shadow position to follow the player.

```
updateShadow() {
    this.shadow.x = this.x + 20;
    this.shadow.y = this.y + 20;
}
```

Every time the player destroys a foe or a shot we show the points. We'll use a bitmap text for that.

```
showPoints(score, color = 0xff0000) {
    let text = this.scene.add
      .bitmapText(this.x + 20, this.y - 30, "starshipped", score, 20, 0xfffd37)
      .setOrigin(0.5);
    this.scene.tweens.add({
      targets: text,
      duration: 2000,
      alpha: { from: 1, to: 0 },
      y: { from: text.y - 10, to: text.y - 100 },
    });
}
```

This will be called when the player dies: we'll show an explosion, shake the camera, and destroy the player.

```
dead() {
    const explosion = this.scene.add
      .circle(this.x, this.y, 10)
      .setStrokeStyle(40, 0xffffff);
    this.scene.tweens.add({
      targets: explosion,
      radius: { from: 10, to: 512 },
      alpha: { from: 1, to: 0.3 },
      duration: 300,
      onComplete: () => {
        explosion.destroy();
      },
    });
    this.scene.cameras.main.shake(500);
    this.death = true;
    this.shadow.destroy();
    new Explosion(this.scene, this.x, this.y, 40);
    super.destroy();
  }
}
```

```
export default Player;
```

Shot

These are players' shots, simple glowing game objects that also include a shadow.

```
const TYPES = {
  chocolate: { color: 0xaf8057, radius: 16, intensity: 0.4 },
  vanila: { color: 0xfff6d5, radius: 16, intensity: 0.4 },
  fruit: { color: 0xffffff, radius: 16, intensity: 0.4 },
  water: { color: 0xffffff, radius: 16, intensity: 0.4 },
  foe: { color: 0x00ff00, radius: 16, intensity: 0.4 },
};

class Shot extends Phaser.GameObjects.PointLight {
  constructor(
    scene, x, y, type = "water",
    playerName, velocityX = 0, velocityY = -500
  ) {
    const { color, radius, intensity } = TYPES[type];
    super(scene, x, y, color, radius, intensity);
    this.name = "shot";
    this.scene = scene;
    this.playerName = playerName;
    scene.add.existing(this);
    scene.physics.add.existing(this);
    this.body.setAllowGravity(false);
    this.body.setVelocityX(velocityX);
    this.body.setVelocityY(velocityY);
    this.body.setCircle(10);
    this.body.setOffset(6, 9);
    this.body.setCollideWorldBounds(true);
    this.body.onWorldBounds = true;
    this.spawnShadow(x, y, velocityX, velocityY);
    this.init();
  }
```

Each shot will have a shadow, which will be a circle with a lower alpha value.

```
  spawnShadow(x, y, velocityX, velocityY) {
    this.shadow = this.scene.add
      .circle(x + 20, y + 20, 10, 0x000000)
      .setAlpha(0.4);
    this.scene.add.existing(this.shadow);
    this.scene.physics.add.existing(this.shadow);
    this.shadow.body.setVelocityX(velocityX);
    this.shadow.body.setVelocityY(velocityY);
  }
```

2. Space Shooter: Starshake

We add a tween to the shot to make it grow and fade out, repeatedly.

```
  init() {
    this.scene.tweens.add({
      targets: this,
      duration: 200,
      intensity: { from: 0.3, to: 0.7 },
      repeat: -1,
    });
  }
}

export default Shot;
```

Shooting pattern

One of the key element in any shooter (and in many other genres) are power-ups. Every time the player catches a power-up the firing pattern will change. Patterns are just different ways of generating shots and this class groups all of them.

```
import Shot from "./shot";

export default class ShootingPatterns {
  constructor(scene, name) {
    this.scene = scene;
    this.name = name;
    this.shootingMethods = {
      water: this.single.bind(this),
      fruit: this.tri.bind(this),
      vanila: this.quintus.bind(this),
      chocolate: this.massacre.bind(this),
    };
  }
```

2. Space Shooter: Starshake — Shooting pattern

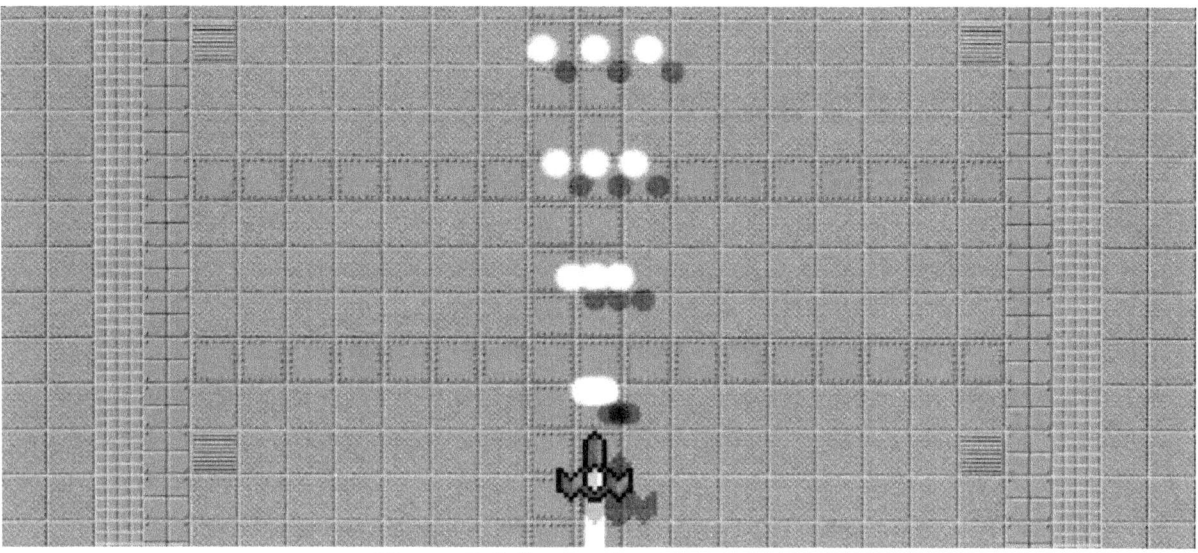

Figure 2.8 Basic shooting pattern.

These are the different functions we will use to shoot. Each one will shoot a different number of shots, with different angles and speeds. The patterns are applied depending on the current power-up.

```javascript
shoot(x, y, powerUp) {
  this.shootingMethods[powerUp](x, y, powerUp);
}

single(x, y, powerUp) {
  this.scene.shots.add(new Shot(this.scene, x, y, powerUp, this.name));
}

tri(x, y, powerUp) {
  this.scene.shots.add(new Shot(this.scene, x, y, powerUp, this.name, -60));
  this.scene.shots.add(new Shot(this.scene, x, y, powerUp, this.name));
  this.scene.shots.add(new Shot(this.scene, x, y, powerUp, this.name, 60));
}

quintus(x, y, powerUp) {
  this.scene.shots.add(new Shot(this.scene, x, y, powerUp, this.name, -300));
  this.scene.shots.add(new Shot(this.scene, x, y, powerUp, this.name, 300));
  this.scene.shots.add(
    new Shot(this.scene, x, y, powerUp, this.name, -300, 500)
  );
  this.scene.shots.add(
    new Shot(this.scene, x, y, powerUp, this.name, 300, 500)
  );
}

massacre(x, y, powerUp) {
  this.scene.shots.add(
    new Shot(this.scene, x, y, powerUp, this.name, 300, 0)
```

```
    );
    this.scene.shots.add(
      new Shot(this.scene, x, y, powerUp, this.name, -300, 0)
    );
    this.scene.shots.add(
      new Shot(this.scene, x, y, powerUp, this.name, 0, 500)
    );
    this.scene.shots.add(new Shot(this.scene, x, y, powerUp, this.name, 30));
    this.scene.shots.add(new Shot(this.scene, x, y, powerUp, this.name, 60));
  }
}
```

These are just a few patterns but we could extend this class as much as we want.

Power Up

Figure 2.9 The sprite sheet for the power-up.

This is a very basic game object that will be generated when a complete fighter formation is destroyed. As soon as the player catches it, the power-up will be applied.

```
class PowerUp extends Phaser.GameObjects.Sprite {
  constructor(scene, x, y, name = "plenny0", power = "fruit") {
    super(scene, x, y, name);
    this.name = name;
    this.power = power;
    this.scene = scene;
    this.id = Math.random();
    this.spawnShadow(x, y);
    scene.add.existing(this);
    scene.physics.add.existing(this);
    this.body.setAllowGravity(false);
    this.body.setCircle(19);
    this.body.setOffset(12, 12);
    this.body.setVelocityX(-100);
    this.init();
  }
```

The power-up also spawns a shadow.

```
  spawnShadow(x, y) {
    this.shadow = this.scene.add
      .image(x + 20, y + 20, "plenny0")
      .setTint(0x000000)
      .setAlpha(0.4);
    this.scene.physics.add.existing(this.shadow);
```

```js
    this.shadow.body.setVelocityX(-100);
  }
```

This sets the animation and movement of the power-up.

```js
  init() {
    this.scene.anims.create({
      key: this.name,
      frames: this.scene.anims.generateFrameNumbers(this.name),
      frameRate: 10,
      repeat: -1,
    });

    this.scene.tweens.add({
      targets: [this],
      duration: 5000,
      x: { from: this.x, to: 0 },
      y: { from: this.y - 10, to: this.y + 10 },
      scale: { from: 0.8, to: 1 },
      repeat: -1,
      yoyo: true,
    });

    this.scene.tweens.add({
      targets: this.shadow,
      duration: 5000,
      x: { from: this.shadow.x, to: 0 },
      y: { from: this.shadow.y - 10, to: this.y + 10 },
      scale: { from: 0.8, to: 1 },
      repeat: -1,
      yoyo: true,
    });

    this.anims.play(this.name, true);
    this.body.setVelocityX(-100);
    this.shadow.body.setVelocityX(-100);
    this.direction = -1;
  }
```

When this element is destroyed, it will also destroy the shadow.

```js
  destroy() {
    this.shadow.destroy();
    super.destroy();
  }
}

export default PowerUp;
```

The game!

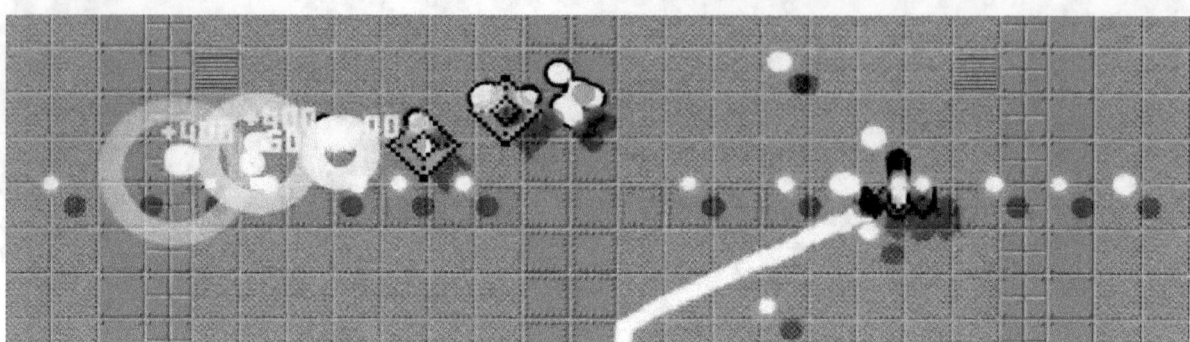

Figure 2.10 Hitting foes with side shots.

Here's the game. A single generic class that takes control of all stages. It follows the same steps we already saw before, but in this case, it needs to define more groups (fighters, shots, power-ups,...) and their collisions. We'll also keep the score and show points each time an enemy is destroyed.

```
import FoeGenerator from "./foe_generator";
import Player from "./player";
import PowerUp from "./powerup";
import SceneEffect from "./scene_effect";

export default class Game extends Phaser.Scene {
  constructor() {
    super({ key: "game" });
    this.player = null;
    this.score = 0;
    this.scoreText = null;
  }
```

We need to initialize the scene with the data we passed from the previous scene, especially the number of the stage to load the correct background. Also, we need to get the current power-up from the registry, although we are not applying it yet.

```
  init(data) {
    this.name = data.name;
    this.number = data.number;
    this.next = data.next;
    this.currentPowerUp = +this.registry.get("currentPowerUp");
  }
```

Here we create and start all the elements of the game. We create the background, the players, the foes, the shots, the power-ups, the scores, the audios and the colliders.

```
create() {
  this.duration = this.time * 1000;
  this.width = this.sys.game.config.width;
  this.height = this.sys.game.config.height;
  this.center_width = this.width / 2;
  this.center_height = this.height / 2;
  new SceneEffect(this).simpleOpen(() => 0);
  this.addBackground();
  this.cameras.main.setBackgroundColor(0x333333);
  this.lights.enable();
  this.lights.setAmbientColor(0x666666);
  this.addScores();
  this.addFoes();
  this.addPlayers();
  this.addPowerUps();
  this.addShots();
  this.loadAudios();
  this.addColliders();
}
```

This is how we create an infinite background. We create a tileSprite with the size of the screen and we set the origin to 0,0. Then we set the scroll factor to 0,1 so it will scroll only in the Y axis.

```
addBackground() {
  this.background = this.add
    .tileSprite(0, 0, this.width, this.height, "stage" + this.number)
    .setOrigin(0)
    .setScrollFactor(0, 1);
}
```

This is the method that will be called from the foe generator when a wave is destroyed. We create a new power-up and we add it to the power-up group.

```
spawnShake() {
  const { x, y } = this.lastDestroyedWaveFoe;
  this.shake = new PowerUp(this, x, y);
  this.powerUps.add(this.shake);
}
```

This adds the score text to the scene. We create a group of scores, one for each player. We add the score text to the group and we set the scroll factor to 0 so it will not scroll with the camera.

Figure 2.11 The score numbers.

```
addScores() {
  this.scores = {
```

```
    player1: {},
    player2: {},
};

this.scores["player1"]["scoreText"] = this.add
    .bitmapText(
        150,
        16,
        "wendy",
        String(this.registry.get("score_player1")).padStart(6, "0"),
        50
    )
    .setOrigin(0.5)
    .setScrollFactor(0);
this.scores["player2"]["scoreText"] = this.add
    .bitmapText(this.width - 150, 16, "wendy", "0".padStart(6, "0"), 50)
    .setOrigin(0.5)
    .setScrollFactor(0);
}
```

This adds the players to the scene. We create a group of players but in this particular implementation, we just add one player.

```
addPlayers() {
    this.trailLayer = this.add.layer();
    this.players = this.add.group();
    this.player = new Player(this, this.center_width, this.center_height);
    this.players.add(this.player);
}
```

Next, we have some functions to add other groups for the game elements.

```
addShots() {
    this.shotsLayer = this.add.layer();
    this.shots = this.add.group();
}

addFoes() {
    this.foeGroup = this.add.group();
    this.foeWaveGroup = this.add.group();
    this.foeShots = this.add.group();
    this.foes = new FoeGenerator(this);
}

addPowerUps() {
    this.available = ["fruit", "vanila", "chocolate"];
    this.powerUps = this.add.group();
}
```

Once we have created all groups of elements, we add the colliders between them.

2. Space Shooter: Starshake

```
addColliders() {
  this.physics.add.collider(
    this.players,
    this.foeGroup,
    this.crashFoe,
    () => {
      return true;
    },
    this
  );

  this.physics.add.collider(
    this.players,
    this.foeWaveGroup,
    this.crashFoe,
    () => {
      return true;
    },
    this
  );

  this.physics.add.overlap(
    this.shots,
    this.foeGroup,
    this.destroyFoe,
    () => {
      return true;
    },
    this
  );

  this.physics.add.overlap(
    this.shots,
    this.foeWaveGroup,
    this.destroyWaveFoe,
    () => {
      return true;
    },
    this
  );

  this.physics.add.collider(
    this.players,
    this.powerUps,
    this.pickPowerUp,
    () => {
      return true;
    },
    this
  );

  this.physics.add.overlap(
    this.players,
```

```
      this.foeShots,
      this.hitPlayer,
      () => {
        return true;
      },
      this
    );

    this.physics.add.collider(
      this.shots,
      this.foeShots,
      this.destroyShot,
      () => {
        return true;
      },
      this
    );
    this.physics.world.on("worldbounds", this.onWorldBounds);
  }
```

This is the callback for the world bounds and we will use it to destroy elements that the game does not need anymore. We check if the element is a shot and if it is, we destroy it. We also destroy the shadow of the shot. We do this because the shadow is not a child of the shot, so it will not be destroyed automatically.

```
onWorldBounds(body, t) {
  const name = body.gameObject.name.toString();
  if (["foeshot", "shot"].includes(name)) {
    body.gameObject.shadow.destroy();
    body.gameObject.destroy();
  }
}
```

This is the callback for the collision between two shots. We destroy both shots and we create an explosion where they meet.

```
destroyShot(shot, foeShot) {
  const point = this.lights.addPointLight(shot.x, shot.y, 0xffffff, 10, 0.7);
  this.tweens.add({
    targets: point,
    duration: 400,
    scale: { from: 1, to: 0 },
  });
  this.playAudio("foexplosion");
  shot.shadow.destroy();
  shot.destroy();
  foeShot.shadow.destroy();
  foeShot.shot();
  this.updateScore(shot.playerName, 50);
}
```

This is called when we destroy a foe that is part of a wave.

```
destroyWaveFoe(shot, foe) {
  this.lastDestroyedWaveFoe = { x: foe.x, y: foe.y };
  this.destroyFoe(shot, foe);
}
```

This is the callback we call when a shot hits a foe. We destroy the shot and we decrease the lives of the foe. If the foe has no more lives, we destroy it and we create an explosion. We also add the points to the score of the player who shot the foe.

```
destroyFoe(shot, foe) {
  foe.lives--;
  this.playAudio("foexplosion");
  const point = this.lights.addPointLight(shot.x, shot.y, 0xffffff, 10, 0.7);
  this.tweens.add({
    targets: point,
    duration: 400,
    scale: { from: 1, to: 0 },
  });
  this.tweens.add({
    targets: foe,
    duration: 400,
    tint: { from: 0xffffff, to: 0xff0000 },
  });
  this.updateScore(shot.playerName, 50);
  this.tweens.add({ targets: foe, y: "-=10", yoyo: true, duration: 100 });

  shot.destroy();
  if (foe.lives === 0) {
    this.playAudio("foedestroy");
    const point = this.lights.addPointLight(
      shot.x,
      shot.y,
      0xffffff,
      10,
      0.7
    );
    this.tweens.add({
      targets: point,
      duration: 400,
      scale: { from: 1, to: 0 },
    });
    this.updateScore(shot.playerName, foe.points);
    foe.dead();
  }
}
```

2. Space Shooter: Starshake — The game!

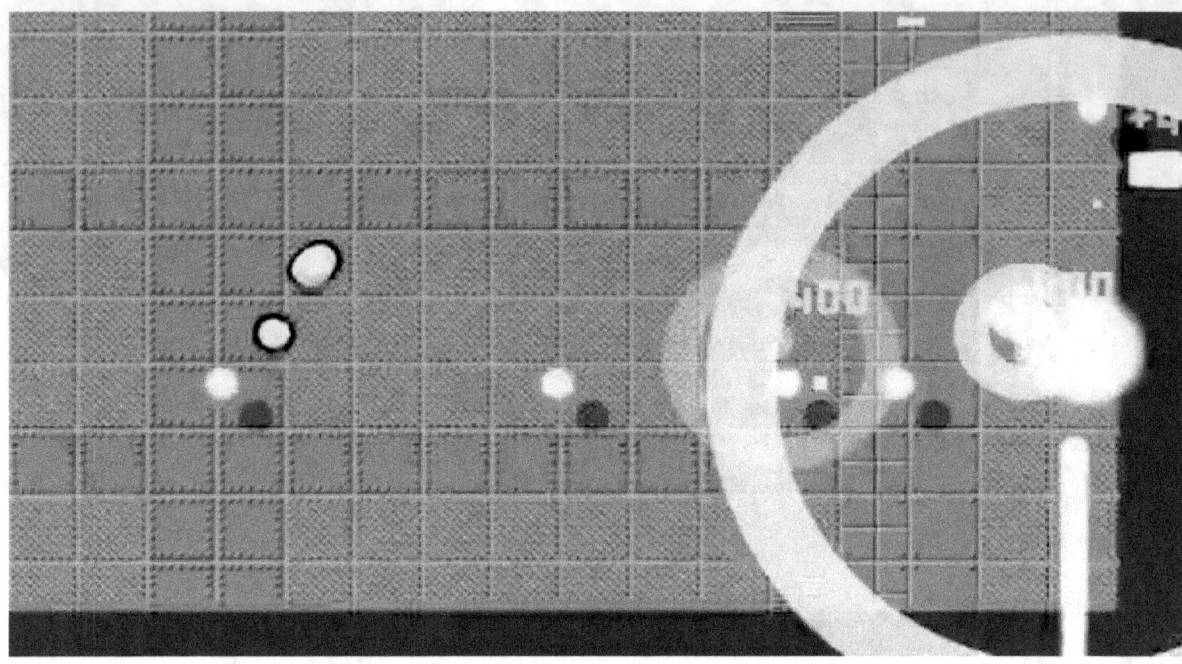

Figure 2.12 Player death: big explosion and camera shake!

This one is called when a foe shot hits the player. Unless the player is blinking (because it just started), we destroy the player and we create an explosion. We also destroy the shadow of the shot. Then we respawn the player.

```
hitPlayer(player, shot) {
  if (player.blinking) return;

  this.players.remove(this.player);
  player.dead();
  this.playAudio("explosion");
  shot.shadow.destroy();
  shot.destroy();
  this.time.delayedCall(1000, () => this.respawnPlayer(), null, this);
}
```

This one is called when a player crashes with a foe. Unless the player is blinking (because it just started), we destroy the player, and the foe and also at the end we respawn the player.

```
crashFoe(player, foe) {
  if (player.blinking) return;
  player.dead();
  this.playAudio("explosion");
  foe.dead();
  this.time.delayedCall(1000, () => this.respawnPlayer(), null, this);
}
```

This is the callback when the player picks up a power-up. We update the power-up of the player and we destroy the power-up. We also create a tween to make the player blink.

```
pickPowerUp(player, powerUp) {
  this.playAudio("stageclear1");
  this.updatePowerUp(player, powerUp);
  this.tweens.add({
    targets: player,
    duration: 200,
    alpha: { from: 0.5, to: 1 },
    scale: { from: 1.4, to: 1 },
    repeat: 3,
  });
  powerUp.destroy();
}
```

This adds a player to the game. We create a tween to make the player blink and then we create a new player.

```
respawnPlayer() {
  this.player = new Player(this, this.center_width, this.center_height);
  this.player.blinking = true;
  this.players.add(this.player);
  this.tweens.add({
    targets: this.player,
    duration: 100,
    alpha: { from: 0, to: 1 },
    repeat: 10,
    onComplete: () => {
      this.player.blinking = false;
    },
  });
}
```

Here we load all the audio, and we add them to the `this.audios` object. Later we can play them with the `playAudio` method.

```
loadAudios() {
  this.audios = {
    shot: this.sound.add("shot"),
    foeshot: this.sound.add("foeshot"),
    explosion: this.sound.add("explosion"),
    foexplosion: this.sound.add("foexplosion"),
    foedestroy: this.sound.add("foedestroy"),
    stageclear1: this.sound.add("stageclear1"),
    stageclear2: this.sound.add("stageclear2"),
    boss: this.sound.add("boss"),
  };
}
```

2. Space Shooter: Starshake

```
playAudio(key) {
  this.audios[key].play();
}
```

The game loop is as simple as this. We update the player and the foes. We also update the background to make it scroll.

```
update() {
  if (this.player) this.player.update();
  this.foes.update();
  this.background.tilePositionY -= 10;
}
```

When the player finishes the stage, we destroy all the elements and we start the transition to the next scene.

```
endScene() {
  this.foeWaveGroup.children.entries.forEach((foe) => foe.shadow.destroy());
  this.foeGroup.children.entries.forEach((foe) => foe.shadow.destroy());
  this.shots.children.entries.forEach((shot) => shot.shadow.destroy());
  this.foeShots.children.entries.forEach((shot) => shot.shadow.destroy());
  this.time.delayedCall(
    2000,
    () => {
      this.finishScene();
    },
    null,
    this
  );
}
```

This is the callback for the end of the scene. We stop all the audio, we stop the scene and we start the transition to the next scene.

```
finishScene() {
  this.game.sound.stopAll();
  this.scene.stop("game");
  const scene = this.number < 5 ? "transition" : "outro";
  this.scene.start(scene, {
    next: "game",
    name: "STAGE",
    number: this.number + 1,
  });
}
```

The power-up looks the same but the effect is different. We keep increasing its value so we can apply the effect to the player. In this game, the power-up applies another shooting pattern.

```
  updatePowerUp(player, powerUp) {
    player.powerUp = this.available[this.currentPowerUp];
    this.currentPowerUp =
      this.currentPowerUp + 1 === this.available.length
        ? this.currentPowerUp
        : this.currentPowerUp + 1;
    this.registry.set("currentPowerUp", this.currentPowerUp);
  }
```

This is the method we use to update the score of the player. We get the score from the registry and we update it. We also create a tween to make the score text blink.

```
  updateScore(playerName, points = 0) {
    const score = +this.registry.get("score_" + playerName) + points;
    this.registry.set("score_" + playerName, score);
    this.scores[playerName]["scoreText"].setText(
      String(score).padStart(6, "0")
    );
    this.tweens.add({
      targets: this.scores[playerName]["scoreText"],
      duration: 200,
      tint: { from: 0x0000ff, to: 0xffffff },
      scale: { from: 1.2, to: 1 },
      repeat: 2,
    });
  }
}
```

Every time the player is destroyed, a huge explosion will be displayed.

Scene Effect

 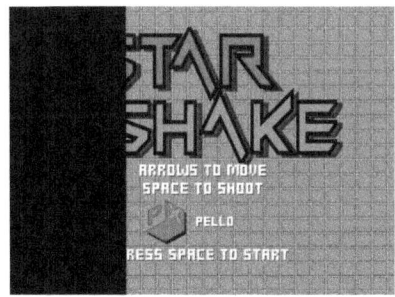 

Figure 2.13 The simple curtain used for transition.

This is just a simple curtain effect every time we change the scene.

```
export default class SceneEffect {
```

2. Space Shooter: Starshake — Scene Effect

```
constructor(scene) {
  this.scene = scene;
}
```

This adds a rectangle to the scene, and then we tween it to make it move from left to right.

```
simpleClose(callback) {
  const rectangleWidth = this.scene.width / 2;
  const rectangle1 = this.scene.add
    .rectangle(
      0 - rectangleWidth,
      0,
      this.scene.width,
      this.scene.height,
      0x000000
    )
    .setOrigin(0.5, 0);

  this.scene.tweens.add({
    targets: rectangle1,
    duration: 500,
    x: { from: -rectangleWidth / 2, to: rectangleWidth },
    onComplete: () => {
      callback();
    },
  });
}
```

This adds a rectangle to the scene, and then we tween it to make it move from right to left.

```
simpleOpen(callback) {
  const rectangleWidth = this.scene.width / 2;
  const rectangle1 = this.scene.add
    .rectangle(
      rectangleWidth,
      0,
      this.scene.width,
      this.scene.height,
      0x000000
    )
    .setOrigin(0.5, 0);

  this.scene.tweens.add({
    targets: rectangle1,
    duration: 500,
    x: { from: rectangleWidth, to: -rectangleWidth },
    onComplete: () => {
      callback();
    },
```

```
    });
}
```

This adds two rectangles to the scene, and then we tween them to make them move from the center to the left and right.

```
close(callback) {
    const rectangleWidth = this.scene.width / 2;
    const rectangle1 = this.scene.add
      .rectangle(
        0 - rectangleWidth,
        0,
        this.scene.width / 2,
        this.scene.height,
        0x000000
      )
      .setOrigin(0.5, 0);
    const rectangle2 = this.scene.add
      .rectangle(
        this.scene.width,
        0,
        this.scene.width / 2,
        this.scene.height,
        0x000000
      )
      .setOrigin(0, 0);
    this.scene.tweens.add(
      {
        targets: rectangle1,
        duration: 1000,
        x: { from: -rectangleWidth / 2, to: rectangleWidth / 2 },
      },
      {
        targets: rectangle2,
        duration: 1000,
        x: { from: this.scene.width, to: rectangleWidth },
        onComplete: () => {
          callback();
        },
      }
    );
}
```

These are very simplest curtain effects, but there are several out there you can apply.

Splash

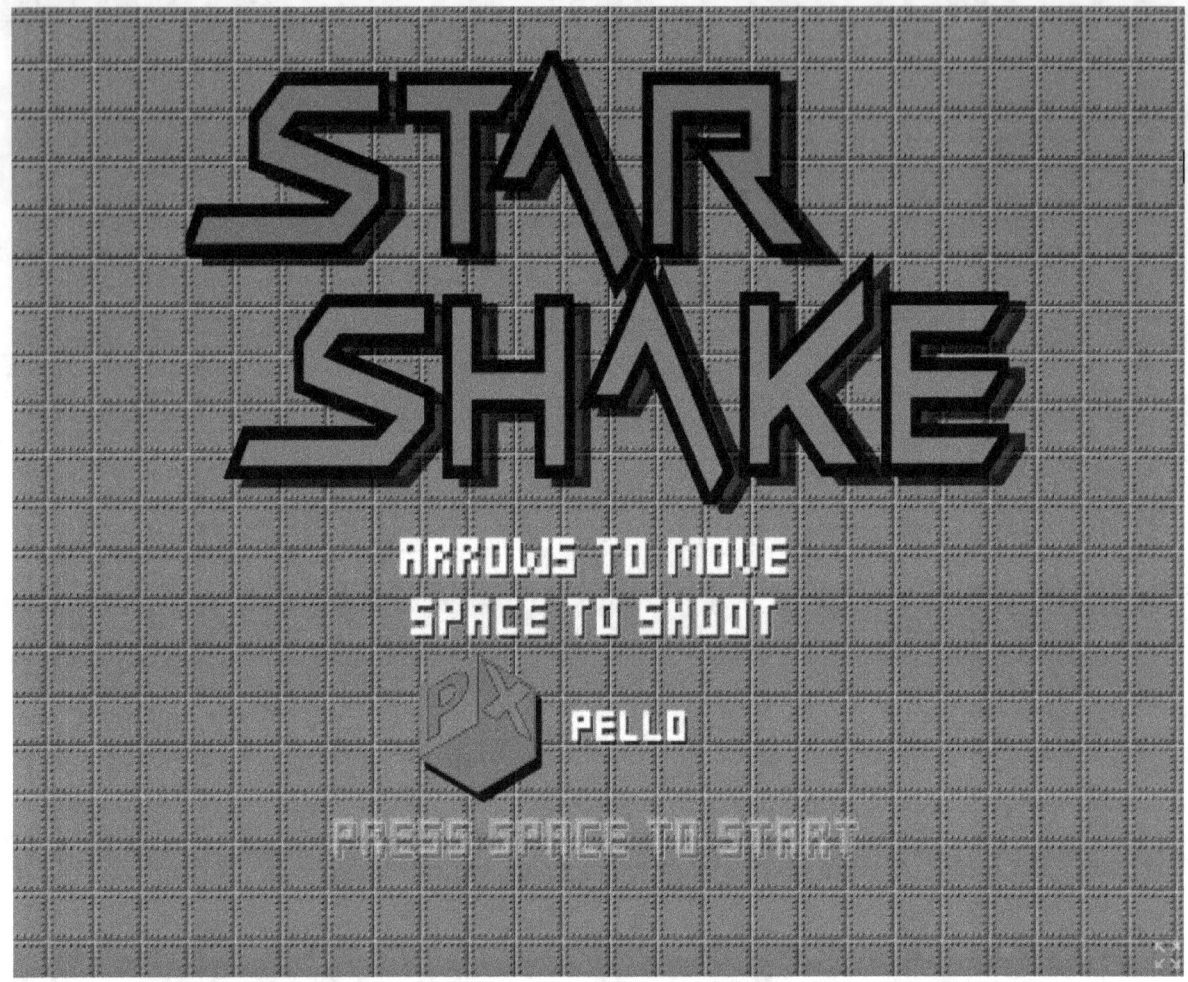

Figure 2.14 Splash screen with blinking "PRESS SPACE TO START".

A good Splash is a key element to sell the game. Not only because it's the first impression of the game but also because it will probably be used as a screenshot or cover for our product. It also sets the tone of your game so do not choose the elements of these screens lightly.

```
import SceneEffect from "./scene_effect";

export default class Splash extends Phaser.Scene {
  constructor() {
    super({ key: "splash" });
  }

  create() {
    this.width = this.sys.game.config.width;
```

2. Space Shooter: Starshake — Splash

```
    this.height = this.sys.game.config.height;
    this.center_width = this.width / 2;
    this.center_height = this.height / 2;
    this.addBackground();
    this.showLogo();
    this.registry.set("currentPowerUp", 0);
    this.time.delayedCall(1000, () => this.showInstructions(), null, this);

    this.input.keyboard.on(
      "keydown-SPACE",
      () => this.transitionToChange(),
      this
    );

    this.playMusic();
  }
```

The background, as the game, is a `tileSprite`, so we can scroll it to make it look like it's moving.

```
  addBackground() {
    this.background = this.add
      .tileSprite(0, 0, this.width, this.height, "background")
      .setOrigin(0)
      .setScrollFactor(0, 1);
  }

  update() {
    this.background.tilePositionY -= 2;
    this.background.tilePositionX += 2;
  }
```

We add one curtain effect to change to another screen:

```
  transitionToChange() {
    new SceneEffect(this).simpleClose(this.startGame.bind(this));
  }

  startGame() {
    if (this.theme) this.theme.stop();
    this.scene.start("transition", {
      next: "game",
      name: "STAGE",
      number: 1,
      time: 30,
    });
  }
```

We add the logo, and then we tween it to make it move up and down.

```
  showLogo() {
```

```
    this.gameLogoShadow = this.add
      .image(this.center_width, 250, "logo")
      .setScale(0.7)
      .setOrigin(0.5);
    this.gameLogoShadow.setOrigin(0.48);
    this.gameLogoShadow.tint = 0x3e4e43;
    this.gameLogoShadow.alpha = 0.6;
    this.gameLogo = this.add
      .image(this.center_width, 250, "logo")
      .setScale(0.7)
      .setOrigin(0.5);

    this.tweens.add({
      targets: [this.gameLogo, this.gameLogoShadow],
      duration: 500,
      y: {
        from: -200,
        to: 250,
      },
    });

    this.tweens.add({
      targets: [this.gameLogo, this.gameLogoShadow],
      duration: 1500,
      y: {
        from: 250,
        to: 200,
      },
      repeat: -1,
      yoyo: true,
    });
}
```

This is the music for the `splash` scene. We'll play it in a loop.

```
playMusic(theme = "splash") {
  this.theme = this.sound.add(theme);
  this.theme.stop();
  this.theme.play({
    mute: false,
    volume: 0.5,
    rate: 1,
    detune: 0,
    seek: 0,
    loop: true,
    delay: 0,
  });
}
```

Here we add the instructions to the scene.

```
showInstructions() {
```

```
    this.add
      .bitmapText(this.center_width, 450, "wendy", "Arrows to move", 60)
      .setOrigin(0.5)
      .setDropShadow(3, 4, 0x222222, 0.7);
    this.add
      .bitmapText(this.center_width, 500, "wendy", "SPACE to shoot", 60)
      .setOrigin(0.5)
      .setDropShadow(3, 4, 0x222222, 0.7);
    this.add
      .sprite(this.center_width - 95, 598, "pello_logo")
      .setOrigin(0.5)
      .setScale(0.3)
      .setTint(0x000000)
      .setAlpha(0.7);
    this.add
      .sprite(this.center_width - 100, 590, "pello_logo")
      .setOrigin(0.5)
      .setScale(0.3);

    this.add
      .bitmapText(this.center_width + 30, 590, "wendy", "PELLO", 50)
      .setOrigin(0.5)
      .setDropShadow(3, 4, 0x222222, 0.7);
    this.space = this.add
      .bitmapText(this.center_width, 680, "wendy", "Press SPACE to start", 60)
      .setOrigin(0.5)
      .setDropShadow(3, 4, 0x222222, 0.7);
    this.tweens.add({
      targets: this.space,
      duration: 300,
      alpha: { from: 0, to: 1 },
      repeat: -1,
      yoyo: true,
    });
  }
}
```

Invest some time in the Splash. I'm sure that you can do it better than me.

Transition page

The transition page is just the previous page we see before the `game` screen. It just shows the number of the stage that is coming next for a few seconds.

```
export default class Transition extends Phaser.Scene {
  constructor() {
    super({ key: "transition" });
  }
```

2. Space Shooter: Starshake — Transition page

```
init(data) {
  this.name = data.name;
  this.number = data.number;
  this.next = data.next;
}
```

Figure 2.15 Transition text.

In the transition, we show a message with the current stage and some advice, and then we load the next scene.

```
create() {
  const messages = [
    "Fire at will",
    "Beware the tanks",
    "Shoot down the UFOs",
    "FINAL BOSS",
  ];

  this.width = this.sys.game.config.width;
  this.height = this.sys.game.config.height;
  this.center_width = this.width / 2;
  this.center_height = this.height / 2;
  this.sound.add("stageclear2").play();
  this.add
    .bitmapText(
      this.center_width,
      this.center_height - 50,
      "wendy",
      messages[this.number - 1],
      100
    )
    .setOrigin(0.5);
  this.add
    .bitmapText(
      this.center_width,
      this.center_height + 50,
      "wendy",
```

2. Space Shooter: Starshake — Transition page

```
            "Ready player 1",
            80
        )
        .setOrigin(0.5);

    this.playMusic("music" + (this.number !== 4 ? this.number : 1));
    this.time.delayedCall(2000, () => this.loadNext(), null, this);
  }

  loadNext() {
    this.scene.start(this.next, {
      name: this.name,
      number: this.number,
      time: this.time,
    });
  }
```

The music of the stage is loaded and played in this transition.

```
  playMusic(theme = "music1") {
    this.theme = this.sound.add(theme);
    this.theme.play({
      mute: false,
      volume: 0.4,
      rate: 1,
      detune: 0,
      seek: 0,
      loop: true,
      delay: 0,
    });
  }
}
```

Despite the timeout, we let the player skip this scene.

Outro

This is just a scene telling what happens when you finish the game and you kill the final boss. This is completely optional but if your game has any type of backstory or message it is worth adding it. After all, this is the scene that only winners will be able to witness so it feels like a reward.

```
export default class Outro extends Phaser.Scene {
  constructor() {
    super({ key: "outro" });
  }

  create() {
```

```
    this.width = this.sys.game.config.width;
    this.height = this.sys.game.config.height;
    this.center_width = this.width / 2;
    this.center_height = this.height / 2;
    this.introLayer = this.add.layer();
    this.splashLayer = this.add.layer();
    this.text = [
      "Score: " + this.registry.get("score_player1"),
      "The evil forces among with",
      "their tyrannical leader GUINXU",
      "were finally wiped out.",
      "Thanks to commander Alva",
      "And the powah of the Plenny Shakes",
      " - press enter - ",
    ];
    this.showHistory();
    this.showPlayer();

    this.input.keyboard.on("keydown-ENTER", this.startSplash, this);
}
```

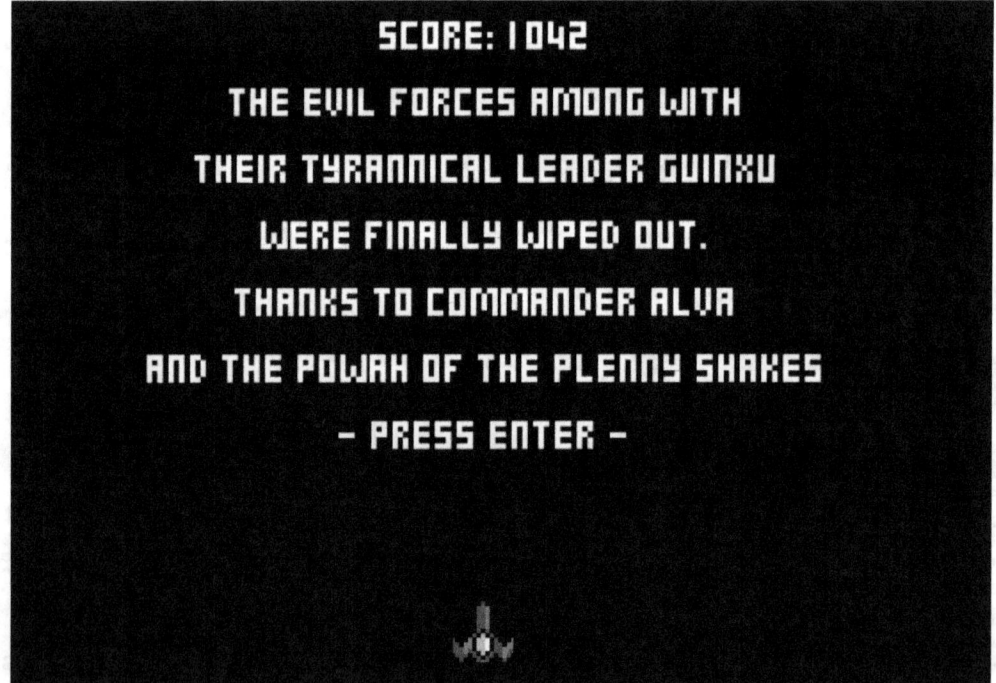

Figure 2.16 This is the outro screen.

These are the functions to show the dramatic story of the game, line by line.

```
showHistory() {
  this.text.forEach((line, i) => {
    this.time.delayedCall(
      (i + 1) * 2000,
      () => this.showLine(line, (i + 1) * 60),
```

```
        null,
        this
      );
    });
    this.time.delayedCall(4000, () => this.showPlayer(), null, this);
  }

  showLine(text, y) {
    let line = this.introLayer.add(
      this.add
        .bitmapText(this.center_width, y, "wendy", text, 50)
        .setOrigin(0.5)
        .setAlpha(0)
    );
    this.tweens.add({
      targets: line,
      duration: 2000,
      alpha: 1,
    });
  }
```

This will just show the `player1` sprite.

```
  showPlayer() {
    this.player1 = this.add
      .sprite(this.center_width, this.height - 200, "player1")
      .setOrigin(0.5);
  }
```

This will start the splash screen.

```
  startSplash() {
    this.scene.start("splash");
  }
}
```

This particular one had a joke about some famous Spanish indie developers.

Other shooter or similar games

U.F.I.S.H.

Source code: https://github.com/pxai/phasergames/tree/master/ufish

Play it here: https://pello.itch.io/ufish

3. Platformer: WallHammer

Source code: https://github.com/pxai/phasergames/tree/master/wallhammer

Play it here: https://pello.itch.io/wallhammer

3. Platformer: WallHammer

It's time for another genre. Now we'll create a platformer game. This genre is very popular and there are many examples out there. We'll create a very simple one, but you can easily extend it to create a more complex game.

This game called WallHammer is a classic platformer where you have to collect coins and avoid bats and zombies. You can block them, but if they touch you, you'll die. You can also collect lunchboxes to get power-ups like speed, better hammer, etc.

Another key element of this platformer is that the player can build new blocks and also destroy them. Also, most of the existing blocks of the scene are breakable which adds some interesting mechanics that players can take advantage of.

Tiled

To build the scenes, we are going to use tiled maps with the Tiled editor. Tiled will allow us to design each scene independently from the code: colliding platform blocks, background and objects will be easily placed making the scene design super easy.

Each scene contains at least three basic layers:

- scene: the platform itself where all present elements will collide with the player and foes.

- objects: the object layer groups locations where we set foes, start and end points for the player, power-ups and any other element that the game requires.

- background: some tiled for decoration purposes.

You can learn more about Tiled in the chapter dedicated to assets.

Init project

This is where we initialize the game with definitions of scenes that should be already familiar: Bootloader, Splash, Transition and a generic Game scene.

```
import Phaser from "phaser";
import Bootloader from "./bootloader";
import Outro from "./outro";
import Splash from "./splash";
import Transition from "./transition";
import Game from "./game";
```

3. Platformer: WallHammer — Init project

```js
const config = {
  width: 1000,
  height: 800,
  scale: {
    mode: Phaser.Scale.FIT,
    autoCenter: Phaser.Scale.CENTER_BOTH,
  },
  autoRound: false,
  parent: "contenedor",
  physics: {
    default: "arcade",
    arcade: {
      gravity: { y: 300 },
      debug: false,
    },
  },
  scene: [Bootloader, Splash, Transition, Game, Outro],
};

const game = new Phaser.Game(config);
```

Again, we'll apply arcade physics.

Loader

In the loader, apart from images, sprites and sounds, we'll also add a new type of element: the tiled maps of the scenes along with the images used for those maps.

```js
export default class Bootloader extends Phaser.Scene {
  constructor() {
    super({ key: "bootloader" });
  }

  preload() {
    this.createBars();
    this.load.on(
      "progress",
      function (value) {
        this.progressBar.clear();
        this.progressBar.fillStyle(0xf09937, 1);
        this.progressBar.fillRect(
          this.cameras.main.width / 4,
          this.cameras.main.height / 2 - 16,
          (this.cameras.main.width / 2) * value,
          16
        );
      },
      this
    );
```

3. Platformer: WallHammer — Loader

```
this.load.on(
  "complete",
  () => {
    this.scene.start("splash");
  },
  this
);
```

Here we load the music for different stages, a couple of images and sound effects:

```
Array(5)
  .fill(0)
  .forEach((_, i) => {
    this.load.audio(`music${i}`, `assets/sounds/music${i}.mp3`);
  });

this.load.image("pello", "assets/images/pello.png");
this.load.image("landscape", "assets/images/landscape.png");

this.load.audio("build", "assets/sounds/build.mp3");
this.load.audio("coin", "assets/sounds/coin.mp3");
this.load.audio("death", "assets/sounds/death.mp3");
this.load.audio("jump", "assets/sounds/jump.mp3");
this.load.audio("kill", "assets/sounds/kill.mp3");
this.load.audio("land", "assets/sounds/land.mp3");
this.load.audio("lunchbox", "assets/sounds/lunchbox.mp3");
this.load.audio("prize", "assets/sounds/prize.mp3");
this.load.audio("stone_fail", "assets/sounds/stone_fail.mp3");
this.load.audio("stone", "assets/sounds/stone.mp3");
this.load.audio("foedeath", "assets/sounds/foedeath.mp3");
this.load.audio("stage", "assets/sounds/stage.mp3");

this.load.audio("splash", "assets/sounds/splash.mp3");

Array(2)
  .fill(0)
  .forEach((_, i) => {
    this.load.image(`brick${i}`, `assets/images/brick${i}.png`);
  });

Array(5)
  .fill(0)
  .forEach((_, i) => {
    this.load.image(
      `platform${i + 2}`,
      `assets/images/platform${i + 2}.png`
    );
  });
```

These are a couple of fonts, one for the game and the other for the splash screen logo:

```
this.load.bitmapFont(
  "pixelFont",
  "assets/fonts/mario.png",
  "assets/fonts/mario.xml"
);
this.load.bitmapFont(
  "hammerfont",
  "assets/fonts/hammer.png",
  "assets/fonts/hammer.xml"
);
```

Here we load the maps for the stages and the images we need for the tiles. They must be the same that we used while editing the tiled maps:

```
Array(5)
  .fill(0)
  .forEach((_, i) => {
    this.load.tilemapTiledJSON(`scene${i}`, `assets/maps/scene${i}.json`);
  });
this.load.image("softbricks", "assets/maps/softbricks.png");
this.load.image("bricks", "assets/maps/bricks.png");
this.load.image("background", "assets/maps/background.png");
```

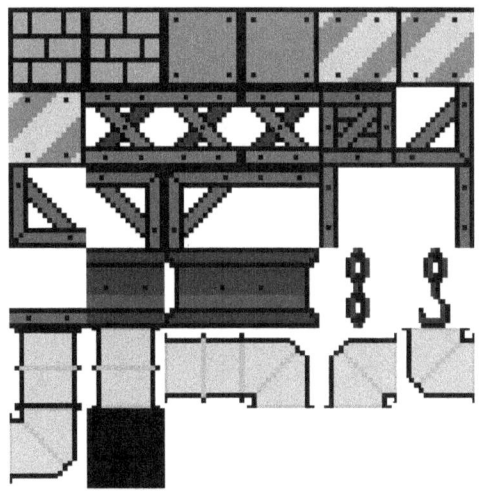

Figure 3.1 These are images for the maps, bricks and background.

These are the sprites for the game objects, starting with the player itself:

```
this.load.spritesheet("walt", "assets/images/walt.png", {
```

3. Platformer: WallHammer — Loader

```
        frameWidth: 64,
        frameHeight: 64,
    });

    this.load.image("chain", "assets/images/chain.png");
    this.load.spritesheet("bat", "assets/images/bat.png", {
        frameWidth: 32,
        frameHeight: 32,
    });
    this.load.spritesheet("zombie", "assets/images/zombie.png", {
        frameWidth: 64,
        frameHeight: 64,
    });
    this.load.spritesheet("coin", "assets/images/coin.png", {
        frameWidth: 64,
        frameHeight: 64,
    });
    this.load.spritesheet("lunchbox", "assets/images/lunchbox.png", {
        frameWidth: 64,
        frameHeight: 64,
    });
    this.load.spritesheet("hammer", "assets/images/hammer.png", {
        frameWidth: 64,
        frameHeight: 64,
    });
    this.load.spritesheet("speed", "assets/images/speed.png", {
        frameWidth: 64,
        frameHeight: 64,
    });
    this.load.spritesheet("boots", "assets/images/boots.png", {
        frameWidth: 64,
        frameHeight: 64,
    });
    this.load.spritesheet("star", "assets/images/star.png", {
        frameWidth: 64,
        frameHeight: 64,
    });
```

Finally, we will use the registry for to keep scores throughout the scenes:

```
    this.registry.set("score", 0);
    this.registry.set("coins", 0);
}

createBars() {
    this.loadBar = this.add.graphics();
    this.loadBar.fillStyle(0xca6702, 1);
    this.loadBar.fillRect(
        this.cameras.main.width / 4 - 2,
```

3. Platformer: WallHammer — Loader

```
      this.cameras.main.height / 2 - 18,
      this.cameras.main.width / 2 + 4,
      20
    );
    this.progressBar = this.add.graphics();
  }
}
```

To avoid repeating commands, we name the scene assets with numbers so we can load them using a for loop.

Bat

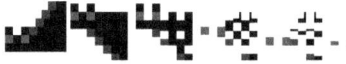

Figure 3.2 The sprites for the bat character.

The bat is the most common and generic enemy here. These are flying animated sprites that cross the scene until they find and obstacle or the player itself. With one touch the player is dead. If they hit any part of the scene platform they will automatically turn and fly in the opposite direction.

```
export default class Bat extends Phaser.Physics.Arcade.Sprite {
  constructor(scene, x, y, type = "right") {
    super(scene, x, y, "bat");
    this.name = "bat";
    this.scene = scene;
    this.scene.physics.add.existing(this);
    this.scene.physics.world.enable(this);
    this.body.setAllowGravity(false);
    this.scene.add.existing(this);
    this.direction = type === "right" ? 1 : -1;

    this.init();
  }
```

This inits the animations for the bat and starts the movement. We also add a listener for the animationcomplete event.

```
  init() {
    this.scene.anims.create({
      key: this.name,
      frames: this.scene.anims.generateFrameNumbers(this.name, {
        start: 0,
        end: 1,
      }),
      frameRate: 5,
```

```
    repeat: -1,
  });

  this.scene.anims.create({
    key: this.name + "death",
    frames: this.scene.anims.generateFrameNumbers(this.name, {
      start: 2,
      end: 5,
    }),
    frameRate: 5,
  });

  this.anims.play(this.name, true);
  this.body.setVelocityX(this.direction * 150);
  this.flipX = this.direction > 0;
  this.on("animationcomplete", this.animationComplete, this);
}

update() {}
```

Turns the bat around and changes the direction:

```
turn() {
  this.direction = -this.direction;
  this.flipX = this.direction > 0;
  this.body.setVelocityX(this.direction * 150);
}
```

This kills the bat "nicely" by playing the death animation.

```
death() {
  this.dead = true;
  this.body.enable = false;
  this.body.rotation = 0;
  this.anims.play(this.name + "death");
}
```

This is called when any animation is completed. If the `death` animation is completed, then it destroys the bat.

```
animationComplete(animation, frame) {
  if (animation.key === this.name + "death") {
    this.destroy();
  }
}
}
```

As you see bats are not very smart so we need to place them at specific heights to be dangerous or just annoying.

3. Platformer: WallHammer

Zombie

Figure 3.3 The sprites for the zombie.

Zombies are the dark side of the player: they are also construction workers but they joined the ranks of the ever-growing army of the undead. They just walk on the ground and as it happens with the bats, they turn when they hit an obstacle.

```
export default class Zombie extends Phaser.Physics.Arcade.Sprite {
  constructor(scene, x, y, type = "right") {
    super(scene, x, y, "zombie");
    this.name = "zombie";
    this.scene = scene;
    this.scene.physics.add.existing(this);
    this.scene.physics.world.enable(this);
    this.body.setAllowGravity(true);
    this.scene.add.existing(this);
    this.direction = type === "right" ? -1 : 1;

    this.init();
  }
```

As we did with the Bat, this inits the animations for the zombies and starts the movement. We also add a listener for the animationcomplete event.

```
  init() {
    this.scene.anims.create({
      key: this.name,
      frames: this.scene.anims.generateFrameNumbers(this.name, {
        start: 0,
        end: 2,
      }),
      frameRate: 5,
      repeat: -1,
    });

    this.scene.anims.create({
      key: this.name + "death",
      frames: this.scene.anims.generateFrameNumbers(this.name, {
        start: 3,
        end: 5,
      }),
      frameRate: 5,
    });
```

3. Platformer: WallHammer — Zombie

```
    this.anims.play(this.name, true);
    this.body.setVelocityX(this.direction * 100);
    this.flipX = this.direction < 0;
    this.on("animationcomplete", this.animationComplete, this);
}
```

Turns the zombie around and changes the direction:

```
turn() {
    this.direction = -this.direction;
    this.flipX = this.direction < 0;
    this.body.setVelocityX(this.direction * 100);
}
```

This kills the zombie "nicely" by playing the death animation.

```
death() {
    this.dead = true;
    this.body.enable = false;
    this.body.rotation = 0;
    this.anims.play(this.name + "death");
}
```

Again, when the death animation is completed, then it destroys the zombie.

```
animationComplete(animation, frame) {
    if (animation.key === this.name + "death") {
        this.destroy();
    }
  }
}
```

Both zombies and bats can be blocked placing a block in their face and they will turn back on collision. Also, the player can kill them with a hammer blow but they must get dangerously close for that.

Turn

Figure 3.4 Turn objects placed to enclose the Zombie.

Turns are invisible game objects that we can place on the stage so we can force foes to turn in specific spots.

```
class Turn extends Phaser.GameObjects.Rectangle {
  constructor(scene, x, y, width = 32, height = 32, type = "") {
    super(scene, x, y, width, height, 0xffffff);
    this.scene = scene;
    this.type = type;
    this.setAlpha(0);
    this.x = x;
    this.y = y;
    scene.add.existing(this);
    scene.physics.add.existing(this);

    this.body.immovable = true;
    this.body.moves = false;
  }
  disable() {
    this.visible = false;
    this.destroy();
  }
  destroy() {
    super.destroy();
  }
}

export default Turn;
```

With the use of this turn, we can enclose the path of foes without adding blocks that affect the player.

Lunchbox

Figure 3.5 Lunchbox object is just a couple of sprites.

Yummy lunchboxes contain random power-ups for the player. They must be placed in the scene map inside the object layer.

```
class LunchBox extends Phaser.GameObjects.Sprite {
  constructor(scene, x, y, name = "lunchbox") {
    super(scene, x, y, name);
    this.scene = scene;
    this.name = name;
    this.setScale(1);
    this.setOrigin(0.5);

    scene.add.existing(this);
    scene.physics.add.existing(this);

    this.body.immovable = true;
    this.body.moves = false;
    this.disabled = false;
    this.init();
  }
```

This first function inits the animations and it adds a little tween effect to make the lunchbox move up and down.

```
init() {
  this.scene.anims.create({
    key: this.name,
    frames: this.scene.anims.generateFrameNumbers(this.name, {
      start: 0,
      end: 0,
    }),
    frameRate: 1,
  });

  this.scene.anims.create({
    key: this.name + "opened",
    frames: this.scene.anims.generateFrameNumbers(this.name, {
      start: 1,
      end: 1,
    }),
    frameRate: 1,
  });
```

3. Platformer: WallHammer

```
    this.anims.play(this.name, true);
    this.scene.tweens.add({
      targets: this,
      duration: 500,
      y: this.y - 20,
      repeat: -1,
      yoyo: true,
    });
}
```

This is called when the player picks up the lunchbox. It plays the opened animation and calls the showPrize method.

```
pick() {
    this.anims.play(this.name + "opened", true);
    this.showPrize();
    this.disabled = true;
    this.scene.time.delayedCall(
      1000,
      () => {
        this.destroy();
        this.prizeSprite.destroy();
      },
      null,
      this
    );
}
```

This method picks a random prize and it shows it to the player when picking up the lunchbox. It plays a tween animation and calls the applyPrize method from the player.

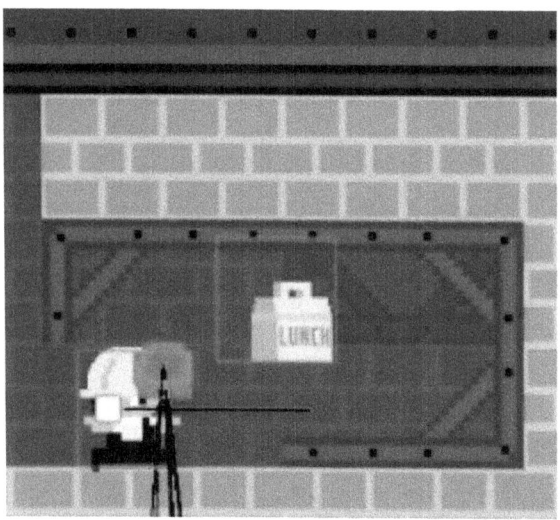

Figure 3.6 Player opens a lunchbox and prize is shown.

3. Platformer: WallHammer — Lunchbox

```javascript
  showPrize() {
    const prize = ["boots", "hammer", "coin", "star", "speed"];
    const selectedPrize = Phaser.Math.RND.pick(prize);
    this.scene.player.applyPrize(selectedPrize);
    this.prizeSprite = this.scene.add
      .sprite(this.x, this.y, selectedPrize)
      .setOrigin(0.5)
      .setScale(0.8);
    this.scene.tweens.add({
      targets: this.prizeSprite,
      duration: 500,
      y: { from: this.y, to: this.y - 64 },
      onComplete: () => {
        this.scene.playAudio("prize");
      },
    });
  }
}

export default LunchBox;
```

To pick up these lunchboxes the player just needs to walk through them. They will automatically open and show a power-up.

Particle

Again we need to show some particles in different moments of the game to provide proper feedback or consequences of actions For example each time the player walks or lands after a jump. Also when breaking blocks or adding new ones. Some particle classes are just squares that shrink and vanish, others are more complex.

This class is used to create the smoke particles. It's a simple rectangle that scales down and fades out.

```javascript
export class Smoke extends Phaser.GameObjects.Rectangle {
  constructor(scene, x, y, width, height, color = 0xffffff, gravity = false) {
    width = width || Phaser.Math.Between(10, 25);
    height = height || Phaser.Math.Between(10, 25);
    super(scene, x, y, width, height, color);
    scene.add.existing(this);
    this.scene = scene;
    this.color = color;
    this.init();
  }

  init() {
    this.scene.tweens.add({
```

```
      targets: this,
      duration: 800,
      scale: { from: 1, to: 0 },
      onComplete: () => {
        this.destroy();
      },
    });
  }
}

// 0xa13000 red brick
// 0xb03e00 orange brick
// 0xb06f00 golden brick
// 0x4d4d4d grey brick
```

This is similar to the previous one but it represents smoke of rock that we will generate when the player breaks something.

```
export class RockSmoke extends Phaser.GameObjects.Rectangle {
  constructor(scene, x, y, width, height, color = 0xffeaab, gravity = false) {
    width = width || Phaser.Math.Between(30, 55);
    height = height || Phaser.Math.Between(30, 55);
    super(scene, x, y, width, height, color);
    scene.add.existing(this);
    scene.physics.add.existing(this);
    this.body.setAllowGravity(false);
    this.body.setVelocityY(-100);
    this.init();
  }

  init() {
    this.scene.tweens.add({
      targets: this,
      duration: 800,
      scale: { from: 1, to: 0 },
      onComplete: () => {
        this.destroy();
      },
    });
  }
}
```

3. Platformer: WallHammer

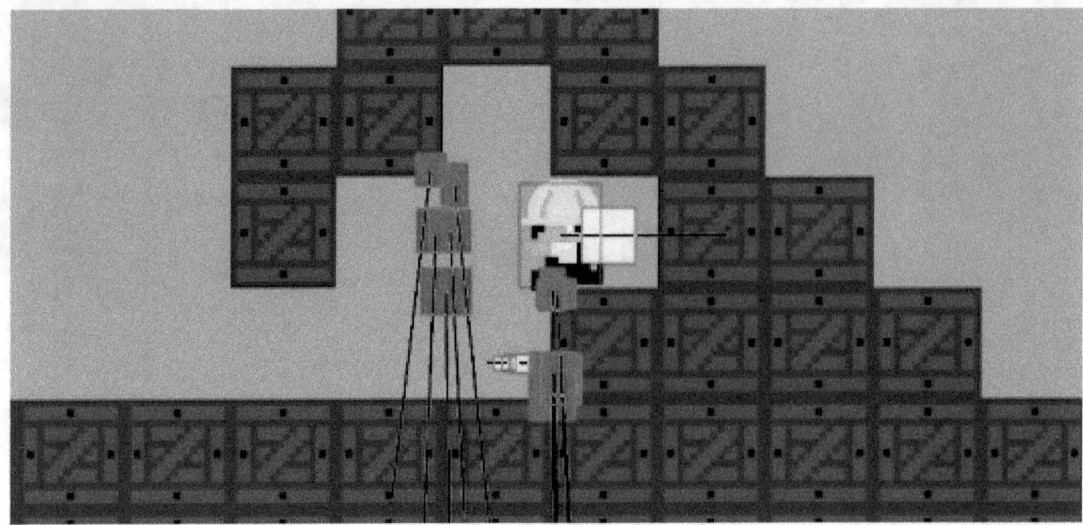

Figure 3.7 Particles for smoke, jump, debris, with or without gravity.

This is similar to the smoke, but it represents the smoke that comes out when the player jumps and it has gravity.

```
export class JumpSmoke extends Phaser.GameObjects.Rectangle {
  constructor(scene, x, y, width, height, color = 0xffeaab, gravity = false) {
    width = width || Phaser.Math.Between(10, 25);
    height = height || Phaser.Math.Between(10, 25);
    super(scene, x, y, width, height, color);
    scene.add.existing(this);
    scene.physics.add.existing(this);
    this.body.setAllowGravity(false);
    this.body.setVelocityX(Phaser.Math.Between(-20, 20));
    this.init();
  }

  init() {
    this.scene.tweens.add({
      targets: this,
      duration: 800,
      scale: { from: 1, to: 0 },
      onComplete: () => {
        this.destroy();
      },
    });
  }
}
```

This represents pieces of rock that we will generate when the player breaks something.

```
export class Debris extends Phaser.GameObjects.Rectangle {
  constructor(scene, x, y, color = 0xb03e00, width, height, gravity = false) {
    width = width || Phaser.Math.Between(15, 30);
```

```
        height = height || Phaser.Math.Between(15, 30);
        super(scene, x, y + 5, width, height, color);
        scene.add.existing(this);
        scene.physics.add.existing(this);
        this.body.setAllowGravity(true);
        this.body.setVelocityX(Phaser.Math.Between(-50, 50));
        this.body.setVelocityY(width * height);
    }
}
```

This particle class was used in many other projects and I should improve it but I'm just a lazy bastard.

Player code

Figure 3.8 The spite sheet for the player contains all his moves.

Here is our hero class. It's a Phaser `Sprite` game object with animations and controls attached to it:

- right/left buttons.
- up: to jump.
- down: to build a brick.
- space: to hit with the hammer.

In this class, we also have methods to add particle effects when walking or jumping, and we also apply power-ups by changing some parameters.

```
import Blow from "./blow";
import Brick from "./brick";
import { JumpSmoke } from "./particle";

class Player extends Phaser.GameObjects.Sprite {
    constructor(scene, x, y, health = 10) {
        super(scene, x, y, "walt");
        this.setOrigin(0.5);
        this.scene = scene;

        this.scene.add.existing(this);
        this.scene.physics.add.existing(this);
        this.cursor = this.scene.input.keyboard.createCursorKeys();
        this.spaceBar = this.scene.input.keyboard.addKey(
            Phaser.Input.Keyboard.KeyCodes.SPACE
```

3. Platformer: WallHammer — Player code

```
    );
    this.down = this.scene.input.keyboard.addKey(
      Phaser.Input.Keyboard.KeyCodes.DOWN
    );
    this.right = true;
    this.body.setGravityY(100);
    this.body.setSize(48, 60);
    this.init();
    this.jumping = false;
    this.building = false;
    this.falling = false;
    this.mjolnir = false;
    this.walkVelocity = 200;
    this.jumpVelocity = -400;
    this.invincible = false;

    this.health = health;

    this.dead = false;

    this.W = this.scene.input.keyboard.addKey(Phaser.Input.Keyboard.KeyCodes.W);
    this.A = this.scene.input.keyboard.addKey(Phaser.Input.Keyboard.KeyCodes.A);
    this.S = this.scene.input.keyboard.addKey(Phaser.Input.Keyboard.KeyCodes.S);
    this.D = this.scene.input.keyboard.addKey(Phaser.Input.Keyboard.KeyCodes.D);
  }
```

Inits the animations for the player: init, idle, walk, jump, death, etc... and it adds a listener for the `animationcomplete` event.

```
init() {
  this.scene.anims.create({
    key: "startidle",
    frames: this.scene.anims.generateFrameNumbers("walt", {
      start: 0,
      end: 1,
    }),
    frameRate: 3,
    repeat: -1,
  });

  this.scene.anims.create({
    key: "playeridle",
    frames: this.scene.anims.generateFrameNumbers("walt", {
      start: 2,
      end: 3,
    }),
    frameRate: 3,
    repeat: -1,
  });

  this.scene.anims.create({
    key: "playerwalk",
```

```js
      frames: this.scene.anims.generateFrameNumbers("walt", {
        start: 4,
        end: 6,
      }),
      frameRate: 10,
      repeat: -1,
    });
    this.scene.anims.create({
      key: "playerjump",
      frames: this.scene.anims.generateFrameNumbers("walt", {
        start: 4,
        end: 4,
      }),
      frameRate: 1,
    });
    this.scene.anims.create({
      key: "playerhammer",
      frames: this.scene.anims.generateFrameNumbers("walt", {
        start: 7,
        end: 8,
      }),
      frameRate: 10,
    });
    this.scene.anims.create({
      key: "playerbuild",
      frames: this.scene.anims.generateFrameNumbers("walt", {
        start: 9,
        end: 10,
      }),
      frameRate: 10,
      repeat: 2,
    });
    this.scene.anims.create({
      key: "playerdead",
      frames: this.scene.anims.generateFrameNumbers("walt", {
        start: 11,
        end: 16,
      }),
      frameRate: 5,
    });

    this.anims.play("startidle", true);

    this.on("animationcomplete", this.animationComplete, this);
  }
```

In the update function, we set the player movement according to the controls. We check if the player is jumping, falling, walking, etc...

3. Platformer: WallHammer

```
update() {
  if (this.dead) return;
  if (this.jumping) {
    if (this.body.velocity.y >= 0) {
      this.body.setGravityY(700);
      this.falling = true;
    }
  }

  if (
    (Phaser.Input.Keyboard.JustDown(this.cursor.up) ||
      Phaser.Input.Keyboard.JustDown(this.W)) &&
    this.body.blocked.down
  ) {
    this.building = false;
    this.body.setVelocityY(this.jumpVelocity);
    this.body.setGravityY(400);
    this.anims.play("playerjump", true);
    this.scene.playAudio("jump");
    this.jumping = true;
    this.jumpSmoke();
  } else if (this.cursor.right.isDown || this.D.isDown) {
    this.building = false;
    if (this.body.blocked.down) {
      this.anims.play("playerwalk", true);
    }
    this.right = true;
    this.flipX = this.body.velocity.x < 0;
    this.body.setVelocityX(this.walkVelocity);
  } else if (this.cursor.left.isDown || this.A.isDown) {
    this.building = false;
    if (this.body.blocked.down) {
      this.anims.play("playerwalk", true);
    }
    this.right = false;
    this.flipX = true;
    this.body.setVelocityX(-this.walkVelocity);
  } else {
    if (this.body.blocked.down) {
      if (this.jumping) {
        this.scene.playAudio("land");
        this.landSmoke();
      }
      this.jumping = false;
      this.falling = false;

      if (!this.building) this.anims.play("playeridle", true);
    }

    this.body.setVelocityX(0);
  }

  if (Phaser.Input.Keyboard.JustDown(this.spaceBar)) this.hammerBlow();
```

3. Platformer: WallHammer — Player code

```
    if (
      Phaser.Input.Keyboard.JustDown(this.cursor.down) ||
      Phaser.Input.Keyboard.JustDown(this.S)
    )
      this.buildBlock();
  }
```

This is called when the player hits the floor. It creates smoke particles. It reuses the jumpSmoke method.

```
  landSmoke() {
    this.jumpSmoke(20);
  }

  jumpSmoke(offsetY = 10, varX) {
    Array(Phaser.Math.Between(3, 6))
      .fill(0)
      .forEach((i) => {
        const offset = varX || Phaser.Math.Between(-1, 1) > 0 ? 1 : -1;
        varX = varX || Phaser.Math.Between(0, 20);
        new JumpSmoke(this.scene, this.x + offset * varX, this.y + offsetY);
      });
  }
```

This is called when the player generates a block. It also creates smoke particles.

```
  buildBlock() {
    this.building = true;
    this.anims.play("playerbuild", true);
    this.scene.playAudio("build");
    const offsetX = this.right ? 64 : -64;
    const offsetY = this.jumpVelocity === -400 ? 0 : -128;
    this.buildSmoke(32, offsetX);
    this.scene.bricks.add(
      new Brick(this.scene, this.x + offsetX, this.y + offsetY)
    );
  }
```

This generates the smoke particles when the player builds a block.

```
  buildSmoke(offsetY = 10, offsetX) {
    Array(Phaser.Math.Between(8, 14))
      .fill(0)
      .forEach((i) => {
        const varX = Phaser.Math.Between(-20, 20);
        new JumpSmoke(this.scene, this.x + (offsetX + varX), this.y + offsetY);
      });
  }
```

This is called when the player creates a blow to destroy something.

3. Platformer: WallHammer

```
hammerBlow() {
  this.building = true;
  this.anims.play("playerhammer", true);
  const offsetX = this.right ? 32 : -32;
  const size = this.mjolnir ? 128 : 32;
  this.scene.blows.add(
    new Blow(this.scene, this.x + offsetX, this.y, size, size)
  );
}
```

This just turns the player in the opposite direction.

```
turn() {
  this.right = !this.right;
}
```

This is called when the player finishes an animation. It checks if the animation is the "playerground", "playerhammer" or "playerbuild" and it plays the idle animation.

```
animationComplete(animation, frame) {
  if (animation.key === "playerground") {
    this.anims.play("playeridle", true);
  }

  if (animation.key === "playerhammer" || animation.key === "playerbuild") {
    this.building = false;
    this.anims.play(this.jumping ? "playerjump" : "playeridle", true);
  }
}
```

This is called when the player is hit by an enemy. It reduces the health and checks if the player is dead.

```
hit() {
  this.health--;
  this.anims.play("playerdead", true);
  this.body.enable = false;
  if (this.health === 0) {
    this.die();
  }
}
```

This is called when the player is dead. It plays the death animation and restarts the scene.

```
die() {
  this.dead = true;
  this.anims.play("playerdead", true);
  this.body.immovable = true;
  this.body.moves = false;
```

```
    this.scene.restartScene();
  }
```

This is called when the player picks up a prize. It checks the prize and calls the corresponding method.

```
  applyPrize(prize) {
    switch (prize) {
      case "speed":
        this.walkVelocity = 330;
        this.flashPlayer();
        break;
      case "hammer":
        this.mjolnir = true;
        this.flashPlayer();
        break;
      case "boots":
        this.jumpVelocity = -600;
        this.flashPlayer();
        break;
      case "coin":
        this.scene.updateCoins();
        break;
      case "star":
        this.invincible = true;
        this.scene.tweens.add({
          targets: this,
          duration: 300,
          alpha: { from: 0.7, to: 1 },
          repeat: -1,
        });
        break;
      default:
        break;
    }
  }
```

This is called when the player picks up a prize. It flashes the player to show the player that he got a prize.

```
  flashPlayer() {
    this.scene.tweens.add({
      targets: this,
      duration: 50,
      scale: { from: 1.2, to: 1 },
      repeat: 10,
    });
  }
}

export default Player;
```

About the controls for the player: it's impossible to satisfy everybody. Gamers tend to have their preferences so you can try to provide alternatives or even configurable controls.

Blow

Figure 3.9 A blow is just a rectangle.

How does the hammer destroy a foe or a brick? Because it generates this `Blow` object: when a blow overlaps with a foe or a brick, it will be destroyed.

```
class Blow extends Phaser.GameObjects.Rectangle {
  constructor(scene, x, y, width = 32, height = 32, type = "") {
    super(scene, x, y, width, height, 0xffffff);
    this.scene = scene;
    this.type = type;
    this.y = y;
    scene.add.existing(this);
    scene.physics.add.existing(this);
    this.body.setAllowGravity(false);
    this.scene.tweens.add({
      targets: this,
      duration: 300,
      scale: { from: 1, to: 0 },
      onComplete: () => {
        this.destroy();
      },
    });
  }
}

export default Blow;
```

When the player gets the hammer power-up, we just create bigger blows!

Platform

Figure 3.10 The platform sprite for size 4.

These are the hanging platforms that we place in our stages. When we edit in Tiled, we can define platforms with a specific name that will set the size and the behavior: platforms can be moved horizontally or vertically.

```js
export default class Platform extends Phaser.GameObjects.Container {
  constructor(scene, x, y, size = 4, demo = false) {
    super(scene, x, y);
    this.x = x;
    this.y = y;
    this.scene = scene;
    this.scene.add.existing(this);
    this.scene.physics.add.existing(this);
    this.body.setAllowGravity(false);
    this.body.setBounce(1);
    this.body.setSize(size * 64, 64);
    this.body.setOffset(-2, -2);

    this.body.immovable = true;
    this.body.moves = false;
    this.chain = new Phaser.GameObjects.Sprite(
      this.scene,
      size * 32 - 32,
      -2048,
      "chain"
    ).setOrigin(0);
    this.add(this.chain);
    this.platform = new Phaser.GameObjects.Sprite(
      this.scene,
      0,
      0,
      "platform" + size
    ).setOrigin(0);
    this.add(this.platform);

    this.init();
  }
```

3. Platformer: WallHammer

Figure 3.11 Randomly generated platforms.

This method generates a random platform. Depending on the result, the platform will move vertically or horizontally or both.

```
init() {
  const type = Phaser.Math.Between(0, 7);
  let offsetX = this.x;
  let offsetY = this.y;

  switch (type) {
    case 0:
      offsetX = Phaser.Math.Between(-50, 50);
      break;
    case 1:
      offsetY = Phaser.Math.Between(-50, 50);
      break;
    case 2:
      offsetX = Phaser.Math.Between(-100, 100);
      offsetY = Phaser.Math.Between(-100, 100);
      break;
    case 3:
    case 4:
    case 5:
    case 6:
    default:
      break;
  }

  this.scene.tweens.add({
    targets: this,
    duration: Phaser.Math.Between(4000, 6000),
    x: { from: this.x, to: offsetX },
```

```
      y: { from: this.y, to: offsetY },
      repeat: -1,
      yoyo: true,
    });
  }
}
```

In this particular implementation of the platforms, there's a problem. When they move horizontally they don't carry the player as you would expect. Something similar happens when the platform goes up/down. We could fix this by changing the friction between the player and platform or keeping the velocity of the player equal to the platform's velocity.

Brick

Figure 3.12 The player generating bricks on the stage.

The Brick class represents a brick sprite created by the player. As explained before, it can also be destroyed if the player needs to.

```
class Brick extends Phaser.GameObjects.Sprite {
  constructor(scene, x, y, name = "brick0") {
    super(scene, x, y, name);
    this.scene = scene;
    this.name = name;

    this.scene.add.existing(this);
    this.scene.physics.add.existing(this);
    this.body.immovable = true;
    this.body.moves = false;
    this.scene.tweens.add({
      targets: this,
      duration: 50,
      x: { from: this.x, to: this.x + Phaser.Math.Between(-7, 7) },
```

```
      y: { from: this.y, to: this.y + Phaser.Math.Between(-7, 7) },
      repeat: 5,
    });
  }
}

export default Brick;
```

This brick will not be affected by gravity but all characters will collide with it.

Coin

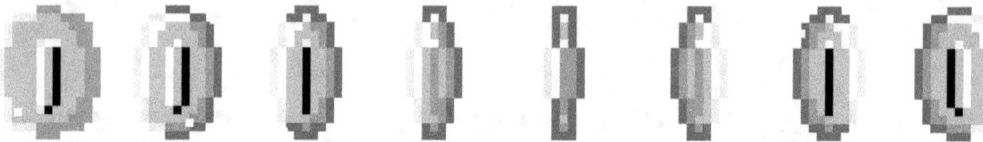

Figure 3.13 The sprite sheet for a desirable shiny coin.

If you break bricks you have a chance to generate coins. The feeling of getting some coins is always great!

```
class Coin extends Phaser.GameObjects.Sprite {
  constructor(scene, x, y, name = "coin") {
    super(scene, x, y, name);
    this.scene = scene;
    this.name = name;
    this.setScale(0.7);
    this.setOrigin(0.5);

    scene.add.existing(this);
    scene.physics.add.existing(this);

    this.body.immovable = true;
    this.body.moves = false;
    this.disabled = false;
    this.init();
  }
```

Inits the animation and it adds a little tween effect to make the coin move up and down.

```
  init() {
    this.scene.anims.create({
      key: this.name,
      frames: this.scene.anims.generateFrameNumbers(this.name, {
        start: 0,
        end: 7,
      }),
```

```
      frameRate: 10,
      repeat: -1,
    });

    this.anims.play(this.name, true);
    this.scene.tweens.add({
      targets: this,
      duration: 500,
      y: this.y - 20,
      repeat: -1,
      yoyo: true,
    });
  }
```

This part adds a tween effect to move the coin toward the score text and then it destroys it

```
  pick() {
    const { x, y } = this.scene.cameras.main.getWorldPoint(
      this.scene.scoreCoinsLogo.x,
      this.scene.scoreCoinsLogo.y
    );

    this.disabled = true;
    this.scene.tweens.add({
      targets: this,
      duration: 500,
      x: { from: this.x, to: x },
      y: { from: this.y, to: y },
      scale: { from: 0.7, to: 0.5 },
      onComplete: () => {
        this.destroy();
      },
    });
  }
}

export default Coin;
```

In this particular game, coins don't give any special advantage, they are here just to provide some dopamine to the player.

3. Platformer: WallHammer

The game!

Figure 3.14 Game in progress.

The Game scene will instantiate the player, foe generator, etc... and most importantly, it will generate the stage based on the tile map. It will also go through the object layer to reflect it and it will be responsible for defining all collisions and overlaps between the player, foes, bricks, blows, etc.

```
import Player from "./player";
import { Debris } from "./particle";
import Bat from "./bat";
import Zombie from "./zombie";
import Turn from "./turn";
import Coin from "./coin";
import LunchBox from "./lunchbox";
import Platform from "./platform";
```

3. Platformer: WallHammer

```
export default class Game extends Phaser.Scene {
  constructor() {
    super({ key: "game" });
    this.player = null;
    this.score = 0;
    this.scoreText = null;
  }

  init(data) {
    this.name = data.name;
    this.number = data.number;
  }

  preload() {}
```

This function creates game elements. It sets the width and height variables, the center of the width and height, and the background color. Then it calls the functions to create the rest of the elements of the game.

```
  create() {
    this.width = this.sys.game.config.width;
    this.height = this.sys.game.config.height;
    this.center_width = this.width / 2;
    this.center_height = this.height / 2;
    this.cameras.main.setBackgroundColor(0x62a2bf); //(0x00b140)//(0x62a2bf)
    this.add.tileSprite(0, 1000, 1024 * 10, 512, "landscape").setOrigin(0.5);
    this.createMap();

    this.cameras.main.setBounds(0, 0, 20920 * 2, 20080 * 2);
    this.physics.world.setBounds(0, 0, 20920 * 2, 20080 * 2);
    this.addPlayer();

    this.cameras.main.startFollow(this.player, true, 0.05, 0.05, 0, 240);
    this.physics.world.enable([this.player]);
    this.addScore();
    this.loadAudios();
    this.playMusic();
  }
```

This function adds the score to the game. It creates the text and the coin icon. It will be updated when the player picks up a coin.

```
  addScore() {
    this.scoreCoins = this.add
      .bitmapText(75, 10, "pixelFont", "x0", 30)
      .setDropShadow(0, 4, 0x222222, 0.9)
      .setOrigin(0)
      .setScrollFactor(0);
    this.scoreCoinsLogo = this.add
      .sprite(50, 25, "coin")
      .setScale(1)
      .setOrigin(0.5);
```

```
    .setScrollFactor(0);
  const coinAnimation = this.anims.create({
    key: "coinscore",
    frames: this.anims.generateFrameNumbers("coin", { start: 0, end: 7 }),
    frameRate: 8,
  });
  this.scoreCoinsLogo.play({ key: "coinscore", repeat: -1 });
}
```

Figure 3.15 The coin score on top of the screen

This function creates the map of the game. It loads the tilemap and the tilesets and it creates the layers and the objects defined on the tilemap. It also creates the groups for the foes, the platforms, the turns, the exits, the lunchboxes, and the bricks. Finally, it calls the function to create the colliders.

```
createMap() {
  this.tileMap = this.make.tilemap({
    key: "scene" + this.number,
    tileWidth: 64,
    tileHeight: 64,
  });
  this.tileSetBg = this.tileMap.addTilesetImage("background");
  this.tileMap.createStaticLayer("background", this.tileSetBg);

  this.tileSet = this.tileMap.addTilesetImage("softbricks");
  this.platform = this.tileMap.createLayer(
    "scene" + this.number,
    this.tileSet
  );
  this.objectsLayer = this.tileMap.getObjectLayer("objects");

  this.platform.setCollisionByExclusion([-1]);

  this.batGroup = this.add.group();
  this.zombieGroup = this.add.group();
  this.foesGroup = this.add.group();
  this.turnGroup = this.add.group();
  this.exitGroup = this.add.group();
  this.platformGroup = this.add.group();
  this.lunchBoxGroup = this.add.group();
  this.bricks = this.add.group();

  this.addsObjects();
  this.addColliders();
}
```

3. Platformer: WallHammer — The game!

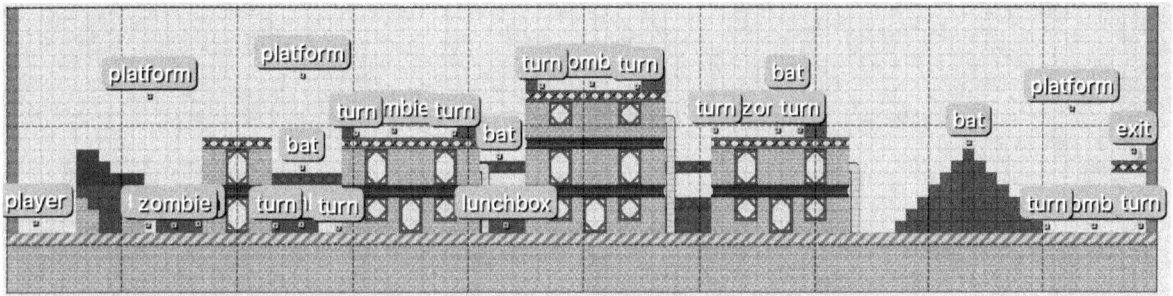

Figure 3.16 View of the first map in the Tiled editor.

This function adds the objects defined on the objects layer of the tilemap to the game. Yeah, I know, I could have used a switch statement here, but lately, I'm trying to avoid them as much as I can.

```
addsObjects() {
  this.objectsLayer.objects.forEach((object) => {
    if (object.name === "bat") {
      let bat = new Bat(this, object.x, object.y, object.type);
      this.batGroup.add(bat);
      this.foesGroup.add(bat);
    }

    if (object.name === "zombie") {
      let zombie = new Zombie(this, object.x, object.y, object.type);
      this.zombieGroup.add(zombie);
      this.foesGroup.add(zombie);
    }

    if (object.name === "platform") {
      this.platformGroup.add(
        new Platform(this, object.x, object.y, object.type)
      );
    }

    if (object.name === "turn") {
      this.turnGroup.add(new Turn(this, object.x, object.y));
    }

    if (object.name === "lunchbox") {
      this.lunchBoxGroup.add(new LunchBox(this, object.x, object.y));
    }

    if (object.name === "text") {
      this.add
        .bitmapText(object.x, object.y, "pixelFont", object.text.text, 30)
        .setDropShadow(2, 4, 0x222222, 0.9)
        .setOrigin(0);
    }

    if (object.name === "exit") {
```

3. Platformer: WallHammer — The game!

```
      this.exitGroup.add(
        new Turn(
          this,
          object.x,
          object.y,
          object.width,
          object.height,
          object.type
        ).setOrigin(0.5)
      );
    }
  });
}
```

Once we have our objects, foes, and platforms in the game, we add the colliders between them.

```
addColliders() {
  this.physics.add.collider(
    this.batGroup,
    this.platform,
    this.turnFoe,
    () => {
      return true;
    },
    this
  );

  this.physics.add.collider(
    this.zombieGroup,
    this.bricks,
    this.turnFoe,
    () => {
      return true;
    },
    this
  );

  this.physics.add.collider(
    this.batGroup,
    this.bricks,
    this.turnFoe,
    () => {
      return true;
    },
    this
  );

  this.physics.add.collider(
    this.zombieGroup,
    this.turnGroup,
    this.turnFoe,
```

3. Platformer: WallHammer — The game!

```
      () => {
        return true;
      },
      this
    );
    this.physics.add.collider(
      this.zombieGroup,
      this.platform,
      this.hitFloor,
      () => {
        return true;
      },
      this
    );
  }
```

This function is called when a foe touches a turn object. It turns the foe.

```
turnFoe(foe, platform) {
  foe.turn();
}
```

This callback is empty but here we could add some effects. It is called when a foe hits the floor.

```
hitFloor() {}
```

We add the player to the game and we add the colliders between the player and the rest of the elements. The starting position of the player is defined on the tilemap.

```
addPlayer() {
  this.elements = this.add.group();
  this.coins = this.add.group();

  const playerPosition = this.objectsLayer.objects.find(
    (object) => object.name === "player"
  );
  this.player = new Player(this, playerPosition.x, playerPosition.y, 0);

  this.physics.add.collider(
    this.player,
    this.platform,
    this.hitFloor,
    () => {
      return true;
    },
    this
  );

  this.physics.add.collider(
```

3. Platformer: WallHammer

```js
    this.player,
    this.platformGroup,
    this.hitFloor,
    () => {
      return true;
    },
    this
);

this.physics.add.collider(
    this.player,
    this.bricks,
    this.hitFloor,
    () => {
      return true;
    },
    this
);

this.physics.add.overlap(
    this.player,
    this.coins,
    this.pickCoin,
    () => {
      return true;
    },
    this
);

this.physics.add.overlap(
    this.player,
    this.lunchBoxGroup,
    this.pickLunchBox,
    () => {
      return true;
    },
    this
);

this.physics.add.overlap(
    this.player,
    this.exitGroup,
    () => {
      this.playAudio("stage");
      this.time.delayedCall(1000, () => this.finishScene(), null, this);
    },
    () => {
      return true;
    },
    this
);

this.blows = this.add.group();
```

3. Platformer: WallHammer

The game!

```javascript
this.physics.add.overlap(
  this.blows,
  this.platform,
  this.blowPlatform,
  () => {
    return true;
  },
  this
);

this.physics.add.overlap(
  this.blows,
  this.bricks,
  this.blowBrick,
  () => {
    return true;
  },
  this
);

this.physics.add.overlap(
  this.blows,
  this.foesGroup,
  this.blowFoe,
  () => {
    return true;
  },
  this
);

this.physics.add.overlap(
  this.bricks,
  this.foesGroup,
  this.foeBlowBrick,
  () => {
    return true;
  },
  this
);

this.physics.add.collider(
  this.player,
  this.batGroup,
  this.hitPlayer,
  () => {
    return true;
  },
  this
);

this.physics.add.collider(
  this.player,
```

```
      this.zombieGroup,
      this.hitPlayer,
      () => {
        return true;
      },
      this
    );
  }
```

Figure 3.17 The collider of bat and player will trigger the hitPlayer function.

This function is called when the player picks up a coin. It disables the coin (to avoid picking it up again while it animates), plays the sound, and updates the score. Same with the lunchbox.

```
pickCoin(player, coin) {
  if (!coin.disabled) {
    coin.pick();
    this.playAudio("coin");
    this.updateCoins();
  }
}

pickLunchBox(player, lunchBox) {
  if (!lunchBox.disabled) {
    this.playAudio("lunchbox");
    lunchBox.pick();
  }
}
```

This function is called when the player touches a foe. If the player is invincible (because of a power-up), then the foe dies. If not, then the player dies.

```
hitPlayer(player, foe) {
  if (player.invincible) {
    foe.death();
    this.playAudio("foedeath");
  } else if (!player.dead && this.number > 0) {
    player.die();
    this.playAudio("death");
  }
```

}

This is called when the player blows a foe up. On the screen, the player generates a blow object and when this collides with a foe, the enemy is destroyed. It plays the sound and kills the foe.

```
blowFoe(blow, foe) {
  this.playAudio("kill");
  this.playAudio("foedeath");
  foe.death();
}
```

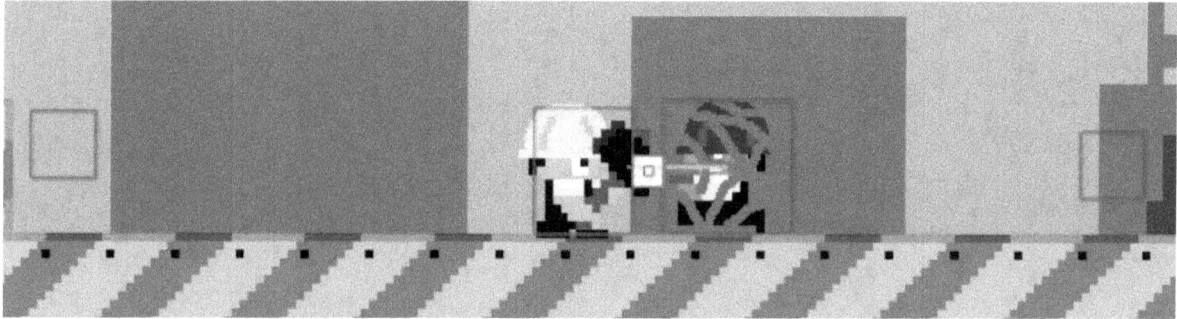

Figure 3.18 The moment where the blow kills a foe.

When a foe touches a brick it turns around and it changes direction.

```
foeBlowBrick(brick, foe) {
  foe.turn();
  Array(Phaser.Math.Between(4, 6))
    .fill(0)
    .forEach((i) => new Debris(this, brick.x, brick.y));
  brick.destroy();
}
```

This is called when the player blows an object of the platform layer on the tilemap. On the screen, the player generates a blow object and when this collides with a brick, if that brick is marked in the map as breakable, the brick is destroyed. It plays the sound and destroys the brick, and at the end, it calls spawnCoin: a function that randomly spawns a coin.

```
blowPlatform(blow, platform) {
  const tile = this.getTile(platform);
  if (this.isBreakable(tile)) {
    this.playAudioRandomly("stone_fail");
    this.playAudioRandomly("stone");
    if (this.player.mjolnir) this.cameras.main.shake(30);
    blow.destroy();
    Array(Phaser.Math.Between(4, 6))
      .fill(0)
```

3. Platformer: WallHammer

```
      .forEach((i) => new Debris(this, tile.pixelX, tile.pixelY));
    this.platform.removeTileAt(tile.x, tile.y);
    this.spawnCoin(tile);
  }
}

getTile(platform) {
  const { x, y } = platform;
  return this.platform.getTileAt(x, y);
}

isBreakable(tile) {
  return tile?.properties["element"] === "break";
}

spawnCoin(tile) {
  if (Phaser.Math.Between(0, 11) > 5) {
    this.time.delayedCall(
      500,
      () => {
        this.coins.add(new Coin(this, tile.pixelX, tile.pixelY));
      },
      null,
      this
    );
  }
}
```

This is similar to the function that blows platforms but it is applied to bricks generated by the player during the game.

```
blowBrick(blow, brick) {
  if (this.player.mjolnir) this.cameras.main.shake(30);
  this.playAudio("stone_fail");
  this.playAudioRandomly("stone");
  blow.destroy();
  Array(Phaser.Math.Between(4, 6))
    .fill(0)
    .forEach((i) => new Debris(this, brick.x, brick.y));
  brick.destroy();
}
```

When the player hits the floor, if it is jumping and it is not falling, then it checks if the tile is breakable. If it is, then it destroys the tile and it plays the sound. Same with the bricks generated by the player. Destroying stuff will generate debris.

```
hitFloor(player, platform) {
  if (
    this.player.jumping &&
    !this.player.falling &&
```

```
        this.player.body.velocity.y === 0
    ) {
      const tile = this.getTile(platform);
      if (this.isBreakable(tile)) {
        this.playAudioRandomly("stone");
        Array(Phaser.Math.Between(4, 6))
          .fill(0)
          .forEach((i) => new Debris(this, tile.pixelX, tile.pixelY));
        this.platform.removeTileAt(tile.x, tile.y);
      } else if (platform?.name === "brick0") {
        this.playAudioRandomly("stone");
        Array(Phaser.Math.Between(4, 6))
          .fill(0)
          .forEach((i) => new Debris(this, platform.x, platform.y));
        platform.destroy();
      }
    }
  }
}
```

This will load all the audio files used in the game. It is called from the `create` function, and so we can use `this.audios` to play the sounds.

```
loadAudios() {
  this.audios = {
    build: this.sound.add("build"),
    coin: this.sound.add("coin"),
    death: this.sound.add("death"),
    jump: this.sound.add("jump"),
    kill: this.sound.add("kill"),
    land: this.sound.add("land"),
    lunchbox: this.sound.add("lunchbox"),
    prize: this.sound.add("prize"),
    stone_fail: this.sound.add("stone_fail"),
    stone: this.sound.add("stone"),
    foedeath: this.sound.add("foedeath"),
    stage: this.sound.add("stage"),
  };
}

playAudio(key) {
  this.audios[key].play();
}
```

This plays the audio with a random volume and rate to add more variety to some sounds that otherwise would sound too repetitive.

```
playAudioRandomly(key) {
  const volume = Phaser.Math.Between(0.8, 1);
  const rate = Phaser.Math.Between(0.8, 1);
  this.audios[key].play({ volume, rate });
}
```

3. Platformer: WallHammer — The game!

This plays the music of the game. It is called from the `create` function, and so we can use `this.theme` to play the music.

```
playMusic(theme = "game") {
  this.theme = this.sound.add("music" + this.number);
  this.theme.stop();
  this.theme.play({
    mute: false,
    volume: 0.7,
    rate: 1,
    detune: 0,
    seek: 0,
    loop: true,
    delay: 0,
  });
}
```

The game loop. It updates the player and checks if the player has fallen from the map (we could add pits for this). If it has, then it restarts the scene.

```
update() {
  this.player.update();
  if (this.number === 3 && this.player.y > 1500) this.restartScene();
}
```

This is called when the player reaches the exit. It stops the music and it starts the transition scene increasing the stage number, so we will load the next map.

```
finishScene() {
  if (this.theme) this.theme.stop();
  this.scene.start("transition", { name: "STAGE", number: this.number + 1 });
}
```

3. Platformer: WallHammer

Figure 3.19 The player about to reach the exit cone.

This is called when the player dies. It stops the music and it starts the transition scene without increasing the stage number.

```
restartScene() {
  this.time.delayedCall(
    1000,
    () => {
      if (this.theme) this.theme.stop();
      this.scene.start("transition", { name: "STAGE", number: this.number });
    },
    null,
    this
  );
}
```

This is called when the player picks up a coin. It updates the score from the registry and it adds a little tween effect to the score text.

```
updateCoins() {
  const coins = +this.registry.get("coins") + 1;
  this.registry.set("coins", coins);
  this.scoreCoins.setText("x" + coins);
  this.tweens.add({
    targets: [this.scoreCoins, this.scoreCoinsLogo],
    scale: { from: 1.4, to: 1 },
    duration: 50,
    repeat: 10,
```

```
        });
    }
}
```

As you can see, if we want to create a platform game with many stages, creating a generic game scene helps a lot. Then the creator can focus on building great stages for the player to enjoy.

The tutorial scene

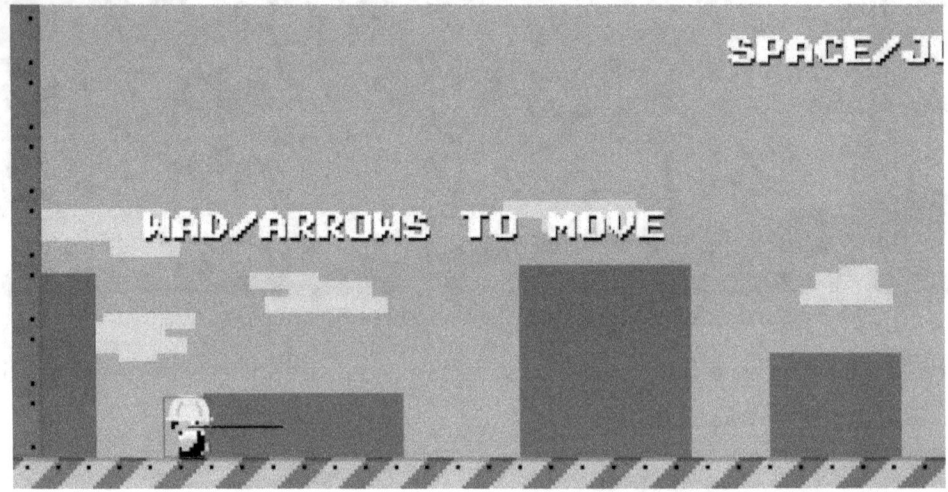

Figure 3.20 Tutorial scene with short instructions.

How can you explain the rules of your game? Walls of text should be forbidden. And people do not like to read instructions, no matter how concise and clear they are. For this game, we have a tutorial scene that allows the player to complete a stage showing instructions as he goes forward: basic controls, building, foes, power-ups, etc.

Always try to engage the player with a tutorial scene. This is the best way to explain and make the player comfortable effortlessly.

Splash

Figure 3.21 Splash screen for Wall Hammer.

As a kid grown in the 80's I tend to very classic splashes. This one adds a bit of style by showing the letters of the title one by one as if they were hammered onto the screen.

```
import { Debris } from "./particle";

export default class Splash extends Phaser.Scene {
  constructor() {
    super({ key: "splash" });
  }

  create() {
    this.width = this.sys.game.config.width;
    this.height = this.sys.game.config.height;
    this.center_width = this.width / 2;
    this.center_height = this.height / 2;
```

3. Platformer: WallHammer — Splash

```js
    this.cameras.main.setBackgroundColor(0x000000);
    this.time.delayedCall(1000, () => this.showInstructions(), null, this);

    this.input.keyboard.on("keydown-SPACE", () => this.startGame(), this);
    this.input.keyboard.on("keydown-ENTER", () => this.startGame(), this);
    this.playMusic();
    this.showTitle();
    this.playAudioRandomly("stone");
}

startGame() {
    if (this.theme) this.theme.stop();
    this.scene.start("transition", {
        next: "game",
        name: "STAGE",
        number: 0,
        time: 30,
    });
}
```

Helper function to show the title letter by letter:

```js
showTitle() {
    "WALL".split("").forEach((letter, i) => {
        this.time.delayedCall(
            200 * (i + 1),
            () => {
                this.playAudioRandomly("stone_fail");

                if (Phaser.Math.Between(0, 5) > 2) this.playAudioRandomly("stone");
                let text = this.add
                    .bitmapText(130 * (i + 1) + 140, 200, "hammerfont", letter, 170)
                    .setTint(0xca6702)
                    .setOrigin(0.5)
                    .setDropShadow(4, 6, 0xf09937, 0.9);
                Array(Phaser.Math.Between(4, 6))
                    .fill(0)
                    .forEach((i) => new Debris(this, text.x, text.y, 0xca6702));
            },
            null,
            this
        );
    });

    "HAMMER".split("").forEach((letter, i) => {
        this.time.delayedCall(
            200 * (i + 1) + 800,
            () => {
                this.playAudioRandomly("stone_fail");
                if (Phaser.Math.Between(0, 5) > 2) this.playAudioRandomly("stone");
                let text = this.add
```

```
            .bitmapText(130 * (i + 1), 350, "hammerfont", letter, 170)
            .setTint(0xca6702)
            .setOrigin(0.5)
            .setDropShadow(4, 6, 0xf09937, 0.9);
          Array(Phaser.Math.Between(4, 6))
            .fill(0)
            .forEach((i) => new Debris(this, text.x, text.y, 0xca6702));
      },
      null,
      this
    );
  });
}
```

Helper function to play audio randomly to add variety.

```
playAudioRandomly(key) {
  const volume = Phaser.Math.Between(0.8, 1);
  const rate = 1;
  this.sound.add(key).play({ volume, rate });
}

playMusic(theme = "splash") {
  this.theme = this.sound.add(theme);
  this.theme.stop();
  this.theme.play({
    mute: false,
    volume: 1,
    rate: 1,
    detune: 0,
    seek: 0,
    loop: true,
    delay: 0,
  });
}
```

This generates the instructions text for the player.

```
showInstructions() {
  this.add
    .bitmapText(this.center_width, 450, "pixelFont", "WASD/Arrows: move", 30)
    .setOrigin(0.5);
  this.add
    .bitmapText(this.center_width, 500, "pixelFont", "S/DOWN: BUILD WALL", 30)
    .setOrigin(0.5);
  this.add
    .bitmapText(this.center_width, 550, "pixelFont", "SPACE: HAMMER", 30)
    .setOrigin(0.5);
  this.add
    .sprite(this.center_width - 120, 620, "pello")
    .setOrigin(0.5)
    .setScale(0.3);
```

```
    this.add
      .bitmapText(this.center_width + 40, 620, "pixelFont", "By PELLO", 15)
      .setOrigin(0.5);
    this.space = this.add
      .bitmapText(
        this.center_width,
        670,
        "pixelFont",
        "Press SPACE to start",
        30
      )
      .setOrigin(0.5);
    this.tweens.add({
      targets: this.space,
      duration: 300,
      alpha: { from: 0, to: 1 },
      repeat: -1,
      yoyo: true,
    });
  }
}
```

I always try to find a nice font for the main title and then I use a simple arcade-type font for instructions, but these choices will always depend on the theme or your style choices. Whatever it is, don't forget to make things readable.

Transition page

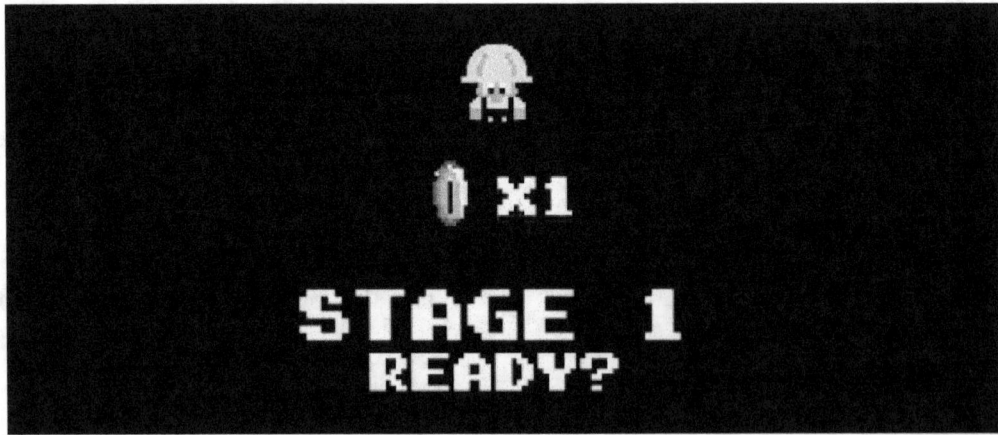

Figure 3.22 Transition stage elements.

This scene is shown before each stage and it just mimics the previous screen that we see before playing in Super Mario or many other games. It's good to show a transition so the player can get ready for the game. Starting suddenly may not feel fair.

3. Platformer: WallHammer

```js
export default class Transition extends Phaser.Scene {
  constructor() {
    super({ key: "transition" });
  }

  init(data) {
    this.name = data.name;
    this.number = data.number;
    this.next = data.next;
  }
```

This creates the elements of the transition screen.

```js
  create() {
    const messages = ["TUTORIAL", "STAGE 1", "STAGE 2", "STAGE 3", "STAGE 4"];
    this.width = this.sys.game.config.width;
    this.height = this.sys.game.config.height;
    this.center_width = this.width / 2;
    this.center_height = this.height / 2;

    if (this.number === 5) this.loadOutro();

    this.addScore();

    this.add.sprite(this.center_width, this.center_height - 170, "walt");
    this.add
      .bitmapText(
        this.center_width,
        this.center_height - 20,
        "pixelFont",
        messages[this.number],
        40
      )
      .setOrigin(0.5);
    this.add
      .bitmapText(
        this.center_width,
        this.center_height + 20,
        "pixelFont",
        "Ready?",
        30
      )
      .setOrigin(0.5);
    this.input.keyboard.on("keydown-ENTER", () => this.loadNext(), this);
    this.input.keyboard.on("keydown-SPACE", () => this.loadNext(), this);
    this.time.delayedCall(
      3000,
      () => {
        this.loadNext();
      },
      null,
      this
```

3. Platformer: WallHammer — Transition page

```
    );
}
```

These functions are used to load the next scene:

```
loadNext() {
  this.scene.start("game", { name: this.name, number: this.number });
}

loadOutro() {
  this.scene.start("outro", { name: this.name, number: this.number });
}
```

Helper function to show the score and coins:

```
addScore() {
  this.scoreCoins = this.add
    .bitmapText(
      this.center_width + 32,
      this.center_height - 100,
      "pixelFont",
      "x" + this.registry.get("coins"),
      30
    )
    .setDropShadow(0, 4, 0x222222, 0.9)
    .setOrigin(0.5)
    .setScrollFactor(0);
  this.scoreCoinsLogo = this.add
    .sprite(this.center_width - 32, this.center_height - 100, "coin")
    .setScale(0.7)
    .setOrigin(0.5)
    .setScrollFactor(0);
  const coinAnimation = this.anims.create({
    key: "coinscore",
    frames: this.anims.generateFrameNumbers("coin", { start: 0, end: 7 }),
    frameRate: 8,
  });
  this.scoreCoinsLogo.play({ key: "coinscore", repeat: -1 });
}
}
```

In transitions, we also have a chance to show points and lives or to develop a story.

Outro

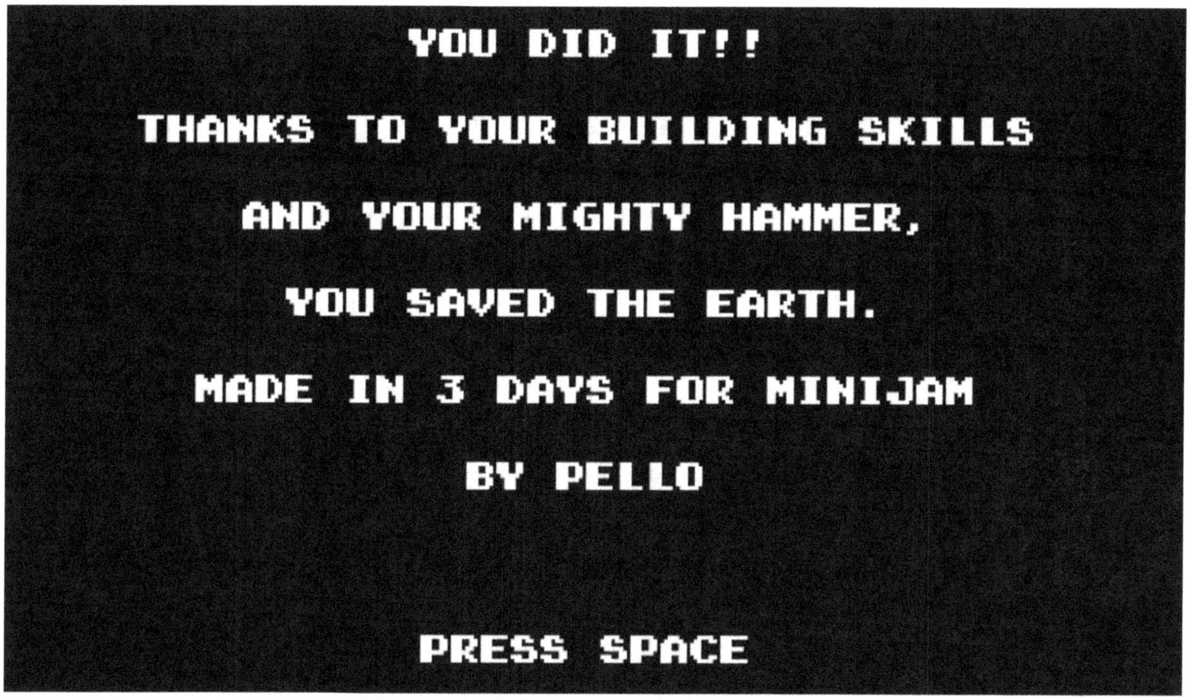

Figure 3.23 The outro is just a text.

After going through a hell of bats and zombies, it is time to reward the player with the achievement he got. Saving the day, the company, the neighborhood or even the world if the hood is not enough.

```
export default class Outro extends Phaser.Scene {
  constructor() {
    super({ key: "outro" });
  }
```

This scene will show some text:

```
create() {
  this.width = this.sys.game.config.width;
  this.height = this.sys.game.config.height;
  this.center_width = this.width / 2;
  this.center_height = this.height / 2;
  this.introLayer = this.add.layer();
  this.splashLayer = this.add.layer();
  this.text = [
    "You did it!!",
    "Thanks to your building skills",
    "and your mighty hammer,",
    "you saved the earth.",
    "Made in 3 days for Minijam",
```

```
      "by Pello",
      "",
      "Press SPACE",
    ];
    this.showHistory();

    this.input.keyboard.on("keydown-SPACE", this.startSplash, this);
    this.input.keyboard.on("keydown-ENTER", this.startSplash, this);
  }

  startSplash() {
    this.scene.start("splash");
  }
```

Helper function to show the text line by line:

```
  showHistory() {
    this.text.forEach((line, i) => {
      this.time.delayedCall(
        (i + 1) * 2000,
        () => this.showLine(line, (i + 1) * 60),
        null,
        this
      );
    });
  }

  showLine(text, y) {
    let line = this.introLayer.add(
      this.add
        .bitmapText(this.center_width, y, "pixelFont", text, 25)
        .setOrigin(0.5)
        .setAlpha(0)
    );
    this.tweens.add({
      targets: line,
      duration: 2000,
      alpha: 1,
    });
  }
}
```

As you may imagine, the real prize for the player is to have fun playing, so try to focus on that first.

Other platformers or similar games

Johnny Depth

Source code: https://github.com/pxai/phasergames/tree/master/johnny_depth

Play it here: https://pello.itch.io/johnny-depth

Weezard

Source code: https://github.com/pxai/phasergames/tree/master/weezard

Play it here: https://pello.itch.io/weezard

Chance Lord

Source code: https://github.com/pxai/phasergames/tree/master/chancelord

Play it here: https://pello.itch.io/chancelord

Raistlin 2

Source code: https://github.com/pxai/phasergames/tree/master/raistlin2

Play it here: https://pello.itch.io/raistlin-2

Atlantis

Source code: https://github.com/pxai/phasergames/tree/master/atlantis

Play it here: https://pello.itch.io/atlantis

Like tears in the rain

Source code: https://github.com/pxai/phasergames/tree/master/tears

Play it here: https://pello.itch.io/like-tears-in-the-rain

4. Puzzles: PushPull

Source code: https://github.com/pxai/phasergames/tree/master/pushpull

Play here: https://pello.itch.io/pushpull

4. Puzzles: PushPull

Puzzle games are a very popular genre, especially in game jams. They are easy to develop and easy to play, but hard to master. They are also very easy to create with Phaser. Also, they give a great chance to create a simple but successful game.

In this chapter, we will create a simple puzzle game called PushPull. The game is inspired by the classic Sokoban game but with a twist. The player can push and pull blocks, and the blocks can be pushed and pulled in any direction. The goal is to push a little block to the exit.

Init project

This has a very simple init with just a few scenes.

```javascript
import Phaser from "phaser";
import Bootloader from "./bootloader";
import Outro from "./outro";
import Splash from "./splash";
import Transition from "./transition";
import Game from "./game";

const config = {
  width: 608,
  height: 608,
  scale: {
    mode: Phaser.Scale.FIT,
    autoCenter: Phaser.Scale.CENTER_BOTH,
  },
  autoRound: false,
  parent: "contenedor",
  physics: {
    default: "arcade",
    arcade: {
      gravity: { y: 0 },
      debug: false,
    },
  },
  plugins: {},
  scene: [Bootloader, Splash, Transition, Game, Outro],
};

const game = new Phaser.Game(config);
```

Loader

The loader is also very simple. We just load a few assets along with very simple tile maps for the stages.

```
export default class Bootloader extends Phaser.Scene {
  constructor() {
    super({ key: "bootloader" });
  }
```

This method loads all the assets of the game organized in different methods.

```
preload() {
  this.createBars();
  this.setLoadEvents();
  this.loadFonts();
  this.loadAudios();
  this.loadImages();
  this.loadSpritesheets();
  this.loadMaps();
  this.setRegistry();
}
```

This loading callback is in charge of updating the progress bar and starting the next scene when the loading is complete.

```
setLoadEvents() {
  this.load.on(
    "progress",
    function (value) {
      this.progressBar.clear();
      this.progressBar.fillStyle(0xa6f316, 1);
      this.progressBar.fillRect(
        this.cameras.main.width / 4,
        this.cameras.main.height / 2 - 16,
        (this.cameras.main.width / 2) * value,
        16
      );
    },
    this
  );
  this.load.on(
    "complete",
    () => {
      this.scene.start("splash");
    },
    this
  );
}
```

4. Puzzles: PushPull

The fonts are loaded in this method.

```
loadFonts() {
  this.load.bitmapFont(
    "mario",
    "assets/fonts/mario.png",
    "assets/fonts/mario.xml"
  );
}
```

It loads the images used in the game.

```
loadImages() {
  this.load.image("pello", "assets/images/pello.png");
  this.load.image("background", "assets/images/background.png");
  this.load.image("tileset_fg", "assets/maps/tileset_fg.png");
  this.load.image("block_red", "assets/images/block_red.png");
  this.load.image("block_green", "assets/images/block_green.png");
  this.load.image("block_blue", "assets/images/block_blue.png");
  this.load.image("block_yellow", "assets/images/block_yellow.png");
  this.load.image("star", "assets/images/star.png");
}
```

This one loads the 9 maps of the game.

```
loadMaps() {
  Array(9)
    .fill(0)
    .forEach((_, i) => {
      this.load.tilemapTiledJSON(`scene${i}`, `assets/maps/scene${i}.json`);
    });
}
```

This method loads the audio files: music and sound effects.

```
loadAudios() {
  this.load.audio("music", "assets/sounds/music.mp3");
  this.load.audio("splash", "assets/sounds/splash.mp3");

  this.load.audio("win", "assets/sounds/win.mp3");
  this.load.audio("hover", "assets/sounds/hover.mp3");
  this.load.audio("select", "assets/sounds/select.mp3");
  this.load.audio("bump", "assets/sounds/bump.mp3");
  this.load.audio("move", "assets/sounds/move.mp3");
}
```

This method loads the sprite sheets used in the game.

```
loadSpritesheets() {
  this.load.spritesheet("spider", "assets/images/spider.png", {
    frameWidth: 32,
```

```
      frameHeight: 32,
    });
    this.load.spritesheet("heart", "assets/images/heart.png", {
      frameWidth: 32,
      frameHeight: 32,
    });
    this.load.spritesheet("frog", "assets/images/frog.png", {
      frameWidth: 32,
      frameHeight: 48,
    });
    this.load.spritesheet("frog2", "assets/images/frog2.png", {
      frameWidth: 48,
      frameHeight: 32,
    });
    this.load.spritesheet("trail", "assets/images/trail.png", {
      frameWidth: 32,
      frameHeight: 32,
    });
    this.load.spritesheet("block", "assets/images/block.png", {
      frameWidth: 48,
      frameHeight: 48,
    });
  }
```

This method sets the initial values of the game registry, to keep track of the score and the number of moves.

```
setRegistry() {
  this.registry.set("score", 0);
  this.registry.set("moves", 0);
}
```

This method creates the loading bars.

```
createBars() {
  this.loadBar = this.add.graphics();
  this.loadBar.fillStyle(0xffe066, 1);
  this.loadBar.fillRect(
    this.cameras.main.width / 4 - 2,
    this.cameras.main.height / 2 - 18,
    this.cameras.main.width / 2 + 4,
    20
  );
  this.progressBar = this.add.graphics();
}
}
```

Each stage is designed in Tiled, making this game very easy to extend with multiple stages.

Block

Figure 4.1 All the different types of blocks.

This is a class that represents a single block. We will group several instances of this to generate different groups, according to map properties.

We will also use this class instance to represents the "player" block, the one that we need to take it out. It will be just **one single red block**. Isolating it in this class is useful to define an overlap with the exit.

```
export default class Block extends Phaser.GameObjects.Sprite {
  constructor(scene, x, y, name = "block_blue", velocity = 100) {
    super(scene, x, y, name);
    this.setOrigin(0, 0);
    this.scene = scene;
    this.name = name;
  }
}
```

There's not much room for feedback and fancy effects here, so we added an extra trailing effect when we moved it. This block can be selected and moved, but that is common in the other big blocks too.

Exit

Figure 4.2 The player has to reach that invisible collider at the exit.

4. Puzzles: PushPull

This is an invisible rectangle object that we place at the exit of the stage so we can detect when we get the little block out of it.

```
export default class Exit extends Phaser.GameObjects.Sprite {
  constructor(scene, x, y, name = "star") {
    super(scene, x, y, "star");
    this.name = name;
    this.setOrigin(0.5);
    this.setAlpha(0);
    scene.add.existing(this);
    scene.physics.add.existing(this);
    this.body.setAllowGravity(false);
  }
}
```

The position of this exit is taken from the tilemap design.

BlockGroup

Figure 4.3 A block group composed by 2x3 yellow blocks.

In this game, there is no regular "Player" class. There are just blocks, of different sizes, and one of them is the little one, which we have to push to the exit. This class is used to represent all the blocks. This also holds all the logic for movements and locks between the stage blocks and boundaries. That is probably the hardest part to program in this project.

```
import Block from "./block";

export default class BlockGroup extends Phaser.GameObjects.Container {
  constructor(
    scene, x, y, w = 2, h = 3,
    color = "blue",
    defaultVelocity = 100
  ) {
    super(scene, x, y);
    this.scene = scene;
    this.w = +w;
```

```
    this.h = +h;
    this.id = Math.random();
    this.name = "block_" + color;
    this.scene.add.existing(this);
    this.scene.physics.add.existing(this);
    this.body.immovable = true;
    this.active = false;
    this.setKeys();
    this.defaultVelocity = defaultVelocity;
    this.createBlock();
    this.allowChangeDirection = true;
    this.scene.events.on("update", this.update, this);
    this.setListeners();
}
```

This method creates the block group based on the size.

```
createBlock() {
  this.body.setSize(this.w * 32, this.h * 32);

  for (let i = 0; i < this.w; i++) {
    for (let j = 0; j < this.h; j++) {
      this.add(new Block(this.scene, i * 32, j * 32, this.name));
    }
  }
}
```

This method sets the keys to move the block group.

```
setKeys() {
  this.cursor = this.scene.input.keyboard.createCursorKeys();
  this.W = this.scene.input.keyboard.addKey(Phaser.Input.Keyboard.KeyCodes.W);
  this.A = this.scene.input.keyboard.addKey(Phaser.Input.Keyboard.KeyCodes.A);
  this.S = this.scene.input.keyboard.addKey(Phaser.Input.Keyboard.KeyCodes.S);
  this.D = this.scene.input.keyboard.addKey(Phaser.Input.Keyboard.KeyCodes.D);
  this.scene.events.on("update", this.update, this);
}
```

This method sets the listeners for the mouse to select blocks. When a block is selected, it becomes the active block. We add some color to it with setTint so the player knows which block is active.

```
setListeners() {
  this.setInteractive(
    new Phaser.Geom.Rectangle(0, 0, 64, 96),
    Phaser.Geom.Rectangle.Contains
  );
  this.on("pointerdown", (pointer) => {
    this.scene.playAudio("select");
    this.iterate((block) => block.setTint(0x306070));
    this.activate();
```

```
    });

    this.on("pointerover", () => {
      this.scene.playAudio("hover");
      this.iterate((block) => block.setTint(0x306070));
    });

    this.on("pointerout", () => {
      this.iterate((block) => block.clearTint());
    });
  }
```

This method activates the block group. It also deactivates the previous active block. The next method does the opposite.

```
activate() {
  if (this.scene.activeBlock) this.scene.activeBlock.deactivate();
  this.active = true;
  this.scene.activeBlock = this;
}

deactivate() {
  this.active = false;
}
```

This method is the game loop for the block group. It detects what key was pressed and it checks if the block group can move in the direction of the key pressed. If it can, it moves the block group and updates the number of moves.

```
update() {
  if (!this.active) return;
  if (
    (Phaser.Input.Keyboard.JustUp(this.S) ||
      Phaser.Input.Keyboard.JustUp(this.cursor.down)) &&
    this.canMoveDown()
  ) {
    this.leaveTrail(this.w * 32, 32);
    this.y += 32;
    this.scene.updateMoves();
  } else if (
    (Phaser.Input.Keyboard.JustUp(this.W) ||
      Phaser.Input.Keyboard.JustUp(this.cursor.up)) &&
    this.canMoveUp()
  ) {
    this.leaveTrail(this.w * 32, 32, 0, (this.h - 1) * 32);
    this.y -= 32;
    this.scene.updateMoves();
  } else if (
    (Phaser.Input.Keyboard.JustUp(this.D) ||
      Phaser.Input.Keyboard.JustUp(this.cursor.right)) &&
```

```
      this.canMoveRight()
    ) {
      this.leaveTrail(32, this.h * 32);
      this.x += 32;
      this.scene.updateMoves();
    } else if (
      (Phaser.Input.Keyboard.JustUp(this.A) ||
        Phaser.Input.Keyboard.JustUp(this.cursor.left)) &&
      this.canMoveLeft()
    ) {
      this.leaveTrail(32, this.h * 32, (this.w - 1) * 32);
      this.x -= 32;
      this.scene.updateMoves();
    }
  }
}
```

This method leaves a trail behind the block group. It is used when the block group moves.

```
leaveTrail(w, h, offsetX = 0, offsetY = 0) {
  this.scene.playAudio("move");
  const trail = this.scene.add
    .rectangle(this.x + offsetX, this.y + offsetY, w, h, 0xcccccc)
    .setOrigin(0);
  this.scene.tweens.add({
    targets: [trail],
    duration: 300,
    alpha: { from: 1, to: 0 },
    onComplete: () => {
      trail.destroy();
    },
  });
}
```

Figure 4.4 We have to check every blocks surroundings to detect overlaps.

This method checks if the block group overlaps with another block group. It is used to check if the block group can move in a certain direction.

```
isOverlap(x = 0, y = 0) {
  const overlaps = this.scene.blocks.children.entries.map((block) => {
    if (block.id === this.id) return false;

    let myBounds = this.getBounds();
    let otherBounds = block.getBounds();
    myBounds.x += 1;
    myBounds.y += 1;
    myBounds.width = this.w * 32 - 2;
    myBounds.height = this.h * 32 - 2;
    myBounds.x += x;
    myBounds.y += y;
    const intersect = Phaser.Geom.Intersects.RectangleToRectangle(
      myBounds,
      otherBounds
    );
    return intersect;
  });
  return !overlaps.every((block) => !block);
}
```

This specific method checks if the block group can move down. It is used by the update method.

```
canMoveDown(distance = 32) {
  if (this.isOverlap(0, 1)) {
    this.scene.playAudio("bump");
    return false;
  }
  distance = this.h * 32;

  const blocks = Array(this.w)
    .fill(0)
    .map((_, i) => {
      return this.scene.platform.getTileAtWorldXY(
        this.x + i * 32,
        this.y + distance
      );
    });

  const canMove = blocks.every((block) => !block);
  if (!canMove) {
    this.scene.playAudio("bump");
  }
  return canMove;
}
```

Same as before, but this time it checks if the block group can move up.

```js
canMoveUp(distance = 32) {
  if (this.isOverlap(0, -1)) {
    this.scene.playAudio("bump");
    return false;
  }
  const blocks = Array(this.w)
    .fill(0)
    .map((_, i) => {
      return this.scene.platform.getTileAtWorldXY(
        this.x + i * 32,
        this.y - 1
      );
    });

  const canMove = blocks.every((block) => !block);
  if (!canMove) {
    this.scene.playAudio("bump");
  }
  return canMove;
}
```

Same as before, but here it checks if the block group can move to the left.

```js
canMoveLeft(distance = 32) {
  if (this.isOverlap(-1, 0)) {
    this.scene.playAudio("bump");
    return false;
  }

  const blocks = Array(this.h)
    .fill(0)
    .map((_, i) => {
      return this.scene.platform.getTileAtWorldXY(
        this.x - distance,
        this.y + i * 32
      );
    });

  const canMove = blocks.every((block) => !block);
  if (!canMove) {
    this.scene.playAudio("bump");
  }
  return canMove;
}
```

... and to the right.

```js
canMoveRight(distance = 32) {
  if (this.isOverlap(1, 0)) {
    this.scene.playAudio("bump");
    return false;
  }
```

```
      distance = this.w * 32;
      const blocks = Array(this.h)
        .fill(0)
        .map((_, i) => {
          return this.scene.platform.getTileAtWorldXY(
            this.x + distance,
            this.y + i * 32
          );
        });
      const canMove = blocks.every((block) => !block);
      if (!canMove) {
        this.scene.playAudio("bump");
      }
      return canMove;
  }
}
```

Blocks are created and placed using the `tilemaps` objects layer.

The game!

Figure 4.5 All the elements of the game.

4. Puzzles: PushPull — The game!

The Game scene orchestrates the whole thing. After creating game elements and loading the scene with the tilemap, it lets the player select blocks and move them. One of the main duties of this scene is to count the number of moves that the player is doing.

```javascript
import BlockGroup from "./block_group";
import Exit from "./exit";

export default class Game extends Phaser.Scene {
  constructor() {
    super({ key: "game" });
    this.player = null;
    this.score = 0;
    this.scoreText = null;
  }

  init(data) {
    this.name = data.name;
    this.number = data.number || 0;
    this.limitedTime = data.limitedTime || 10;
  }

  preload() {}
```

This method is called when the scene starts. We set the width and height variables as well as the center width and height; then we set the background color, and we disable the context menu of the mouse. And then we add the elements we need: maps with blocks, audio files, texts, and the pointer.

```javascript
  create() {
    this.width = this.sys.game.config.width;
    this.height = this.sys.game.config.height;
    this.center_width = this.width / 2;
    this.center_height = this.height / 2;
    this.cameras.main.setBackgroundColor(0x000000);
    this.input.mouse.disableContextMenu();
    this.addPointer();

    this.addMap();
    this.addMoves();
    this.addRetry();

    this.loadAudios();
    this.showTexts();
    this.solved = false;
  }
```

We add the retry key to restart the scene.

```javascript
  addRetry() {
```

4. Puzzles: PushPull — The game!

```
    this.R = this.input.keyboard.addKey(Phaser.Input.Keyboard.KeyCodes.R);
}
```

This method adds the moves text and the total moves.

```
addMoves() {
  this.movesText = this.add
    .bitmapText(this.center_width, 32, "mario", "0", 30)
    .setOrigin(0.5)
    .setTint(0xffe066)
    .setDropShadow(3, 4, 0x75b947, 0.7);
  this.totalMoves = 0;
}
```

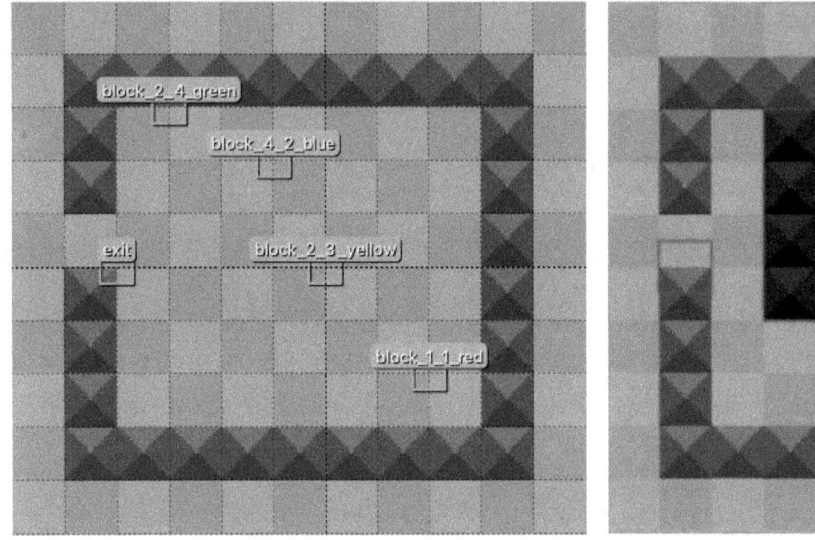

Figure 4.6 The tiled map and the rendered version on the screen.

This generates the map with the blocks and the exits. Depending on the number of the scene, it loads a different map.

```
addMap() {
  this.tileMap = this.make.tilemap({
    key: `scene${this.number}`,
    tileWidth: 32,
    tileHeight: 32,
  });
  this.tileSetBg = this.tileMap.addTilesetImage("tileset_fg");
  this.tileMap.createStaticLayer("background", this.tileSetBg);

  this.tileSet = this.tileMap.addTilesetImage("tileset_fg");
  this.platform = this.tileMap.createLayer(
    `scene${this.number}`,
    this.tileSet
```

4. Puzzles: PushPull — The game!

```
    );
    this.objectsLayer = this.tileMap.getObjectLayer("objects");
    this.platform.setCollisionByExclusion([-1]);
    this.physics.world.setBounds(0, 0, this.width, this.height);
    this.exits = this.add.group();
    this.blocks = this.add.group();
    this.texts = [];

    this.addObjects();
}
```

Adds objects to the game: blocks and exits. The blocks are added to the group blocks and the exits to the group exits. The block_1_1 block is the player.

```
addObjects() {
    this.objectsLayer.objects.forEach((object) => {
        if (object.name.startsWith("block")) {
            const [name, width, height, color] = object.name.split("_");
            this.activeBlock = new BlockGroup(
                this,
                object.x,
                object.y,
                width,
                height,
                color
            );
            this.blocks.add(this.activeBlock);
            if (object.name.startsWith("block_1_1")) {
                this.addPlayer(this.activeBlock);
            }
        }

        if (object.name.startsWith("exit")) {
            this.exits.add(new Exit(this, object.x - 16, object.y));
        }
    });
}
```

If the scene has some texts, we show them. This is helpful to explain to the player what to do in a tutorial scene.

```
showTexts() {
    if (this.number > 0) return;
    const texts = [
        "Select cubes",
        "Pull/push them with WASD/Arrows",
        "MOVE the red to exit",
    ];
    texts.forEach((text, i) => {
        this.add
            .bitmapText(this.center_width, 425 + 35 * i, "mario", text, 15)
```

4. Puzzles: PushPull — The game!

```
        .setOrigin(0.5)
        .setTint(0xffe066)
        .setDropShadow(1, 2, 0xbf2522, 0.7);
    });
}
```

This method adds the player -which is just another block- to the game. It also adds an overlap between the player and the exits. If the player overlaps with an exit, the method `hitExit` is called.

```
addPlayer(block) {
    this.player = block;
    this.physics.add.overlap(
        this.player,
        this.exits,
        this.hitExit,
        () => {
            return true;
        },
        this
    );
}

hitBlockBlock(block, platform) {}
```

This is called when the player touches the exit of the scene. It destroys the exit and calls the `finishScene` method.

```
hitExit(player, exit) {
    this.player.active = false;
    exit.destroy();

    this.finishScene();
}
```

This method sets the pointer (the mouse in a computer) to `this.pointer` and disables the context menu of the mouse.

```
addPointer() {
    this.pointer = this.input.activePointer;
    this.input.mouse.disableContextMenu();
}
```

The next method loads the audio, it plays them normally and the last one plays an audio with a random rate and detune.

```
loadAudios() {
    this.audios = {
        bump: this.sound.add("bump"),
```

```
      hover: this.sound.add("hover"),
      select: this.sound.add("select"),
      move: this.sound.add("move"),
      win: this.sound.add("win"),
    };
  }

  playAudio(key) {
    this.audios[key].play();
  }

  playRandom(key, volume = 1) {
    this.audios[key].play({
      rate: Phaser.Math.Between(1, 1.5),
      detune: Phaser.Math.Between(-1000, 1000),
      delay: 0,
      volume,
    });
  }
```

The game loop just detects if R was pressed to restart the scene.

```
update() {
  if (Phaser.Input.Keyboard.JustDown(this.R)) {
    this.restartScene();
  }
}
```

Figure 4.7 Text over the screen when the stage is cleared.

4. Puzzles: PushPull — The game!

This method is called when the player touches the exit of the scene. It destroys the exit and calls the `finishScene` method. It also adds a text with the number of moves and the time it took to finish the scene.

```
finishScene() {
  if (this.solved) return;

  this.playAudio("win");
  this.solved = true;
  const totalMoves = +this.registry.get("moves") + this.totalMoves;
  this.registry.set("moves", totalMoves);

  this.winText = this.add
    .bitmapText(this.center_width, -100, "mario", "STAGE CLEARED!", 30)
    .setOrigin(0.5)
    .setTint(0xffe066)
    .setDropShadow(2, 3, 0x75b947, 0.7);
  this.tweens.add({
    targets: this.winText,
    duration: 500,
    y: { from: this.winText.y, to: this.center_height },
  });
  this.tweens.add({
    targets: [this.winText, this.movesText],
    duration: 100,
    scale: { from: 1, to: 1.1 },
    repeat: -1,
    yoyo: true,
  });
  this.time.delayedCall(
    2000,
    () => {
      this.scene.start("transition", {
        next: "underwater",
        name: "STAGE",
        number: this.number + 1,
      });
    },
    null,
    this
  );
}
```

This method restarts the scene.

```
restartScene() {
  this.scene.start("game", {
    next: "underwater",
    name: "STAGE",
    number: this.number,
  });
```

}

This method updates the number of moves. It is called when the player moves the block group. It is the score of the game after all.

```
updateMoves() {
  this.totalMoves++;
  this.movesText.setText(this.totalMoves);
  this.tweens.add({
    targets: [this.timerText],
    duration: 200,
    alpha: { from: 0.6, to: 1 },
    repeat: -1,
  });
}
}
```

In the selections and collisions, the game scene also adds some sounds to provide some feedback. Adding these sounds, as we'll repeat over and over makes the game feel way better; it's just a little effort for the programmer that always pays off.

Splash

Figure 4.8 The Splash screen for the game.

Another simple Splash screen with a big title and arcade-like fonts everywhere. After all, it's just a relaxing puzzle game without time limits so we are not selling any frenzy thing.

```
export default class Splash extends Phaser.Scene {
  constructor() {
    super({ key: "splash" });
```

4. Puzzles: PushPull

```
}
```

We create the elements of the splash scene: the background, the title, the start button, and the instructions.

```
create() {
  this.width = this.sys.game.config.width;
  this.height = this.sys.game.config.height;
  this.center_width = this.width / 2;
  this.center_height = this.height / 2;
  this.background = this.add
    .tileSprite(0, 0, 1024, 1024, "background")
    .setOrigin(0);

  this.cameras.main.setBackgroundColor(0x3c97a6);

  this.time.delayedCall(1000, () => this.showInstructions(), null, this);
  this.addStartButton();
  this.input.keyboard.on("keydown-SPACE", () => this.startGame(), this);
  this.playMusic();

  this.showTitle();
  this.addStartButton();
}
```

We use the game loop to animate the background diagonally.

```
update() {
  this.background.tilePositionX += 1;
  this.background.tilePositionY += 1;
}
```

When the game starts, we stop the music and start the transition scene with a new music file.

```
startGame() {
  if (this.theme) this.theme.stop();
  this.playGameMusic();
  this.scene.start("transition", { name: "STAGE", number: 0 });
}

playGameMusic(theme = "music") {
  this.theme = this.sound.add(theme);
  this.theme.stop();
  this.theme.play({
    mute: false,
    volume: 0.2,
    rate: 1,
    detune: 0,
    seek: 0,
    loop: true,
```

4. Puzzles: PushPull

```
      delay: 0,
    });
}
```

These functions show the game title which consists of a couple of bitmap texts that are tweened.

```
showTitle() {
  this.gameLogo1 = this.add
    .bitmapText(this.center_width - 1000, 100, "mario", "Push", 120)
    .setOrigin(0.5)
    .setTint(0xffffff)
    .setDropShadow(3, 4, 0x75b947, 0.7);
  this.gameLogo2 = this.add
    .bitmapText(this.center_width + 1000, 220, "mario", "Pull", 120)
    .setOrigin(0.5)
    .setTint(0xffe066)
    .setDropShadow(2, 3, 0x693600, 0.7);

  this.titleTweens();
}

titleTweens() {
  this.tweens.add({
    targets: [this.gameLogo2],
    duration: 1000,
    x: { from: this.gameLogo2.x, to: this.center_width },
    onComplete: () => {
      this.tweens.add({
        targets: [this.gameLogo2],
        duration: 1000,
        x: "-=20",
        repeat: -1,
        ease: "Linear",
      });
    },
  });
  this.tweens.add({
    targets: [this.gameLogo1],
    duration: 1000,
    x: { from: this.gameLogo1.x, to: this.center_width },
    onComplete: () => {
      this.tweens.add({
        targets: [this.gameLogo1],
        duration: 1000,
        x: "+=20",
        repeat: -1,
        ease: "Linear",
      });
    },
  });
}
```

4. Puzzles: PushPull — Splash

This plays the music of the splash scene in a loop.

```
playMusic(theme = "splash") {
  this.theme = this.sound.add(theme);
  this.theme.stop();
  this.theme.play({
    mute: false,
    volume: 0.5,
    rate: 1,
    detune: 0,
    seek: 0,
    loop: true,
    delay: 0,
  });
}
```

This adds a start button that can be clicked with the mouse or touched with a finger.

```
addStartButton() {
  this.startButton = this.add
    .bitmapText(this.center_width, 500, "mario", "start", 30)
    .setOrigin(0.5)
    .setTint(0xffe066)
    .setDropShadow(2, 3, 0x693600, 0.7);
  this.startButton.setInteractive();
  this.startButton.on("pointerdown", () => {
    this.sound.add("move").play();
    this.startGame();
  });

  this.startButton.on("pointerover", () => {
    this.startButton.setTint(0x3e6875);
  });

  this.startButton.on("pointerout", () => {
    this.startButton.setTint(0xffe066);
  });
  this.tweens.add({
    targets: this.space,
    duration: 300,
    alpha: { from: 0, to: 1 },
    repeat: -1,
    yoyo: true,
  });
}
```

This just shows the author's information and a space key that blinks.

```
showInstructions() {
  this.add
    .sprite(this.center_width - 80, 400, "pello")
    .setOrigin(0.5)
```

```
      .setScale(0.5);
    this.add
      .bitmapText(this.center_width + 40, 400, "mario", "By PELLO", 15)
      .setOrigin(0.5);

    this.tweens.add({
      targets: this.space,
      duration: 300,
      alpha: { from: 0, to: 1 },
      repeat: -1,
      yoyo: true,
    });
  }
}
```

This game uses mouse input so we let the player click on the letters to start. As we did before, instead of explaining anything here, we use a very simple first stage as a tutorial.

Transition page

We use these scenes again as transitions from one stage to another.

```
export default class Transition extends Phaser.Scene {
  constructor() {
    super({ key: "transition" });
  }

  init(data) {
    this.name = data.name;
    this.number = data.number;
  }
```

Figure 4.9 Simple transition text between stages.

4. Puzzles: PushPull — Transition page

We just show the name of the stage and the word "Ready?". If the stage is the last one, we start the outro scene.

```javascript
create() {
  const messages = [
    "Tutorial",
    "Stage0",
    "Stage1",
    "Stage2",
    "Stage3",
    "Stage4",
    "Stage5",
    "Stage6",
    "Stage7",
    "Outro",
  ];

  this.width = this.sys.game.config.width;
  this.height = this.sys.game.config.height;
  this.center_width = this.width / 2;
  this.center_height = this.height / 2;
  this.cameras.main.setBackgroundColor(0x3c97a6);

  if (this.number === 9) {
    this.scene.start("outro", { name: this.name, number: this.number });
  }

  this.add
    .bitmapText(
      this.center_width,
      this.center_height - 20,
      "mario",
      messages[this.number],
      40
    )
    .setOrigin(0.5)
    .setTint(0xa6f316)
    .setDropShadow(2, 3, 0x75b947, 0.7);
  this.add
    .bitmapText(
      this.center_width,
      this.center_height + 20,
      "mario",
      "Ready?",
      30
    )
    .setOrigin(0.5)
    .setTint(0xa6f316)
    .setDropShadow(2, 3, 0x75b947, 0.7);
  this.time.delayedCall(1000, () => this.loadNext(), null, this);
}
```

```
loadNext() {
  this.scene.start("game", {
    name: this.name,
    number: this.number,
    limitedTime: 10 + this.number * 3,
  });
}
}
```

In this case, it's important to show the stage number so the player can be aware of his progress.

Outro

Figure 4.10 outro screen.

There is not much story here, so we can use the outro to show the number of moves used by the player.

```
export default class Outro extends Phaser.Scene {
  constructor() {
    super({ key: "outro" });
  }

  create() {
    this.width = this.sys.game.config.width;
    this.height = this.sys.game.config.height;
    this.center_width = this.width / 2;
    this.center_height = this.height / 2;
    this.introLayer = this.add.layer();
    this.cameras.main.setBackgroundColor(0x3c97a6);
    this.splashLayer = this.add.layer();
```

4. Puzzles: PushPull — Outro

```
    this.showCount();

    this.addStartButton();
    this.input.keyboard.on("keydown-SPACE", this.startSplash, this);
    this.input.keyboard.on("keydown-ENTER", this.startSplash, this);
  }
```

This will show the total moves during the game.

```
showCount() {
  this.winText = this.add
    .bitmapText(
      this.center_width,
      -100,
      "mario",
      "TOTAL MOVES: " + this.registry.get("moves"),
      30
    )
    .setOrigin(0.5)
    .setTint(0xffe066)
    .setDropShadow(2, 3, 0x75b947, 0.7);
  this.tweens.add({
    targets: this.winText,
    duration: 500,
    y: { from: this.winText.y, to: this.center_height },
  });
  this.tweens.add({
    targets: this.winText,
    duration: 100,
    scale: { from: 1, to: 1.1 },
    repeat: -1,
    yoyo: true,
  });
}
```

This adds a start button that can be clicked with the mouse or touched with a finger.

```
addStartButton() {
  this.startButton = this.add
    .bitmapText(this.center_width, 500, "mario", "Click to start", 30)
    .setOrigin(0.5)
    .setTint(0x9a5000)
    .setDropShadow(2, 3, 0x693600, 0.7);
  this.startButton.setInteractive();
  this.startButton.on("pointerdown", () => {
    this.startSplash();
  });

  this.startButton.on("pointerover", () => {
    this.startButton.setTint(0x3e6875);
  });
```

```
    this.startButton.on("pointerout", () => {
      this.startButton.setTint(0xffffff);
    });

    this.tweens.add({
      targets: this.space,
      duration: 300,
      alpha: { from: 0, to: 1 },
      repeat: -1,
      yoyo: true,
    });
  }
```

This starts the splash scene.

```
  startSplash() {
    this.sound.stopAll();
    this.scene.start("splash");
  }
}
```

In this type of puzzle game, it's interesting to offer a scoreboard so players can compete to finish it in the least number of moves possible. Check the Cookbook chapter to find the examples of scoreboards.

Other puzzles or similar games

Keep Rolling

Source code: https://github.com/pxai/phasergames/tree/master/keeprolling

Play it here: https://pello.itch.io/keep-rolling

Puddle Escape

Source code: https://github.com/pxai/phasergames/tree/master/froggy

Play it here: https://pello.itch.io/puddle-escape

Power Grid

Source code: https://github.com/pxai/phasergames/tree/master/cars

Play it here: https://pello.itch.io/make-way

Shogun Killer

Source code: https://github.com/pxai/phasergames/tree/master/ninjagolf

Play it here: https://pello.itch.io/shogun-killer

5. Roguelike: Bobble Dungeon

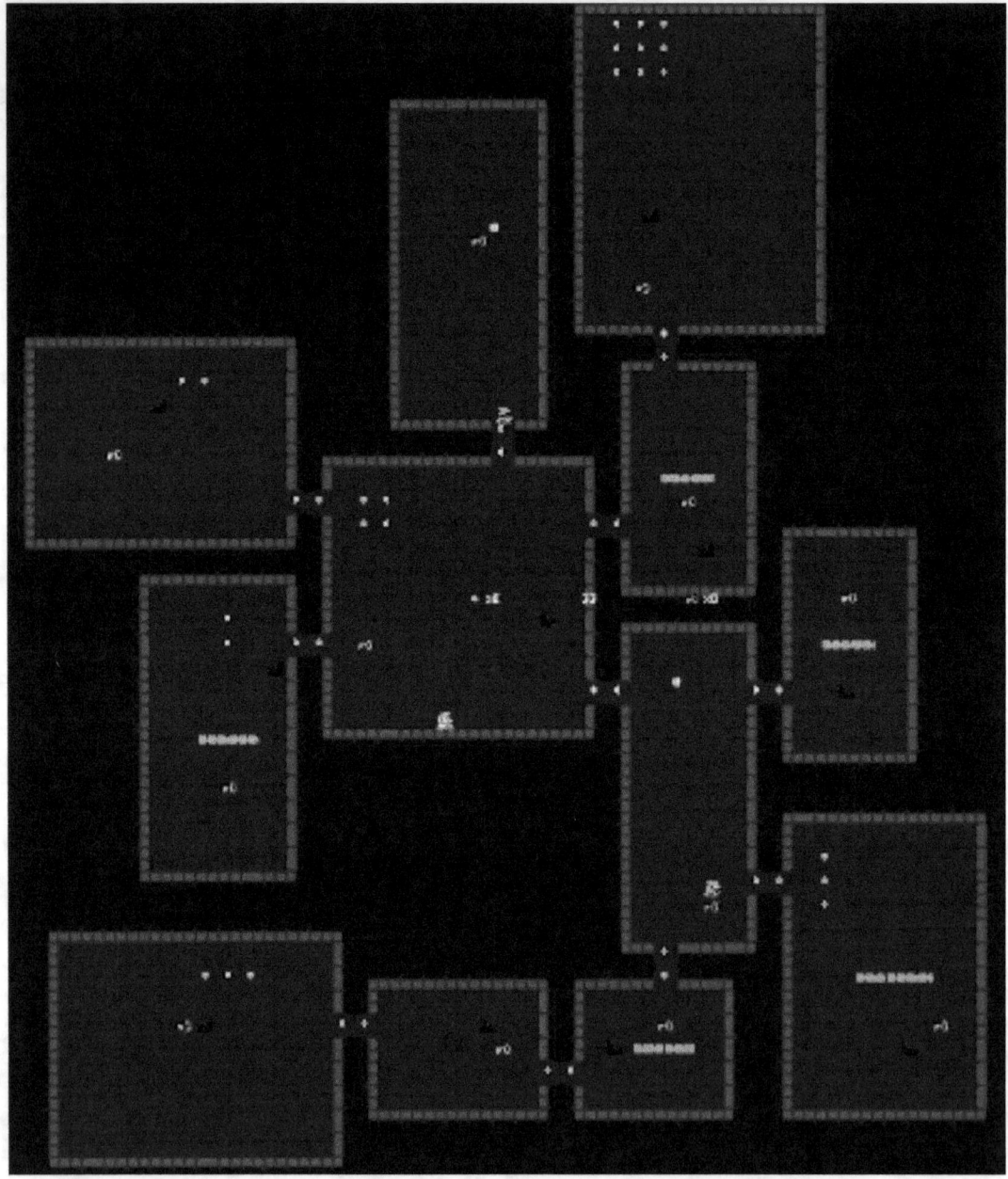

Source code: https://github.com/pxai/phasergames/tree/master/dungeon

Play it here: https://pello.itch.io/dungeonbobble

5. Roguelike: Bobble Dungeon

Roguelikes are a specific sub-genre of fantasy games where the player moves through dungeons, fights monsters, collects items and levels up. The most famous roguelike is probably Nethack, but there are many others. The main characteristics of roguelikes are:

- Turn-based gameplay.
- Randomly generated dungeons.
- Infinite playability.
- Increasing difficulty and player level development.

In this chapter, we'll create a roguelike game with Phaser. We'll use the same techniques that we've learned in the previous chapters, but we'll add some new ones too. We'll use a tilemap to create the dungeon, and we'll use Matter physics to move the player and the enemies.

This particular dungeon will have gravity so the player will need to climb up through the walls or use bubbles. Bubbles can be used to trap foes for some time or to jump on them.

Init project

This time we'll use a more complex init with a few scenes. In this case, we'll be setting `matter` physics, which means that we'll be using the Matter.js physics engine instead of the simple arcade one. Matter.js is a very popular physics engine that is used in many games and it allows us to create more complex physics interactions.

As happens when you use something different, we'll have to learn a few new things, but it's not that hard and the benefits and possibilities that this library will give you are immense.

```
import Phaser from "phaser";
import Bootloader from "./bootloader";
import Outro from "./outro";
import Splash from "./splash";
import Transition from "./transition";
import Game from "./game";
import PhaserMatterCollisionPlugin from "phaser-matter-collision-plugin";
import { MatterGravityFixPlugin } from "./matter_gravity_fix";

const config = {
```

```
    width: 600,
    height: 600,
    scale: {
      mode: Phaser.Scale.FIT,
      autoCenter: Phaser.Scale.CENTER_BOTH,
    },
    autoRound: false,
    parent: "contenedor",
    physics: {
      default: "matter",
      matter: {
        debug: false,
      },
    },
    plugins: {
      scene: [
        {
          plugin: PhaserMatterCollisionPlugin, // The plugin class
          key: "matterCollision", // Where to store in Scene.Systems, e.g.
scene.sys.matterCollision
          mapping: "matterCollision", // Where to store in the Scene, e.g.
scene.matterCollision
        },
        {
          key: "MatterGravityFixPlugin",
          plugin: MatterGravityFixPlugin,
          mapping: "matterGravityFix",
          start: true,
        },
      ],
    },
    scene: [Bootloader, Splash, Transition, Game, Outro],
};

const game = new Phaser.Game(config);
```

Loader

As always, we use this special class just to show the loading bar and load all the assets that we need. This time we don't need several maps, just some tile images that will be used by our dungeon generator.

```
export default class Bootloader extends Phaser.Scene {
  constructor() {
    super({ key: "bootloader" });
  }
```

5. Roguelike: Bobble Dungeon   Loader

Once again we use the scene `preload` method to call the different methods that will load the game assets.

```
preload() {
  this.createBars();
  this.setLoadEvents();
  this.loadFonts();
  this.loadImages();
  this.loadMaps();
  this.loadAudios();
  this.loadSpritesheets();
}
```

As we showed before, this method takes care of the loading bar and the progress bar using load events.

```
setLoadEvents() {
  this.load.on(
    "progress",
    function (value) {
      this.progressBar.clear();
      this.progressBar.fillStyle(0x0088aa, 1);
      this.progressBar.fillRect(
        this.cameras.main.width / 4,
        this.cameras.main.height / 2 - 16,
        (this.cameras.main.width / 2) * value,
        16
      );
    },
    this
  );

  this.load.on(
    "complete",
    () => {
      this.scene.start("splash");
    },
    this
  );
}
```

The fonts are loaded in this method. We'll call them `default`. Later we could add other fonts but with the same "default" name in case we want to try different fonts.

```
loadFonts() {
  this.load.bitmapFont(
    "default",
    "assets/fonts/pico.png",
    "assets/fonts/pico.xml"
  );
```

}

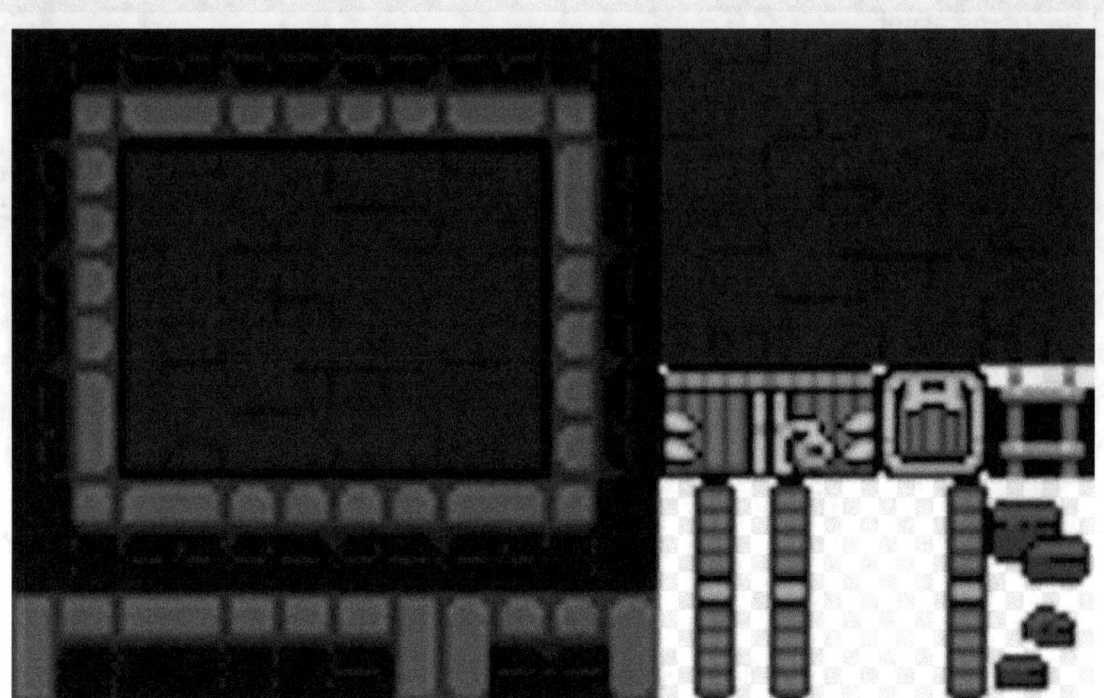

Figure 5.1 These are the images used to generate the dungeon.

This one loads the static images.

```
loadImages() {
  this.load.image("pello", "assets/images/pello_ok.png");
  this.load.image("fireball", "assets/images/fireball.png");
  this.load.image("tiles", "assets/maps/pixel-poem-tiles.png");
  this.load.image("block", "assets/images/block.png");
  this.load.image("seesaw", "assets/images/seesaw.png");
  this.load.image("bubble", "assets/images/bubble.png");
  this.load.image("platform", "assets/images/platform.png");
}
```

This loads the level map. In this game, we just use one empty map that we'll fill with the different elements of the game using a dungeon generator class.

```
loadMaps() {
  this.load.tilemapTiledJSON("scene0", "assets/maps/level.json");
}
```

This loads the audio files: music and sound effects.

```
loadAudios() {
  Array(5)
    .fill(0)
    .forEach((_, i) => {
      this.load.audio(`climb${i}`, `assets/sounds/climb${i}.mp3`);
```

```
    });

    this.load.audio("splash", "assets/sounds/splash.mp3");
    this.load.audio("music", "assets/sounds/music.mp3");
    this.load.audio("jump", "assets/sounds/jump.mp3");
    this.load.audio("bubble", "assets/sounds/bubble.mp3");
    this.load.audio("trap", "assets/sounds/trap.mp3");
    this.load.audio("crash", "assets/sounds/crash.mp3");
    this.load.audio("fireball", "assets/sounds/fireball.mp3");
    this.load.audio("win", "assets/sounds/win.mp3");
    this.load.audio("start", "assets/sounds/start.mp3");
    this.load.audio("death", "assets/sounds/death.mp3");
}
```

This part loads sprite sheets for game objects that need animations or variations.

```
loadSpritesheets() {
    this.load.spritesheet("player", "assets/images/player.png", {
        frameWidth: 48,
        frameHeight: 48,
    });
    this.load.spritesheet("dust", "assets/images/dust.png", {
        frameWidth: 32,
        frameHeight: 32,
    });
    this.load.spritesheet("coin", "assets/images/coin.png", {
        frameWidth: 32,
        frameHeight: 32,
    });
    this.load.spritesheet("keys", "assets/images/keys.png", {
        frameWidth: 48,
        frameHeight: 48,
    });
    this.load.spritesheet("bat", "assets/images/bat.png", {
        frameWidth: 32,
        frameHeight: 32,
    });
    this.load.spritesheet("wizard", "assets/images/wizard.png", {
        frameWidth: 48,
        frameHeight: 48,
    });
}
```

This one adds the load bar to the scene.

```
createBars() {
    this.loadBar = this.add.graphics();
    this.loadBar.fillStyle(0x00aafb, 1);
    this.loadBar.fillRect(
        this.cameras.main.width / 4 - 2,
        this.cameras.main.height / 2 - 18,
        this.cameras.main.width / 2 + 4,
```

```
      20
    );
    this.progressBar = this.add.graphics();
  }
}
```

Also, notice that in this particular game, I was paying homage to Bubble Bobble because this was used for a jam whose theme was *famous games parodies*. It's easy to find sprites for any well-known or classic games.

Bat

Do you remember the bat we used in the WallHammer platform game? it's here again. This time is moving with matter physics, and it also uses a tween to automatically turn.

```
import Bubble from "./bubble";

export default class Bat extends Phaser.Physics.Matter.Sprite {
  constructor(scene, x, y, texture = "bat", ground) {
    super(scene.matter.world, x, y, texture, 0);
    this.label = "bat";
    this.scene = scene;
    this.scene.add.existing(this);
    this.startX = x;
    this.direction = Phaser.Math.RND.pick([-1, 1]);
    this.setFixedRotation();
    this.setIgnoreGravity(true);
    this.addCollisions();
    this.init();
  }
```

Initiate the bat animation and movement. Also, add the update event to the scene so it will update in this class.

```
  init() {
    this.scene.anims.create({
      key: this.label,
      frames: this.scene.anims.generateFrameNumbers(this.label, {
        start: 0,
        end: 1,
      }),
      frameRate: 5,
      repeat: -1,
    });

    this.scene.anims.create({
```

5. Roguelike: Bobble Dungeon — Bat

```
    key: this.label + "death",
    frames: this.scene.anims.generateFrameNumbers(this.label, {
      start: 2,
      end: 5,
    }),
    frameRate: 5,
  });

  this.anims.play(this.label, true);
  this.on("animationcomplete", this.animationComplete, this);
  this.setVelocityX(this.direction * 5);
  this.scene.events.on("update", this.update, this);
}
```

We add the collision event to the scene so we can handle the collision with the bat and the bubble.

```
addCollisions() {
  this.unsubscribeBatCollide = this.scene.matterCollision.addOnCollideStart({
    objectA: this,
    callback: this.onBatCollide,
    context: this,
  });
}

onBatCollide({ gameObjectA, gameObjectB }) {
  if (gameObjectB instanceof Bubble) {
    gameObjectB.load("bat");
    this.destroy();
  }
}
```

Update the bat movement. If the bat is not moving anymore, we turn it around.

```
update() {
  if (!this.active) return;
  if (Math.abs(this.body.velocity.x) <= 0.5) this.turn();
}
```

This function turns the bat around and sets the velocity to the new direction.

```
turn() {
  this.direction = -this.direction;
  this.flipX = this.direction > 0;
  this.setFlipX(this.direction > 0);
  this.setVelocityX(this.direction * 5);
}
```

We don't destroy the bat directly, we kill the bat and play the death animation.

```
death() {
```

```
    this.dead = true;
    this.anims.play(this.label + "death");
  }
}
```

This destroys the bat after the death animation is complete.

```
animationComplete(animation, frame) {
  if (animation.key === this.label + "death") {
    this.destroy();
  }
}
}
```

We could have changed this bat with any other sprite though.

Bubble

Figure 5.2 The bubble sprite.

Bubbles are `Sprite` game objects generated by the player itself. These elements go floating up and they have two effects:

1. They are solid for the players and they can be used as lifts.

2. They trap the foes for a few seconds.

```
import Bat from "./bat";
import Wizard from "./wizard";

export default class Bubble extends Phaser.Physics.Matter.Sprite {
  constructor(scene, x, y, offset, options = { isStatic: true }) {
    super(scene.matter.world, x + offset, y, "bubble", 0, options);
    this.offset = offset;
    this.setFriction(1, 0, Infinity);
    this.startX = x;
    this.startY = y;
    this.scene = scene;
    scene.add.existing(this);
    this.moveVertically();
    this.scene.events.on("update", this.update, this);
  }
```

Figure 5.3 A bubble with a captured bat.

This function loads the sprite that will be inside the bubble. It also creates a tween to make it rotate.

```
load(sprite) {
  this.scene.playAudio("trap");
  this.loaded = this.scene.add
    .sprite(this.x, this.y, sprite)
    .setOrigin(0.5)
    .setScale(0.6);
  this.loaded.name = sprite;
  this.loadedTween = this.scene.tweens.add({
    targets: this.loaded,
    rotation: "+=5",
    yoyo: true,
    repeat: -1,
  });
}
```

This method moves the bubble horizontally. It happens when the bubble is launched.

```
moveHorizontally() {
  this.scene.tweens.add({
    targets: this,
    scaleX: { from: 1, to: 0.9 },
    yoyo: true,
    repeat: -1,
    duration: 200,
  });
  this.scene.tweens.addCounter({
    from: 0,
    to: Phaser.Math.Between(-400, 400),
    duration: 3500,
    ease: Phaser.Math.Easing.Sine.InOut,
    onUpdate: (tween, target) => {
      const x = this.startX + target.value;
```

5. Roguelike: Bobble Dungeon

```
      const dx = x - this.x;
      this.x = x;
      this.setVelocityX(dx);
    },
    onComplete: () => {
      this.scene.time.delayedCall(
        1000,
        () => {
          this.destroy();
        },
        null,
        this
      );
    },
  });
}
```

This one moves the bubble vertically. It moves the bubble with a tween and then it destroys it.

```
moveVertically() {
  this.blob = this.scene.tweens.add({
    targets: this,
    scaleX: { from: 1, to: 0.9 },
    yoyo: true,
    repeat: -1,
    duration: 200,
  });
  this.scene.tweens.addCounter({
    from: 0,
    to: -300,
    duration: 4500,
    ease: Phaser.Math.Easing.Sine.InOut,
    onUpdate: (tween, target) => {
      const y = this.startY + target.value;
      const dy = y - this.y;
      this.y = y;
      this.setVelocityY(dy);
    },
    onComplete: () => {
      this.blob.destroy();
      this.scene.time.delayedCall(
        1000,
        () => {
          this.destroy();
        },
        null,
        this
      );
    },
  });
}
```

5. Roguelike: Bobble Dungeon — Bubble

When a bubble is destroyed, we respawn the sprite that was inside it, setting it free.

```
respawn() {
  this.loadedTween.destroy();
  if (this.loaded.name === "wizard") {
    new Wizard(this.scene, this.x, this.y);
  } else if (this.loaded.name === "bat") {
    new Bat(this.scene, this.x, this.y);
  }
  this.loaded.destroy();
  this.loaded = null;
}
```

We update the position of the sprite that was inside the bubble.

```
update() {
  if (!this.active) return;
  if (this.loaded) {
    this.loaded.x = this.x;
    this.loaded.y = this.y;
  }
}
```

This is called when the bubble is destroyed. We play the crash sound and respawn the sprite that was inside it and finally we actually destroy the bubble game object.

```
destroy() {
  if (!this.scene) return;
  this.scene.playAudio("crash");
  if (this.loaded) this.respawn();
  super.destroy();
}
```

Depending on the place we use them the bubble can bring the foes out of the dungeon. Is that a bug or a feature? Well, we could change that easily making the bubble collide with the walls, but it's also a nice feature.

Coin

Figure 5.4 The sprite sheet for the coin.

5. Roguelike: Bobble Dungeon   Coin

Can you imagine a dungeon without treasures or something to loot? As soon as the player touches them they will be added to the score and of course, we'll play a catchy sound when we get them.

```javascript
export default class Coin extends Phaser.Physics.Matter.Sprite {
  constructor(scene, x, y, texture = "coin", options = { isStatic: true }) {
    super(scene.matter.world, x, y, texture, 0, options);
    this.scene = scene;
    this.label = "coin";
    scene.add.existing(this);
    this.init();
  }
```

The coin animation is created and played. Also, we add a tween to make it move up and down to make it more appealing.

```javascript
init() {
  this.scene.anims.create({
    key: this.label,
    frames: this.scene.anims.generateFrameNumbers(this.label, {
      start: 0,
      end: 3,
    }),
    frameRate: 10,
    repeat: -1,
  });
  this.anims.play(this.label, true);
  this.tween = this.scene.tweens.add({
    targets: this,
    duration: 300,
    y: "-=5",
    repeat: -1,
    yoyo: true,
  });
}
```

When the coin is collected, we stop the tween and destroy the coin.

```javascript
destroy() {
  this.tween.stop();
  super.destroy();
  }
}
```

These coins are generated automatically in each room.

Key

Figure 5.5 The two types of keys.

There's a key in each dungeon and the player has to collect all of them to win the game. It's quite similar to the coin.

```js
export default class key extends Phaser.Physics.Matter.Sprite {
  constructor(scene, x, y, texture = "keys", options = { isStatic: true }) {
    super(
      scene.matter.world,
      x,
      y,
      texture,
      Phaser.Math.RND.pick([0, 1]),
      options
    );
    this.scene = scene;
    this.label = "keys";
    scene.add.existing(this);

    this.init();
  }
```

As we did with the coin, we create the animation and add a tween to make it move up and down. We could possibly do something different here, like make it rotate. Or just reuse the same class as the coin.

```js
  init() {
    this.tween = this.scene.tweens.add({
      targets: this,
      duration: 300,
      y: "-=5",
      repeat: -1,
      yoyo: true,
    });
  }

  destroy() {
    this.tween.stop();
    super.destroy();
  }
}
```

Dust

Figure 5.6 Particles generated as trail and landing dust, animated and fading.

We want to offer a lot of feedback while the player runs and jumps so we make use of this Dust class.

```
export default class Dust extends Phaser.GameObjects.Sprite {
  constructor(scene, x, y, name = "dust", tween = false) {
    super(scene, x, y, name);
    this.scene = scene;
    this.name = name;
    this.setScale(0.5);
    this.scene.add.existing(this);
    this.init(tween);
  }
```

This dust is a simple sprite that plays an animation and then destroys itself. It's used when the player lands, slides on a wall, or jumps. We can optionally add a tween to make it fade out.

```
  init(tween) {
    if (tween) {
      this.scene.tweens.add({
        targets: this,
        duration: Phaser.Math.Between(500, 1000),
        alpha: { from: 1, to: 0 },
        onComplete: () => {
          this.destroy();
        },
      });
    }

    this.scene.anims.create({
      key: this.name,
      frames: this.scene.anims.generateFrameNumbers(this.name, {
```

```
      start: 0,
      end: 10,
    }),
    frameRate: 10,
  });
  this.on("animationcomplete", this.animationComplete, this);
  this.anims.play(this.name, true);
  }

  animationComplete() {
    this.destroy();
  }
}
```

Fireball

Figure 5.7 The fireball sprite.

Fireballs are sprites launched by the wizards. They also use matter physics and they can kill the player instantly.

```
export default class Fireball extends Phaser.Physics.Matter.Sprite {
  constructor(scene, x, y, direction) {
    super(scene.matter.world, x, y, "fireball", 0);
    this.label = "fireball";
    this.scene = scene;
    this.direction = direction;
    scene.add.existing(this);
    this.setIgnoreGravity(true);
    this.setVelocityX(5 * this.direction);
    this.setVelocityY(Phaser.Math.Between(0, -8));
    this.setBounce(1);
    this.init();
  }
```

We create the animation for the fireball and add the update event to the scene so it will update in this class.

```
  init() {
    this.scene.events.on("update", this.update, this);
    this.tween = this.scene.tweens.add({
      targets: this,
      duration: 200,
      scale: { from: 0.9, to: 1 },
      repeat: -1,
    });
    this.scene.time.delayedCall(
```

```
      3000,
      () => {
        this.destroy();
      },
      null,
      this
    );
  }

  update() {
    if (this.scene?.gameOver) return;
  }

  destroy() {
    this.tween.destroy();
    super.destroy();
  }
}
```

The wizard launches fireballs at the player but these can also bounce off the walls to make them more dangerous.

Wizard

Figure 5.8 The Wizard sprite sheet.

These are static characters that dwell the dungeons, but beware of them. They launch fireballs repeatedly in unpredictable directions.

```
import Fireball from "./fireball";
import Bubble from "./bubble";

export default class Wizard extends Phaser.Physics.Matter.Sprite {
  constructor(scene, x, y, texture = "wizard", ground) {
    super(scene.matter.world, x, y, texture, 0);
    this.label = "wizard";
    this.scene = scene;
    this.scene.add.existing(this);
    this.startX = x;
    this.direction = Phaser.Math.RND.pick([-1, 1]);

    this.setFixedRotation();
    this.addCollisions();
    this.init();
  }
```

This function inits the wizard. It creates the animations and it also creates a timer that will be used to shoot the fireballs.

```
init() {
  this.scene.anims.create({
    key: this.label,
    frames: this.scene.anims.generateFrameNumbers(this.label, {
      start: 0,
      end: 5,
    }),
    frameRate: 5,
    repeat: -1,
  });

  this.anims.play(this.label, true);

  this.timer = this.scene.time.addEvent({
    delay: 3000,
    callback: this.directShot,
    callbackScope: this,
    loop: true,
  });
}
```

As we did with the player and the bat, we create this callback to handle the collision with the bubble.

```
addCollisions() {
  this.unsubscribeBatCollide = this.scene.matterCollision.addOnCollideStart({
    objectA: this,
    callback: this.onWizardCollide,
    context: this,
  });
}
```

This will be called when the bubble hits the wizard. We "load" the wizard inside the bubble and destroy the wizard.

```
onWizardCollide({ gameObjectA, gameObjectB }) {
  if (gameObjectB instanceof Bubble) {
    gameObjectB.load("wizard");
    this.destroy();
  }
}
```

The wizard will try to shoot directly at the player. It will shoot a fireball and then turn around.

```
directShot() {
  this.scene.playAudio("fireball");
```

```
    const distance = Phaser.Math.Distance.BetweenPoints(
      this.scene.player,
      this
    );
    this.anims.play("wizardshot", true);
    const fireball = new Fireball(this.scene, this.x, this.y, this.direction);
    this.delayedTurn = this.scene.time.delayedCall(
      1000,
      () => {
        this.turn();
      },
      null,
      this
    );
  }
```

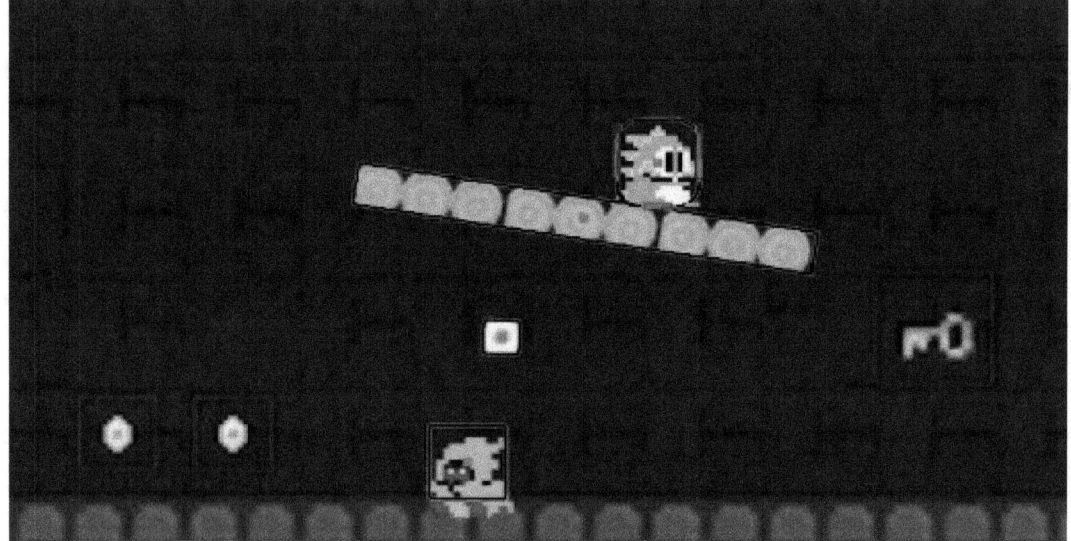

Figure 5.9 The Wizard shooting a fireball to player's position.

This method takes care of turning the wizard around.

```
turn() {
  this.direction = -this.direction;
  this.flipX = this.direction > 0;
  this.setFlipX(this.direction > 0);
  this.setVelocityX(this.direction * 5);
}
```

This will be called when the wizard is destroyed. We destroy the timer and the delayed turn before destroying the wizard.

```
destroy() {
  if (this.timer) this.timer.destroy();
  if (this.delayedTurn) this.delayedTurn.destroy();
  if (this.fireball) this.fireball.destroy();
```

```
      super.destroy();
    }
  }
```

We could have made the wizards walk to both sides too.

Matter Gravity Fix

This is a very specific fix code that we need when using Matter with Phaser, especially to have objects that are not affected by gravity.

```
export class MatterGravityFixPlugin extends Phaser.Plugins.ScenePlugin {
  constructor(scene, pluginManager) {
    super(scene, pluginManager);
  }
  boot() {
    const Matter = Phaser.Physics.Matter.Matter;
    this.applyGravityFix(Matter);
  }
```

This does the trick to fix the gravity issue. It overrides the _bodiesApplyGravity function in the Matter.Engine class.

```
  applyGravityFix(Matter) {
    Matter.Engine._bodiesApplyGravity = function (bodies, gravity) {
      var gravityScale =
          typeof gravity.scale !== "undefined" ? gravity.scale : 0.001,
        bodiesLength = bodies.length;

      if ((gravity.x === 0 && gravity.y === 0) || gravityScale === 0) {
        return;
      }

      for (var i = 0; i < bodiesLength; i++) {
        var body = bodies[i];

        if (body.ignoreGravity || body.isStatic || body.isSleeping) {
          continue;
        }
        body.force.y += body.mass * gravity.y * gravityScale;
        body.force.x += body.mass * gravity.x * gravityScale;
      }
    };
  }
}
```

Thanks to this fix we can have flying bats in our game.

Dungeon generator

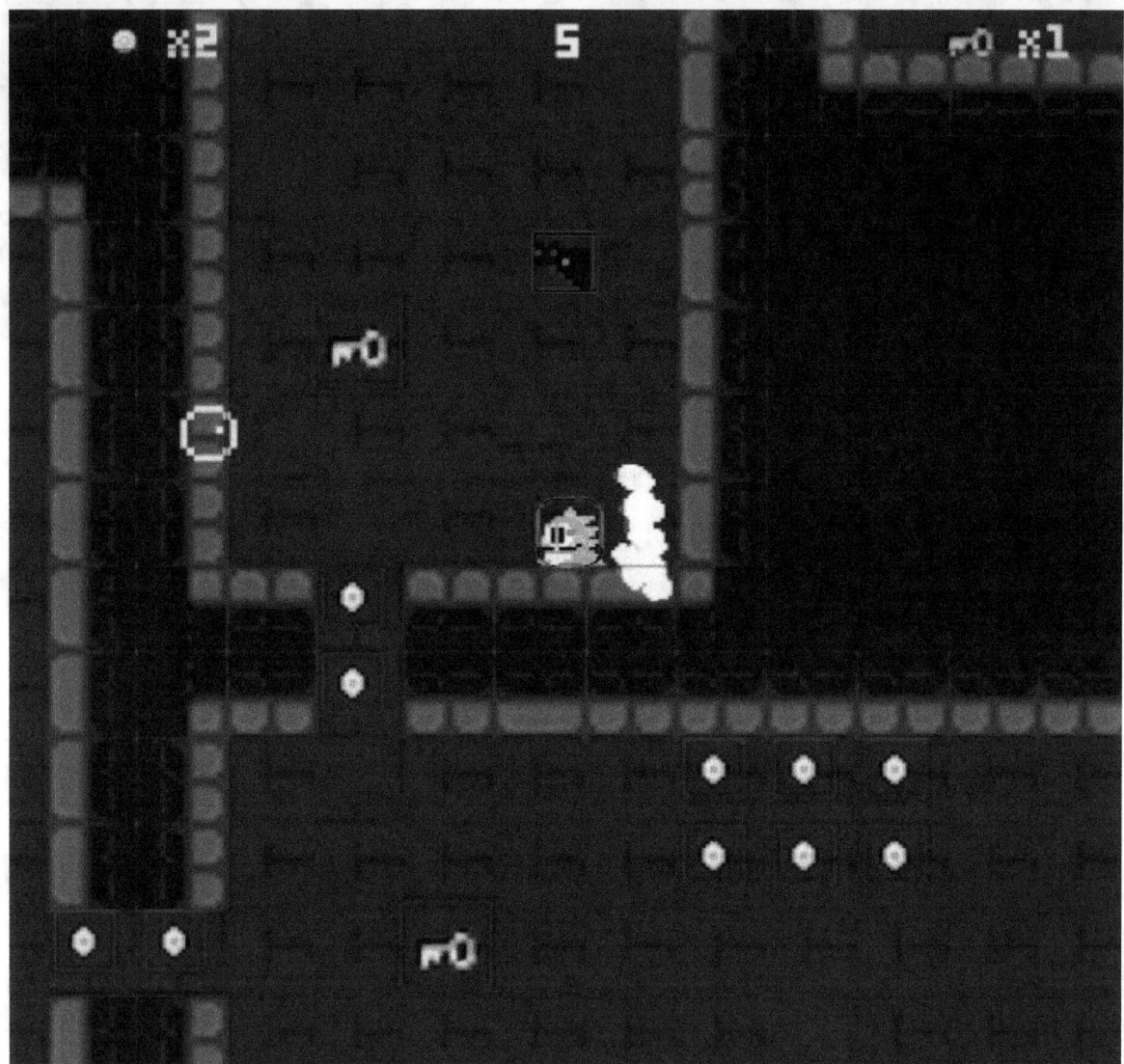

Figure 5.10 Each room in the dungeon will have doors, a key and coins.

Well, this is the key class in this project. It uses an existing library for dungeon generation and does all the heavy lifting. We "just" need to give some parameters and most importantly to specify the tiles that we'll use for walls, corners, doors, etc. It's highly customizable and it works really well.

```
import Dungeon from "@mikewesthad/dungeon";
import Coin from "./coin";
import Key from "./key";
```

5. Roguelike: Bobble Dungeon — Dungeon generator

```
import Bat from "./bat";
import Wizard from "./wizard";
import SeeSaw from "./seesaw";

export default class DungeonGenerator {
  constructor(scene) {
    this.scene = scene;
    this.generate();
  }
```

This is the method that generates the whole dungeon. It's divided into different methods to make it more readable but basically, it generates the dungeon, and the map and then it places the different elements on the map.

```
  generate() {
    this.generateDungeon();
    this.generateMap();
    // Watch the player and layer for collisions, for the duration of the scene:
    //this.physics.add.collider(this.player.sprite, layer);

    this.dungeon.rooms.forEach((room) => {
      // These room properties are all in grid units (not pixels units)
      const { x, y, width, height } = room;
      // Fill the room (minus the walls) with mostly clean floor tiles (90% of the time), but
      // occasionally place a dirty tile (10% of the time).
      this.groundLayer.weightedRandomize(
        [
          { index: 17, weight: 9 }, // 9/10 times, use index 17
          { index: [7, 8, 9, 17, 18, 19], weight: 1 }, // 1/10 times, randomly pick 7, 8, 9, 17, 18, 19
        ],
        x + 1,
        y + 1,
        width - 2,
        height - 2
      );

      this.placeCorners(room);
      this.placeWalls(room);

      const doors = room.getDoorLocations(); // Returns an array of {x, y} objects
      this.addDoors(room, doors, x, y);
      this.addKey(room);
      this.addFoes(room);
      this.addCoins(room);
      this.addSeeSaw(room);
    });
  }
```

5. Roguelike: Bobble Dungeon — Dungeon generator

This method generates the dungeon using the @mikewesthad/dungeon dungeon generator library. We just need to pass the width and height of the dungeon and some options. You can check the documentation of the library to see all the options available.

```
generateDungeon() {
  this.dungeon = new Dungeon({
    width: 50,
    height: 50,
    doorPadding: 2,
    rooms: {
      width: { min: 7, max: 15 },
      height: { min: 7, max: 15 },
      maxRooms: 12,
    },
  });
}
```

This method adds a specific tilemap to our dungeon, with its layers and collisions.

```
generateMap() {
  this.map = this.scene.make.tilemap({
    tileWidth: 48,
    tileHeight: 48,
    width: this.dungeon.width,
    height: this.dungeon.height,
  });
  const tileset = this.map.addTilesetImage("tiles", null, 48, 48, 0, 0); // 1px margin, 2px spacing
  this.groundLayer = this.map.createBlankLayer("Layer 1", tileset);
  this.stuffLayer = this.map.createBlankLayer("Stuff", tileset);

  // Get a 2D array of tile indices (using -1 to not render empty tiles) and place them into the
  // blank layer
  const mappedTiles = this.dungeon.getMappedTiles({
    empty: -1,
    floor: -1,
    door: 3,
    wall: 0,
  });
  this.groundLayer.putTilesAt(mappedTiles, 0, 0);
  this.groundLayer.setCollision(0);
  this.groundLayer.setCollisionByProperty({ collides: true });
  this.scene.matter.world.convertTilemapLayer(this.groundLayer);
}
```

This method places the corners of the room. We use the tile index to place the corner tiles.

```
placeCorners(room) {
```

```js
    const { left, right, top, bottom } = room;
    this.groundLayer.putTileAt(0, left, top);
    this.groundLayer.putTileAt(5, right, top);
    this.groundLayer.putTileAt(45, right, bottom);
    this.groundLayer.putTileAt(40, left, bottom);
  }
```

This method places the walls of the room. We use the tile index to place the wall tiles. It uses a weighted randomize method to place the tiles which means that we can give more weight (frequency) to some tiles than others.

```js
  placeWalls(room) {
    const { width, height, left, right, top, bottom } = room;
    this.groundLayer.weightedRandomize(
      [
        { index: 2, weight: 4 },
        { index: [1, 2, 3, 4], weight: 1 },
      ],
      left + 1,
      top,
      width - 2,
      1
    );
    this.groundLayer.weightedRandomize(
      [
        { index: 42, weight: 4 },
        { index: [41, 42, 43, 44], weight: 1 },
      ],
      left + 1,
      bottom,
      width - 2,
      1
    );
    this.groundLayer.weightedRandomize(
      [
        { index: 10, weight: 4 },
        { index: [10, 20, 30], weight: 1 },
      ],
      left,
      top + 1,
      1,
      height - 2
    );
    this.groundLayer.weightedRandomize(
      [
        { index: 15, weight: 4 },
        { index: [15, 25, 35], weight: 1 },
      ],
      right,
      top + 1,
      1,
```

```
      height - 2
    );
}
```

As the name implies, this one adds the doors to the room. We also use the tile index to place the door tiles.

```
addDoors(room, doors, x, y) {
  for (let i = 0; i < doors.length; i++) {
    const worldPosition = this.groundLayer.tileToWorldXY(
      x + doors[i].x,
      y + doors[i].y
    );
    new Coin(this.scene, worldPosition.x + 20, worldPosition.y + 20);
    if (doors[i].y === 0) {
      this.groundLayer.putTilesAt([[7], [7]], x + doors[i].x, y + doors[i].y);
    } else if (doors[i].y === room.height - 1) {
      this.groundLayer.putTilesAt([[7], [7]], x + doors[i].x, y + doors[i].y);
    } else if (doors[i].x === 0) {
      this.groundLayer.putTilesAt([[7]], x + doors[i].x, y + doors[i].y);
    } else if (doors[i].x === room.width - 1) {
      this.groundLayer.putTilesAt([[7]], x + doors[i].x, y + doors[i].y);
    }
  }
}
```

Each room must have a key that the player has to collect. This method adds the key to the room.

```
addKey(room) {
  const keyX = Phaser.Math.Between(room.left + 2, room.right - 2);
  const keyY = Phaser.Math.Between(room.top + 2, room.bottom - 2);
  const worldPosition = this.groundLayer.tileToWorldXY(keyX, keyY);
  new Key(this.scene, worldPosition.x + 22, worldPosition.y + 22);
}
```

Randomly, some rooms may have a seesaw. This method adds the seesaw to the center of the room.

```
addSeeSaw(room) {
  if (Phaser.Math.Between(0, 10) < 7) return;
  const worldPosition = this.groundLayer.tileToWorldXY(
    room.centerX,
    room.centerY
  );
  new SeeSaw(
    this.scene,
    worldPosition.x + 22,
    worldPosition.y + 22,
    room.width
```

```
    );
}
```

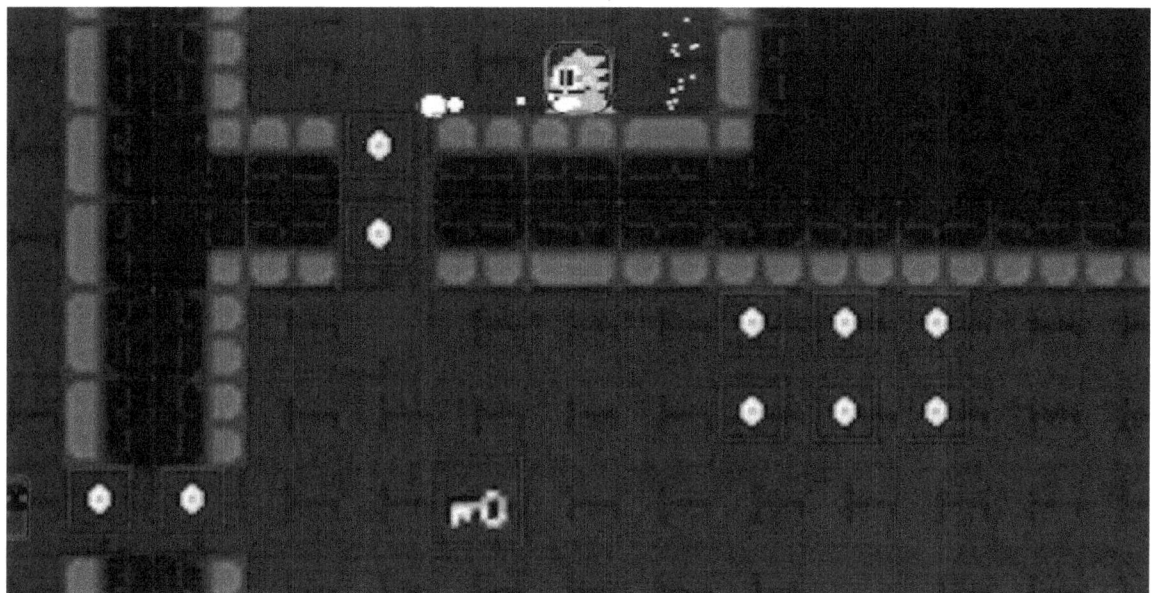

Figure 5.11 Coins generated at the doors and on top.

Coins are randomly placed in the room. We use a random method to decide where to place the coins. It uses other helper methods to place the coins in different positions.

```
addCoins(room) {
  const where = Phaser.Math.RND.pick([
    "top",
    "bottom",
    "left",
    "right",
    "none",
  ]);
  const width = parseInt(room.width / 3) - Phaser.Math.Between(1, 2);
  const height = parseInt(room.height / 3) - Phaser.Math.Between(1, 2);
  switch (where) {
    case "top":
      this.addCoinsTop(room, width, height);
      break;
    case "bottom":
      this.addCoinsdBottom(room, width, height);
      break;
    case "left":
      this.addCoinsdLeft(room, width, height);
      break;
    case "right":
      this.addCoinsdRight(room, width, height);
      break;
    default:
      break;
```

5. Roguelike: Bobble Dungeon — Dungeon generator

```
    }
}
```

This specific functions will place the coins in the corner they belong to:

```
addCoinsTop(room, width, height) {
  const keyY = room.top + Phaser.Math.Between(1, 2);
  const keyX = room.left + Phaser.Math.Between(1, 2);

  Array(width)
    .fill()
    .forEach((x, i) => {
      Array(height)
        .fill()
        .forEach((y, j) => {
          const worldPosition = this.groundLayer.tileToWorldXY(
            keyX + i,
            keyY + j
          );
          new Coin(this.scene, worldPosition.x + 20, worldPosition.y + 20);
        });
    });
}

addCoinsdBottom(room, width, height) {
  const keyY = room.bottom - Phaser.Math.Between(1, 2);
  const keyX = room.left + Phaser.Math.Between(1, 2);

  Array(width)
    .fill()
    .forEach((x, i) => {
      Array(height)
        .fill()
        .forEach((y, j) => {
          const worldPosition = this.groundLayer.tileToWorldXY(
            keyX + i,
            keyY - j
          );
          new Coin(this.scene, worldPosition.x + 20, worldPosition.y + 20);
        });
    });
}

addCoinsdLeft(room, width, height) {
  const keyY = room.top + Phaser.Math.Between(3, 4);
  const keyX = room.left + Phaser.Math.Between(1, 2);

  Array(width)
    .fill()
    .forEach((x, i) => {
```

```js
      Array(height)
        .fill()
        .forEach((y, j) => {
          const worldPosition = this.groundLayer.tileToWorldXY(
            keyX + i,
            keyY - j
          );
          new Coin(this.scene, worldPosition.x + 20, worldPosition.y + 20);
        });
    });
}

addCoinsdRight(room, width, height) {
  const keyY = room.top + Phaser.Math.Between(1, 2);
  const keyX = room.right - Phaser.Math.Between(3, 4);

  Array(width)
    .fill()
    .forEach((x, i) => {
      Array(height)
        .fill()
        .forEach((y, j) => {
          const worldPosition = this.groundLayer.tileToWorldXY(
            keyX - i,
            keyY + j
          );
          new Coin(this.scene, worldPosition.x + 20, worldPosition.y + 20);
        });
    });
}
```

This is the function that we will use to add both Wizards and Bats on the stage:

```js
addFoes(room) {
  const keyX = Phaser.Math.Between(room.left + 2, room.right - 2);
  const keyY = Phaser.Math.Between(room.top + 2, room.bottom - 2);

  const worldPosition = this.groundLayer.tileToWorldXY(keyX, keyY);

  if (Phaser.Math.Between(0, 5) > 4) {
    new Wizard(
      this.scene,
      worldPosition.x + 22,
      worldPosition.y + 22,
      this.groundLayer
    );
  } else {
    new Bat(
      this.scene,
      worldPosition.x + 22,
      worldPosition.y + 22,
      this.groundLayer
```

```
      );
    }
  }
}
```

This one adds the top traps or spikes to the room. Finally is not used in the game but it's a good example of how to add more elements to the dungeon.

```
addTopTraps(room) {
  const { x, y, width, height, left, right, top, bottom, tiles } = room;

  const topTiles = tiles[0];
  topTiles.forEach((tile, i) => {
    if (tile === 1 && i > 0 && i < right)
      this.groundLayer.putTileAt(5, i + left, top + 1);
  });
}
```

Following the roguelike rules, in this game, the scene is generated each time you play.

See-Saw

Figure 5.12 Base seesaw sprite.

See-saws are another type of element that Matter.js physics allows you to create. These platforms are fixed in the center so when the player jumps on them they will rotate according to the weight balance.

```
export default class SeeSaw {
  constructor(scene, x, y, numTiles = 5) {
    const platform = scene.add.tileSprite(
      x,
      y,
      (32 * numTiles) / 2,
      18,
      "seesaw"
    );
    scene.matter.add.gameObject(platform, {
      restitution: 0, // No bounciness
      frictionAir: 0.2, // Spin forever without slowing down from air resistance
      friction: 0.2, // A little extra friction so the player sticks better
      // Density sets the mass and inertia based on area - 0.001 is the default. We're going lower
      // here so that the platform tips/rotates easily
      density: 0.0005,
```

```
    });

    const { Constraint } = Phaser.Physics.Matter.Matter;

    const constraint = Constraint.create({
      pointA: { x: platform.x, y: platform.y },
      bodyB: platform.body,
      length: 0,
    });

    scene.matter.world.add(constraint);
    const sign = Math.random() < 0.5 ? -1 : 1;
  }
}
```

Visually we just need a sprite to see them and in this case, the sprite is repeated to cover the length of the element.

Player

Figure 5.13 Our cute player sprite sheet.

This is "just" another player class with animations and controls attached to it but pay attention! In this game, we are using Matter physics so functions for moving are a bit different. Also, the player is a composite object with more than one sensor so we can apply different effects depending on what we touch. For example, the side sensors will allow the player to detect walls and be able to climb them jumping.

```
import Bubble from "./bubble";
import Dust from "./particle";

export default class Player {
  constructor(scene, x, y) {
    this.scene = scene;
    this.label = "player";
    this.moveForce = 0.01;
    this.invincible = true;
    this.isTouching = { left: false, right: false, ground: false };
    this.canJump = true;
    this.jumpCooldownTimer = null;
    this.canShoot = true;
    this.shootCooldownTimer = null;
    this.onWall = false;
```

```
    this.init(x, y);
    this.addControls();
}
```

The init method is called from the constructor and in this case, it has several jobs. This is just a conventional class that contains a compound body: it consists of different bodies for the player, and we need to add them to the Matter world. We also need to add the player sprite to the scene and set up the animations.

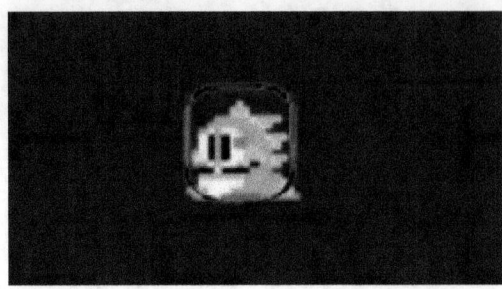

Figure 5.14 Player has a main body and 3 sensors.

Finally, we need to add the colliders and events that will be used to control the player. If you set the debug to `true` you'll see the different bodies that make up the player. The ones on the sides are used to detect collisions with walls and be able to climb up.

```
init(x, y) {
    // Before Matter's update, reset our record of what surfaces the player is touching.
    this.scene.matter.world.on("beforeupdate", this.resetTouching, this);
    this.sprite = this.scene.matter.add.sprite(0, 0, "player", 0);

    const { Body, Bodies } = Phaser.Physics.Matter.Matter; // Native Matter modules
    const { width: w, height: h } = this.sprite;

    const mainBody = Bodies.rectangle(0, 5, w - 14, h - 10, {
      chamfer: { radius: 10 },
    });
    this.sensors = {
      bottom: Bodies.rectangle(0, h * 0.5, w * 0.25, 2, { isSensor: true }),
      left: Bodies.rectangle(-w * 0.35, 0, 2, h * 0.5, { isSensor: true }),
      right: Bodies.rectangle(w * 0.35, 0, 2, h * 0.5, { isSensor: true }),
    };
    const compoundBody = Body.create({
      parts: [
        mainBody,
        this.sensors.bottom,
        this.sensors.left,
        this.sensors.right,
      ],
      frictionStatic: 0,
```

```
      frictionAir: 0.02,
      friction: 0.1,
      render: { sprite: { xOffset: 0.5, yOffset: 0.5 } },
    });
    this.sprite
      .setExistingBody(compoundBody)
      .setFixedRotation() // Sets inertia to infinity so the player can't rotate
      .setPosition(x, y);

    this.addEvents();
    this.addColliders();
    this.addAnimations();
    this.initInvincible();
  }
```

We attach this class to the scene events, so we can update the player on every frame. We also add the destroy method to the scene events, so we can clean up the player when the scene is destroyed.

```
addEvents() {
  this.scene.events.on("update", this.update, this);
  this.scene.events.once("shutdown", this.destroy, this);
  this.scene.events.once("destroy", this.destroy, this);
}
```

These are the collider events that will be used to control the player. We use the MatterCollision plugin to detect collisions between the player and the walls. We also use the onSensorCollide method to detect collisions with the sensors that we added to the player. This is used to detect collisions with the walls and the ground.

```
addColliders() {
  this.scene.matterCollision.addOnCollideStart({
    objectA: [this.sensors.bottom, this.sensors.left, this.sensors.right],
    callback: this.onSensorCollide,
    context: this,
  });
  this.scene.matterCollision.addOnCollideActive({
    objectA: [this.sensors.bottom, this.sensors.left, this.sensors.right],
    callback: this.onSensorCollide,
    context: this,
  });
}
```

These define the different animation states to the player: idle, walking, shooting, etc.

```
addAnimations() {
  this.scene.anims.create({
    key: "playeridle",
    frames: this.scene.anims.generateFrameNumbers(this.label, {
```

```
        start: 0,
        end: 1,
      }),
      frameRate: 5,
      repeat: -1,
    });

    this.scene.anims.create({
      key: "playerwalk",
      frames: this.scene.anims.generateFrameNumbers(this.label, {
        start: 0,
        end: 3,
      }),
      frameRate: 6,
    });

    this.scene.anims.create({
      key: "playershot",
      frames: this.scene.anims.generateFrameNumbers(this.label, {
        start: 4,
        end: 5,
      }),
      frameRate: 4,
    });
    this.sprite.anims.play("playeridle", true);
    this.sprite.on("animationcomplete", this.animationComplete, this);
  }
```

When the player is just created, it's invincible for a short time. This is done by a flag and changing the alpha of the sprite, so it blinks.

```
initInvincible() {
  this.scene.tweens.add({
    targets: this.sprite,
    alpha: { from: 0.5, to: 1 },
    duration: 200,
    repeat: 10,
    onComplete: () => {
      this.invincible = false;
    },
  });
}
```

This is the method that is called when the player collides with something. We use it to detect collisions with the walls and the ground. We also use it to detect collisions with the sensors that we added to the player.

```
onSensorCollide({ bodyA, bodyB, pair }) {
    if (bodyB.isSensor) return; // We only care about collisions with physical objects
```

```js
      if (bodyA === this.sensors.left) {
        this.friction();
        this.onWall = true;
        this.isTouching.left = true;
        if (pair.separation > 0.5) this.sprite.x += pair.separation - 0.5;
      } else if (bodyA === this.sensors.right) {
        this.friction();
        this.onWall = true;
        this.isTouching.right = true;
        if (pair.separation > 0.5) this.sprite.x -= pair.separation - 0.5;
      } else if (bodyA === this.sensors.bottom) {
        this.land();
        this.isTouching.ground = true;
      }
    }
```

This is used to reset the `isTouching` flags so we can determine if the player is on the ground or not.

```js
  resetTouching() {
    this.isTouching.left = false;
    this.isTouching.right = false;
    this.isTouching.ground = false;
  }
```

This is used to add the controls to the player: WASD keys and we can also use the cursor keys to move the player and shoot bubbles.

```js
  addControls() {
    this.cursor = this.scene.input.keyboard.createCursorKeys();
    this.W = this.scene.input.keyboard.addKey(Phaser.Input.Keyboard.KeyCodes.W);
    this.A = this.scene.input.keyboard.addKey(Phaser.Input.Keyboard.KeyCodes.A);
    this.S = this.scene.input.keyboard.addKey(Phaser.Input.Keyboard.KeyCodes.S);
    this.D = this.scene.input.keyboard.addKey(Phaser.Input.Keyboard.KeyCodes.D);
  }
```

This is the game loop for the player. This is called on every frame. We check the input and move the player accordingly. We also check if the player is on the ground or not, and if it is, we allow it to jump. We also check if the player is in the air and touching a wall, so we can allow it to climb up.

```js
  update() {
    this.isOnGround = this.isTouching.ground;
    this.isInAir = !this.isOnGround;
    this.moveForce = this.isOnGround ? 0.01 : 0.005;

    if (this.D.isDown || this.cursor.right.isDown) {
      this.sprite.setFlipX(true);
      if (!(this.isInAir && this.isTouching.right)) {
        this.step();
```

5. Roguelike: Bobble Dungeon — Player

```
      this.sprite.anims.play("playerwalk", true);
      this.sprite.setVelocityX(5);
    }
  } else if (this.A.isDown || this.cursor.left.isDown) {
    this.sprite.setFlipX(false);
    if (!(this.isInAir && this.isTouching.left)) {
      this.step();
      this.sprite.anims.play("playerwalk", true);
      this.sprite.setVelocityX(-5);
    }
  } else {
    if (this.sprite.anims.currentAnim.key !== "playershot")
      this.sprite.anims.play("playeridle", true);
  }

  if (this.sprite.body.velocity.x > 7) this.sprite.setVelocityX(7);
  else if (this.sprite.body.velocity.x < -7) this.sprite.setVelocityX(-7);

  this.checkJump();
  this.checkShoot();
}
```

If the player is jumping, we add a cooldown timer so it can't jump again until it touches the ground.

```
checkJump() {
  if (
    ((this.canJump && this.isOnGround) || this.onWall) &&
    (this.W.isDown || this.cursor.up.isDown)
  ) {
    this.sprite.setVelocityY(-8);
    this.scene.playAudio("jump");
    this.canJump = false;
    this.onWall = false;
    this.jumpCooldownTimer = this.scene.time.addEvent({
      delay: 250,
      callback: () => (this.canJump = true),
    });
  }
}
```

Same as we did with the jump, here we add a cooldown timer to the shooting so the player can't shoot again until the cooldown is over.

```
checkShoot() {
  if (
    this.canShoot &&
    (Phaser.Input.Keyboard.JustDown(this.cursor.down) ||
      Phaser.Input.Keyboard.JustDown(this.W))
  ) {
    const offset = this.sprite.flipX ? 128 : -128;
```

```js
      this.sprite.anims.play("playershot", true);
      this.scene.playAudio("bubble");
      this.canShoot = false;
      new Bubble(this.scene, this.sprite.x, this.sprite.y, offset);
      this.shootCooldownTimer = this.scene.time.addEvent({
        delay: 500,
        callback: () => (this.canShoot = true),
      });
    }
  }
```

When the player is killed, apart from destroying the sprite, we also remove the events and colliders that we added to it.

```js
destroy() {
  this.scene.playAudio("death");
  this.destroyed = true;

  this.scene.events.off("update", this.update, this);
  this.scene.events.off("shutdown", this.destroy, this);
  this.scene.events.off("destroy", this.destroy, this);
  if (this.scene.matter.world) {
    this.scene.matter.world.off("beforeupdate", this.resetTouching, this);
  }

  const sensors = [
    this.sensors.bottom,
    this.sensors.left,
    this.sensors.right,
  ];
  this.scene.matterCollision.removeOnCollideStart({ objectA: sensors });
  this.scene.matterCollision.removeOnCollideActive({ objectA: sensors });

  if (this.jumpCooldownTimer) this.jumpCooldownTimer.destroy();

  this.sprite.destroy();
}
```

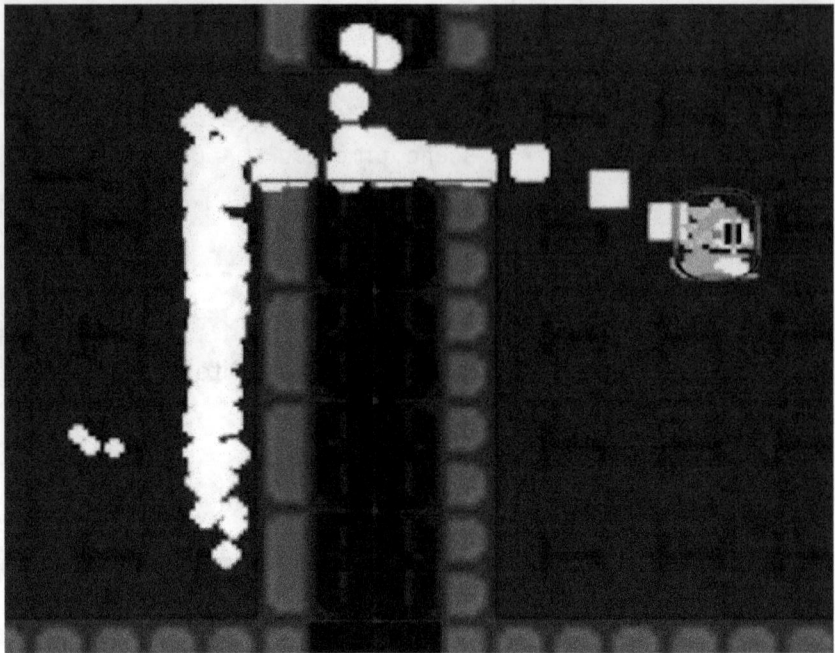

Figure 5.15 Sensors will detect friction against walls and the ground.

Every time the player moves, we add a few dust particles to the scene. This is done by creating a new Dust object. The same happens when the player is on the wall or landing after a jump. Probably there's a good chance to refactor this but in this particular case, for a couple of lines maybe it's not worth it.

```
step() {
  if (Phaser.Math.Between(0, 5) > 4) {
    this.scene.trailLayer.add(
      new Dust(
        this.scene,
        this.sprite.x,
        this.sprite.y + Phaser.Math.Between(10, 16)
      )
    );
  }
}

friction() {
  Array(Phaser.Math.Between(2, 4))
    .fill(0)
    .forEach((i) => {
      new Dust(
        this.scene,
        this.sprite.x + Phaser.Math.Between(-8, 8),
        this.sprite.y + Phaser.Math.Between(-32, 32)
      );
    });
}
```

```
land() {
  if (this.sprite.body.velocity.y < 1) return;
  Array(Phaser.Math.Between(3, 6))
    .fill(0)
    .forEach((i) => {
      new Dust(
        this.scene,
        this.sprite.x + Phaser.Math.Between(-32, 32),
        this.sprite.y + Phaser.Math.Between(10, 16)
      );
    });
}
```

This is called when the player dies, creating an explosion of dust particles.

```
explosion() {
  Array(Phaser.Math.Between(10, 15))
    .fill(0)
    .forEach((i) => {
      new Dust(
        this.scene,
        this.sprite.x + Phaser.Math.Between(-32, 32),
        this.sprite.y + Phaser.Math.Between(20, 36)
      );
    });
}
```

This is called when the player finishes the shooting animation. We use it to play the idle animation again.

```
  animationComplete(animation, frame) {
    if (animation.key === "playershot") {
      this.sprite.anims.play("playeridle", true);
    }
  }
}
```

If you try the game you'll feel like climbing is too powerful but hey, you can always tweak the powers of your character.

The game!

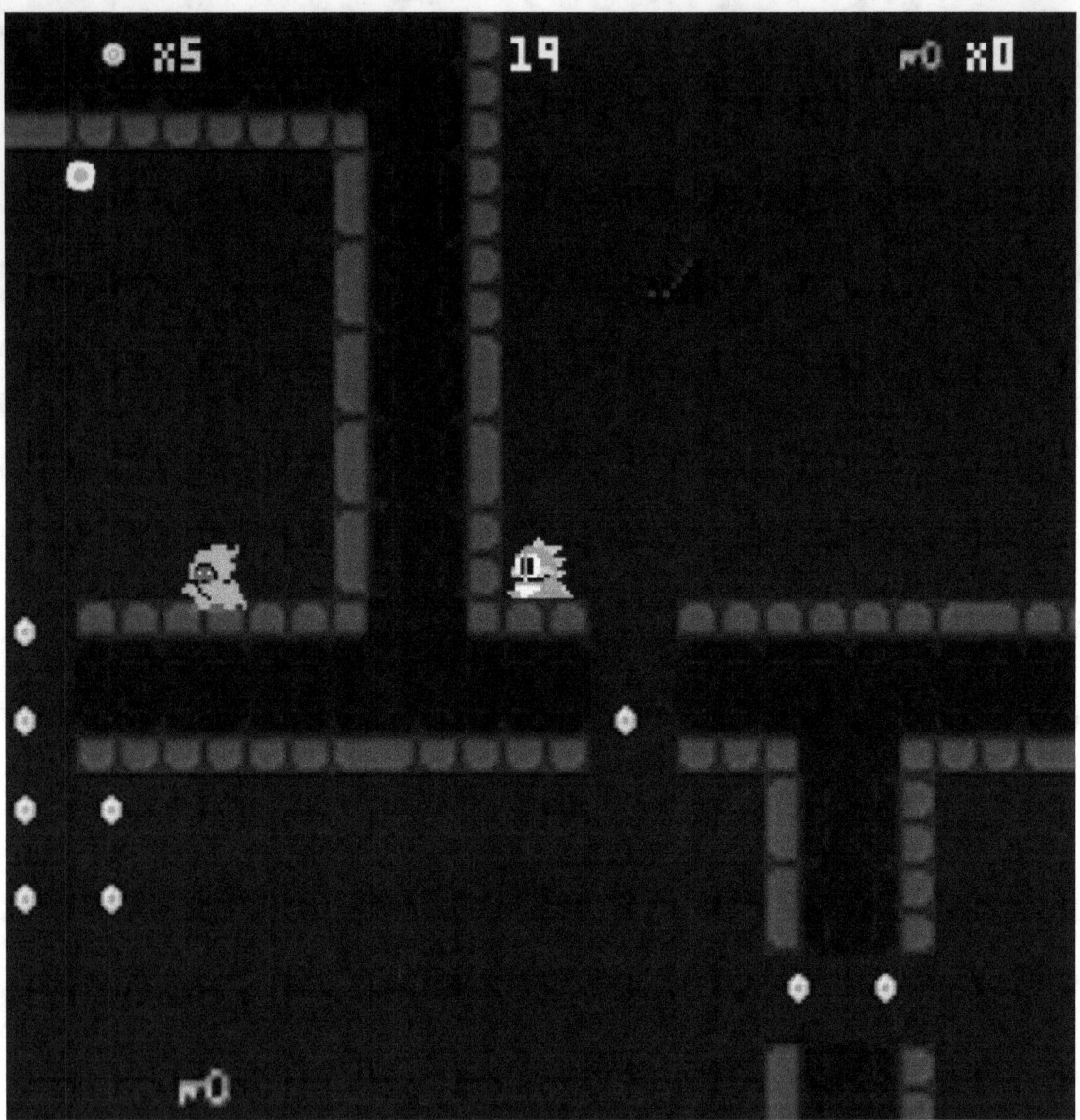

Figure 5.16 Game in progress.

This is again the scene that puts everything together. The player, the dungeon generator and most importantly, the definition of collisions and interactions. That is the part that is different from the previous games with arcade physics, and to be honest the most annoying part of using Matter.js in Phaser.

```
import Player from "./player";
```

5. Roguelike: Bobble Dungeon

```
import DungeonGenerator from "./dungeon_generator";

export default class Game extends Phaser.Scene {
  constructor() {
    super({ key: "game" });
    this.player = null;
    this.score = 0;
    this.scoreText = null;
  }

  init(data) {
    this.name = data.name;
    this.number = data.number;
  }

  preload() {
    this.registry.set("seconds", 0);
    this.registry.set("coins", 0);
    this.registry.set("keys", 0);
  }
```

From this, we create the whole thing. We call the methods to add the map, the player, the collisions, the camera and the scores.

```
create() {
  this.width = this.sys.game.config.width;
  this.height = this.sys.game.config.height;
  this.center_width = this.width / 2;
  this.center_height = this.height / 2;

  this.addMap();
  this.addPlayer();
  this.addCollisions();
  this.addCamera();
  this.addScores();
  this.loadAudios();
}
```

This method creates the map using the `DungeonGenerator` class.

```
addMap() {
  this.dungeon = new DungeonGenerator(this);
  this.input.keyboard.on("keydown-ENTER", () => this.finishScene(), this);
}
```

Figure 5.17 Scores for coins, time and keys.

This method adds the scores to the scene. We add the coins, the seconds, the keys and the timer. We'll update them with other methods.

```
addScores() {
  this.add
    .sprite(62, 26, "coin", 0)
    .setOrigin(0.5)
    .setScrollFactor(0)
    .setScale(0.8);
  this.scoreCoins = this.add
    .bitmapText(100, 24, "default", "x0", 15)
    .setOrigin(0.5)
    .setScrollFactor(0);
  this.scoreSeconds = this.add
    .bitmapText(this.center_width, 24, "default", "0", 15)
    .setOrigin(0.5)
    .setScrollFactor(0);
  this.add
    .sprite(this.width - 90, 24, "keys", 0)
    .setOrigin(0.5)
    .setScrollFactor(0)
    .setScale(0.8);
  this.scoreKeys = this.add
    .bitmapText(this.width - 48, 24, "default", "x0", 15)
    .setOrigin(0.5)
    .setScrollFactor(0);
  this.timer = this.time.addEvent({
    delay: 1000,
    callback: () => {
      this.updateSeconds();
    },
    callbackScope: this,
    loop: true,
  });
}
```

This method adds the player to the scene. It creates a new Player object along with a trail layer that will be used to draw the trail of the player.

```
addPlayer() {
  this.trailLayer = this.add.layer();
  this.player = new Player(
    this,
    this.dungeon.map.widthInPixels / 2,
    this.dungeon.map.heightInPixels / 2,
    100
  );
}
```

This method sets up the collisions between the player and anything else. Basically, it sets a callback function that will be called when the player collides with something.

5. Roguelike: Bobble Dungeon — The game!

```
addCollisions() {
  this.unsubscribePlayerCollide = this.matterCollision.addOnCollideStart({
    objectA: this.player.sprite,
    callback: this.onPlayerCollide,
    context: this,
  });

  this.matter.world.on("collisionstart", (event) => {
    event.pairs.forEach((pair) => {
      const bodyA = pair.bodyA;
      const bodyB = pair.bodyB;
    });
  });
}
```

This is the callback that we call when the player collides with something. We check the label of the object that the player collides with and call the corresponding method.

```
onPlayerCollide({ gameObjectA, gameObjectB }) {
  if (!gameObjectB) return;
  if (gameObjectB.label === "coin") this.playerPicksCoin(gameObjectB);
  if (gameObjectB.label === "keys") this.playerPicksKey(gameObjectB);
  if (gameObjectB.label === "bat") this.playerHitsFoe(gameObjectB);
  if (gameObjectB.label === "wizard") this.playerHitsFoe(gameObjectB);
  if (gameObjectB.label === "fireball") this.playerHitsFoe(gameObjectB);
  if (!(gameObjectB instanceof Phaser.Tilemaps.Tile)) return;

  const tile = gameObjectB;

  if (tile.properties.isLethal) {
    this.unsubscribePlayerCollide();
    this.restartScene();
  }
}
```

This is called when a player picks up a coin. It destroys the coin and updates the score.

```
playerPicksCoin(coin) {
  this.showPoints(coin.x, coin.y, 1, this.scoreCoins);
  coin.destroy();
  this.updateCoins();
  this.playAudio("coin");
}
```

Same as the previous one but with the key.

```
playerPicksKey(key) {
  this.updateKeys();
  this.showPoints(
    key.x,
    key.y,
```

```
        this.registry.get("keys") + "/" + this.dungeon.dungeon.rooms.length,
        this.scoreKeys
    );
    key.destroy();
}
```

Unless the player is invincible (blinking at the beginning), this is called when the player hits any foe. It kills the player, destroys the foe, and restarts the scene.

```
playerHitsFoe(foe) {
    if (this.player.invincible) return;
    this.player.explosion();
    foe.destroy();
    this.restartScene();
}
```

Every time we need to show points, we call this method. It creates a text element, adds a tween to it, and destroys it when the tween is finished.

```
showPoints(x, y, score, textElement, color = 0xffffff) {
    let text = this.add
        .bitmapText(x + 20, y - 80, "default", "+" + score, 10)
        .setDropShadow(2, 3, color, 0.7)
        .setOrigin(0.5);
    this.tweens.add({
        targets: text,
        duration: 1000,
        alpha: { from: 1, to: 0 },
        x: {
            from: text.x + Phaser.Math.Between(-10, 10),
            to: text.x + Phaser.Math.Between(-40, 40),
        },
        y: { from: text.y - 10, to: text.y - 60 },
        onComplete: () => {
            text.destroy();
        },
    });

    this.textUpdateEffect(textElement, color);
}
```

5. Roguelike: Bobble Dungeon — The game!

Figure 5.18 As soon as we touch and pick up the coins the points will show up.

This method adds the camera to the scene and the background color. It sets the bounds of the camera to the size of the map and makes it follow the player.

```
addCamera() {
  this.cameras.main.setBounds(
    0,
    0,
    this.dungeon.map.widthInPixels,
    this.dungeon.map.heightInPixels
  );
  this.cameras.main.startFollow(this.player.sprite, false, 0.5, 0.5);
  this.cameras.main.setBackgroundColor(0x25131a);
}
```

As we did in other games, here we add the audio files to the scene along with a method to play them.

```
loadAudios() {
  this.audios = {
    jump: this.sound.add("jump"),
    bubble: this.sound.add("bubble"),
    trap: this.sound.add("trap"),
    crash: this.sound.add("crash"),
    fireball: this.sound.add("fireball"),
    death: this.sound.add("death"),
    coin: this.sound.add("start"),
  };
}

playAudio(key) {
  this.audios[key].play();
}
```

This method is called when the player dies. It makes the camera shake and fade out and then restarts the scene.

```
restartScene() {
```

5. Roguelike: Bobble Dungeon — The game!

```
    this.player.sprite.visible = false;
    this.cameras.main.shake(100);
    this.cameras.main.fade(250, 0, 0, 0);
    this.cameras.main.once("camerafadeoutcomplete", () => this.scene.restart());
}
```

If a player finishes the stage, we fade out the camera and start the outro scene.

```
finishScene() {
    this.cameras.main.fade(250, 0, 0, 0);
    this.cameras.main.once("camerafadeoutcomplete", () => {
        this.scene.start("outro", {
            next: "underwater",
            name: "STAGE",
            number: this.number + 1,
        });
    });
}
```

This method is called every second. It updates the seconds and the timer because, for any competitive player, time is the most important thing. We could add a scoreboard at the end ordered by time.

```
updateSeconds(points = 1) {
    const seconds = +this.registry.get("seconds") + points;
    this.registry.set("seconds", seconds);
    this.scoreSeconds.setText(seconds);
}
```

The next two functions update the coins and keys scores. In the case of the keys, if the player has collected all the keys, we finish the scene.

```
updateCoins(points = 1) {
    const coins = +this.registry.get("coins") + points;
    this.registry.set("coins", coins);
    this.scoreCoins.setText("x" + coins);
}

updateKeys(points = 1) {
    const keys = +this.registry.get("keys") + points;
    this.registry.set("keys", keys);
    this.scoreKeys.setText("x" + keys);
    if (keys === this.dungeon.dungeon.rooms.length) {
        this.finishScene();
    }
}
```

We have this method to update the text elements when we add points to the score. In this class is not used currently but we could use it later or in other classes.

```
  textUpdateEffect(textElement, color) {
    textElement.setTint(color);
    const prev = textElement.y;
    this.tweens.add({
      targets: textElement,
      duration: 100,
      alpha: { from: 1, to: 0.8 },
      scale: { from: 1.2, to: 1 },
      repeat: 5,
      onComplete: () => {
        textElement.setTint(0xffffff);
        textElement.y = prev;
      },
    });
  }
}
```

Apart from collisions, the game scene also controls the end condition by keeping the count of collected keys. Also, each time the player dies it will restart the scene regenerating a new dungeon map. Another feature that we add to the scene is the timer. This will be changing each second and we will save it in the registry to show it later on the outro Scene.

Splash

Figure 5.19 The Splash screen for Dungeon Bobble

This is a humble Splash screen where we just want to show our main character chased by a foe. Splash screens can have more than text and static images. They are scenes with game loops so don't forget that we are allowed to add characters, animate them and make a fun splash.

```
export default class Splash extends Phaser.Scene {
  constructor() {
    super({ key: "splash" });
  }
```

5. Roguelike: Bobble Dungeon

As always, we create everything we need on the scene from the `create` method.

```
create() {
  this.width = this.sys.game.config.width;
  this.height = this.sys.game.config.height;
  this.center_width = this.width / 2;
  this.center_height = this.height / 2;

  this.backLayer = this.add.layer();
  this.cameras.main.setBackgroundColor(0x000000);
  this.showTitle();
  this.addPlayerAndFoe();
  this.addAnimationTweens();

  this.time.delayedCall(1000, () => this.showInstructions(), null, this);

  this.input.keyboard.on("keydown-SPACE", () => this.startGame(), this);
  this.input.keyboard.on("keydown-ENTER", () => this.startGame(), this);
  this.playMusic();
}

startGame() {
  if (this.theme) this.theme.stop();
  this.scene.start("transition");
}
```

This shows the title of the game. It's a bitmap text with a shadow and a tween to make it move. We could improve this looping over an array.

```
showTitle() {
  this.textShadow1 = this.add
    .bitmapText(this.center_width, 100, "default", "DUNGEON", 85)
    .setTint(0xff787a)
    .setOrigin(0.5);
  this.textShadow2 = this.add
    .bitmapText(this.center_width, 250, "default", "BOBBLE", 85)
    .setTint(0xff787a)
    .setOrigin(0.5);
  this.text1 = this.add
    .bitmapText(this.center_width, 100, "default", "DUNGEON", 85)
    .setTint(0x302030)
    .setOrigin(0.5);
  this.text2 = this.add
    .bitmapText(this.center_width, 250, "default", "BOBBLE", 85)
    .setTint(0x302030)
    .setOrigin(0.5);
  this.text11 = this.add
    .bitmapText(this.center_width, 100, "default", "DUNGEON", 88)
    .setTint(0x00aafb)
    .setOrigin(0.5);
  this.text22 = this.add
    .bitmapText(this.center_width, 250, "default", "BOBBLE", 88)
```

5. Roguelike: Bobble Dungeon — Splash

```
      .setTint(0x00aafb)
      .setOrigin(0.5);
    this.tweens.add({
      targets: [this.textShadow1, this.textShadow2],
      duration: 1000,
      x: "+=10",
      y: "+=10",
      yoyo: true,
      repeat: -1,
    });
}
```

This method plays the music of the scene. It's a looped music with a volume of 0.3.

```
playMusic(theme = "splash") {
  this.theme = this.sound.add(theme);
  this.theme.stop();
  this.theme.play({
    mute: false,
    volume: 0.3,
    rate: 1,
    detune: 0,
    seek: 0,
    loop: true,
    delay: 0,
  });
}
```

This method shows the instructions of the game, the classic controls, the author, and a blinking text to start the game.

```
showInstructions() {
  this.add
    .bitmapText(this.center_width, 430, "default", "WASD/Arrows: move", 30)
    .setDropShadow(1, 1, 0xff787a, 0.7)
    .setOrigin(0.5);
  this.add
    .sprite(this.center_width - 60, 490, "pello")
    .setOrigin(0.5)
    .setScale(0.3);
  this.add
    .bitmapText(this.center_width + 40, 490, "default", "By PELLO", 15)
    .setDropShadow(1, 1, 0xff787a, 0.7)
    .setOrigin(0.5);
  this.space = this.add
    .bitmapText(this.center_width, 550, "default", "Press SPACE to start", 25)
    .setDropShadow(1, 1, 0x3d253b, 0.7)
    .setOrigin(0.5);
  this.tweens.add({
    targets: this.space,
    duration: 300,
```

```
      alpha: { from: 0, to: 1 },
      repeat: -1,
      yoyo: true,
    });
  }
```

This method adds the player and the foe to the scene and creates the animations for both.

```
addPlayerAndFoe() {
  this.player = this.add.sprite(this.width - 100, 350, "player").setScale(2);
  this.anims.create({
    key: "playeridle",
    frames: this.anims.generateFrameNumbers("player", { start: 0, end: 3 }),
    frameRate: 5,
    repeat: -1,
  });
  this.player.anims.play("playeridle");
  this.foe = this.add.sprite(this.width, 350, "wizard").setScale(2);
  this.anims.create({
    key: "foe",
    frames: this.anims.generateFrameNumbers("wizard", { start: 0, end: 4 }),
    frameRate: 5,
    repeat: -1,
  });
  this.foe.anims.play("foe");
}
```

We also add some tweens to the player and the foe to make them move. The interesting part is how we can use the tweens to simulate a walk cycle. We just need to change the x value of the target and flip the sprite.

```
addAnimationTweens() {
  this.tweens.add({
    targets: [this.player],
    x: { from: this.player.x, to: 0 },
    duration: 2500,
    yoyo: true,
    repeat: -1,
    onYoyo: () => {
      this.player.flipX = !this.player.flipX;
    },
    onRepeat: () => {
      this.player.flipX = !this.player.flipX;
    },
  });

  this.tweens.add({
    targets: [this.foe],
    x: { from: this.foe.x, to: 100 },
```

```
      duration: 2500,
      yoyo: true,
      repeat: -1,
      onYoyo: () => {
        this.foe.flipX = !this.foe.flipX;
      },
      onRepeat: () => {
        this.foe.flipX = !this.foe.flipX;
      },
    });
  }
}
```

The letters also have a little dynamic shadow effect that is easy to achieve.

Transition page

Figure 5.20 Simple text explaining the goal of the game.

The gameplay is quite frantic here so even if there's just one stage we'll show this transition to get the player ready.

```
export default class Transition extends Phaser.Scene {
  constructor() {
    super({ key: "transition" });
  }
```

In this short transition before the game, we show the instructions and the keys to press to start the game. This scene becomes the prelude right before the game to get the player ready.

```
  create() {
```

```js
    this.sound.stopAll();
    this.width = this.sys.game.config.width;
    this.height = this.sys.game.config.height;
    this.center_width = this.width / 2;
    this.center_height = this.height / 2;
    this.sound.add("start").play();
    this.playMusic();
    this.key = this.add
      .sprite(this.center_width, this.center_height - 120, "keys", 0)
      .setOrigin(0.5)
      .setScale(2);

    this.add
      .bitmapText(
        this.center_width,
        this.center_height - 20,
        "default",
        "GET ALL KEYS",
        30
      )
      .setOrigin(0.5);
    this.add
      .bitmapText(
        this.center_width,
        this.center_height + 40,
        "default",
        "from all rooms!",
        25
      )
      .setOrigin(0.5);
    this.input.keyboard.on("keydown-ENTER", () => this.loadNext(), this);
    this.input.keyboard.on("keydown-SPACE", () => this.loadNext(), this);
    this.time.delayedCall(1000, () => this.loadNext(), null, this);
  }

  loadNext() {
    this.scene.start("game");
  }
```

We play the music in a loop from the transition. This way the music doesn't stop when the player goes to the game and dies. Once the player is in the game scene, if he dies he will be respawned in that scene and this music should continue playing, so it will not stop and start all the time.

```js
  playMusic(theme = "music") {
    this.theme = this.sound.add(theme);
    this.theme.stop();
    this.theme.play({
      mute: false,
      volume: 0.2,
      rate: 1,
```

```
        detune: 0,
        seek: 0,
        loop: true,
        delay: 0,
      });
    }
  }
```

The transition is only shown between splash and game. When the game is restarted every time the player dies we won't bother him anymore.

Outro

Figure 5.21 This is how the outro looks like.

This outro scene will be used to show what the player achieved:

- Completion time.
- Collected coins. We could also show killed foes, but hey... poor guys.

```
export default class Outro extends Phaser.Scene {
  constructor() {
    super({ key: "outro" });
  }
```

```js
init(data) {
  this.name = data.name;
  this.number = data.number;
  this.next = data.next;
}
```

First, we add all elements to the scene: player image, score, text, and the input to restart the game.

```js
create() {
  this.width = this.sys.game.config.width;
  this.height = this.sys.game.config.height;
  this.center_width = this.width / 2;
  this.center_height = this.height / 2;
  this.showPlayer();
  this.sound.add("win").play();
  this.scoreCoins = this.add
    .bitmapText(
      this.center_width,
      50,
      "default",
      "Coins: " + this.registry.get("coins"),
      25
    )
    .setOrigin(0.5)
    .setScrollFactor(0);
  this.scoreSeconds = this.add
    .bitmapText(
      this.center_width,
      100,
      "default",
      "Time: " + this.registry.get("seconds"),
      25
    )
    .setOrigin(0.5)
    .setScrollFactor(0);
  this.add
    .bitmapText(
      this.center_width,
      this.center_height - 20,
      "default",
      "YOU DID IT!!",
      40
    )
    .setOrigin(0.5);
  this.add
    .bitmapText(
      this.center_width,
      this.center_height + 40,
      "default",
      "Press space to restart",
```

5. Roguelike: Bobble Dungeon

```
      25
    )
    .setOrigin(0.5);
  this.input.keyboard.on("keydown-ENTER", () => this.loadNext(), this);
  this.input.keyboard.on("keydown-SPACE", () => this.loadNext(), this);
}

loadNext() {
  this.scene.start("splash");
}
```

We show the player image and play the idle animation.

```
showPlayer() {
  this.player = this.add
    .sprite(this.center_width, this.center_height - 120, "player")
    .setOrigin(0.5)
    .setScale(3);
  this.anims.create({
    key: "playeridle",
    frames: this.anims.generateFrameNumbers("player", { start: 0, end: 1 }),
    frameRate: 5,
    repeat: -1,
  });

  this.player.anims.play("playeridle");
}
```

This would be also a good game to keep a scoreboard.

Other roguelike or similar games

Drill Bill

Source code: https://github.com/pxai/phasergames/tree/master/drill

Play it here: https://pello.itch.io/drill-bill

Greedy Willie

Source code: https://github.com/pxai/phasergames/tree/master/greedywilly

Play it here: https://pello.itch.io/greedy-willie

Spooky

Source code: https://github.com/pxai/phasergames/tree/master/pumpkin

Play it here: https://pello.itch.io/spooky

Other games using matter physics

Lucky Shot

Source code: https://github.com/pxai/phasergames/tree/master/lucky

Play it here: https://pello.itch.io/lucky-shot

5. Roguelike: Bobble Dungeon — Other games using matter physics

Moriarty

Source code: https://github.com/pxai/phasergames/tree/master/moriarty

Play it here: https://pello.itch.io/moriarty

6. Tell me a story: Marstranded

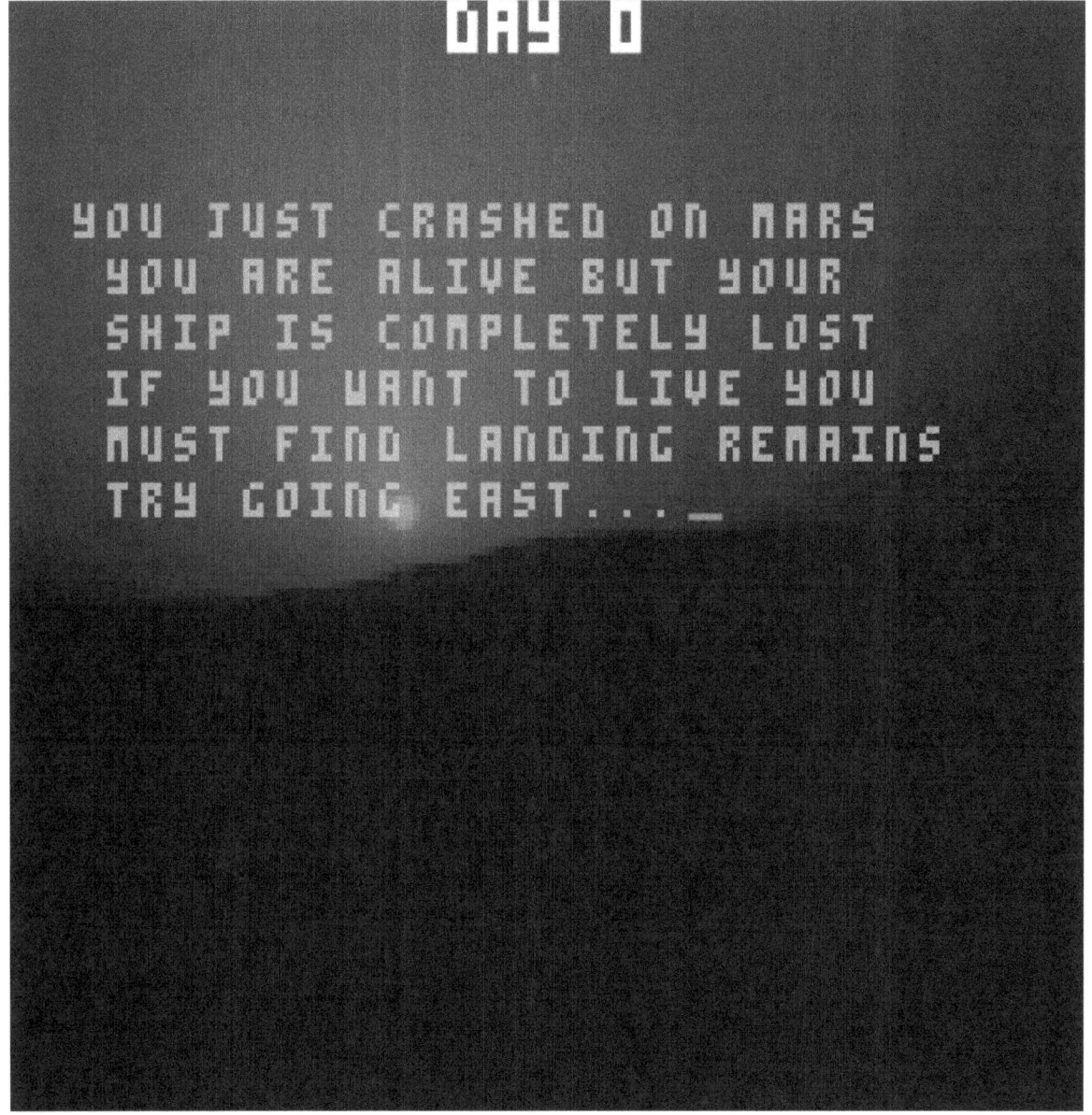

Source code: https://github.com/pxai/phasergames/tree/master/marstranded

Play it here: https://pello.itch.io/marstranded

One of the interesting things about games is that they can also tell stories. That's not something exclusive of books or movies. The fact is that games can tell stories in a way that is unique to them. And most importantly, a background story can make a game more interesting and engaging.

In this chapter, we'll create a simple game that tells a story. We'll use a few techniques that we've learned in the previous chapters, and once again we'll add some new ones too. The story is divided into different stages created with tile maps. There will be collisions, objects, traps and foes. But everything will be very simple. The goal is to tell a story and involve the player, not to create a complex game.

The story, as the name already suggests, is about an astronaut that has crashed on Mars. The player has to help her to survive and to find a way to go back home. The story is told on a few screens. The first one is a splash screen with the title and the credits. Then we have a transition screen that gives some context and clues for each stage. After we complete each stage, we'll get a new transition screen with a new clue. Finally, when we complete the last stage, we'll get the outro screen. The style of the game is a rip-off of Cold Scream, with symbolic graphics instead of animated characters: that is why it relies heavily on backstory and ambiance.

Init project

From the code perspective, this is a pretty straightforward game, with splash, transitions, and a game scene with maps.

```
import Phaser from "phaser";
import Bootloader from "./bootloader";
import Outro from "./outro";
import Splash from "./splash";
import Transition from "./transition";
import Game from "./game";

const config = {
  width: 800,
  height: 800,
  scale: {
    mode: Phaser.Scale.FIT,
    autoCenter: Phaser.Scale.CENTER_BOTH,
  },
  autoRound: false,
  parent: "contenedor",
```

```
    physics: {
      default: "arcade",
      arcade: {
        gravity: { y: 300 },
        debug: false,
      },
    },
    scene: [Bootloader, Splash, Transition, Game, Outro],
};

const game = new Phaser.Game(config);
```

We'll be using a [library](#) that implements A* algorithm to find the best path between two points. This is a very popular algorithm that is used in many games. It's not part of Phaser, but it's very easy to use it. We'll see how to use it later.

Loader

This scene will take care of loading a lot of assets. This game uses a lot of sounds as recordings to tell the story. We'll also load a few tile maps and images.

```
export default class Bootloader extends Phaser.Scene {
  constructor() {
    super({ key: "bootloader" });
  }
```

Once again we load all the assets in the preload method, organizing them in the usual order and starting from the progress bar.

```
  preload() {
    this.createBars();
    this.setLoadEvents();
    this.loadFonts();
    this.loadImages();
    this.loadMaps();
    this.loadAudios();
    this.loadSpritesheets();
    this.setRegistry();
  }
```

This will be the method that will be in charge of updating the progress bar as the assets are loaded. The colors used in the bar are the same that we use in the game and the splash screen.

```
  setLoadEvents() {
```

6. Tell me a story: Marstranded

```js
    this.load.on(
      "progress",
      function (value) {
        this.progressBar.clear();
        this.progressBar.fillStyle(0xae2012, 1);
        this.progressBar.fillRect(
          this.cameras.main.width / 4,
          this.cameras.main.height / 2 - 16,
          (this.cameras.main.width / 2) * value,
          16
        );
      },
      this
    );
    this.load.on(
      "complete",
      () => {
        this.scene.start("splash");
      },
      this
    );
  }
```

In this game, there's only one minimalistic, computer-like font, so we only need to load one bitmap font.

```js
loadFonts() {
  this.load.bitmapFont(
    "pico",
    "assets/fonts/pico.png",
    "assets/fonts/pico.xml"
  );
}
```

These are the fixed images of the game. A couple of them are backgrounds used in the game transitions.

```js
loadImages() {
  this.load.image("body", "assets/images/body.png");
  this.load.image("landscape", "assets/images/landscape.png");
  this.load.image("record", "assets/images/record.png");
  this.load.image("hole", "assets/images/hole.png");
  this.load.image("pello", "assets/images/pello_ok.png");
  this.load.image("mars", "assets/maps/mars64.png");
  this.load.image("background", "assets/maps/mars.png");
}
```

Figure 6.1 Tile image used for Mars.

This game contains different tiled maps. As the game advances, the style will change slightly, with a more complex and darker style at the end.

```
loadMaps() {
  Array(7)
    .fill(0)
    .forEach((_, i) => {
      this.load.tilemapTiledJSON(`scene${i}`, `assets/maps/scene${i}.json`);
    });
}
```

There are many audios in this game because we need to create a very immersive atmosphere and we require sound recordings for the diaries and the officer's messages.

```
loadAudios() {
  this.load.audio("mars_background", "assets/sounds/mars_background.mp3");
  this.load.audio("step", "assets/sounds/step.mp3");
  this.load.audio("creepy", "assets/sounds/creepy.mp3");
  this.load.audio("heartbeat", "assets/sounds/heartbeat.mp3");
  this.load.audio("breath", "assets/sounds/breath.mp3");
  this.load.audio("blip", "assets/sounds/blip.mp3");
  this.load.audio("ohmygod", "assets/sounds/ohmygod.mp3");
  this.load.audio("kill", "assets/sounds/kill.mp3");
  this.load.audio("tracker", "assets/sounds/tracker.mp3");
  this.load.audio("holeshout", "assets/sounds/holeshout.mp3");
  this.load.audio("oxygen", "assets/sounds/oxygen.mp3");
  this.load.audio("monster", "assets/sounds/monster.mp3");
  this.load.audio("killed", "assets/sounds/killed.mp3");
  this.load.audio("creepy_static", "assets/sounds/creepy_static.mp3");
  this.load.audio("shock", "assets/sounds/shock.mp3");
  this.load.audio("cave", "assets/sounds/cave.mp3");
  this.load.audio("type", "assets/sounds/type.mp3");

  Array(4)
    .fill(0)
    .forEach((_, i) => {
      this.load.audio(`static${i}`, `assets/sounds/static${i}.mp3`);
```

6. Tell me a story: Marstranded

```
    });

    Array(6)
      .fill(0)
      .forEach((_, i) => {
        this.load.audio(
          `diary    1 `,
          `assets/sounds/diary/diary${i + 1}.mp3`
        );
      });

    Array(6)
      .fill(0)
      .forEach((_, i) => {
        this.load.audio(
          `officer    1 `,
          `assets/sounds/officer/officer${i + 1}.mp3`
        );
      });
  }
```

These are the sprites, not many because of the style of the game. Uh-oh, there's a monster!

```
loadSpritesheets() {
  this.load.spritesheet("player", "assets/images/player.png", {
    frameWidth: 64,
    frameHeight: 64,
  });
  this.load.spritesheet("debris", "assets/images/debris.png", {
    frameWidth: 64,
    frameHeight: 64,
  });
  this.load.spritesheet("step", "assets/images/step.png", {
    frameWidth: 64,
    frameHeight: 64,
  });
  this.load.spritesheet("wave", "assets/images/wave.png", {
    frameWidth: 64,
    frameHeight: 64,
  });
  this.load.spritesheet("drone", "assets/images/drone.png", {
    frameWidth: 64,
    frameHeight: 64,
  });
  this.load.spritesheet("monster", "assets/images/monster.png", {
    frameWidth: 128,
    frameHeight: 64,
  });
}
```

6. Tell me a story: Marstranded — Loader

This method will set the initial value of the game's registry. The score will be set to 0. We could use it to measure completion time or the steps required.

```
setRegistry() {
  this.registry.set("score", 0);
}
```

This is the background of the progress bar. It's a simple rectangle with a border and it also uses one of the game's colors.

```
createBars() {
  this.loadBar = this.add.graphics();
  this.loadBar.fillStyle(0x6b140b, 1);
  this.loadBar.fillRect(
    this.cameras.main.width / 4 - 2,
    this.cameras.main.height / 2 - 18,
    this.cameras.main.width / 2 + 4,
    20
  );
  this.progressBar = this.add.graphics();
}
```

The audios were generated in simple text-to-speech websites. There are many of them, and they are very easy to use. We just need to write the text and select the voice. Then we can download the audio file and use it in our game. After that, the sound file was uploaded to a website that adds filters to audio so they can sound like a robot, a radio transmission, a telephone call, etc. This is a very simple way to add some variety to the voices.

Hole

Figure 6.2 The hole sprite, only visible when the player dies.

Holes are invisible sprites that work as traps for the player. They are placed in the Tiled editor and they are used to kill the player when he falls into them, and they consist in two parts: the surrounding and the hole itself. The surroundings are just a rectangle that is used to trigger the hole detector. The hole is also an invisible sprite that is used to detect the collision with the player. When the player touches the hole, the hole sprite is revealed while the player screams in agony.

```
export default class Hole extends Phaser.GameObjects.Sprite {
  constructor(scene, x, y) {
    super(scene, x, y, "hole");
    this.name = "hole";
    this.setOrigin(0);
    this.setAlpha(0);
    this.scene = scene;
    scene.add.existing(this);
    scene.physics.add.existing(this);
    this.body.setAllowGravity(false);
  }
}
```

As the story explains in the transitions, the player will be able to detect when they are close to them. These elements are particularly simple yet very effective in this kind of game.

Drone

Figure 6.3 The killer drone

Drones are sprite objects that represent a Mars robot vehicle that went rogue and they will try to kill you. The interesting part here is that they are moved autonomously toward the player avoiding obstacles! How is that possible? Easy, using an implementation of A* path searching algorithm. When each map is loaded, the game scene will also create a logical grid of the scenario and that will be used by the drone to move from its actual position to the player. That means that even if the player moves, drones will also recalculate their paths to her. This feature can be also useful for roguelikes or even games like Pacman, so you don't need to take care of the enemies.

```
import EasyStar from "easystarjs";

export default class Drone extends Phaser.GameObjects.Sprite {
  constructor(scene, x, y, grid) {
    super(scene, x, y, "drone");
    this.name = "drone";
    this.setScale(1);
```

```
    this.grid = grid;
    this.scene = scene;
    scene.add.existing(this);
    scene.physics.add.existing(this);
    this.body.setAllowGravity(false);
    this.easystar = new EasyStar.js();
    this.init();
}
```

Here we have to pay attention to the fact that we are using the EasyStar library to calculate the path of the drone: we have to set the grid and the acceptable tiles for the pathfinding algorithm. We also have to set the animation of the drone and the event that will trigger the movement of the drone. When it starts moving it will also reproduce the sound of the drone.

```
init() {
    this.easystar.setGrid(this.grid);
    this.easystar.setAcceptableTiles([0]);
    this.scene.events.on("update", this.update, this);
    this.scene.tweens.add({
        targets: this,
        duration: 500,
        repeat: -1,
        scale: { from: 0.95, to: 1 },
        yoyo: true,
    });

    this.scene.anims.create({
        key: this.name,
        frames: this.scene.anims.generateFrameNumbers(this.name, {
            start: 0,
            end: 3,
        }),
        frameRate: 5,
        repeat: -1,
    });

    this.anims.play(this.name, true);
    this.flipX = this.direction < 0;

    this.scene.time.delayedCall(
        Phaser.Math.Between(3000, 5000),
        () => {
            this.scene.playAudio("kill");
            this.launchMove();
        },
        null,
        this
    );
}
```

This starts the movement of the drone:

```
launchMove() {
  if (!this.scene) return;
  this.delayedMove = this.scene.time.addEvent({
    delay: 2000, // ms
    callback: this.move.bind(this),
    startAt: 0,
    callbackScope: this,
    loop: true,
  });
}
```

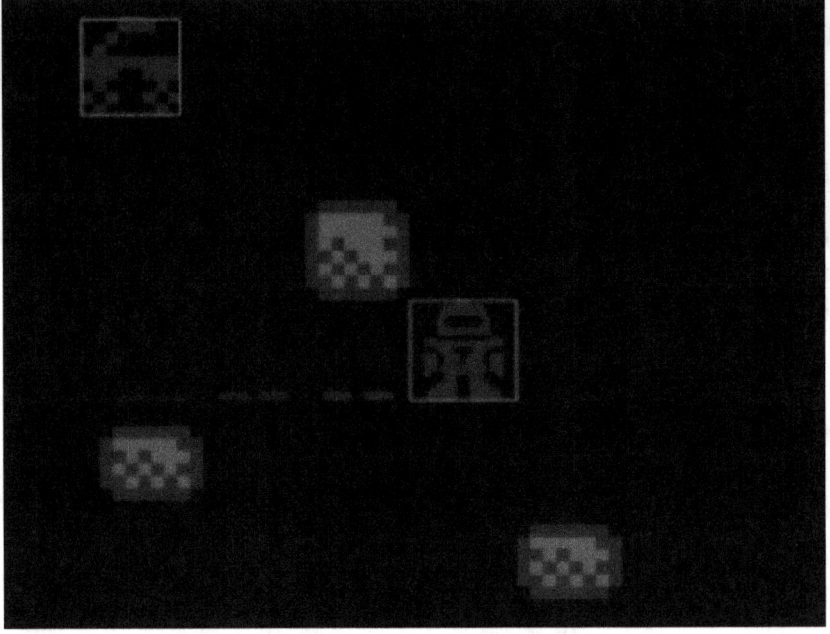

Figure 6.4 The drone is getting close!

This function uses EasyStar to calculate the path and then we will call a function to move the drone.

```
move() {
  try {
    if (!this.scene.player) return;
    if (this.moveTimeline) this.moveTimeline.destroy();

    this.easystar.findPath(
      Math.floor(this.x / 64),
      Math.floor(this.y / 64),
      Math.floor(this.scene.player.x / 64),
      Math.floor(this.scene.player.y / 64),
      this.moveIt.bind(this)
    );
```

6. Tell me a story: Marstranded — Drone

```
      this.easystar.setIterationsPerCalculation(10000);
      this.easystar.enableSync();
      this.easystar.calculate();
    } catch (err) {
      console.log("Cant move yet: ", err);
    }
  }
}
```

And finally, this function will move the drone through the calculated path. At the end of the path, it will call the `launchMove` function again, so the drone can recalculate the path even if the player changes her position.

```
moveIt(path) {
  if (path === null) {
    console.log("hello sneaky pete");
  } else {
    let tweens = [];
    this.i = 0;
    this.path = path;
    for (let i = 0; i < path.length - 1; i++) {
      if (this.scene.player.dead) return;
      let ex = path[i + 1].x * 64;
      let ey = path[i + 1].y * 64;
      tweens.push({
        targets: this,
        duration: 400,
        x: ex,
        y: ey,
      });
    }

    this.moveTimeline = this.scene.tweens.timeline({
      tweens: tweens,
      onComplete: () => {
        this.delayedMove.remove();
        if (this.alpha > 0 && !this.scene.player.dead) this.launchMove();
      },
    });
  }
}
```

These movable enemies are really dangerous. Not only because they can directly hunt down the player and kill her, but also because they can force her to run desperately and fall into a trap.

Object

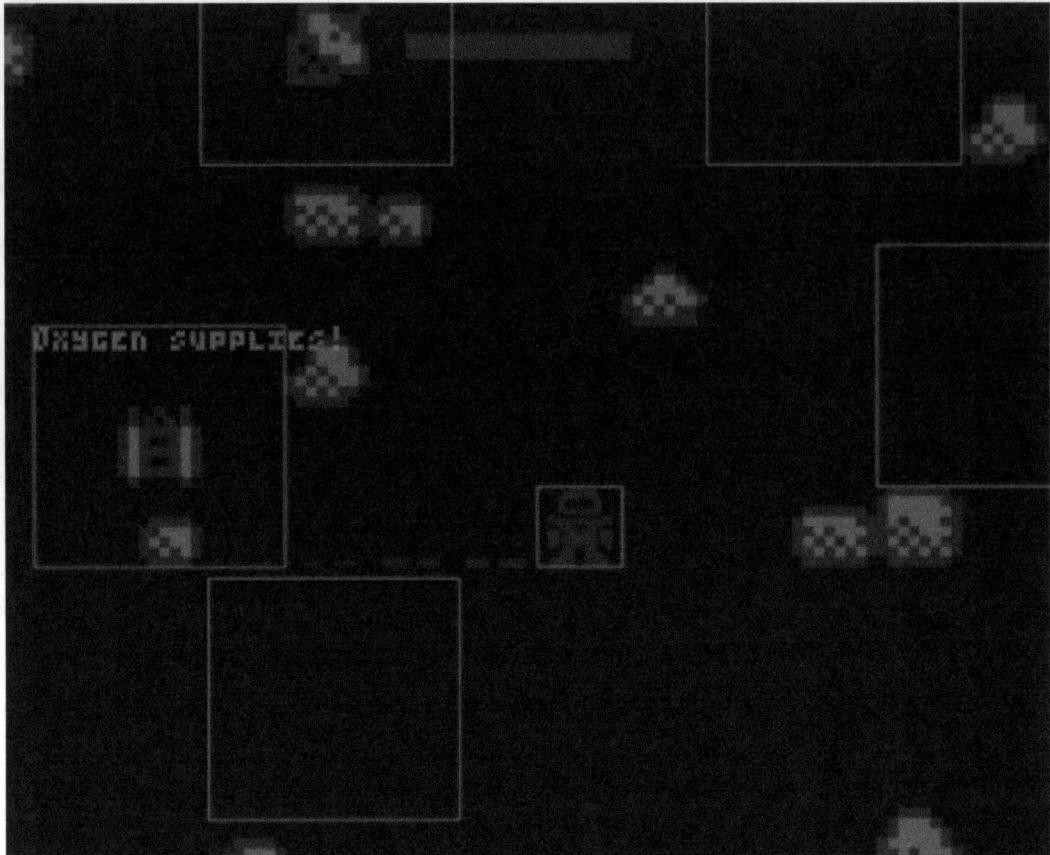

Figure 6.5 Objects are all over the stage.

This represents a generic object that can be used as several items in the game. As soon as the player touches an object, we can create different effects depending on the type: notes, radio transmissions, oxygen supplies, etc. It also includes the exit sensor.

```
import Hole from "./hole";
import Braun from "./braun";

export default class Object extends Phaser.GameObjects.Rectangle {
  constructor(scene, x, y, type, description, extra = "") {
    super(scene, x, y, 64 * 3, 64 * 3);
    this.scene = scene;
    this.setOrigin(0);
    this.type = type;
    this.description = description;
    this.extra = extra;
    scene.add.existing(this);
    scene.physics.add.existing(this);
    this.body.setAllowGravity(false);
    this.activated = false;
  }
```

This function decides what to do when the player touches the object, depending on its type.

```
touch() {
  switch (this.type) {
    case "note":
      this.showNote(this.description);
      break;
    case "radio":
      this.useRadio();
      break;
    case "exit":
      this.exitScene();
      break;
    case "hole":
      this.activateHole();
      break;
    case "oxygen":
      this.useOxygen();
      break;
    case "braun":
      this.activateBraun();
      break;
    case "ending":
      this.revealEnding();
      break;
    default:
      break;
  }
}
```

This will show a text on the screen.

```
showNote(note) {
  const objectText = this.scene.add.bitmapText(
    this.x,
    this.y,
    "pico",
    note,
    15
  );
  this.scene.tweens.add({
    targets: objectText,
    alpha: { from: 1, to: 0 },
    duration: 6000,
    ease: "Sine",
    onComplete: () => {
      objectText.destroy();
    },
  });
}
```

6. Tell me a story: Marstranded

This is also a text that is shown when the player reaches the exit.

```
showExit(note) {
  const objectText = this.scene.add.bitmapText(
    this.x - 128,
    this.y - 64,
    "pico",
    note,
    25
  );
  this.scene.tweens.add({
    targets: objectText,
    alpha: { from: 0.8, to: 1 },
    duration: 100,
    repeat: 5,
  });
}
```

This function will play a random static sound:

```
useRadio() {
  this.officerAudio = this.scene.sound.add(this.description);
  this.officerAudio.play();
  this.officerAudio.on(
    "complete",
    function () {
      this.scene.playRandomStatic();
      if (this.extra) this.scene.sound.add(this.extra).play();
    }.bind(this)
  );
}
```

When the player reaches the exit, we need to do a few things: show the exit message, play the static sound and finish the scene.

```
exitScene() {
  this.showExit(this.description);
  this.showNote(this.extra);
  this.scene.finishScene();
}
```

Anytime the player touches the oxygen supplies, we need to show a message and refill the oxygen.

```
useOxygen() {
  this.showNote("Oxygen supplies!");
  this.scene.player.oxygen = 100;
  this.scene.updateOxygen();
  this.scene.playAudio("oxygen");
}
```

Figure 6.6 Event fired when player touches the oxygen item.

Well, well... you can guess what happens here, right?

```
revealEnding() {
  const ohmy = this.scene.sound.add("ohmygod");
  ohmy.play();
  this.scene.cameras.main.shake(10000);
  this.showExit(this.description);
  this.scene.sound.add("monster").play({ volume: 1.5, rate: 0.8 });
  const monster = this.scene.add
    .sprite(this.x + 128, this.y + 128, "monster")
    .setOrigin(0.5);
  this.scene.anims.create({
    key: "monster",
    frames: this.scene.anims.generateFrameNumbers("monster", {
      start: 0,
      end: 5,
    }),
    frameRate: 3,
  });
  monster.anims.play("monster", true);
  ohmy.on(
    "complete",
    function () {
      this.scene.breathing.pause();
      this.scene.playAudio("holeshout");
      this.scene.finishScene(false);
    }.bind(this)
  );
}
```

When the player touches the hole location, we need to create a new hole in the scene, and the player will die.

```
activateHole() {
  this.scene.holes.add(new Hole(this.scene, this.x + 64, this.y + 64));
}
```

Finally, when the player reaches a certain point, we need to activate "Braun".

```
activateBraun() {
  this.showExit(this.description);
  this.scene.playAudio("shock");
  new Braun(this.scene, this.x + 128, this.y + 64);
  }
}
```

Items that a player can find are crucial in story-telling games, not just as keys or power-ups, but also as elements to build the story itself triggering different types of events.

Utils

This is just a class to show texts as if it was typed one character at a time. It is a simple but very fitting effect for a sci-fi game like this.

```
export default class Utils {
  constructor(scene) {
    this.scene = scene;
  }
```

This is the `typeText` method. It will create a bitmap text for each character in the string, and will animate them in a timeline. The text will be typed in the screen, with a typewriter effect.

```
  typeText(text, font, x, y = 150, tint = 0x06e18a, size = 40) {
    let characters = [];
    let jump = 0;
    let line = 0;
    let last = 0;
    text.split("").forEach((character, i) => {
      if (character === "\n") {
        jump += 2;
        line = 0;
      }
      last = i;
```

```js
      characters.push(
        this.scene.add
          .bitmapText(
            x - 350 + line++ * 25,
            y + jump * size,
            font,
            character,
            size
          )
          .setTint(tint)
          .setAlpha(0)
      );
    });
    const ending = this.scene.add
      .rectangle(x - 335 + line * 25, y + 25 + jump * size, 25, 5, tint)
      .setOrigin(0.5)
      .setAlpha(0);
    const timeline = this.scene.tweens.createTimeline();
    this.typeAudio = this.scene.sound.add("type");

    characters.forEach((character, i) => {
      timeline.add({
        targets: character,
        alpha: { from: 0, to: 0.5 },
        duration: 100,
      });
    });
    timeline.add({
      targets: ending,
      alpha: { from: 0, to: 0.8 },
      duration: 100,
      repeat: 5,
      yoyo: true,
      onStart: () => {
        this.typeAudio.stop();
      },
    });
    this.typeAudio.play({
      mute: false,
      volume: 1,
      rate: 1,
      detune: 0,
      seek: 0,
      loop: true,
      delay: 0,
    });
    timeline.play();
    characters.push(ending);
    return characters;
  }
```

This removes the typed text from the screen.

```
  removeTyped(texts) {
    texts.flat().forEach((char) => char.destroy());
  }
}
```

This is a simple effect that can be used in many other games.

Player

Figure 6.7 Officer Tereshkova.

Here she is, our hero Tereshkova. The player here is quite simple and she just moves in the four directions. But try not to run! The player has a limitation of oxygen and moves because the faster she moves the quicker she depletes the oxygen reserve. We could add some dust effect while moving but for a Martian game like this, we added footsteps effect. The movements are really simple in the game, there is no animation but trailing footsteps that vanish after a few seconds. As with all the elements of the game, the player looks like a symbol, that's why she is represented as an icon.

```
import Step from "./step";

export default class Player extends Phaser.GameObjects.Sprite {
  constructor(scene, x, y, oxygen = 100) {
    super(scene, x, y, "player");
    this.scene = scene;
    this.setOrigin(0);
    this.setScale(1);
    this.scene.add.existing(this);
    this.scene.physics.add.existing(this);
    this.body.setAllowGravity(false);
    this.dead = false;
    this.init();
    this.shells = 0;
    this.lastDirection = 0;
    this.steps = 0;
    this.stepDelta = 0;
    this.moveDelta = 0;
    this.rate = 0.2;
    this.previousRate = 0.2;
    this.oxygen = oxygen;
    this.locked = false;
```

}

Here we add the controls for the player and the events to update the player's position and breath.

```
init() {
  this.addControls();
  this.scene.events.on("update", this.update, this);
}

addControls() {
  this.cursor = this.scene.input.keyboard.createCursorKeys();
  this.W = this.scene.input.keyboard.addKey(Phaser.Input.Keyboard.KeyCodes.W);
  this.A = this.scene.input.keyboard.addKey(Phaser.Input.Keyboard.KeyCodes.A);
  this.S = this.scene.input.keyboard.addKey(Phaser.Input.Keyboard.KeyCodes.S);
  this.D = this.scene.input.keyboard.addKey(Phaser.Input.Keyboard.KeyCodes.D);
}
```

In the update function, we check the player's input and update the player's position and breath as always. But in this particular game, we move the player with a tween, so we have to check if the player is locked to avoid multiple movements at the same time.

```
update(time, delta) {
  if (this.dead) return;
  if (this.locked) return;
  this.stepDelta += delta;
  this.moveDelta += delta;

  if (
    (Phaser.Input.Keyboard.JustDown(this.W) ||
      Phaser.Input.Keyboard.JustDown(this.cursor.up)) &&
    this.canMoveUp()
  ) {
    this.moveDelta = 0;
    const { x, y } = this;
    this.locked = true;
    this.scene.tweens.add({
      targets: this,
      y: "-=64",
      duration: 200,
      onComplete: () => {
        this.locked = false;
      },
    });
    this.step(x, y);
  } else if (
    (Phaser.Input.Keyboard.JustDown(this.D) ||
      Phaser.Input.Keyboard.JustDown(this.cursor.right)) &&
    this.canMoveRight()
  ) {
```

```
      this.moveDelta = 0;
      const { x, y } = this;
      this.locked = true;
      this.scene.tweens.add({
        targets: this,
        x: "+=64",
        duration: 200,
        onComplete: () => {
          this.locked = false;
        },
      });
      this.step(x, y);
    } else if (
      (Phaser.Input.Keyboard.JustDown(this.A) ||
        Phaser.Input.Keyboard.JustDown(this.cursor.left)) &&
      this.canMoveLeft()
    ) {
      this.moveDelta = 0;
      const { x, y } = this;
      this.locked = true;
      this.scene.tweens.add({
        targets: this,
        x: "-=64",
        duration: 200,
        onComplete: () => {
          this.locked = false;
        },
      });
      this.step(x, y);
    } else if (
      (Phaser.Input.Keyboard.JustDown(this.S) ||
        Phaser.Input.Keyboard.JustDown(this.cursor.down)) &&
      this.canMoveDown()
    ) {
      this.moveDelta = 0;
      const { x, y } = this;
      this.locked = true;
      this.scene.tweens.add({
        targets: this,
        y: "+=64",
        duration: 200,
        onComplete: () => {
          this.locked = false;
        },
      });
      this.step(x, y);
    }

    this.adaptBreath();
  }
```

Figure 6.8 Before the player moves we check for obstacles.

The next functions, lets us know if the player can move in a certain direction. We check if the tile in front of the player is empty and if the player has waited enough time to move again.

```
canMoveUp() {
  return (
    !this.scene.platform.getTileAtWorldXY(this.x, this.y - 1) &&
    this.moveDelta > 200
  );
}

canMoveRight() {
  return (
    !this.scene.platform.getTileAtWorldXY(this.x + 64, this.y) &&
    this.moveDelta > 200
  );
}

canMoveDown() {
  return (
    !this.scene.platform.getTileAtWorldXY(this.x, this.y + 64) &&
    this.moveDelta > 200
  );
}

canMoveLeft() {
  return (
    !this.scene.platform.getTileAtWorldXY(this.x - 1, this.y) &&
    this.moveDelta > 200
  );
```

}
```

This function adds a step to the player and creates a new step sprite in the scene. It also plays a random sound to simulate the player's steps.

```
step(x, y) {
  this.steps++;
  this.scene.smokeLayer.add(new Step(this.scene, x, y));
  this.scene.playRandom("step", 1);
}
```

This is another important function to add some tension. It adapts the breathing of the player depending on the steps she has taken. Depending on the step rate, the player will breathe faster or slower. If the player has not taken any steps, the player will breathe normally. The player will also consume oxygen depending on the steps she has taken.

```
adaptBreath() {
  if (this.stepDelta > 2000) {
    if (this.steps > 2) {
      this.previousRate = this.rate;
      this.rate = this.steps < 11 ? this.steps / 10 : 1;
      this.scene.breath(this.rate);
      this.updateOxygen(this.steps + Math.round(this.steps / 2));
    } else if (this.rate !== this.previousRate) {
      this.previousRate = this.rate;
      this.rate = this.rate > 0.2 ? this.rate - 0.1 : 0.2;
      this.scene.breath(this.rate);
      this.scene.updateOxygen(this.steps);
    } else {
      this.scene.updateOxygen(this.steps);
    }
    this.steps = this.stepDelta = 0;
  }
}
```

As the player moves, she will consume oxygen. If the player runs out of oxygen, she will die.

```
updateOxygen(waste) {
  if (waste >= this.oxygen) {
    this.oxygen = 0;
    this.death();
  } else {
    this.oxygen -= waste;
  }
  this.scene.updateOxygen();
}
```
```

This function will be called when the player dies. It will stop the player's body and restart the scene.

```
death() {
  this.dead = true;
  this.body.stop();
  this.body.enable = false;
  this.scene.restartScene();
  }
}
```

We use some breathing sounds as feedback for this and that is a part of the storytelling. Also, the game does not have great visuals so we try to rely on sounds for a more immersive experience.

As single indie developers, we may not be able to create a realistic 3D character with detailed textures and smooth movements. The elements that try to get the user into the game are the story, the ambiance and the sounds. As we can't use professional voices (unless we pay an actor or we use an AI), we could use text-to-speech software with different voices: children, women and men. The problem with those voices is their lack of feelings so in this case, we could add some filters to make the voices sound like radio transmissions. Cheap and effective enough for a weekend jam.

Braun

Well... there is a class called Braun, that's interesting. As you can imagine, this class represents Dr. Braun, the target of the game. Well, it seems to be a simple sprite.

```
export default class Braun extends Phaser.GameObjects.Sprite {
  constructor(scene, x, y) {
    super(scene, x, y, "body");
    this.name = "body";
    this.setOrigin(0);
    this.rotation = 1.6;
    this.scene = scene;
    scene.add.existing(this);
  }
}
```

After all, should we expect that Doctor Braun is alive? We won't spoil the game at this point, right?

Game

Figure 6.9 Game in progress.

Hey, the good news is that the game, technically, is pretty straightforward. Mars is but a map that changes on every stage. As the player advances, the stages will have more dangers and the day will become darker. But a single class can take care of all the scenarios, including the last one.

```
import Player from "./player";
import Object from "./object";
import Drone from "./drone";
import HorrifiPostFx from "phaser3-rex-plugins/plugins/horrifipipeline.js";

export default class Game extends Phaser.Scene {
  constructor() {
    super({ key: "game" });
    this.player = null;
    this.score = 0;
    this.scoreText = null;
  }

  init(data) {
    this.name = data.name;
    this.number = data.number;
  }
```

This creates the elements of the game. The background colors are relevant because they are used to set a darker color as the game progresses.

```js
create() {
  this.backgroundColors = [
    0xae2012, 0x961c10, 0x50120a, 0x40120a, 0x30120a, 0x2f120a, 0x000000,
  ];
  this.width = this.sys.game.config.width;
  this.height = this.sys.game.config.height;
  this.center_width = this.width / 2;
  this.center_height = this.height / 2;
  this.cameras.main.setBackgroundColor(this.backgroundColors[this.number]);

  this.addLight();
  this.createMap();
  this.smokeLayer = this.add.layer();
  this.addPlayer();
  this.addOxygen();

  // this.input.keyboard.on("keydown-ENTER", () => this.skipThis(), this);
  // for testing
  this.cameras.main.startFollow(this.player, true, 0.05, 0.05, 0, 0);
  this.loadAudios();
  this.addEffects();
  this.playMusic();
}
```

The oxygen bar is the only UI element in the game. It's a rectangle that changes its width according to the player's oxygen level.

```js
addOxygen() {
  this.oxygenBar = this.add
    .rectangle(this.center_width, 40, this.player.oxygen * 1.8, 20, 0x6b140b)
    .setOrigin(0.5)
    .setScrollFactor(0);
}
```

This is the method that will add the post-processing effects to the game. The game uses the HorrifiPostFx plugin, which is a custom plugin that adds a horror effect to the game.

```js
addEffects() {
  this.cameras.main.setPostPipeline(HorrifiPostFx);
}
```

This method will add the day text to the game. It is not used in the final version of the game, but maybe it could be useful for a future version.

```js
addDay() {
  this.dayText = this.add
    .bitmapText(20, 10, "pico", "Day " + (this.number + 1), 20)
    .setTint(0x6b140b)
    .setOrigin(0)
```

```
    .setScrollFactor(0)
    .setDropShadow(0, 2, 0x6b302a, 0.9);
}
```

We have this method to add the light system to the game. But it's not used in the final version of the game. It could be useful for the last scene though. You can check the Camp Night game to see how it's used.

```
addLight() {
  this.lights.disable();
  this.lights.setAmbientColor(0xae2012); // 0x707070
  this.playerLight = this.lights
    .addLight(0, 100, 100)
    .setColor(0xffffff)
    .setIntensity(3.0);
}
```

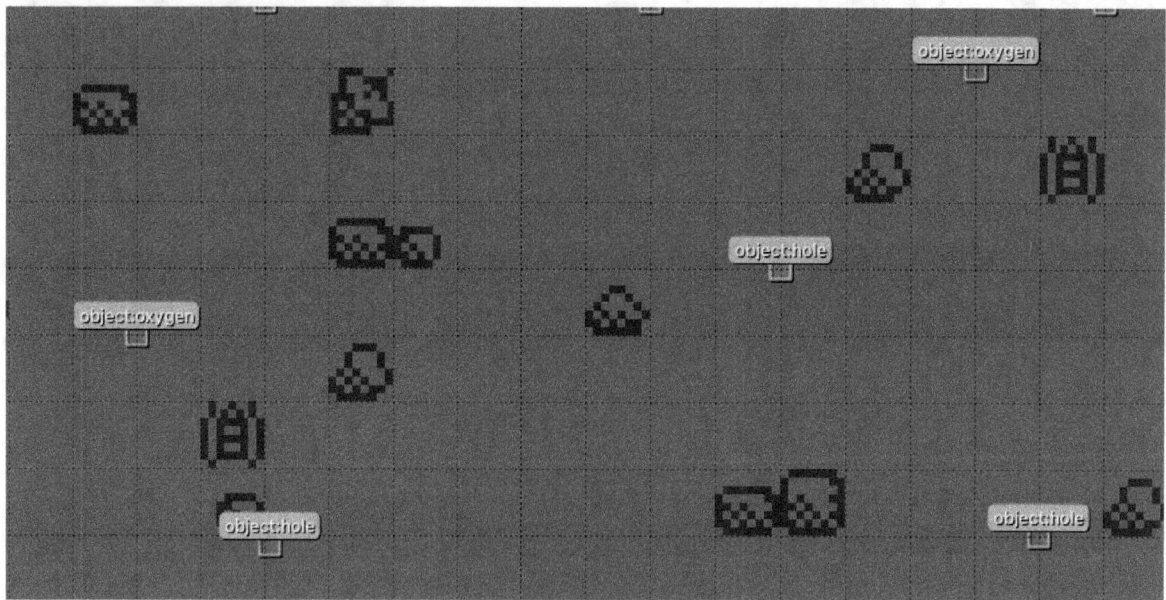

Figure 6.10 Detail of the stage 2 map.

This game uses also tiled maps: with a main layer, a border layer, and an objects layer. The main layer is the one where the player can walk and it will have some obstacles. The objects layer is used to add the objects to the game, like the oxygen tanks and the holes.

```
createMap() {
  this.tileMap = this.make.tilemap({
    key: "scene" + this.number,
    tileWidth: 64,
    tileHeight: 64,
  });
  this.tileSetBg = this.tileMap.addTilesetImage("mars");
  this.tileSet = this.tileMap.addTilesetImage("mars");
```

```js
    this.platform = this.tileMap.createLayer(
      "scene" + this.number,
      this.tileSet
    );
    this.border = this.tileMap.createLayer("border", this.tileSet);
    this.objectsLayer = this.tileMap.getObjectLayer("objects");
    this.border.setCollisionByExclusion([-1]);
    this.platform.setCollisionByExclusion([-1]);

    this.holes = this.add.group();
    this.foes = this.add.group();
    this.objects = this.add.group();
    this.createGrid();
    this.addObjects();
}
```

This method will add the objects to the game: we group most of them as "objects" and the drones as "foes". In the `Object` class, we will take care of treating the objects according to their type.

```js
addObjects() {
    this.objectsLayer.objects.forEach((object) => {
      if (object.name.startsWith("object")) {
        const [name, type, description, extra] = object.name.split(":");
        this.objects.add(
          new Object(this, object.x, object.y, type, description, extra)
        );
      }

      if (object.name.startsWith("drone")) {
        this.foes.add(new Drone(this, object.x, object.y, this.grid));
      }
    });
}
```

This method will create a grid of 40x40 cells. It will be used by the drones to move around the map.

```js
createGrid() {
    this.grid = [];

    Array(40)
      .fill(0)
      .forEach((_, i) => {
        this.grid[i] = [];
        Array(40)
          .fill(0)
          .forEach((_, j) => {
            let rock = this.platform.getTileAt(Math.floor(j), Math.floor(i));
            let wall = this.border.getTileAt(Math.floor(j), Math.floor(i));
```

```
            this.grid[i][j] = rock || wall ? 1 : 0;
        });
    });
}
```

Here we add the player element to the game. We also add the collisions between the player and the platform, the objects, the foes, and the holes.

```
addPlayer() {
    this.trailLayer = this.add.layer();
    const playerPosition = this.objectsLayer.objects.find(
        (object) => object.name === "player"
    );
    this.player = new Player(this, playerPosition.x, playerPosition.y);

    this.physics.add.collider(
        this.player,
        this.platform,
        this.hitFloor,
        () => {
            return true;
        },
        this
    );

    this.physics.add.overlap(
        this.player,
        this.objects,
        this.touchObject,
        () => {
            return true;
        },
        this
    );

    this.physics.add.overlap(
        this.player,
        this.foes,
        this.playerHitByFoe,
        () => {
            return true;
        },
        this
    );

    this.physics.add.overlap(
        this.player,
        this.holes,
        this.playerHitHole,
        () => {
            return true;
        },
```

```
      this
    );
  }
```

```
  hitFloor(player, platform) {}
```

This is the method that will be called when the player touches an object. It will call the touch method of the object.

```
  touchObject(player, object) {
    if (object.type === "hole") this.playTracker();
    if (!object.activated) {
      object.activated = true;
      object.touch();
    }
  }
```

If the player is hit by a foe (drone), it will die and the scene will restart.

```
  playerHitByFoe(player, foe) {
    this.cameras.main.shake(100);
    this.playAudio("killed");
    player.death();
    this.restartScene();
  }
```

When the player hits the hole, it will die and the scene will restart.

```
  playerHitHole(player, hole) {
    if (!player.dead) {
      this.playAudio("holeshout");
      hole.setAlpha(1);
      player.setAlpha(0);
      this.cameras.main.shake(50);
      player.death();
      this.restartScene();
    }
  }
```

This is the function that loads the audio files. The tracker has a special treatment because it will be played in a loop when the player is close to a hole.

```
  loadAudios() {
    this.audios = {
      mars_background: this.sound.add("mars_background"),
      step: this.sound.add("step"),
      kill: this.sound.add("kill"),
      blip: this.sound.add("blip"),
      ohmygod: this.sound.add("ohmygod"),
      holeshout: this.sound.add("holeshout"),
```

```
    oxygen: this.sound.add("oxygen"),
    shock: this.sound.add("shock"),
    killed: this.sound.add("killed"),
  };
  this.tracker = this.sound.add("tracker");
}

playTracker() {
  if (!this.tracker.isPlaying) this.tracker.play();
}
```

We will use this function to play static sound files (4 different files) adding some variations to the rate, delay, and volume:

```
playRandomStatic() {
  const file =
    this.number < 6 ? "static" + Phaser.Math.Between(0, 3) : "creepy_static";
  this.sound.add(file).play({
    rate: Phaser.Math.Between(9, 11) / 10,
    delay: 0,
    volume: Phaser.Math.Between(5, 10) / 10,
  });
}
```

These are the functions to play the sounds, normally or with some random variations.

```
playAudio(key) {
  this.audios[key].play();
}

playRandom(key, volume = 1) {
  this.audios[key].play({
    rate: Phaser.Math.Between(0.9, 1),
    detune: Phaser.Math.Between(-500, 500),
    delay: 0,
    volume,
  });
}
```

This function will be used to play the officer's messages. It will play a specific sound file according to the number of the scene.

```
playOfficer() {
  this.sound.add(`officer${this.number}`).play();
}
```

Here we play several sounds at the same time: the background sound, and the creepy sound. It also starts the breathing sound.

```
playMusic() {
```

6. Tell me a story: Marstranded

```js
    const theme = this.number < 6 ? "mars_background" : "cave";
    this.theme = this.sound.add(theme);
    this.theme.stop();
    this.theme.play({
      mute: false,
      volume: 1.5,
      rate: 1,
      detune: 0,
      seek: 0,
      loop: true,
      delay: 0,
    });
    this.sound.add("creepy").play({
      mute: false,
      volume: 1,
      rate: 1,
      detune: 0,
      seek: 0,
      loop: true,
      delay: 0,
    });
    this.breathing = this.sound.add("breath");
    this.breath(0.2);
  }
```

This function will be used to play the breathing sound. It will be called with a specific rate and volume. In the end, it will be restarted again.

```js
  breath(rate = 0.2, volume = 0.4) {
    const duration = Phaser.Math.Between(500, 1000);
    this.tweens.add({
      targets: this.breathing,
      volume: 0,
      duration,
      onComplete: () => {
        this.breathing.play({ rate, volume });
      },
    });
  }
```

If the player dies, the scene will restart. We show a failure message and a black rectangle that will fade in.

```js
  restartScene() {
    const x = this.cameras.main.worldView.centerX;
    const y = this.cameras.main.worldView.centerY;

    this.fadeBlack = this.add
      .rectangle(x - 100, y - 50, 10000, 11000, 0x000000)
      .setOrigin(0.5);
    this.failure = this.add
```

```
        .bitmapText(x, y, "pico", "FAILURE", 40)
        .setTint(0x6b140b)
        .setOrigin(0.5)
        .setDropShadow(0, 2, 0x6b302a, 0.9);

    this.tweens.add({
      targets: [this.failure, this.fadeBlack],
      alpha: { from: 0, to: 1 },
      duration: 2000,
    });
    this.time.delayedCall(
      3000,
      () => {
        this.sound.stopAll();
        this.scene.start("transition", { number: this.number });
      },
      null,
      this
    );
}
```

Figure 6.11 The player reaches the exit object!

If the player reaches the exit object, we finish the scene. We disable the player, play a sound, and show a black rectangle that will fade in.

```
finishScene(mute = true) {
  const x = this.cameras.main.worldView.centerX;
  const y = this.cameras.main.worldView.centerY;

  this.fadeBlack = this.add
    .rectangle(x - 100, y - 50, 2000, 2000, 0x000000)
    .setOrigin(0.5);
```

```
    this.tweens.add({
      targets: [this.fadeBlack],
      alpha: { from: 0, to: 1 },
      duration: 3000,
    });

    this.player.dead = true;
    this.player.body.stop();
    if (this.mute) this.sound.add("blip").play();
    this.time.delayedCall(
      3000,
      () => {
        if (this.mute) this.sound.stopAll();
        this.scene.start("transition", {
          next: "underwater",
          name: "STAGE",
          number: this.number + 1,
        });
      },
      null,
      this
    );
  }
```

This function will update the oxygen bar as the player moves.

```
  updateOxygen() {
    this.oxygenBar.width = this.player.oxygen * 1.8;
  }
```

We have this function to skip the scene. It will be used for testing purposes.

```
  skipThis() {
    this.player.dead = true;
    this.player.body.stop();
    this.theme.stop();
    this.scene.start("transition", { number: this.number + 1 });
  }
}
```

The map has no limits, but if the user goes to an empty land we somehow suggest that he went off the stage. We could add some warning there, but anyway, that is a way the transition page gives some indication before the game starts.

In this case, there's no score to keep. At the end of each stage, we just move forward to the next through a transition.

Splash

Figure 6.12 Splash screen.

This is a very simple splash with creepy sounds to set the tone: it is a black screen showing the characters of the name Marstranded one by one with the sound of footsteps and some dust effect. In the background, we will hear some "Martian" wind gusts and eerie music.

```
import { ShotSmoke } from "./particle";

export default class Splash extends Phaser.Scene {
  constructor() {
    super({ key: "splash" });
  }
```

This creates the elements of the splash screen.

```
  create() {
    this.width = this.sys.game.config.width;
    this.height = this.sys.game.config.height;
    this.center_width = this.width / 2;
    this.center_height = this.height / 2;
    this.cameras.main.setBackgroundColor(0x000000);
    this.smokeLayer = this.add.layer();
    this.showTitle();
```

6. Tell me a story: Marstranded

```
    this.time.delayedCall(1000, () => this.showInstructions(), null, this);

    this.input.keyboard.on("keydown-SPACE", () => this.startGame(), this);
    this.playMusic();
}
```

The title of the game is created with a delay between each letter, and the smoke effect is created simulating footsteps on the red planet.

```
showTitle() {
  this.step = this.sound.add("step");
  "MARSTRANDED".split("").forEach((letter, i) => {
    this.time.delayedCall(
      600 * (i + 1),
      () => {
        let text = this.add
          .bitmapText(70 * i + 50, 200, "pico", letter, 70)
          .setTint(0x6b140b)
          .setOrigin(0.5)
          .setDropShadow(0, 4, 0x6b302a, 0.9);
        Array(Phaser.Math.Between(2, 4))
          .fill(0)
          .forEach((j) => {
            this.smokeLayer.add(
              new ShotSmoke(
                this,
                70 * i + 80 + Phaser.Math.Between(-30, 30),
                200 + Phaser.Math.Between(-30, 30),
                0,
                -1,
                0x6b302a
              )
            );
          });
        this.step.play({ rate: 0.8 });
        this.step.resume();
      },
      null,
      this
    );
  });
}
```

This method is called when the player presses the space bar to start the game. It stops the music and starts the transition to the game.

```
startGame() {
  if (this.theme) this.theme.stop();
  this.sound.add("blip").play();
  this.scene.start("transition", {
    next: "game",
```

```
      name: "STAGE",
      number: 0,
      time: 30,
    });
}
```

We add some background sound instead of music, but it's a looped sound file after all.

```
playMusic(theme = "mars_background") {
    this.theme = this.sound.add(theme);
    this.theme.stop();
    this.theme.play({
      mute: false,
      volume: 2,
      rate: 1,
      detune: 0,
      seek: 0,
      loop: true,
      delay: 0,
    });
}
```

Below the title, we show the instructions to start the game and the author's name.

```
showInstructions() {
    this.add
      .bitmapText(this.center_width, 450, "pico", "WASD/Arrows", 40)
      .setTint(0x6b140b)
      .setOrigin(0.5)
      .setDropShadow(0, 3, 0x6b302a, 0.9);
    this.add
      .sprite(this.center_width - 140, 355, "pello")
      .setOrigin(0.5)
      .setScale(0.5);
    this.add
      .bitmapText(this.center_width + 60, 350, "pico", "By PELLO", 35)
      .setTint(0x6b140b)
      .setOrigin(0.5)
      .setDropShadow(0, 3, 0x6b302a, 0.9);
    this.space = this.add
      .bitmapText(this.center_width, 520, "pico", "SPACE start", 30)
      .setTint(0x6b140b)
      .setOrigin(0.5)
      .setDropShadow(0, 2, 0x6b302a, 0.9);
    this.tweens.add({
      targets: this.space,
      duration: 300,
      alpha: { from: 0, to: 1 },
      repeat: -1,
      yoyo: true,
    });
}
```

}

The splash does not show much but it should tell that you are about to play a terror story.

Transition page

Figure 6.13 The transition page playing the audio record.

In the transition, we provide information to the player. In the first one, it will be a typed text but then transitions will start with a recording saying something. At the end of the recording, a single phrase will tell the player the direction they need to go. In this scene, we also add some "music" that resonates with Carpenter's *The Thing*.

We add the option to skip the transition, users will always be thankful for having that choice.

```
import Utils from "./utils";

export default class Transition extends Phaser.Scene {
  constructor() {
    super({ key: "transition" });
  }

  init(data) {
    this.number = data.number;
  }
```

We create the elements of the transitions. We have to add the sound of the diary, the creepy sound, and the mission objective.

```
  create() {
```

```
    this.missions = [
      "",
      "Go north, locate containers.",
      "Find landing zone. North East.",
      "Locate landing, South East.",
      "Go East, locate containers.",
      "Other landings: North East",
      "Find out ship origin...",
    ];

    this.utils = new Utils(this);
    this.width = this.sys.game.config.width;
    this.height = this.sys.game.config.height;
    this.center_width = this.width / 2;
    this.center_height = this.height / 2;
    this.add.tileSprite(0, 0, 800, 600, "landscape").setOrigin(0);

    if (this.number === 7) {
      this.scene.start("outro", { number: this.number });
    } else {
      this.sound.stopAll();
    }

    this.showInstructions();

    this.input.keyboard.on("keydown-ENTER", () => this.loadNext(), this);
    this.input.keyboard.on("keydown-SPACE", () => this.loadNext(), this);
}
```

This is the method that will show the instructions for the next scene. It will show the day, the audio record of the captain, and the mission objective.

```
showInstructions() {
  const listOfDays = Array(8)
    .fill(0)
    .map((_, i) => `DAY    `);
  this.text1 = this.add
    .bitmapText(this.center_width, 20, "pico", listOfDays[this.number], 30)
    .setOrigin(0.5)
    .setAlpha(0);
  this.text2 = this.add
    .bitmapText(
      this.center_width,
      70,
      "pico",
      "AUDIO RECORD OF CAPTAIN BRAUN",
      20
    )
    .setOrigin(0.5)
    .setAlpha(0);

  if (this.number > 0) {
```

```
      this.showSceneInstructions();
    } else {
      this.showFirstInstructions();
    }
  }
```

The next methods are used to show the instructions for the next scene. In the case of the first screen, it adds some extra effects.

```
showSceneInstructions() {
  this.tweens.add({
    targets: [this.text1, this.text2, this.play],
    duration: 1000,
    alpha: { from: 0, to: 1 },
    onComplete: () => {
      this.playDiary();
    },
  });
}

showFirstInstructions() {
  this.playBackground();
  this.text2 = this.add
    .bitmapText(this.center_width, 70, "pico", "THE CRASH", 20)
    .setOrigin(0.5)
    .setAlpha(0);
  this.playCreepy();
  this.tweens.add({
    targets: [this.text1],
    duration: 2000,
    alpha: { from: 0, to: 1 },
    onComplete: () => {
      this.playIntro();
    },
  });
}
```

This is the function that will show the intro of the game. It's a text that will be typed on the screen.

```
playIntro() {
  const text =
    "YOU JUST CRASHED ON MARS\n" +
    "YOU ARE ALIVE BUT YOUR\n" +
    "SHIP IS COMPLETELY LOST\n" +
    "IF YOU WANT TO LIVE YOU\n" +
    "MUST FIND LANDING REMAINS\n" +
    "TRY GOING EAST...";

  this.utils.typeText(text, "pico", this.center_width, 150, 0xffffff, 20);
}
```

6. Tell me a story: Marstranded — Transition page

This is the background sound of the transition. It's a looped sound.

```javascript
playBackground() {
  const theme = "mars_background";
  this.theme = this.sound.add(theme);
  this.theme.stop();
  this.theme.play({
    mute: false,
    volume: 1,
    rate: 1,
    detune: 0,
    seek: 0,
    loop: true,
    delay: 0,
  });
}
```

This is the audio record of the captain. It will be played along with an animation of a sound wave (not tied to the sound itself, but to the time of the animation).

```javascript
playDiary() {
  this.wave = this.add.sprite(this.center_width, 200, "wave").setOrigin(0.5);
  this.anims.create({
    key: "wave",
    frames: this.anims.generateFrameNumbers("wave", { start: 0, end: 4 }),
    frameRate: 20,
    repeat: -1,
  });
  this.wave.anims.play("wave", true);
  this.recording = this.sound.add(`diary  this.number}`);
  this.recording.on(
    "complete",
    function () {
      this.wave.destroy();
      this.showMission();
      this.playCreepy();
    }.bind(this)
  );
  this.recording.play();
}
```

This will be used to play a specific creepy sound at the end. Probably we could reuse the playBackground method.

```javascript
playCreepy() {
  this.creepy = this.sound.add("creepy");
  this.creepy.play({
    mute: false,
    volume: 0.9,
    rate: 0.9,
    detune: 0,
```

```
      seek: 0,
      loop: true,
      delay: 0,
  });
}
```

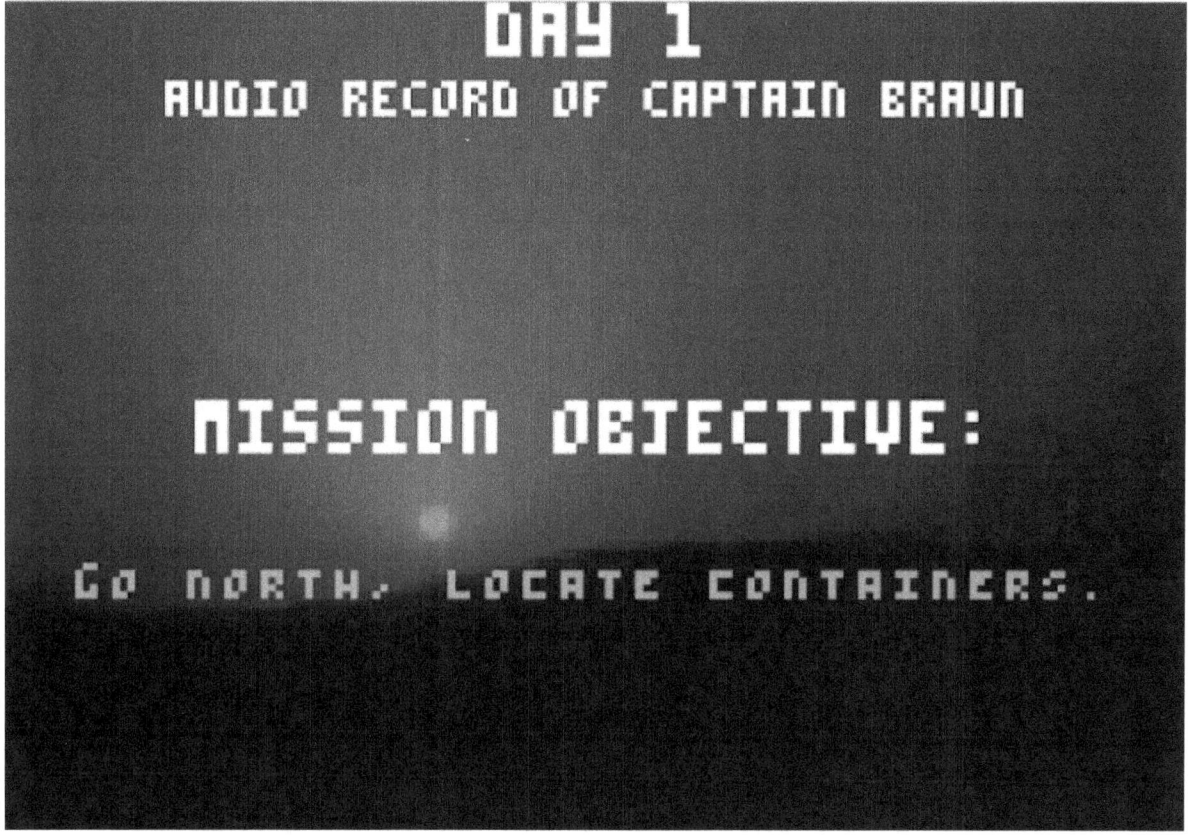

Figure 6.14 When the audio is over, the objective is revealed.

This is the mission objective. It will be shown on the screen.

```
showMission() {
  this.text3 = this.add
    .bitmapText(this.center_width, 300, "pico", "MISSION OBJECTIVE:", 30)
    .setOrigin(0.5);
  this.utils.typeText(
    this.missions[this.number],
    "pico",
    this.center_width,
    400,
    0xffffff,
    20
  );
}
```

6. Tell me a story: Marstranded — Transition page

When the transition information finishes or the user presses the space bar, we will start the next scene.

```
loadNext() {
    this.sound.add("blip").play();
    this.sound.stopAll();
    this.scene.start("game", { number: this.number });
  }
}
```

In this particular game, Transitions are essential. Not only because they provide the instructions for the next stage, but also because this is the place where we build the story for the player.

Transitions can be skipped too if necessary.

Outro

Well, in a game like this, there must be an outro. It is quite simple but I won't give any more details. At the end, this closing scene will be shown with the same music as in the transitions.

```
import Utils from "./utils";

export default class Outro extends Phaser.Scene {
  constructor() {
    super({ key: "outro" });
  }
```

The outro is similar to the splash screen, but it has a different background and a different title. It also has a different music theme.

```
create() {
    this.width = this.sys.game.config.width;
    this.height = this.sys.game.config.height;
    this.center_width = this.width / 2;
    this.center_height = this.height / 2;
    this.introLayer = this.add.layer();
    this.splashLayer = this.add.layer();

    this.add.tileSprite(0, 0, 800, 600, "landscape").setOrigin(0);
    this.utils = new Utils(this);
    this.title = this.add
      .bitmapText(
        this.center_width,
```

```
      this.center_height + 100,
      "pico",
      "MARSTRANDED",
      60
    )
    .setTint(0x6b140b)
    .setAlpha(0)
    .setDropShadow(0, 4, 0x6b302a, 0.9)
    .setOrigin(0.5);
  this.tweens.add({
    targets: this.title,
    alpha: { from: 0, to: 1 },
    duration: 4000,
  });

  this.input.keyboard.on("keydown-SPACE", this.startSplash, this);
  this.input.keyboard.on("keydown-ENTER", this.startSplash, this);
}
```

Figure 6.15 The outro comes after the final revelation.

We set again the background sound:

```
playMusic(theme = "mars_background") {
  this.theme = this.sound.add(theme);
  this.theme.stop();
  this.theme.play({
    mute: false,
```

```
        volume: 1.5,
        rate: 1,
        detune: 0,
        seek: 0,
        loop: true,
        delay: 0,
    });
}
```

This function will start the splash screen.

```
startSplash() {
    this.sound.stopAll();
    this.scene.start("splash");
}
}
```

In the end, the player must feel that he had an experience but also that he was told a story. How does the story end? Check it out.

Remember. Books tell stories. Movies and series also tell great stories. Guess what, games can also tell you a story, where the player can be directly involved. Nowadays there are games as huge as any Hollywood production. But even a humble game can have its own universe, its own world and characters, its own story. So apart from sprites and sounds, another important asset you should consider is a backstory of your game. That will not only give a sense of the whole experience but also engage the user.

Other story telling games

Camp Night

Source code: https://github.com/pxai/phasergames/tree/master/camping

Play it here: https://pello.itch.io/camp-night

7. Multiplayer games

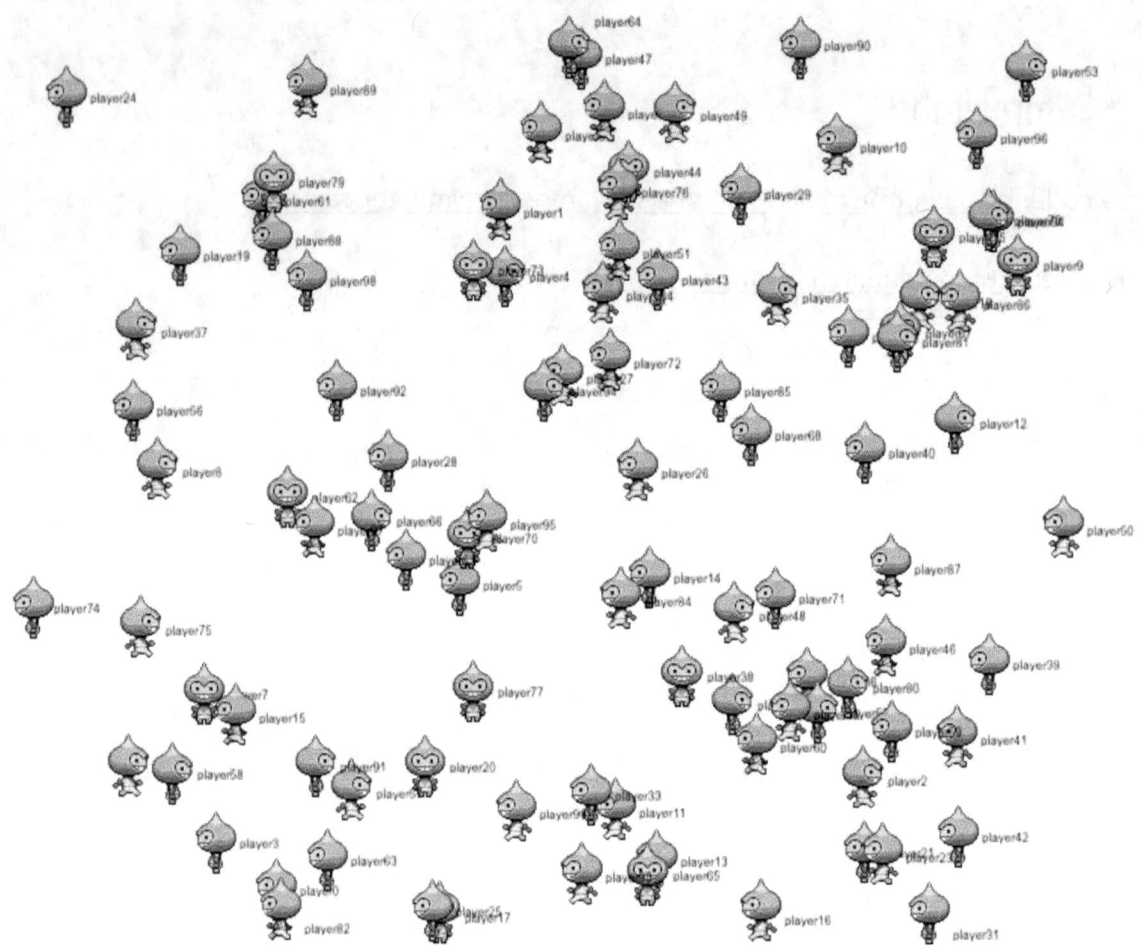

7. Multiplayer games

This is a topic that deserves a book on its own. As we do with the rest of the examples, we are providing a couple of simple projects for you to discover and let you explore on your own. In this case, the games are pretty simple and we will focus on the elements that enable the multiplayer experience. Everything you know about scenes, game objects and controls still applies. Now you just need to take into account that there will be external events and more players.

We are presenting two types of games: a real-time multiplayer game and a simple game to play on Twitch with chat users.

Blastemup: multiplayer with websockets.

Source code: https://github.com/pxai/phasergames/tree/master/blastemup

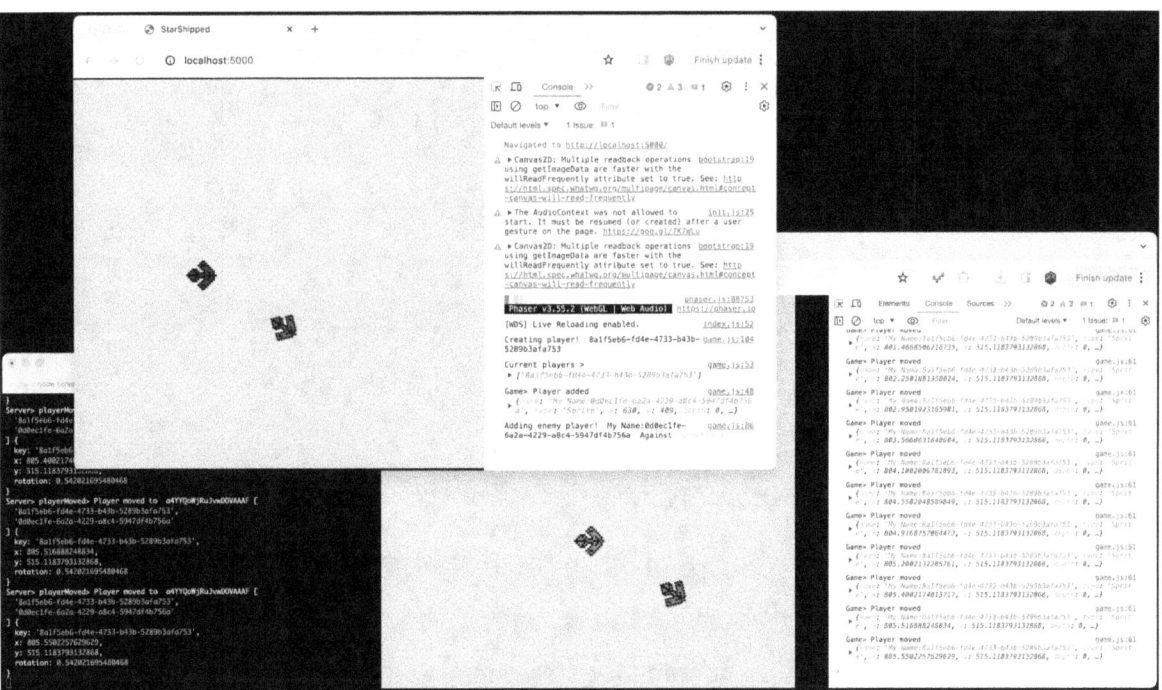

Figure 7.1 Blast Em Up in action.

This is a very simple game, no more than a proof of concept to show the minimum to have multiple players on the screen. In the game, players just move and destroy each other by collision. Yeah, it sucks, but let's focus on the mechanisms that we need to manage multiple players.

7. Multiplayer games — Blastemup: multiplayer with websockets.

The server

To understand what the communications are done, we should see the server first. This is a NodeJS-based Express server with Websockets capability using the socket.io package.

```javascript
const express = require("express");
const app = express();
const http = require("http").Server(app);
const io = require("socket.io")(http);
```

We set up a very basic express server. By default, we will serve the `index.html` page built by our Webpack build script on the front end. Anything inside `dist` will be served automatically, so the game JavaScript and assets will be served statically as well.

```javascript
app.get("/", function (request, response) {
  response.sendFile(__dirname + "/dist/index.html");
});

app.use("/", express.static("dist"));

http.listen(5000, function () {
  console.log("Server ready, listening on port ", 5000);
});

const players = {};
```

This is where we set all the events that our server will listen to. It will react like this:

- Is a new user connected? Notify it to the rest of the players to generate it as a new enemy.

- Is a player disconnected? Notify the rest of the players to destroy this enemy.

- Has the player moved? Notify it to the rest of the players so they can update the position of the enemy.

For debugging purposes, we left some logs on these events.

```javascript
io.on("connection", function (socket) {
  socket.on("newPlayer", function (newPlayer) {
    console.log("New player joined with state:", newPlayer);
    const [name, key] = newPlayer.name.split(":");
    players[key] = newPlayer;

    socket.emit("currentPlayers", players);
    socket.broadcast.emit("newPlayer", newPlayer);
```

```
  });

  socket.on("playerDisconnected", function (key) {
    delete players[key];
    console.log("Serve > player destroyed: ", key);

    socket.broadcast.emit("playerDisconnected", key);
  });

  socket.on("playerIsMoving", function (position_data) {
    console.log("Server> playerMoved> Player moved to ", position_data);
    const key = position_data?.key;
    if (players[key] == undefined) return;
    players[key].x = position_data.x;
    players[key].y = position_data.y;
    players[key].rotation = position_data.rotation;

    socket.broadcast.emit("playerMoved", players[key]);
  });
});
```

To play the game properly through the server, players must connect to this server with the browser.

The player

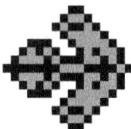

Figure 7.2 The sprite of the ship.

The players (the local and the rest of enemy players) are represented by this class. To identify all of them, it adds a unique uuid to the name. Alternatively, we could make use of the socket ID for that purpose. It does not do much, only the movement is different from what we have seen before, moving forward and using rotation to turn.

```
import Particle from "./particle";

class Player extends Phaser.GameObjects.Sprite {
  constructor(scene, x, y, name) {
    super(scene, x, y, "ship1_1");
    this.scene = scene;
    this.name = name;
    this.tint = Math.random() * 0xffffff;
    scene.add.existing(this);
    scene.physics.add.existing(this);
```

```
    this.body.setAllowGravity(false);
    this.body.setCircle(26);
    this.body.setOffset(6, 9);
    this.body.setBounce(0.8);
    this.angle = 0;
    this.speed = 0;
    this.friction = 0.95;
    this.death = false;
    this.init();
}
```

This `init` sets the controls for cursor keys. Also sets default properties for body.

```
init() {
    this.cursor = this.scene.input.keyboard.createCursorKeys();
    this.scene.events.on("update", this.update, this);
    this.body.setDrag(300);
    this.body.setAngularDrag(400);
    this.body.setMaxVelocity(600);
    this.upDelta = 0;
}
```

This is a getter so we can get the unique identifier from the name of the player.

```
get key() {
    return this.name.split(":")[1];
}
```

The update loop is used to move the spaceship according to the user input. When the player moves to right/left the body of the ship will rotate, when moving up it will gain velocity. Randomly, a trailing particle will be added.

```
update(timestep, delta) {
  if (this.death) return;
  if (this.cursor.left.isDown) {
    this.body.setAngularVelocity(-150);
  } else if (this.cursor.right.isDown) {
    this.body.setAngularVelocity(150);
  } else {
    this.body.setAngularVelocity(0);
  }

  if (this.cursor.up.isDown) {
    this.upDelta += delta;
    if (this.upDelta > 200) {
      this.upDelta = 0;
    }
    this.body.setVelocity(
      Math.cos(this.rotation) * 300,
      Math.sin(this.rotation) * 300
    );
```

```
      } else {
        this.body.setAcceleration(0);
      }

      if (Phaser.Math.Between(1, 4) > 1) {
        this.scene.thrust.add(
          new Particle(this.scene, this.x, this.y, 0xffffff, 10)
        );
      }
    }

    destroy() {
      this.death = true;
      super.destroy();
    }
  }

  export default Player;
```

Here we could add a shooting mechanism, but bear in mind that shots and their movement will need to be notified to the server.

The game

Finally, the game: this is where we put the server and the player together. In this particular case, you should pay attention to the function that sets the callbacks for the communication events.

```
import Phaser from "phaser";
import Player from "./player";

import {
  NEW_PLAYER,
  CURRENT_PLAYERS,
  PLAYER_DISCONNECTED,
  PLAYER_MOVED,
  PLAYER_IS_MOVING,
} from "./status";

export default class Game extends Phaser.Scene {
  constructor() {
    super({ key: "game" });
  }

  create() {
    this.id = null;
```

7. Multiplayer games   Blastemup: multiplayer with websockets.

```
    this.startSockets();
    this.loadAudios();
    this.addColliders();
}
```

Next is where the connection with the server is established and we set listeners for events that we will receive from that server. Through those listeners, we will be aware of new players, player movement and player destroy events. We need to add that .bind(this) to this event callback to make the elements of this class reachable. In this case, we separate the group of enemies in a hash and their physical group with this.enemyPlayers to set the collisions. But we could just use the physical group.

```
startSockets() {
  this.socket = io();
  this.addPlayer();
  this.enemies = {};
  this.enemyPlayers = this.physics.add.group();

  this.socket.on(
    NEW_PLAYER,
    function (playerInfo) {
      this.addEnemyPlayers(playerInfo);
    }.bind(this)
  );

  this.socket.on(
    CURRENT_PLAYERS,
    function (players) {
      Object.keys(players).forEach((key) => {
        if (!this.enemies[key] && key !== this.player.key)
          this.addEnemyPlayers(players[key]);
      });
    }.bind(this)
  );

  this.socket.on(
    PLAYER_MOVED,
    function (playerInfo) {
      const [name, key] = playerInfo.name.split(":");
      if (this.enemies[key]) {
        this.enemies[key].setRotation(playerInfo.rotation);
        this.enemies[key].setPosition(playerInfo.x, playerInfo.y);
      }
    }.bind(this)
  );

  this.socket.on(
    PLAYER_DISCONNECTED,
    function (key) {
      this.enemyPlayers.getChildren().forEach(function (otherPlayer) {
```

```
        if (key === otherPlayer.key) {
          otherPlayer.destroy();
        }
      });
    }.bind(this)
  );
}
```

When a new enemy event is received, we'll add this new game object to this player's screen.

```
addEnemyPlayers(enemyPlayer) {
  const [name, key] = enemyPlayer.name.split(":");
  console.log("Adding enemy player! ", enemyPlayer.name, " Against ", key);
  const enemy = new Player(
    this,
    enemyPlayer.x,
    enemyPlayer.y,
    enemyPlayer.name
  );
  this.enemies[enemy.key] = enemy;
  this.enemyPlayers.add(enemy);
}
```

When we add our local player to the game, we must notify the server about it! We are setting a generic game here, but we could add a custom name provided by the remote user.

```
addPlayer() {
  this.thrust = this.add.layer();
  const x = 600 + Phaser.Math.Between(-100, 100);
  const y = 500 + Phaser.Math.Between(-100, 100);
  this.player = new Player(this, x, y, "MyName:" + crypto.randomUUID());
  console.log("Creating player! ", this.player.key);
  this.socket.emit(NEW_PLAYER, this.player);
  this.setCamera();
}

setCamera() {
  this.cameras.main.setBackgroundColor(0xcccccc);
  this.cameras.main.startFollow(this.player, true, 0.05, 0.05, 0, 100);
}
```

This is the only collider in this simplified game. If the player hits any other ship, both ships will be destroyed.

```
addColliders() {
  this.physics.add.overlap(
    this.player,
    this.enemyPlayers,
```

```
      this.playerCollision.bind(this)
    );
  }

  playerCollision(player, foe) {
    console.log("Collision! ");
    this.socket.emit(PLAYER_DISCONNECTED, player.key);
    player.destroy();
    foe.destroy();
  }
```

In the game loop, we check if the player position has changed. If it has, we notify the server about it, so other players can reproduce the movement.

```
update() {
  if (this.player) {
    const currPosition = {
      x: this.player.x,
      y: this.player.y,
      rotation: this.player.rotation,
    };
    if (
      this.player.oldPosition &&
      (currPosition.x !== this.player.oldPosition.x ||
        currPosition.y !== this.player.oldPosition.y ||
        currPosition.rotation !== this.player.oldPosition.rotation)
    ) {
      this.socket.emit(PLAYER_IS_MOVING, {
        key: this.player.key,
        ...currPosition,
      });
    }

    this.player.oldPosition = currPosition;
  }
}
```

The rest of the game is the same as usual.

```
loadAudios() {
  this.audios = {
    pick: this.sound.add("pick"),
    shot: this.sound.add("shot"),
    foeshot: this.sound.add("foeshot"),
    explosion: this.sound.add("explosion"),
    asteroid: this.sound.add("asteroid"),
  };
}

playAudio(key) {
  this.audios[key].play({ volume: 0.2 });
```

```
  }

  startGame() {
    if (this.theme) this.theme.stop();
    this.scene.start("game");
  }

  destroy() {
    if (this.player) this.socket.emit(PLAYER_DISCONNECTED, this.player.key);
    super.destroy();
  }
}
```

Well, once you get how it is done, adding shots and common maps shouldn't be difficult and we leave that to you. There are several issues like lag, keep-alive, deployment... but that would go beyond the scope of this book.

Running it

To run and try this game, we need to:

- Build the phaser game code and publish it in a directory.
- Run the server and serve the game built by Phaser.

The user should connect to the server! In this example, it would be `https://localhost:5000` locally. The server provides the game along with the socket.io library. You can open multiple local browsers to try it. Every time you reload the browser you should see a new ship. You should add a *keep-alive* mechanism to let the server know when a player is disconnected.

You can check the example code and the Webpack configuration in the sourcecode.

Zenbaki: a game for Twitch chat.

Figure 7.3 Zenbaki chat game in progress.

Source code: https://github.com/pxai/phasergames/tree/master/zenbaki

Play it here: https://pello.itch.io/zenbaki

A simple web-based game for Twitch chat that does not require any registration. Anybody in the chat can play just by sending commands. Players will see a number in the circle and a simple operation below (+, -, *, /). Try to be the first to guess the result and write it on the chat. You'll get points every time you guess the result, but beware! If you are wrong you'll lose everything and the game will be over.

To play this game, a channel owner must run it locally, sharing the screen with the running game on the stream.

This game was developed for the Numerica game jam promoted by RothioTome, where many Numerica-like games were created along with other games for Twitch chat.

Web Page

Figure 7.4 HTML page to start the game.

7. Multiplayer games — Zenbaki: a game for Twitch chat.

This is an HTML screen with a little form where the channel owner can set some values and then start the game. The most important detail is to specify the channel where the commands will be read from.

```html
<!DOCTYPE html>
<html>
<head>
  <meta charset="utf-8">
  <meta name="viewport" content="width=device-width">
  <link rel="stylesheet" href="assets/css/styles.css">
  <style>
    @import url('https://fonts.cdnfonts.com/css/gang-of-three');
  </style>
  <title>ZenBaki</title>
</head>
<body>

  <div class="container">
    <div class="logo">
      <div class="floating-div left"></div>
      <div class="round">
        <div class="number">Z</div>
      </div>
      <div class="floating-div right"></div>
    </div>
    <div class="title">
      ZenBaki
    </div>
    <div class="form-container">
        <header>
          <h2>Options</h2>
        </header>
        <form action="game.html">
            <div><label for="channel">Channel</label></div>
            <div><input type="text" name="channel" id="channel" value="devdiaries"></div>
            <div><label for="background">Background Color</label></div>
            <div><input type="color" name="background" id="background", value = '#00b140'></div>
            <div><label for="foreground">Foreground Color</label></div>
            <div><input type="color" name="foreground" id="foreground", value = '#F0EAD6'></div>
            <br />
            <div><input type="submit", value = 'PLAY'></div>
        </form>
        <footer>
        </footer>
    </div>
    <div>
      <a href="https://pello.itch.io">By Pello</a>
    </div>
```

```html
    <div class="list-row" id="listBlock">
      <div class="list">
          <h2>Game Rules</h2>
          <ul>
              <li class="list-item">You will see a number...</li>
              <li class="list-item">...and an operation below.</li>
              <li class="list-item">Guess the result</li>
              <li class="list-item">and write it on the chat!</li>
          </ul>
      </div>
    </div>
</div>

    <script>
       const listBlock = document.getElementById('listBlock');

       function toggleList() {
           listBlock.style.display = listBlock.style.display === 'none' || listBlock.style.display !== 'flex' ? 'flex' : 'none';
       }

    </script>
</body>
</html>
```

The background color is necessary in case the channel owner wants to add some transparency filter to the game. By default, the well-known green of the chroma screens is set.

This is the page that the channel owner will use to launch the game locally. Once the game is running and shared on the stream, his channel users will be able to play by sending chat messages.

Init

This is a simple init file like the previous ones where we define the scenes and the settings of the game.

```
import Phaser from "phaser";
import Bootloader from "./bootloader";
import Game from "./game";

const config = {
  width: 260,
  height: 380,
```

7. Multiplayer games   Zenbaki: a game for Twitch chat.

```js
  scale: {
    autoCenter: Phaser.Scale.CENTER_BOTH,
  },
  autoRound: false,
  parent: "contenedor",
  physics: {
    default: "arcade",
    arcade: {
      gravity: { y: 300 },
      debug: false,
    },
  },
  scene: [Bootloader, Game],
};

const game = new Phaser.Game(config);
```

Bootloader

Here we load the assets of the game, we define the game scene and we load everything.

```js
export default class Bootloader extends Phaser.Scene {
  constructor() {
    super({ key: "bootloader" });
  }
```

We don't have much to preload so we load all assets here.

```js
  preload() {
    this.createBars();
    this.setLoadEvents();

    Array(15)
      .fill(0)
      .forEach((_, i) => {
        this.load.image(`cloud${i}`, `assets/images/cloud${i}.png`);
      });
    this.load.image("pello", "assets/images/pello.png");
    this.load.image("sensei", "assets/images/sensei.png");

    this.load.audio("win", "assets/sounds/win.mp3");
    this.load.audio("drip", "assets/sounds/drip.mp3");
    this.load.audio("fail", "assets/sounds/fail.mp3");
    this.load.bitmapFont(
      "mainFont",
      "assets/fonts/hiro.png",
      "assets/fonts/hiro.xml"
    );
```

```js
    this.registry.set("score", 0);
  }
```

Again we move load events to this method to avoid cluttering the preload method.

```js
setLoadEvents() {
  this.load.on(
    "progress",
    function (value) {
      this.progressBar.clear();
      this.progressBar.fillStyle(0x88d24c, 1);
      this.progressBar.fillRect(
        this.cameras.main.width / 4,
        this.cameras.main.height / 2 - 16,
        (this.cameras.main.width / 2) * value,
        16
      );
    },
    this
  );
  this.load.on(
    "complete",
    () => {
      this.scene.start("game");
    },
    this
  );
}
```

We add the load bar and the progress bar to the scene.

```js
createBars() {
  this.loadBar = this.add.graphics();
  this.loadBar.fillStyle(0x008483, 1);
  this.loadBar.fillRect(
    this.cameras.main.width / 4 - 2,
    this.cameras.main.height / 2 - 18,
    this.cameras.main.width / 2 + 4,
    20
  );
  this.progressBar = this.add.graphics();
}
}
```

Player

This class just represents each player. It won't be a visible player in this case, but just a class to hold the name and points of each player.

7. Multiplayer games   Zenbaki: a game for Twitch chat.

```javascript
class Player {
  constructor(scene, name) {
    this.scene = scene;
    this.name = name;
    this.score = 0;
    this.lastMessage = null;
    this.dead = false;
    this.penalties = 0;
  }
```

We can use this function to check if the player has spammed the chat. We will use it to avoid players spamming the game with chat messages.

```javascript
  hasSpammed() {
    if (!this.lastMessage) return false;

    const current = new Date();
    const timeDifferenceInMilliseconds = current - this.lastMessage;
    return timeDifferenceInMilliseconds / 1000 < this.scene.spamTimeWait;
  }
```

We could optionally penalize the user for spamming or whatever we want to do. With this mechanism, we just ignore the messages for 10 seconds.

```javascript
  setPenalty() {
    this.penalties++;
    this.score = 0;
    this.dead = true;
    this.scene.time.delayedCall(
      10000 * this.penalties,
      () => {
        this.dead = false;
      },
      null,
      this
    );
  }
}

export default Player;
```

Game

The game just shows the current operation. Players must try to be the first to guess the result and they will be rewarded with points. If they fail, the round will be over.

```javascript
import Player from "./player";
```

7. Multiplayer games   Zenbaki: a game for Twitch chat.

```javascript
import Chat from "./chat";

export default class Game extends Phaser.Scene {
  constructor() {
    super({ key: "game" });
    this.player = null;
    this.score = 0;
    this.scoreText = null;
    this.nextOperator = "";
    this.lastMessage = null;
    this.number = "";
    this.counter = 0;
    this.failed = false;
  }
```

We use preload in this case only to get the background color from the URL parameters. We could also get the foreground color, but we will use the default one if it's not specified. We also calculate the first result.

```javascript
  preload() {
    const urlParams = new URLSearchParams(window.location.search);
    let parambg = urlParams.get("background") || "#00b140";
    parambg = parseInt(parambg.substring(1), 16);
    this.backgroundColor = "0x" + parambg.toString(16);

    let paramfg = urlParams.get("foreground") || "#F0EAD6";
    paramfg = parseInt(paramfg.substring(1), 16);
    this.foregroundColor = "0x" + paramfg.toString(16);

    this.spamTimeWait = 2;
    this.result = Phaser.Math.Between(1, 9);
  }
```

We create the elements of the game. This one is quite simple. We just create the chat, and the UI and load the audio files.

```javascript
  create() {
    this.width = this.sys.game.config.width;
    this.height = this.sys.game.config.height;
    this.center_width = this.width / 2;
    this.center_height = this.height / 2;
    this.cameras.main.setBackgroundColor(+this.foregroundColor);
    this.allPlayers = {};

    this.addChat();
    this.loadAudios();
    this.addUI();
  }
```

7. Multiplayer games   Zenbaki: a game for Twitch chat.

Figure 7.5 The current number and the operation below.

This creates an instance of the chat client and allows us to receive messages from the chat.

```
addChat() {
  this.chat = new Chat(this);
}
```

This is called from the chat when the connection is ready. We will create the next operation when the game is connected to the chat channel.

```
loadGame() {
  this.generateNextOperation();
}
```

The game has a very simple interface. We just show the current number, the next operation and the score. We also add some clouds to make it look nicer.

```
addUI() {
  this.circle = this.add.circle(
    this.center_width,
    this.center_height - 50,
    100,
    0xf22c2e
```

```
    );
    this.numberText = this.add
      .bitmapText(
        this.center_width,
        this.center_height - 50,
        "mainFont",
        this.number,
        120
      )
      .setOrigin(0.5)
      .setTint(0x000000);
    this.operatorText = this.add
      .bitmapText(
        this.center_width,
        this.center_height + 80,
        "mainFont",
        `${this.nextOperator}${this.number}`,
        50
      )
      .setOrigin(0.5)
      .setTint(0x000000);
    this.addClouds();
    this.addScore();
    this.byText = this.add
      .bitmapText(
        this.center_width,
        this.height - 10,
        "mainFont",
        "by Pello",
        10
      )
      .setOrigin(0.5)
      .setTint(0x000000);
}
```

This is the function that will generate random clouds and move them across the screen. We use tweens to move them and destroy them when they are out of the screen. Then we call the function again to generate new clouds.

```
addClouds() {
  this.cloudLeft = this.add
    .image(
      this.center_width - 100,
      this.center_height - 120 + Phaser.Math.Between(-15, 15),
      "cloud" + Phaser.Math.Between(1, 14)
    )
    .setScale(Phaser.Math.Between(5, 9) * 0.1);
  this.cloudRight = this.add
    .image(
      this.center_width + 100,
      this.center_height + 30 + Phaser.Math.Between(-15, 15),
```

```
        "cloud" + Phaser.Math.Between(1, 14)
      )
      .setScale(Phaser.Math.Between(4, 6) * 0.1);
    this.tweens.add({
      targets: [this.cloudLeft],
      x: { from: -156, to: this.width + 156 },
      duration: 30000,
      onComplete: () => {
        this.cloudLeft.destroy();
      },
    });

    this.tweens.add({
      targets: this.cloudRight,
      x: { from: this.width + 156, to: -156 },
      duration: 30000,
      onComplete: () => {
        this.cloudLeft.destroy();
        this.addClouds();
      },
    });
  }
```

This is the function that will show the score while on the game screen. We will show the top 3 players ranked by points.

```
addScore() {
  const scoreBoard = this.createScoreBoard();
  this.add
    .bitmapText(this.center_width, 25, "mainFont", "zenbaki", 25)
    .setOrigin(0.5)
    .setTint(0x000000);
  scoreBoard.slice(0, 3).forEach((player, i) => {
    const winnerText = `${i + 1}. ${player.name}: ${player.score}`;
    this.add
      .bitmapText(this.center_width, 100 + i * 50, "mainFont", winnerText, 30)
      .setOrigin(0.5)
      .setTint(this.foregroundColor)
      .setDropShadow(1, 2, 0xbf2522, 0.7);
  });

  this.scoreText1 = this.add
    .bitmapText(
      this.center_width,
      this.center_height + 130,
      "mainFont",
      "",
      20
    )
    .setOrigin(0.5)
    .setTint(0x000000);
  this.scoreText2 = this.add
```

```
      .bitmapText(
        this.center_width,
        this.center_height + 160,
        "mainFont",
        "",
        25
      )
      .setOrigin(0.5)
      .setTint(0x000000);
  }
```

When a new player tries to guess or joins the channel, we'll add it to `allPlayers` array. If the player already exists, we'll return the existing player.

```
addPlayer(name) {
  if (this.allPlayers[name]) return this.allPlayers[name];
  const player = new Player(this, name);
  this.allPlayers[name] = player;
  this.chat.say(`Player ${name} joins game!`);
  return player;
}
```

This is the function that will be called when a player tries to guess the number. We will check if the player exists and if it does, we will check if the player has spammed the chat. If it hasn't, we will check if the number is correct. If it is, we will add the score to the player and generate a new operation. If it's not, we will penalize the player and show a message.

```
guess(playerName, number) {
  if (this.failed) return;
  console.log("Game> guess: ", playerName, number);

  const player = this.addPlayer(playerName);
  if (player.dead) return;
  if (player.hasSpammed()) return;
  player.lastMessage = new Date();

  console.log("Game> guess go on: ", playerName, number);

  if (this.result === parseInt(number)) {
    const score = this.calculateScore();
    player.score += score;
    this.showScore(playerName, score);
    this.generateNextOperation();
    console.log("Player", playerName, "guess", number);
  } else if (this.number === parseInt(number)) {
    console.log("Player, ", playerName, " is too slow");
  } else {
    this.cameras.main.shake(100, 0.01);
```

```
    this.playAudio("fail");
    this.failed = true;
    player.setPenalty();
    this.showShame(playerName);
    this.chat.say(`Player ${playerName} failed! Shame on you!`);
  }
}
```

These are the points that we will add to the player score depending on the operator. We will add 1 point for "+", 2 for -, 4 for * and 5 for /.

```
calculateScore() {
  const operatorPoints = { "+": 1, "-": 2, "*": 4, "/": 5 };
  return this.counter + operatorPoints[this.nextOperator];
}
```

We use the loadAudio/playAudios mechanism again:

```
loadAudios() {
  this.audios = {
    win: this.sound.add("win"),
    drip: this.sound.add("drip"),
    fail: this.sound.add("fail"),
  };
}

playAudio(key) {
  this.audios[key].play({
    volume: 0.5,
  });
}
```

This will cover the game screen and show the result of the game. We will show the top 5 players ordered by points.

```
showResult() {
  const scoreBoard = this.createScoreBoard();
  this.scoreRectangle = this.add
    .rectangle(0, 0, this.width, this.height, this.foregroundColor, 0.9)
    .setOrigin(0, 0);
  this.scores = this.add.group();
  this.sensei = this.add
    .image(this.center_width, this.height - 60, "sensei")
    .setOrigin(0.5)
    .setScale(0.4);
  this.scores.add(this.sensei);
  this.scores.add(
    this.add
      .bitmapText(this.center_width, 60, "mainFont", "Senseis:", 30)
      .setOrigin(0.5)
      .setTint(0x000000)
```

```
  );
  scoreBoard.slice(0, 5).forEach((player, i) => {
    const winnerText = `${i + 1}.  ${player.name}, ${player.score}`;
    this.scores.add(
      this.add
        .bitmapText(
          this.center_width,
          100 + i * 20,
          "mainFont",
          winnerText,
          15
        )
        .setOrigin(0.5)
        .setTint(0x000000)
    );
  });

  this.removeResult();
}
```

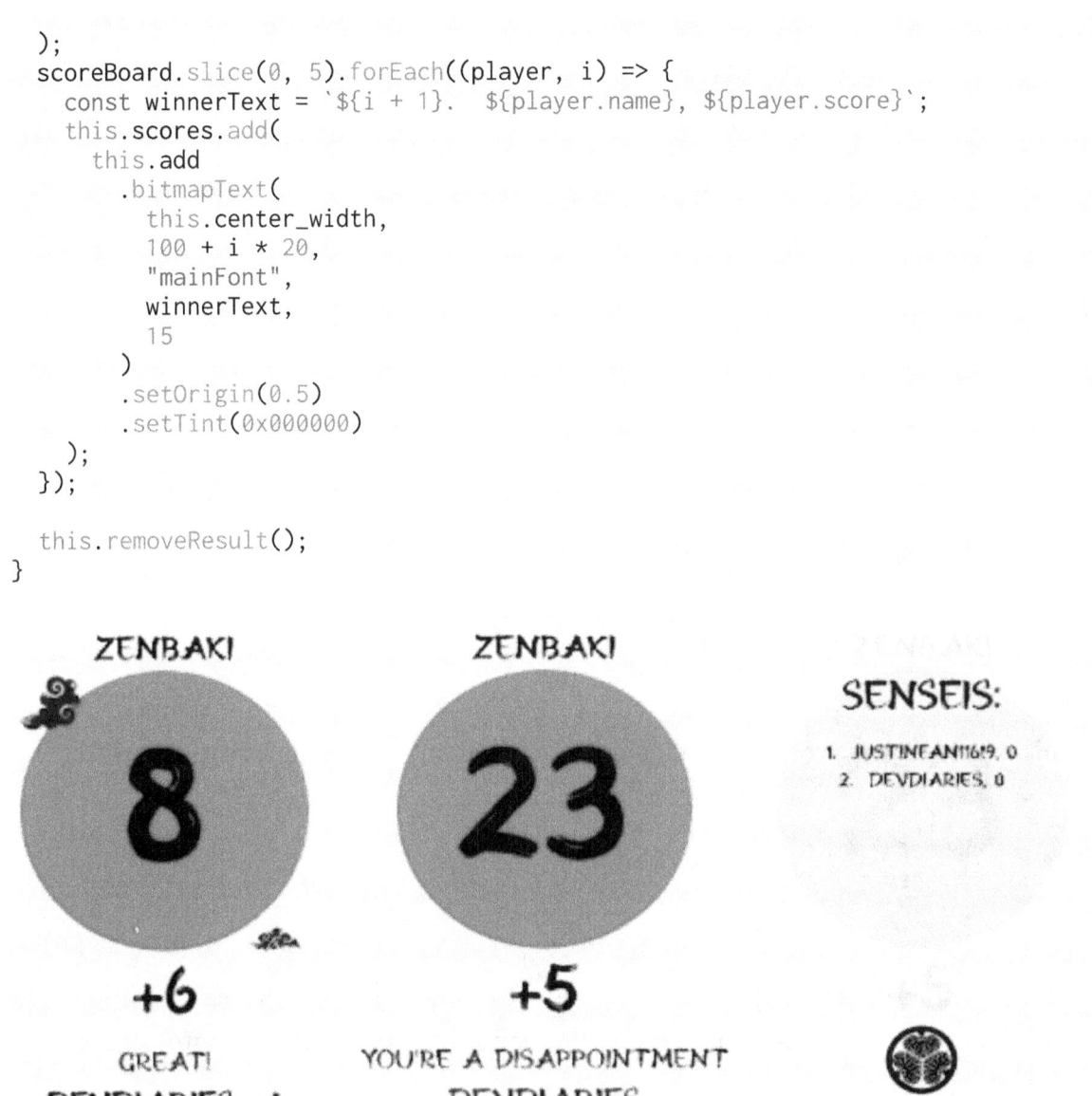

Figure 7.6 Three reactions: correct result, failure, and scoreboard overlay.

Once we show the result, we will remove it after 5 seconds.

```
removeResult() {
  this.time.delayedCall(
    5000,
    () => {
      this.tweens.add({
        targets: [this.scoreRectangle, this.scores, this.sensei],
        duration: 1000,
        alpha: { from: 1, to: 0 },
```

```
        onComplete: () => {
          this.scoreRectangle.destroy();
          this.scores.getChildren().forEach(function (child) {
            child.destroy();
          }, this);
          this.scores.clear(true, true);
        },
      });
      this.resetScore();
      this.generateNextOperation();
    },
    null,
    this
  );
}
```

This will order the players by score:

```
createScoreBoard() {
  return [...Object.values(this.allPlayers)].sort(
    (player1, player2) => player2.score - player1.score
  );
}
```

This will reset the score and the counter and will set the failed flag to `false`.

```
resetScore() {
  this.number = 0;
  this.counter = 0;
  this.failed = false;
}
```

We'll call this function to generate the next operation. We will increase the counter, set the number to the result, generate a new operand and a new operator and calculate the result.

```
generateNextOperation() {
  this.counter++;
  this.number = this.result;
  this.nextOperand = Phaser.Math.Between(1, 9);
  this.nextOperator = this.selectOperator();
  this.result = parseInt(
    eval(this.number + this.nextOperator + this.nextOperand)
  );
  console.log(
    "Current: ",
    this.number,
    " operator: ",
    this.nextOperator,
    " nextNumber: ",
    this.nextOperand,
```

```
      ", Result: ",
      this.result
    );
    this.showNextOperation(this.nextOperator, this.nextOperand);
    this.playAudio("drip");
  }
```

To select the next operator to use, we take into account the number, the next operand and the result. We will try to avoid big negative numbers and numbers bigger than 100, and also divisions that don't result in an integer.

```
  selectOperator() {
    if (this.number % this.nextOperand === 0 && this.nextOperand !== 1) {
      return Phaser.Math.RND.pick(["+", "-", "+", "-", "/"]);
    } else if (this.number + this.nextOperand >= 100) {
      return Phaser.Math.RND.pick(["-"]);
    } else if (this.number - this.nextOperand <= -100) {
      return Phaser.Math.RND.pick(["+"]);
    } else if (Math.abs(this.number * this.nextOperand) < 100) {
      return Phaser.Math.RND.pick(["+", "-", "+", "-", "*"]);
    } else {
      return Phaser.Math.RND.pick(["+", "-", "+", "-"]);
    }
  }
}
```

If a player guesses the result correctly, we will show a message with the player's name and the score.

```
  showScore(playerName, score) {
    this.scoreText1.setText(`Great!`).setAlpha(1);
    this.scoreText2.setText(`${playerName} +${score}`).setAlpha(1);
    this.tweens.add({
      targets: [this.scoreText1],
      alpha: { from: 1, to: 0 },
      ease: "Linear",
      duration: 3000,
    });
  }
```

If a player fails, we will show a message to the player and then we will reveal the current scoreboard.

```
  showShame(playerName) {
    const rants = [
      "You're a disgrace",
      "Shame on you",
      "You dishonor us all",
      "You're a disappointment",
      "You're a failure",
      "You dishonor this dojo",
```

```
    ];
    this.scoreText1.setText(Phaser.Math.RND.pick(rants)).setAlpha(1);
    this.scoreText2.setText(`${playerName}`).setAlpha(1);
    this.tweens.add({
      targets: [this.scoreText1, this.scoreText2],
      alpha: { from: 1, to: 0 },
      ease: "Linear",
      duration: 3000,
      onComplete: () => {
        this.showResult();
      },
    });
  }
```

This shows the current number and the next operation.

```
  showNextOperation(operator, nextNumber) {
    this.numberText.setText(this.number);
    this.operatorText.setText(`${operator}${nextNumber}`);
  }
}
```

The biggest issue with this type of game is that you may have several users trying to guess. This implementation just considers one winner, but you can try other approaches.

Chat

This is the differential class in the game. As the name implies, this class takes care of chat connection and parsing commands. The settings for the connection are taken from the URL string that is set in the initial HTML splash form.

Once the connection is established, this class just parses and passes commands to the game.

```
const tmi = require("tmi.js");

export default class Chat {
  constructor(scene, username, password, channels) {
    this.scene = scene;
    this._username = username;
    this._password = password;

    const urlParams = new URLSearchParams(window.location.search);
    this.channel = urlParams.get("channel") || "devdiaries";
    this.feedback = urlParams.get("feedback") == "1";
    this.maxPlayers = this.isValidNumberWithMax(urlParams.get("maxplayers"))
      ? +urlParams.get("maxplayers")
```

```
      : 500;
    this.init();
  }
```

This is where we create the connection to the chat. We just specify the channel, but we could add and identity to log in with a user and send messages to the channel or do chat actions during the game like temporary bans. With just the channel connection, we will be able to read the chat and act accordingly, which could be enough for some games.

```
  init() {
    console.log(
      "Chat channel: ",
      this.channel,
      "feedback: ",
      this.feedback,
      "maxPlayers: ",
      this.maxPlayers
    );
    this.client = new tmi.Client({
      options: { debug: false },
      // identity: {
      //     username: "devdiaries", // We could actually log in with a user
      //     password: NOPE   // and send messages or do actions
      // },
      channels: [this.channel],
    });

    this.client
      .connect()
      .then((ok) => {
        console.log("Connected!, loading game");
        this.scene.loadGame();
      })
      .catch(console.error);

    this.setOnJoinListener();
    this.setOnMessageListener();
    this.setOnChatListener;
  }
```

We add a listener to the join event, so we can add the player to the game when they join the chat.

```
  setOnJoinListener() {
    this.client.on("join", (channel, username, self) => {
      console.log("Somebody joined the chat: ", channel, username);
      if (self) {
        this.scene.addPlayer(username);
      }
```

```
  });
}
```

Messages to the chat can come with two different events: message or chat. We will process them both in the same way, but we need different event callbacks because the data comes in different formats.

```
setOnMessageListener() {
  this.client.on("message", (channel, tags, message, self) => {
    console.log(`Message: ${tags.username} just ${message}`);
    this.processMessage(tags.username, message);
  });
}

setOnChatListener() {
  this.client.on("chat", async (channel, user, message, self) => {
    if (user.mod) {
      // User is a mod.
    }
    const messageParts = message.toLowerCase().split(" ");
    console.log("Received chat: ", channel, user, messageParts);

    this.processMessage(user["display-name"], message);
  });
}
```

Once we isolate the username and the message, we can process the message. In this case, we will check if the message is a number and if it is, we will send it to the game to check if it is the correct answer.

```
processMessage(username, message) {
  if (this.isValidNumber(message)) {
    this.scene.guess(username, +message);
  }
}
```

We are not using this function but I will leave it here, in case you want to send actions to the chat, like /me does.

```
sendAction(channel, msg) {
  console.log("Sending action: ", this.feedback, channel, msg);
  if (!this.feedback) return;
  this.client.action(channel, msg);
}
```

We are not using this function either, but this is what you do in case you want to send messages to the chat:

```
  say(msg) {
    if (!this.feedback) return;
    this.client.say(this.channel, msg);
  }
```

We use these two functions to validate the number sent by the user. It must be a number within a limit.

```
  isValidNumberWithMax(number, limit = 100) {
    return this.isValidNumber(number) && +number > 0 && +number <= limit;
  }

  isValidNumber(number) {
    return !isNaN(number);
  }
}
```

This example connection just uses read-only privileges on the chat channel. You can go further and set users with special permission to let the game post messages and even perform commands like temporal bans or any other action that you may consider making a part of the game.

Other Twitch games

WarChat: A worms-like game

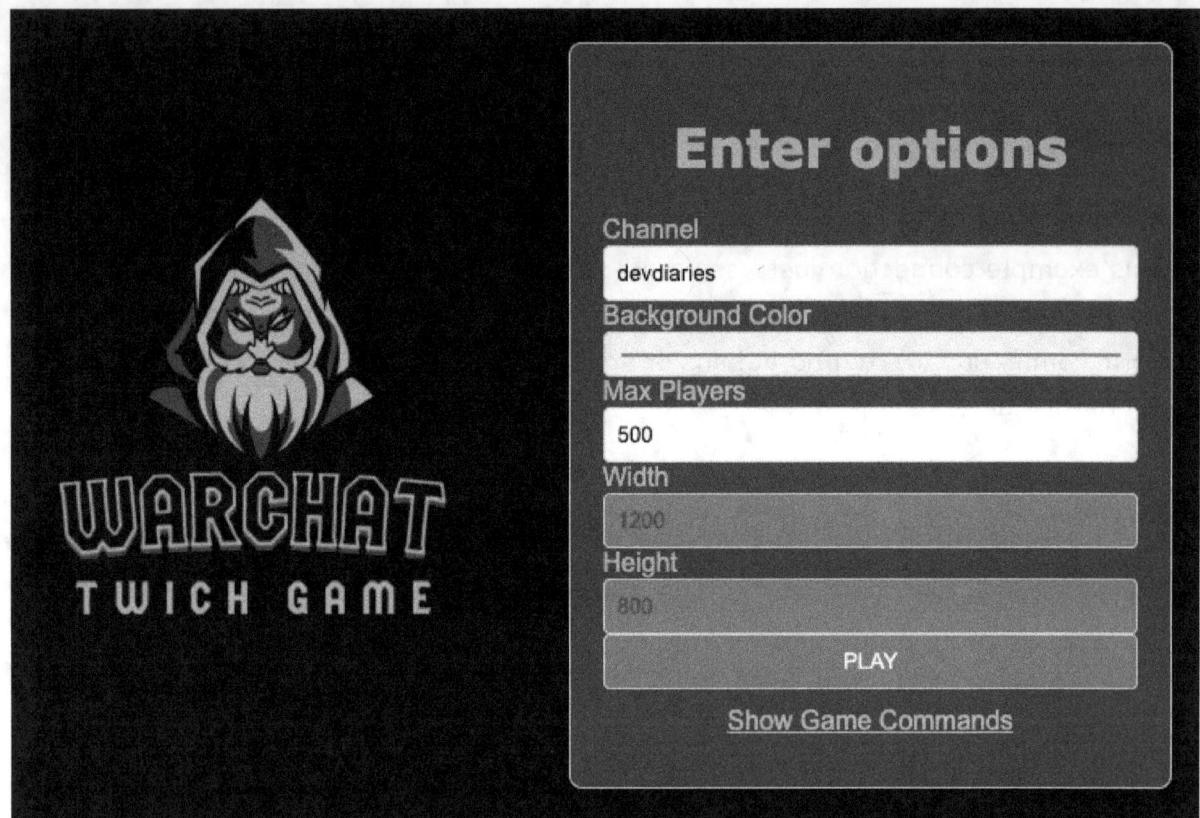

Figure 7.7 Launch web page for WatChat,

Zenbaki is just a casual game, but you can bring the experience further making a better use of Phaser possibilities. Check out WarChat, another game for Twitch that uses the chat to send commands. In this particular case, it gets commands from users (direction and angle) to attack each other.

Figure 7.8 WarChat game scene.

Source code: https://github.com/pxai/phasergames/tree/master/warchat

Play it here: https://pello.itch.io/warchat

Chatgasol

Source code: https://github.com/pxai/phasergames/tree/master/chatgasol

Play it here: https://pello.itch.io/chatgasol

Chatdefense

Source code: https://github.com/pxai/phasergames/tree/master/chatdefense

Play it here: https://pello.itch.io/chatdefense

8. 3D: Fate

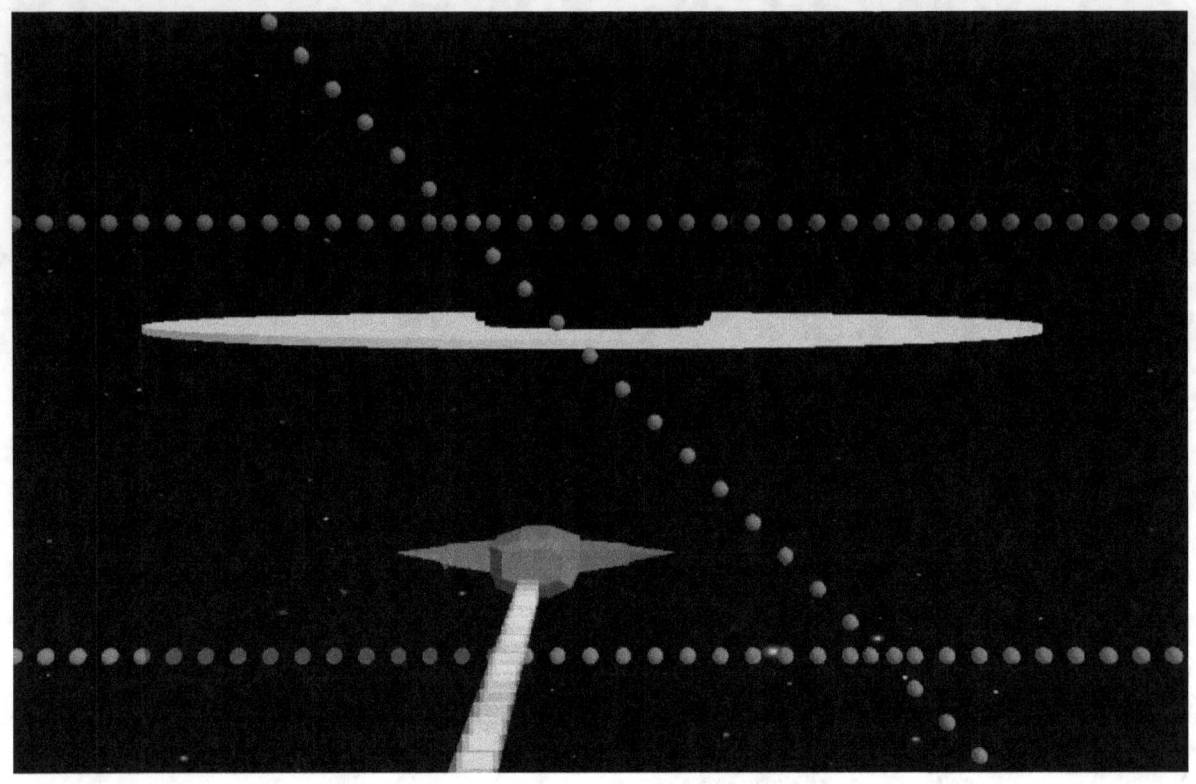

Source code: https://github.com/pxai/phasergames/tree/master/fate

Play it here: https://pello.itch.io/fate

8. 3D: Fate

3D in a Phaser game? Yes, it is possible. The enable3d library is not very well documented and even to create a simple game like this I had to work hard trying and failing many times. But ultimately I was able to create a very simple 3D bullet hell. This is a spectacular game genre where the player is bombarded with massive bullet waves that take different shapes and patterns.

This game has also a bit of a backstory. Did you think that Yuri Gagarin, the first man who went to space, died in an accident? No way! He was sent on a secret mission beyond our solar system to study a neutrino star. The supremacy of soviet science lies in your hands, Commander Gagarin.

Figure 8.1 The inspiration for this game.

Init

This time the init will be a bit different, as we need to set the game to be 3D.

```
import * as Phaser from "phaser";
import { enable3d, Canvas } from "@enable3d/phaser-extension";
import Bootloader from "./bootloader";
import Outro from "./outro";
import GameOver from "./game_over";
import Splash from "./splash";
import Story from "./story";
import Game from "./game";

const config = {
  type: Phaser.WEBGL,
```

```
      transparent: true,
      scale: {
        mode: Phaser.Scale.FIT,
        autoCenter: Phaser.Scale.CENTER_BOTH,
        width: 1280,
        height: 720,
      },
      scene: [Bootloader, Story, Splash, Game, Outro, GameOver],
      ...Canvas(),
};
```

We need this specific way to load the game because we are using the 3D extension.

```
window.addEventListener("load", () => {
  enable3d(() => new Phaser.Game(config)).withPhysics("./assets/ammo");
});
```

Also, notice that the last command differs from the previous ones we were using in simple 2D games with arcade physics or matter physics.

Bootloader

We can alternate ordinary 2D scenes so we can use our bootloader to load assets in different methods. Pay attention to the new type of assets: videos!

```
import { Scene3D } from "@enable3d/phaser-extension";

export default class Bootloader extends Scene3D {
  constructor() {
    super({ key: "bootloader" });
  }
```

We use the `preload` method to call the methods to load all our assets.

```
  preload() {
    this.createBars();
    this.setLoadEvents();
    this.loadFonts();
    this.loadImages();
    this.loadAudios();
    this.loadVideos();
    this.setRegistry();
  }
```

This is a method to set the events that will be triggered when the loading is progressing and when it is complete.

```
setLoadEvents() {
  this.load.on(
    "progress",
    function (value) {
      this.progressBar.clear();
      this.progressBar.fillStyle(0x03a062, 1);
      this.progressBar.fillRect(
        this.cameras.main.width / 4,
        this.cameras.main.height / 2 - 16,
        (this.cameras.main.width / 2) * value,
        16
      );
    },
    this
  );
  this.load.on(
    "complete",
    () => {
      this.scene.start("story");
    },
    this
  );
}
```

This is a method to load the fonts.

```
loadFonts() {
  this.load.bitmapFont(
    "pixelFont",
    "assets/fonts/mario.png",
    "assets/fonts/mario.xml"
  );
  this.load.bitmapFont(
    "computer",
    "assets/fonts/computer.png",
    "assets/fonts/computer.xml"
  );
}
```

We load this logo that looks old to match the style of the splash.

```
loadImages() {
  this.load.image("pello_logo_old", "assets/images/pello_logo_old.png");
}
```

We need to keep track of the deviation -hits- and the number of probes.

```
setRegistry() {
  this.registry.set("deviation", "0");
  this.registry.set("probes", "20");
}
```

8. 3D: Fate — Bootloader

We load the sounds and the music.

```
loadAudios() {
  Array(4)
    .fill(0)
    .forEach((e, i) => {
      this.load.audio(`thunder${i}`, `./assets/sounds/thunder${i}.mp3`);
    });
  Array(2)
    .fill(0)
    .forEach((e, i) => {
      this.load.audio(`passby${i}`, `./assets/sounds/passby${i}.mp3`);
    });
  Array(4)
    .fill(0)
    .forEach((_, i) => {
      this.load.audio(`hit${i + 1}`, `assets/sounds/hit${i + 1}.mp3`);
    });
  this.load.image("logo", "assets/images/logo.png");
  this.load.audio("hymn", "assets/sounds/hymn.mp3");
  this.load.audio("music", "assets/sounds/music.mp3");
  this.load.audio("type", "assets/sounds/type.mp3");
  this.load.audio("shot", "assets/sounds/shot.mp3");
  this.load.audio("voice_start", "assets/sounds/voice_start.mp3");
  this.load.audio("voice_drop", "assets/sounds/voice_drop.mp3");
  this.load.audio("voice_hit", "assets/sounds/voice_hit.mp3");
}
```

In this game, we are using videos! They will be played in the presentation scene that comes before the splash.

```
loadVideos() {
  Array(4)
    .fill(0)
    .forEach((e, i) => {
      this.load.video(
        `video    `,
        `./assets/videos/video${i}.mp4`,
        "loadeddata",
        false,
        true
      );
    });
}
```

As you may already now, this is a method to create the loading bars.

```
createBars() {
  this.loadBar = this.add.graphics();
  this.loadBar.fillStyle(0x06e18a, 1);
  this.loadBar.fillRect(
```

```
      this.cameras.main.width / 4 - 2,
      this.cameras.main.height / 2 - 18,
      this.cameras.main.width / 2 + 4,
      20
    );
    this.progressBar = this.add.graphics();
  }
}
```

In this particular case, after the bootloader, we will show a story scene.

Story

This is a scene that we show before the splash screen. It starts with some text explaining an enigma and then it changes to a video with credits. Pretty much as we would see in any movie. The videos change as we show more information about the game.

```
import { Scene3D } from "@enable3d/phaser-extension";
import Utils from "./utils";

export default class Story extends Scene3D {
  constructor() {
    super({ key: "story" });
  }
```

This creates the scene that shows the story, which consists of a series of texts and videos. It can be skipped by pressing the space bar.

```
  create() {
    this.game.sound.stopAll();
    this.width = this.sys.game.config.width;
    this.height = this.sys.game.config.height;
    this.center_width = this.width / 2;
    this.center_height = this.height / 2;
    this.utils = new Utils(this);
    this.loadAudios();
    this.showIntro();
    this.cameras.main.setBackgroundColor(0x000000);
    this.input.keyboard.on("keydown-SPACE", () => this.startGame(), this);
  }
```

If the player presses the space bar, we start the game by cutting the typing and the music.

```
  startGame() {
```

```
    if (this.utils.typeAudio) this.utils.typeAudio.stop();
    if (this.theme) this.theme.stop();
    this.scene.start("splash");
}
```

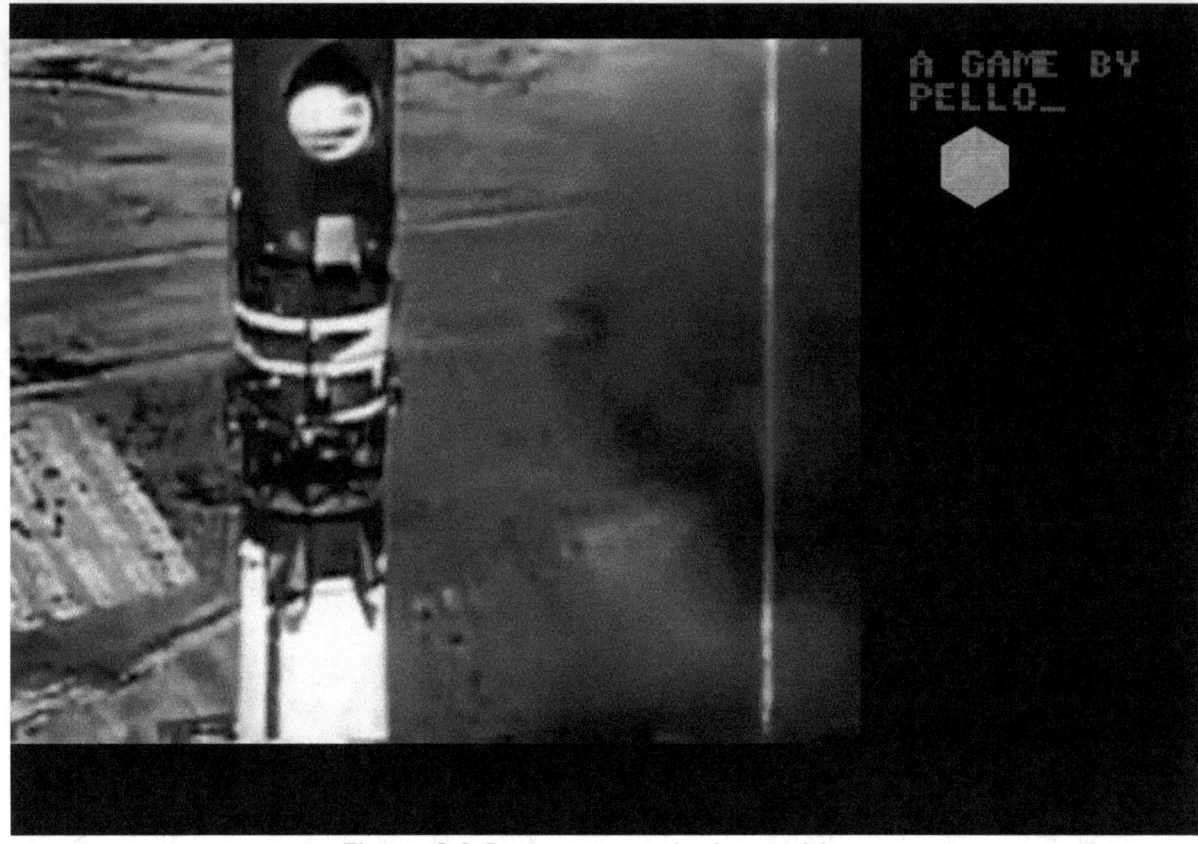

Figure 8.2 Story screen playing a video.

With this method, we load the music that will be played during the story. The next method loads audio files (just the type) and then we have a method to play them.

```
playMusic(theme = "hymn") {
    this.theme = this.sound.add(theme);
    this.theme.stop();
    this.theme.play({
        mute: false,
        volume: 0.7,
        rate: 1,
        detune: 0,
        seek: 0,
        loop: true,
        delay: 0,
    });
}

loadAudios() {
```

```
    this.audios = {
      type: this.sound.add("type"),
    };
  }

  playAudio(key) {
    this.audios[key].play();
  }
```

Figure 8.3 The intro text on screen.

This is a text intro that is shown before the videos. It is typed and then removed.

```
showIntro() {
  let text1, text2;
  text1 = this.utils.typeText(
    " IN 1968 YURI GAGARIN DIED\nDURING A ROUTINE FLIGHT",
    "computer",
    this.center_width,
    this.center_height
  );
  this.time.delayedCall(
    5500,
    () => {
      text2 = this.utils.typeText(
        " OR SO THEY MADE US BELIEVE...",
        "computer",
        this.center_width,
        this.center_height + 100
      );
    },
    null,
    this
  );

  this.time.delayedCall(7000, () => this.playMusic(), null, this);
  this.time.delayedCall(
    10000,
    () => {
      this.utils.removeTyped([text1, text2]);
      this.aGameBy();
    },
```

```
      null,
      this
    );
}
```

This function generates the first part of the video. The programmer logo, some text and the first video.

```
aGameBy() {
  let text2;
  let text1 = this.utils.typeText(" A GAME BY\nPELLO", "computer", 1250, 10);
  let pelloLogo = this.add
    .image(990, 120, "pello_logo_old")
    .setScale(0.2)
    .setOrigin(0.5);
  let video = this.add.video(400, 300, "video0");

  this.time.delayedCall(
    5000,
    () => {
      this.utils.removeTyped([text1]);
      pelloLogo.destroy();
      text2 = this.utils.typeText(
        " MINIJAM #96\nFATE",
        "computer",
        1250,
        400
      );
    },
    null,
    this
  );

  this.time.delayedCall(9000, () => {
    this.utils.removeTyped([text2]);
    video.stop();
    video.destroy();
    this.tools();
  });

  video.play(true);
}
```

This is the second part of the video. It shows the tools used to create the game.

```
tools() {
  let text2;
  let text1 = this.utils.typeText(
    " TOOLS: PHASER AND ENABLE3D",
    "computer",
    550,
```

8. 3D: Fate

```js
      10
    );
    let video = this.add.video(this.center_width, 500, "video1").setOrigin(0.5);

    this.time.delayedCall(
      5000,
      () => {
        this.utils.removeTyped([text1]);
        text2 = this.utils.typeText(" MY FIRST 3D GAME!", "computer", 550, 50);
      },
      null,
      this
    );

    this.time.delayedCall(9000, () => {
      this.utils.removeTyped([text2]);
      video.stop();
      video.destroy();
      this.otherTools();
    });

    video.play(true);
  }
```

This is the third part of the video. It shows other tools used to create the game and the amount of coffee consumed.

```js
  otherTools() {
    let text2;
    let text1 = this.utils.typeText(
      " VSCODE, GULP, BLENDER, FFMPEG,...",
      "computer",
      550,
      500
    );
    let video = this.add.video(this.center_width, 100, "video2").setOrigin(0.5);

    this.time.delayedCall(
      5000,
      () => {
        this.utils.removeTyped([text1]);
        text2 = this.utils.typeText(
          " GAZILLIONS OF COFFEE WERE CONSUMED",
          "computer",
          550,
          600
        );
      },
      null,
      this
    );
```

8. 3D: Fate

```
  this.time.delayedCall(10000, () => {
    this.utils.removeTyped([text2]);
    video.stop();
    video.destroy();
    this.lastVideo();
  });

  video.play(true);
}
```

Finally, another video and more credits for the music.

```
lastVideo() {
  let text2;
  let text1 = this.utils.typeText(
    " MUSIC: SACRED WAR, BY THE RED ARMY CHOIR",
    "computer",
    400,
    50
  );
  let video = this.add.video(this.center_width, 400, "video3").setOrigin(0.5);

  this.time.delayedCall(
    5000,
    () => {
      this.utils.removeTyped([text1]);
      text2 = this.utils.typeText(
        " EVOLUTION, BY BENSOUND",
        "computer",
        550,
        100
      );
    },
    null,
    this
  );

  this.time.delayedCall(10000, () => {
    this.utils.removeTyped([text2]);
    video.stop();
    video.destroy();
    this.explanation();
  });

  video.play(true);
}
```

This is a long text that explains the story of the game. Characters are typed one by one.

```
explanation() {
```

```
    this.tweens.add({
      targets: this.theme,
      volume: { from: 1, to: 0 },
      duration: 16000,
    });
    const text =
      " GAGARIN WAS SENT ON A SECRET MISSION\nBEYOND THE OORT CLOUD, " +
      "PROPELLED BY\nNUCLEAR DETONATIONS.\n\nHE HAS NOW PASSED THE FRONTIER OF\nOUR SOLAR SYSTEM\n" +
      "HIS MISSION:\nTO SET 20 PROBES AND RECOLLECT DATA\nFROM THE DEADLIEST STELLAR OBJECT:\n" +
      "A NEUTRINO STAR!\n\nHE HAS TO AVOID INCOMING DEBRIS\nAND GET AS CLOSE AS POSSIBLE TO THE STAR.\n" +
      "THAT WILL MEAN CERTAIN DEATH, BUT ALSO\nA MASSIVE ACHIEVEMENT " +
      "FOR SOVIET SCIENTISTS!\n\n" +
      "THE FATAL FATE OF GAGARIN IS NOW TIED\nTO THE GLORIOUS FATE " +
      "OF MOTHER RUSSIA...\n\n\nSPACE TO CONTINUE";
    let text1 = this.utils.typeText(text, "computer", 450, 50);
  }
}
```

Apart from doing a movie-like intro, this simple trick is great for supporting the backstory of our hero Yuri Gagarin.

Bullet Hell

This is a utility class used to generate different bullet waves. This particular game uses very simple patterns but it could be extended at will.

```
export default class BulletHell {
  constructor() {
    this._functions = [
      this.flat,
      this.tlaf,
      this.horizontal,
      this.multiWave,
      this.cos,
      this.tan,
      this.ripple,
    ];
  }

  get functions() {
    return this._functions;
  }
```

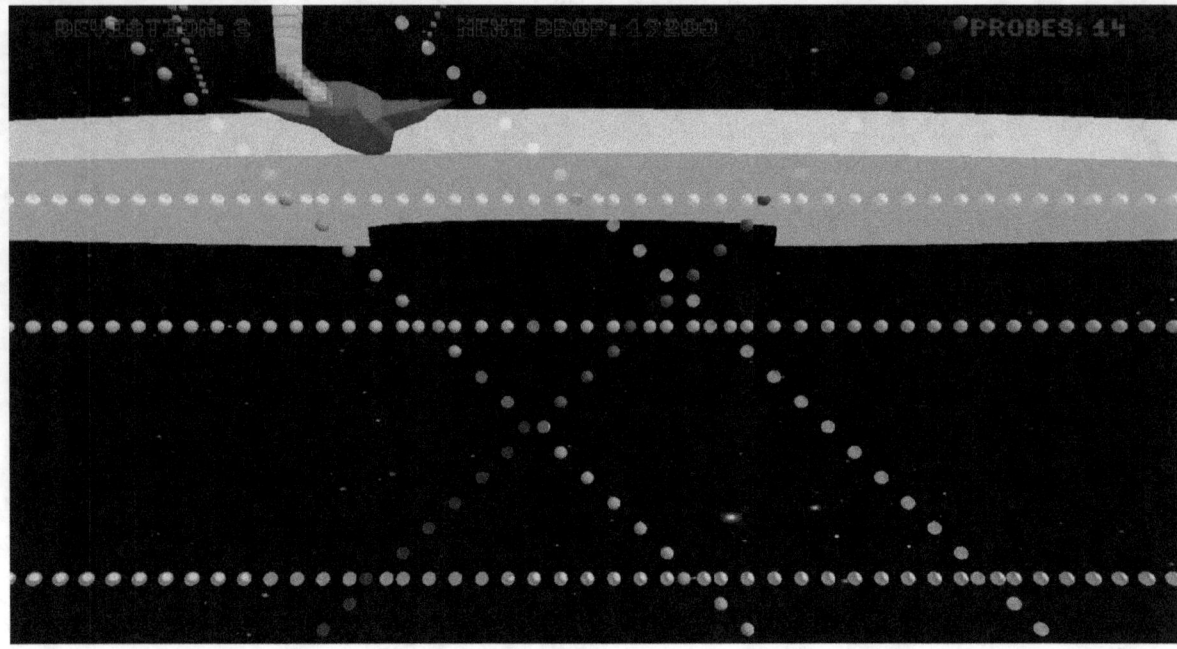

Figure 8.4 Patterns will get increasingly worse.

These are different functions that we will use to generate the path of the bullets. They're quite simple, but you can create your own functions to generate more complex paths. We will use the x, y, z and `time` parameters to generate different patterns.

```
sin(x, time) {
  return Math.sin(x);
}

flat(x, y, z) {
  return x + z;
}

tlaf(x, y, z) {
  return -x - z;
}

horizontal(x, y, z) {
  return z;
}

wave(x, time) {
  return Math.sin(Math.PI * (x + time));
}

multiWave(x, time) {
  return Math.sin(Math.PI * (x + time));
}

cos(x, time, z) {
```

```
    return Math.cos(x) * Phaser.Math.Between(0.1, 0.9);
  }

  tan(x, time, z) {
    return Math.tan(x);
  }

  ripple(x, time, z) {
    return Math.sin(time * x * (Math.PI / 360));
  }
}
```

As you can imagine, our best friend for bullet hells is math. Did you hate trigonometry at school? No, you shouldn't have! Maths and physics are your best friends here!

Lightning

This class generates a lightning effect. It's a 2D effect, where we just alternate black and white rectangles in front of the player with a thundering noise. Yeah, in the vacuum there are no sounds but imagine a completely silent game.

```
export default class Lightning {
  constructor(scene) {
    this.scene = scene;
  }
```

In this method, we create a timeline to show the lightning effect. We use the lightningEffect rectangle to show the lightning and the lightsOut rectangle to darken the screen.

```
  lightning() {
    if (Phaser.Math.Between(1, 11) < 10) return;
    const timeline = this.scene.tweens.createTimeline();
    timeline.add({
      targets: this.scene.lightningEffect,
      alpha: { from: 0, to: 1 },
      duration: 100,
      repeat: 3,
    });
    if (this.scene.lights.out) {
      timeline.add({
        targets: this.scene.lightsOut,
        alpha: { from: 1, to: 0.5 },
        duration: 500,
      });
    }
```

```
    timeline.add({
      targets: this.scene.lightningEffect,
      alpha: { from: 1, to: 0 },
      duration: 2000,
    });
    if (this.scene.lights.out) {
      timeline.add({
        targets: this.scene.lightsOut,
        alpha: { from: 0.5, to: 1 },
        duration: 500,
      });
    }

    timeline.play();
    this.scene.playRandom("thunder" + Phaser.Math.Between(0, 3));
  }
}
```

Is there lightning when you get close to a neutrino star? Well, only Gagarin knows but it's a simple but nice effect that we could add that makes us believe that we are in a really dangerous environment.

Utils

Figure 8.5 Utils for the typing effect.

We reuse this typing effect again for transition scenes.

```
export default class Utils {
  constructor(scene) {
    this.scene = scene;
  }

  typeText(text, font, x, y = 150, tint = 0x06e18a, size = 40) {
    let characters = [];
    let jump = 0;
    let line = 0;
    let last = 0;
```

```
    text.split("").forEach((character, i) => {
      if (character === "\n") {
        jump++;
        line = 0;
      }
      last = i;
      characters.push(
        this.scene.add
          .bitmapText(
            x - 350 + line++ * 25,
            y + (jump * size) / 1.3,
            font,
            character,
            size
          )
          .setTint(tint)
          .setAlpha(0)
      );
    });
    const ending = this.scene.add
      .rectangle(x - 335 + line * 25, y + 25 + (jump * size) / 1.3, 25, 5, tint)
      .setOrigin(0.5)
      .setAlpha(0);
    const timeline = this.scene.tweens.createTimeline();
    this.typeAudio = this.scene.sound.add("type");

    characters.forEach((character, i) => {
      timeline.add({
        targets: character,
        alpha: { from: 0, to: 0.5 },
        duration: 100,
      });
    });
    timeline.add({
      targets: ending,
      alpha: { from: 0, to: 0.8 },
      duration: 100,
      repeat: 5,
      yoyo: true,
      onStart: () => {
        this.typeAudio.stop();
      },
    });
    this.typeAudio.play({
      mute: false,
      volume: 1,
      rate: 1,
      detune: 0,
      seek: 0,
      loop: true,
      delay: 0,
    });
    timeline.play();
```

```
    characters.push(ending);
    return characters;
  }
```

This simple method will destroy all the characters of the text.

```
  removeTyped(texts) {
    texts.flat().forEach((char) => char.destroy());
  }
}
```

Splash

Figure 8.6 Splash screen after the intro.

The splash screen is really simple. It starts with the music of the game that will be played in a loop while we play. It also shows the instructions with the typing effect.

```
import { Scene3D } from "@enable3d/phaser-extension";
```

8. 3D: Fate

```js
import Utils from "./utils";

export default class Splash extends Scene3D {
  constructor() {
    super({ key: "splash" });
  }
```

This will create the elements of the splash screen. This screen is a normal scene that is shown before the game starts. It shows the logo and the basic instructions.

```js
  create() {
    this.width = this.sys.game.config.width;
    this.height = this.sys.game.config.height;
    this.center_width = this.width / 2;
    this.center_height = this.height / 2;
    this.utils = new Utils(this);
    this.showLogo();
    this.showInstructions();
    this.input.keyboard.on("keydown-SPACE", () => this.loadNext(), this);
    this.playMusic();
  }
```

We use this method to play the music. In this game, the music theme starts in the splash screen and it is played during the game.

```js
  playMusic(theme = "music") {
    this.theme = this.sound.add(theme);
    this.theme.stop();
    this.theme.play({
      mute: false,
      volume: 0.5,
      rate: 1,
      detune: 0,
      seek: 0,
      loop: true,
      delay: 0,
    });
  }
```

This is just the logo of the game, which is just a text.

```js
  showLogo() {
    this.logo = this.add
      .image(this.center_width, 170, "logo")
      .setOrigin(0.5)
      .setScale(0.7)
      .setAlpha(0);
    this.tweens.add({
      targets: this.logo,
      duration: 3000,
      alpha: { from: 0, to: 1 },
```

```
    });
}
```

These are the instructions for the game. We use again the Utils class to show the text letter by letter.

```
showInstructions() {
  let text1, text2;
  text1 = this.utils.typeText(
    "ARROWS + W + S\nMOUSE FOR POV\n",
    "computer",
    this.center_width + 190,
    this.center_height
  );
  this.time.delayedCall(
    2000,
    () => {
      text2 = this.utils.typeText(
        " PRESS SPACE",
        "computer",
        this.center_width + 190,
        this.center_height + 100
      );
    },
    null,
    this
  );

  this.time.delayedCall(
    4000,
    () => {
      let text3 = this.utils.typeText(
        " A GAME BY PELLO",
        "computer",
        this.center_width + 140,
        this.center_height + 200
      );
      let pelloLogo = this.add
        .image(this.center_width, this.center_height + 300, "pello_logo_old")
        .setScale(0.2)
        .setOrigin(0.5);
    },
    null,
    this
  );
}
```

This is the method that will start the game.

```
loadNext() {
  if (this.utils.typeAudio) this.utils.typeAudio.stop();
```

```
    this.scene.start("game");
  }
}
```

From the splash scene, we jump directly to the game!

Game

The game! It is defined as a 3D scene, but we can also use everything we learned about regular 2D scenes when it comes to text, sounds, and simple images. We will need to set up the 3D at the beginning and everything related to 3D will be preceded with the word `third`.

Then we will generate 3D elements in the scene: the neutrino star, the ship and the incoming bullet waves. Obviously, the collision detection will also differ from previous games.

```
import { Scene3D, ExtendedObject3D, THREE } from "@enable3d/phaser-extension";
import { ThreeGraphics } from "@enable3d/three-graphics";
import { Euler } from "three";
import BulletHell from "./bullet_hell";
import Lightning from "./lightning";

export default class Game extends Scene3D {
  constructor() {
    super({ key: "game" });
    this.player = null;
    this.score = 0;
    this.scoreText = null;
  }
```

This is where we set the scene to become a 3D scene. We also load other assets that we will use in the game.

```
  init(data) {
    this.accessThirdDimension({ gravity: { x: 0, y: 0, z: 0 } });
    this.third.load.preload("stars", "assets/images/stars.png");
    this.third.load.preload("nebulaset", "assets/images/nebulaset.png");
  }
```

This will be called when the scene starts. We create the star, the player, the bullets, the score and the controls. Everything related to 3D is accessed through `this.third`.

```
  create() {
```

8. 3D: Fate

```
    this.bulletHell = new BulletHell();
    this.x = -500;

    // creates a nice scene : remove -orbitControls
    this.third.warpSpeed("-ground", "-grid", "-sky", "-light");
    this.setLights();
    this.createBottom();
    this.third.camera.position.set(0, 0, 20);
    this.third.camera.lookAt(0, 0, 0);
    this.third.load
      .texture("nebulaset")
      .then((sky) => (this.third.scene.background = sky));
    this.particles = [];
    this.waves = [];
    this.remaining = 20000;
    this.addWaveEvent = this.time.addEvent({
      delay: 3000,
      callback: this.addWave,
      callbackScope: this,
      loop: true,
    });
    this.addClockEvent = this.time.addEvent({
      delay: 50,
      callback: this.updateClock,
      callbackScope: this,
      loop: true,
    });
    this.setCenters();
    //enable physics debugging
    //this.third.physics.debug.enable()
    this.setLightning();
    this.setNeutrinoStar();

    this.loadAudios();

    this.prepareShip();

    this.setScores();
    this.cursor = this.input.keyboard.createCursorKeys();
    this.W = this.input.keyboard.addKey(Phaser.Input.Keyboard.KeyCodes.W);
    this.S = this.input.keyboard.addKey(Phaser.Input.Keyboard.KeyCodes.S);
    this.playAudio("voice_start");
  }
```

This will set up the lightning effect with a rectangle that will be shown when the lightning is triggered.

```
setLightning() {
  this.lightsOut = this.add
    .rectangle(0, 40, this.width, this.height + 100, 0x0)
    .setOrigin(0);
  this.lightsOut.setAlpha(0);
```

8. 3D: Fate

```
    this.lightningEffect = this.add
      .rectangle(0, 40, this.width, this.height + 100, 0xffffff)
      .setOrigin(0);
    this.lightningEffect.setAlpha(0);
    this.lightning = new Lightning(this);
  }
```

This adds the light sources to the scene. This is 3D so we have infinite possibilities to set light sources and types wherever we want. We are using a spotlight and a directional light.

```
  setLights() {
    this.spot = this.third.lights.spotLight({
      color: "blue",
      angle: Math.PI / 8,
    });

    this.directional = this.third.lights.directionalLight({ intensity: 0.5 });
    this.directional.position.set(5, 5, 5);

    this.third.lights.hemisphereLight({ intensity: 0.7 });

    const d = 4;
    this.directional.shadow.camera.top = d;
    this.directional.shadow.camera.bottom = -d;
    this.directional.shadow.camera.left = -d;
    this.directional.shadow.camera.right = d;
  }
```

The neutrino star is the main element of the game. It is a sphere that is in the center of the scene. It has a front and a back part. The back part is the one that is used to detect collisions. It tries to imitate a black hole.

```
  setNeutrinoStar() {
    this.torus = this.addRing(0);
    this.proximity = 0;
    this.star = this.third.add.sphere(
      { name: "neutrinoStarBack", radius: 22, x: 0, y: 14.5, z: -150 },
      { lambert: { color: 0xffffe0, transparent: true, opacity: 0.5 } }
    );
    this.third.physics.add.existing(this.star);
    this.star.body.setCollisionFlags(2);
    this.starFront = this.third.add.sphere(
      { name: "neutrinoStarBack", radius: 17, x: 0, y: 12, z: -120 },
      { lambert: { color: "black", transparent: false } }
    );
    this.third.physics.add.existing(this.starFront);
    this.starFront.body.setCollisionFlags(2);
  }
```

8. 3D: Fate

This adds the rings that are around the neutrino star. They are just cylinders with a texture.

```
addRings() {
  this.rings = Array(20)
    .fill(0)
    .map((ring, i) => {
      this.addRing(i);
    });
}

addRing(i) {
  let torus = this.third.add.cylinder(
    {
      x: 0,
      y: 12,
      z: -120,
      height: 1,
      radiusSegments: 200,
      radiusBottom: 75 * (i + 1),
      radiusTop: 75 * (i + 1),
    },
    { lambert: { color: 0xffffe0, transparent: true, opacity: 0.8 } }
  );

  torus.rotation.set(0.1, 0, 0);
  this.third.physics.add.existing(torus, { shape: "hacd" });
  torus.body.setCollisionFlags(6);

  return torus;
}
```

We use this helper method to set the "center" of the screen.

```
setCenters() {
  this.width = this.cameras.main.width;
  this.height = this.cameras.main.height;
  this.center_width = this.width / 2;
  this.center_height = this.height / 2;
}
```

We use this method to update the deviation. The deviation is the number of times that the player has been hit by a particle.

```
updateClock() {
  if (this.remaining < 0) {
    this.remaining = 20000;
    this.releaseProbe();
  } else {
    this.nextDropText.setText("NEXT DROP: " + this.remaining);
  }
```

```
      this.remaining -= 50;
  }
```

This creates a background which is a texture that is repeated. It is a simple way to create a background.

```
createBottom() {
  this.third.load.texture("stars").then((grass) => {
    grass.wrapS = grass.wrapT = 1000; // RepeatWrapping
    grass.offset.set(0, 0);
    grass.repeat.set(2, 2);

    // BUG: To add shadows to your ground, set transparent = true
    this.ground = this.third.physics.add.ground(
      { width: 2000, height: 2000, y: -50 },
      { phong: { map: grass, transparent: true } }
    );
  });
}
```

The probes are like the elements we use to measure the progress of the ship. We use a registry variable to keep track of the number of probes. When the ship reaches the star, it should release the last probe and the game will end with a victory!

```
releaseProbe() {
  this.updateProbes(-1);
  this.tweens.add({
    targets: this.probesText,
    duration: 400,
    alpha: { from: 0.5, to: 1 },
    repeat: 5,
  });
}
```

DEVIATION: 2   **NEXT DROP: 9900**   **PROBES: 13**

Figure 8.7 The scoreboard on top.

The scores are just some text that we show on the screen. We use the registry to keep track of the deviation and the probes.

```
setScores() {
  this.deviationText = this.add
    .bitmapText(
      175,
      30,
      "computer",
      "DEVIATION: " + this.registry.get("deviation"),
      30
    )
```

8. 3D: Fate Game

```
      .setTint(0x03a062)
      .setOrigin(0.5);
    this.nextDropText = this.add
      .bitmapText(
        this.center_width,
        30,
        "computer",
        "NEXT DROP: " + this.remaining,
        30
      )
      .setTint(0x03a062)
      .setOrigin(0.5);
    this.probesText = this.add
      .bitmapText(
        this.width - 150,
        30,
        "computer",
        "PROBES: " + this.registry.get("probes"),
        30
      )
      .setTint(0x03a062)
      .setOrigin(0.5);
}
```

Before we actually add the ship object to the scene, we need to load it. We use the GLTF loader to load the ship model.

```
prepareShip() {
  this.third.load.gltf("./assets/objects/ship.glb").then((gltf) => {
    this.object = new ExtendedObject3D();
    this.object.add(gltf.scene);

    const shapes = [
      "box",
      "compound",
      "hull",
      "hacd",
      "convexMesh",
      "concaveMesh",
    ];

    const material = this.third.add.material({
      standard: { color: 0xcc0000, transparent: false, opacity: 1 },
    });

    this.object.traverse((child) => {
      if (child.isMesh && child.material.isMaterial) {
        child.material = material;
      }
    });
    this.ship = this.createShip("convexMesh", 0, this.object);
    this.setShipColliderWithParticles();
```

```
  });
}
```

This is the function that adds the ship object to the scene.

```
createShip(shape, i, object3d) {
  this.left = false;
  const object = new ExtendedObject3D();

  object.add(object3d.clone());
  object.position.set(i, -2, 10);
  object.rotation.set(0, Math.PI, 0);

  let options = { addChildren: false, shape };

  this.third.add.existing(object);
  this.third.physics.add.existing(object, options);
  object.body.needUpdate = true;
  object.body.setLinearFactor(0, 0, 0);
  object.body.setAngularFactor(1, 1, 0);
  object.body.setFriction(20, 20, 20);
  object.body.setCollisionFlags(2); // Dynamic body: 0, kinematic: 2

  return object;
}
```

This will detect the collision between the ship and the particles. If the ship collides with a particle it will take hits.

```
setShipColliderWithParticles() {
  this.ship.body.on.collision((otherObject, event) => {
    if (/particle/.test(otherObject.name)) {
      this.updateDeviation(1);
      this.cameras.main.shake(500);
      this.playAudio(`hit${Phaser.Math.Between(1  4)}`);
      this.third.destroy(this.ship);
      this.ship = this.createShip("convexMesh", 0, this.object);
      this.setShipColliderWithParticles();
    }
  });
}
```

Here we load the audio files used in the game. Same as usual, we will use `playAudio` and `playRandom` to play them.

```
loadAudios() {
  this.audios = {
    thunder0: this.sound.add("thunder0"),
    thunder1: this.sound.add("thunder1"),
    thunder2: this.sound.add("thunder2"),
    thunder3: this.sound.add("thunder3"),
```

8. 3D: Fate

```
      passby0: this.sound.add("passby0"),
      passby1: this.sound.add("passby1"),
      shot: this.sound.add("shot"),
      hit1: this.sound.add("hit1"),
      hit2: this.sound.add("hit2"),
      hit3: this.sound.add("hit3"),
      hit4: this.sound.add("hit4"),
      voice_start: this.sound.add("voice_start"),
      voice_drop: this.sound.add("voice_drop"),
      voice_hit: this.sound.add("voice_hit"),
    };
  }

  playAudio(key) {
    this.audios[key].play();
  }

  playRandom(key) {
    this.audios[key].play({
      rate: Phaser.Math.Between(1, 1.5),
      detune: Phaser.Math.Between(-1000, 1000),
      delay: 0,
    });
  }
```

This is the game loop and it is quite simple. It will move the ship in the direction of the pressed keys. It will also move the neutrino star and the rings, because guess what... the ship is not really moving forward: we move the star towards the ship.

```
  update(time, delta) {
    this.currentTime = time;

    if (this.ship && this.ship.body) {
      let { x, y, z } = this.ship.position;
      if (this.cursor.up.isDown && this.ship.position.y < 6 / (z / 5)) {
        y = y + 0.1;
        this.createWingTrails();
      } else if (
        this.cursor.down.isDown &&
        this.ship.position.y > -7 / (z / 5)
      ) {
        y = y - 0.1;
        this.createWingTrails();
      }

      if (this.cursor.left.isDown && this.ship.position.x > -7 / (z / 6)) {
        x = x - 0.1;
        this.ship.rotation.set(0, Math.PI, -0.2);
        this.createWingTrails(true);
      } else if (
        this.cursor.right.isDown &&
```

8. 3D: Fate

```
        this.ship.position.x < 7 / (z / 6)
      ) {
        x = x + 0.1;
        this.ship.rotation.set(0, Math.PI, 0.2);
        this.createWingTrails(false);
      }

      if (!this.cursor.right.isDown && !this.cursor.left.isDown) {
        this.ship.rotation.set(0, Math.PI, 0);
      }

      if (this.W.isDown && this.ship.position.z > 7) {
        this.ship.position.set(x, y, z - 0.1);
        z = z - 0.1;
      } else if (this.S.isDown && this.ship.position.z < 15) {
        this.ship.position.set(x, y, z + 0.1);
        z = z + 0.1;
      }

      this.ship.position.set(x, y, z);
      this.ship.body.needUpdate = true;
      this.createTrail();
    }

    if (this.ground) {
      this.ground.setRotationFromEuler(new Euler(0, 0, 1));
    }

    if (this.star) {
      this.star.material.opacity = 0.5 / Math.sin(time * 3);
      let offset = Math.sin(time) / 10;
      this.starFront.position.set(
        this.starFront.position.x + offset,
        this.starFront.position.y + offset,
        this.starFront.position.z + offset + this.proximity
      );
      this.starFront.rotation.set(0, time, 0);

      this.starFront.body.needUpdate = true;

      this.star.position.set(
        this.star.position.x + offset,
        this.star.position.y + offset,
        this.star.position.z + offset + this.proximity
      );

      this.star.body.needUpdate = true;
      this.proximity += 0.000001;

      this.torus.rotation.set(0.1, delta, 0);
      this.torus.position.set(
        this.torus.position.x,
        this.torus.position.y,
```

```
      this.star.position.z + this.proximity
    );
    this.torus.body.needUpdate = true;
  }
}
```

Figure 8.8 Main trail and secondary trails from the wings.

We will create a trail as we did in other games: generating boxes in the ship position that will be destroyed after a while.

```
createTrail() {
  const color = Phaser.Math.Between(-1, 1) > 0 ? 0xadd8e6 : 0xffffff;
  const trail = this.third.add.box(
    {
      x: this.ship.position.x,
      y: this.ship.position.y + 0.3,
      z: this.ship.position.z + 1,
      width: 0.2,
      height: 0.2,
      depth: 0.2,
    },
    { lambert: { color, transparent: true, opacity: 0.4 } }
  );
  this.third.physics.add.existing(trail);
  trail.body.setVelocityZ(15);
  this.tweens.add({
    targets: trail,
    duration: 600,
    scale: { from: 1, to: 0 },
    repeat: 1,
    onComplete: () => {
      this.destroyParticle(trail);
    },
  });
}
```

This adds some trails to the ship wings. The trails are just boxes that will be destroyed after a while.

```
createWingTrails(toTheLeft = null) {
  const color = Phaser.Math.Between(-1, 1) > 0 ? 0xadd8e6 : 0xffffff;
  const [m1, m2] =
    toTheLeft === null ? [0, 0] : toTheLeft ? [-0.3, 0.3] : [0.3, -0.3];

  const trail1 = this.third.add.box(
    {
      x: this.ship.position.x + 1.3,
      y: this.ship.position.y + 0.5 + m2,
      z: this.ship.position.z + 0.5,
      width: 0.05,
      height: 0.05,
      depth: 0.05,
    },
    { lambert: { color, transparent: true, opacity: 0.4 } }
  );
  const trail2 = this.third.add.box(
    {
      x: this.ship.position.x - 1.3,
      y: this.ship.position.y + 0.5 + m1,
      z: this.ship.position.z + 0.5,
      width: 0.05,
      height: 0.05,
      depth: 0.05,
    },
    { lambert: { color, transparent: true, opacity: 0.4 } }
  );

  this.third.physics.add.existing(trail1);
  this.third.physics.add.existing(trail2);
  trail1.body.setVelocityZ(15);
  trail2.body.setVelocityZ(15);
  this.tweens.add({
    targets: [trail1, trail2],
    duration: 600,
    scale: { from: 1, to: 0 },
    repeat: 1,
    onComplete: () => {
      this.destroyParticle(trail1);
      this.destroyParticle(trail2);
    },
  });
}
```

This is the function that creates a wave to the scene. It will create a wave of particles that will move from the back to the front of the screen. At the end, it will remove the wave and play a sound.

8. 3D: Fate

```
addWave(start = -25, zed = false) {
  this.lightning.lightning();
  const { f1, f2, c } = this.applyFunctionsInterval();

  for (let j = 0; j < c; j++) {
    let waveFunction = this.bulletHell.functions[Phaser.Math.Between(f1, f2)];
    let randomHeight = Phaser.Math.Between(-10, 10);
    let color = Phaser.Math.Between(0x111111, 0xffffff);
    let wave = Array(50)
      .fill(0)
      .map((particle, i) => {
        let x = start + i;
        let y = waveFunction(x, 16 * i, randomHeight);

        let box = this.third.add.sphere(
          {
            name: "particle" + Math.random(),
            radius: 0.25,
            x,
            y,
            z: start - (zed ? x : 0),
          },
          { lambert: { color } }
        );

        this.third.physics.add.existing(box);
        this.particles.push(box);
        box.body.setVelocityZ(15);

        return box;
      });
    this.playAudio("shot");

    this.waves.push(wave);
    this.time.delayedCall(
      4000,
      () => this.playRandom("passby" + Phaser.Math.Between(0, 1)),
      null,
      this
    );
    this.time.delayedCall(6000, () => this.removeWave(), null, this);
  }
}
```

Depending on the number of probes, we will apply a different function to the wave. This is to make the game more difficult as the player progresses.

```
applyFunctionsInterval() {
  return {
    20: { f1: 0, f2: 3, c: 3 },
    19: { f1: 0, f2: 4, c: 3 },
    18: { f1: 0, f2: 3, c: 4 },
```

```
    17: { f1: 0, f2: 3, c: 5 },
    16: { f1: 0, f2: 3, c: 6 },
    15: { f1: 0, f2: 3, c: 6 },
    14: { f1: 0, f2: 3, c: 6 },
    13: { f1: 0, f2: 3, c: 6 },
    12: { f1: 0, f2: 4, c: 4 },
    11: { f1: 0, f2: 4, c: 4 },
    10: { f1: 0, f2: 4, c: 4 },
    9: { f1: 0, f2: 4, c: 5 },
    8: { f1: 0, f2: 4, c: 5 },
    7: { f1: 0, f2: 5, c: 4 },
    6: { f1: 0, f2: 5, c: 5 },
    5: { f1: 0, f2: 5, c: 5 },
    4: { f1: 0, f2: 5, c: 6 },
    3: { f1: 0, f2: 6, c: 5 },
    2: { f1: 0, f2: 6, c: 5 },
    1: { f1: 0, f2: 6, c: 6 },
    0: { f1: 0, f2: 6, c: 6 },
  }[this.registry.get("probes")];
}
```

When a wave passes, we need to remove the particles from the scene and destroy them.

```
removeWave() {
  const wave = this.waves.shift();
  wave.forEach((particle) => this.destroyParticle(particle));
}

destroyParticle(particle) {
  particle.userData.dead = true;
  particle.visible = false;
  this.third.physics.destroy(particle);
  particle = null;
}
```

We use this method to finish the scene and change to another one. Depending on the result, it can be the outro or the game over.

```
finishScene(name = "outro") {
  this.scene.start(name);
}
```

We use this method to update the deviation. The deviation is the number of times that the player has been hit by a particle.

```
updateDeviation(points = 0) {
  const deviation = +this.registry.get("deviation") + points;
  this.registry.set("deviation", deviation);
  this.playAudio("voice_hit");
```

```
    this.deviationText.setText(
      "DEVIATION: " + Number(deviation).toLocaleString()
    );
    if (deviation === 20) {
      this.finishScene("game_over");
    }
  }
}
```

This is the same as the previous one but for the probes. It will also play a sound of a radio transmission.

```
updateProbes(points = 0) {
  const probes = +this.registry.get("probes") + points;
  this.registry.set("probes", probes);
  this.playAudio("voice_drop");
  this.probesText.setText("PROBES: " + Number(probes).toLocaleString());
  if (probes === 0) {
    this.finishScene("outro");
  }
 }
}
```

Apart from the specific 3D elements, it's just a scene and the logic of the game loop remains the same.

GameOver

If the player fails, we'll show this scene with some message.

```
export default class GameOver extends Phaser.Scene {
  constructor() {
    super({ key: "game_over" });
  }
```

This creates the elements that we will show when the player loses the game.

```
create() {
  this.cameras.main.setBackgroundColor(0x000000);
  this.width = this.sys.game.config.width;
  this.height = this.sys.game.config.height;
  this.center_width = this.width / 2;
  this.center_height = this.height / 2;
  this.introLayer = this.add.layer();
  this.splashLayer = this.add.layer();
  this.text = [
    "GAME OVER",
    "You failed to deliver the probes",
```

```
    "you survived but the mission failed!",
    "Go back to the solar system,",
    "The gulag of the dark side of the moon",
    "awaits for reeducation...",
  ];
  this.showHistory();

  this.input.keyboard.on("keydown-SPACE", this.startSplash, this);
  this.input.keyboard.on("keydown-ENTER", this.startSplash, this);
}
```

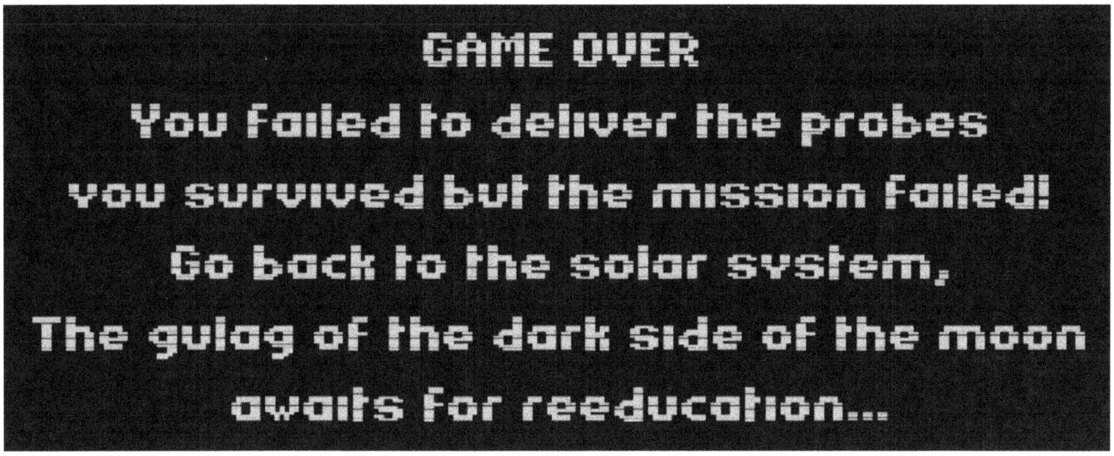

Figure 8.9 Game over screen.

We show the message for the failed mission.

```
showHistory() {
  this.text.forEach((line, i) => {
    this.time.delayedCall(
      (i + 1) * 2000,
      () => this.showLine(line, (i + 1) * 60),
      null,
      this
    );
  });
}

showLine(text, y) {
  let line = this.introLayer.add(
    this.add
      .bitmapText(this.center_width, y, "computer", text, 45)
      .setTint(0x06e18a)
      .setOrigin(0.5)
      .setAlpha(0)
  );
  this.tweens.add({
    targets: line,
    duration: 2000,
    alpha: 1,
```

This is the method that will start the splash scene.

```
startSplash() {
  location.reload();
  this.scene.start("bootstrap");
}
}
```

The text is shown line by line in this case.

Outro

If our dear Gagarin completes the mission we show another message.

```
export default class Outro extends Phaser.Scene {
  constructor() {
    super({ key: "outro" });
  }
```

This outro is shown when the player wins the game. It just shows a few lines of text and then it starts the game again.

```
  create() {
    this.cameras.main.setBackgroundColor(0x000000);
    this.width = this.sys.game.config.width;
    this.height = this.sys.game.config.height;
    this.center_width = this.width / 2;
    this.center_height = this.height / 2;
    this.introLayer = this.add.layer();
    this.splashLayer = this.add.layer();
    this.text = [
      "This feels like falling",
      "and collapsing at the same time...",
      "I'm glad that I succeded",
      "By the way...",
      "I see no god inside here.",
    ];
    this.showHistory();
    this.input.keyboard.on("keydown-SPACE", this.startAgain, this);
    this.input.keyboard.on("keydown-ENTER", this.startAgain, this);
  }

  startAgain() {
    this.scene.start("bootstrap");
  }
```

8. 3D: Fate — Outro

We use this function again to show the text line by line.

```
showHistory() {
  this.text.forEach((line, i) => {
    this.time.delayedCall(
      (i + 1) * 2000,
      () => this.showLine(line, (i + 1) * 60),
      null,
      this
    );
  });
}

showLine(text, y) {
  let line = this.introLayer.add(
    this.add
      .bitmapText(this.center_width, y, "computer", text, 35)
      .setOrigin(0.5)
      .setAlpha(0)
  );
  this.tweens.add({
    targets: line,
    duration: 2000,
    alpha: 1,
  });
}
```

Reference

https://enable3d.io/

https://github.com/enable3d/enable3d-website/blob/master/src/examples/first-phaser-game-3d-version.html

https://catlikecoding.com/unity/tutorials/basics/mathematical-surfaces/

9. Deep dive into Phaser

Let's get into more deeper of the Phaser ocean. If you're curious about how Phaser working behind the scenes, tune in!

What is Phaser?

Phaser is an HTML5 game framework designed specifically for web browsers. It is built using, and relying on, web technologies. And the games it creates are meant to be played in desktop or mobile browsers, or apps capable of running web games, such as Discord, SnapChat, Facebook and more. There are ways to convert browser games to native mobile or desktop apps using 3rd party tools, and many Phaser developers have done this successfully. However, Phasers primary focus is, and always will be, the web.

Phaser is a 2D game framework. This means that both its features and internal design are based entirely around creating lightning fast 2D games. It does not include 3D rendering or 3D physics as built-in features.

Again, there are ways to integrate 3rd party libraries to provide this, but Phaser itself is 2D and our documentation and examples reflect this.

Phaser was developed in JavaScript, because this is the language of the web browser. As such, you will need to code your game using either JavaScript or TypeScript. All of our examples and documentation are provided in JavaScript, but we also provide TypeScript definitions.

Phaser is made available as a JavaScript library. This can be downloaded, linked from a Content Delivery Network (CDN), or installed via any of the standard JavaScript package managers, such as npm. Phaser is not a desktop application. You do not 'install' it and there is no 'Phaser IDE'. It is a JavaScript library that you include in your own web pages, or bundle. You then write your game code in JavaScript and run them together in a web browser.

Phaser has been in active development for over 10 years. There is a small but dedicated full-time team behind it, who are constantly striving to make it the best it can be, while keeping it easy to learn. It is used by developers around the world and has been used to create many thousands of games, from small prototypes to full-scale commercial titles with millions of players. Because of its maturity, Phaser is a stable and reliable framework. It is not a 'fad'. When changes are made, they're for the benefit of the framework as whole, not just to chase a 'trendy' new technology.

To this end it's important to understand when Phaser is not a suitable choice:

- You want to make your game fully in 3D.
- You want to publish your game on a modern console, such as PS5, XBox or Nintendo Switch.
- You don't want to learn JavaScript or deal with JavaScript libraries and need a visual / no-code based editor.
- You want to use cutting-edge browser features that aren't yet widely supported.

If any of the above apply to you, then Phaser isn't the right choice for your game. There are plenty of other frameworks and tools that will be a better fit. However, if you're looking to make a 2D game for the web, then we firmly believe that Phaser is a great choice.

The Core Concepts of Phaser

Before we jump in to any code it's worth spending a few minutes to understand the core concepts of Phaser.

Here we'll cover the terminology used, the structure of a Phaser game and how the various parts fit together. This will be a high-level overview. Later chapters will get deeper into the systems, but it's important to understand these concepts before you start coding.

Events

Events are a way for one system to send a signal, that other systems may listen for and then act upon. For example, if the player clicks their mouse on your game, that will internally emit a sequence of events within Phaser. Or if the Loader finishes downloading a file, that will emit a related event.

Events are a core part of Phaser and you'll find them used throughout the framework. They are used both internally, for one system to talk to another, and externally, for your game code to listen for and respond to.

There are hundreds of such events that Phaser will emit during the course of a game.

Events are always emitted by what is known as an Event Emitter. Most systems and Game Objects within Phaser are Event Emitters, meaning they can emit events directly and you can hook event handlers to them.

We adopted this practise because events are extremely common in the web browser. Most browser APIs are event-driven, so it made sense to follow this pattern. It also means that you can easily extend Phaser by adding your own events, or listening for existing ones and responding to them.

Game

If you look at any Phaser example you'll see they all create an instance of the Phaser.Game class. Indeed, without it, nothing will actually happen. This one class can be considered as the heart of your game, for without it, nothing will run.

Typically, you only ever have one instance of a Phaser game at any given time. The Game class itself doesn't do a great deal, and beyond creating it, you rarely ever interact with it. Yet it's responsible for creating and updating all of the internal systems that your game needs while it is executing.

Even if you're creating the type of game that consists of lots of smaller games (think Mario Party, or Wario Ware), you'll still only ever have one instance of the Phaser Game class itself.

Renderer

The Renderer is the part of Phaser that is responsible for drawing everything you see on the screen. Phaser ships with two different renderers: Canvas and WebGL. By default, Phaser will query the browser to see if it supports running WebGL. If it does, then it will create a WebGL renderer, otherwise it will fall back to

Canvas. You can also force Phaser to use a specific renderer, if you wish, via the game configuration. For maximum compatibility Phaser uses a WebGL1 based renderer. A move to a WebGPU is planned for Phaser4.

Some features are only available in WebGL. For example, the ability to use Shaders or special effects onGame Objects. WebGL is also optimized for rendering extremely large amounts of Game Objects to the screen via the GPU, something canvas struggles with.

However, Canvas is still a very capable renderer and can sometimes be a better choice for games that don't require the advanced features of WebGL, or in hardware constrained environments.

Scenes

Phaser uses the concept of Scenes to allow you to divide your game up into logical sections. A Scene can be as large, or as small, as you like. Typical uses for a Scene would be a Loading Screen, a Main Menu, a Game

Level, a Boss Fight, an in-game Item Shop, a High Score Table, etc. You can have as many Scenes in your game as you like. When you are starting out, you'll probably only have one or two, but as your game grows in complexity, you'll find yourself adding more.

It's important to understand that you do not have to have one Scene per file. You can, if you like, but it's not a requirement. You can have all of your Scenes in a single file, or you can have one file per Scene. It's entirely up to you.

Internally, there is a Scene Manager. This Manager is what you interact with when you add, remove or switch between Scenes. It's also responsible for updating and rendering the Scenes. You have full control over the order in which the Scenes are rendered in your game. For example, it's a common practise to have a Scene dedicated entirely to handling the UI for your game, that is rendered above all other Scenes.

We will look at the life-cycle of a Scene in more detail in a later chapter, but for now it's worth understanding that you can pause, resume and sleep a Scene at will, and that you can easily run multiple Scenes at the same time, if you wish.

In versions of Phaser prior to v3, Scenes were called States. The two terms are conceptually interchangeable, but Scene is the correct term to use and expect to see in Phaser 3. If you find any reference to States in code or a tutorial you've found online, it's for Phaser 2 and likely won't work in Phaser 3.

Game Objects

The main purpose of a Scene is to contain Game Objects. These are the building blocks of your game and Phaser has a lot of Game Objects available for you to use. Some of the more common ones include: Sprites,

Text, Images, Particle Emitters, Containers, Graphics, Tilemaps, and more. You can create as many Game Objects as you like. A Game Object always belongs to the Scene in which it was created. It is born and it dies there and cannot be moved to another Scene.

Games Objects are typically created via the Game Object Factory. This factory is available for direct use from within a Scene. For example, to create a Sprite you would call `this.add.sprite()`. add is an alias to the factory and sprite is a function within it. The factory is responsible for creating the Game Object, adding it to the Scene and returning it to you.

Internally, Phaser has a base Game Object class from which all other Game Objects inherit. This base Game

Object does not display anything, or even have a position within the game world. It simply provides the core functionality that all Game Objects need. Each individual type of Game Object then adds its own features.

For example, the Sprite Game Object will add components for position, scale, rotation, textures and animation.

Because Game Objects are made from a set of components, it's possible to extend them and create your own custom Game Objects. This is a very powerful feature of Phaser and one that we'll explore in detail later in this guide.

Chainable Methods

Lots of methods in Phaser are chainable. This means that you can call one method after another, without having to store the Game Object in a temporary variable. For example, if you have a Sprite and want to set its position, scale and rotation, you can chain the calls together like this:

```
sprite.setPosition(x, y).setScale(2).setRotation(0.5);
```

This works because each of the methods returns a reference to the Game Object itself. So, when you call setPosition it returns the Sprite, which you can then call setScale on, and so on.

When you see a method in the Phaser API that begins with set in the majority of cases it means it's chainable. This is a very common JavaScript convention and one that we use heavily in Phaser.

Game World

The Game World is the space in which all of your Game Objects live. It's a virtual space that has no fixed size. You can think of it as a giant canvas that you can draw on. Game Objects that have the Transform

Component (which is most of them) have the ability to set their x and y coordinates. These values control their placement within the Game World.

Although the Game World is technically infinite, that doesn't mean your game has to be. You can still easily create 'single screen' games in Phaser. Or you can create games that extend only in one direction, such as a horizontal endless-runner. Or you can create games that scroll in all directions, such as a top-down RPG. It's entirely up to you.

The Game World is not an object or class within Phaser. It's simply a concept that you can use to help visualize where your Game Objects are in relation to each other.

Cameras

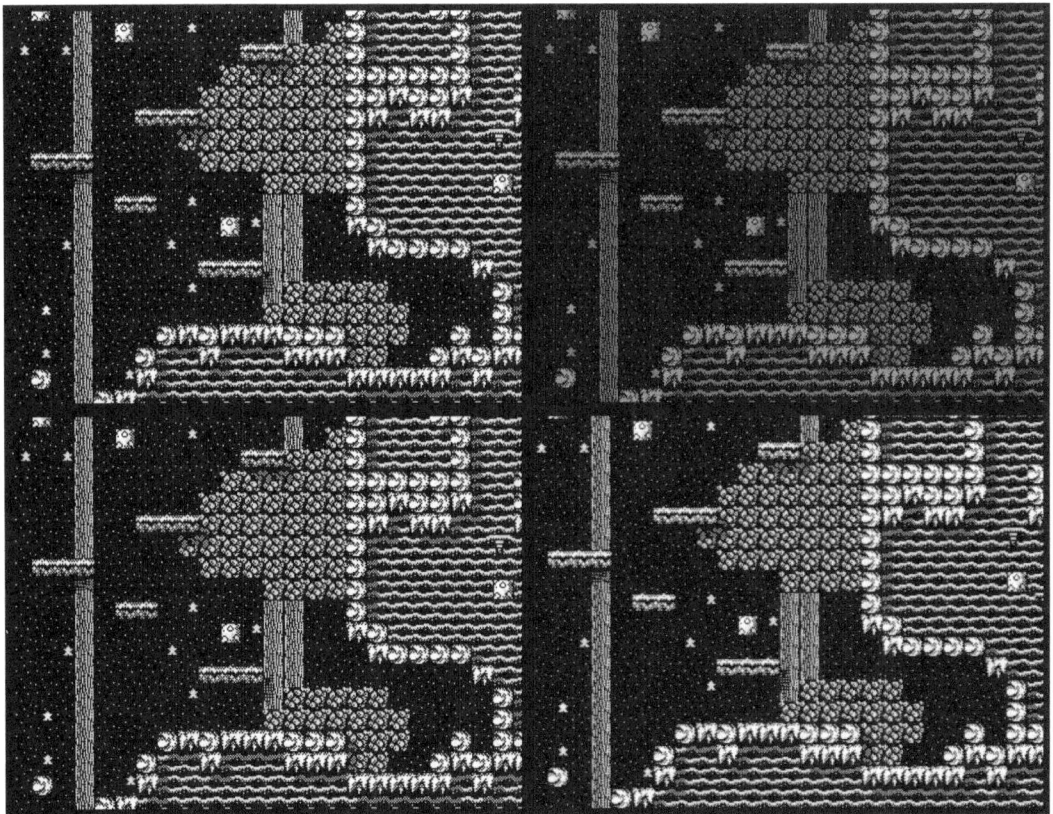

Figure 9.1 Cameras

Phaser has a built-in Camera system. A Camera is a way to control which part of your Game World you are currently looking at. You can move the camera around the world, and that in turn will influence which Game

Objects are displayed, based on their world position. By default, a Scene creates a single Camera ready for you to use. It must always have at least one Camera, otherwise nothing will render.

You can add as many extra Cameras as you like. You can also control the position, size, rotation, scaling and viewport of each Camera. Common uses of being able to have multiple cameras are for creating split-screen games, or games with picture-in-picture effects.

Cameras can also be given a bounds. This is a rectangular area that the Camera cannot scroll outside of. By default, a Camera has no bounds, so it can freely scroll anywhere. However in practise you will likely need to constrain the Camera to a fixed area of your Game World, and the Camera Bounds are how you do this.

Input

Phaser maintains a unified input system that works across all browsers and devices. By unified we mean that you don't have to worry about whether the user is on a desktop with a mouse, or a mobile device with touch input, or even a touch capable desktop. All you need to do is listen for, and respond to, the input events that

Phaser provides. You can also respond to input events from both keyboards and gamepads. Internally there is a global Input Manager and every Scene has an instance of the Input Plugin. The Input

Manager is responsible for listening for native DOM events, such as mouse movement, touch gestures and keyboard presses. It then passes these events on to the Input Plugins, which in turn processes them.

By default, Game Objects in Phaser do not process input. This is because not all Game Objects need to respond to input. For example, a background image or game logo likely doesn't need to respond to input, but a button does. Therefore, you must enable input processing on the Game Objects that you specifically want to respond to input.

Once enabled for input, a Game Object will then listen for input events from the Input Plugin and check to see if it has been 'clicked', or not. There are lots of events that can be emitted, such as pointer up and down events, drag events, scroll wheel events, etc. We'll explore these in more detail later in this guide, along with how the input system works internally. For now, it's enough to know that you can enable input on almost any Game Object and then respond to the events it emits as your game requires.

Loader

The Loader, as the name implies, is responsible for loading any external assets that your game may require.

Common asset types include images, texture atlases, sprite sheets, fonts, audio files and JSON data, but there are many more that Phaser can handle.

By default, every Scene has access to its own Loader instance. The Loader works on a queue-basis, which means you can add as many 'load requests' to it as you like and they all get added to an internal queue. You then tell the Loader to start and it will work through the queue, loading each asset in turn.

Scenes have a special method available to you called 'preload'. This method is called automatically by Phaser when the Scene starts. It's a good place to add all of your game assets to the Loader and you'll see this convention used heavily in our examples and third-party tutorials. However, you can also add assets to the Loader at any point in your game, not just from within the preload method.

When you add a file to the loader, you have to give it a string-based key. This is a unique identifier for that file and its related resource. For example, if you load an image and give it the key 'player', then you identify that image by the key 'player' from that point on. The keys are case-sensitive and their uniqueness is applied per file type. I.e. a sound file could have the key 'player' as well as an image file. String-based keys is a very important concept in Phaser and you'll see it used throughout the framework.

The files are loaded via built-in browser APIs, which often allows for many files to be downloaded in parallel, depending on the browser and server settings. The Loader is specialised in loading files based on network requests and across a network. It is not for loading files from the local file system, something that all modern web browsers prohibit for security reasons.

As with most systems in Phaser, there are lots of events you can listen for that come from the Loader. These events are naturally centered around the loading progress: such as which files have completed, or maybe failed, and how far along the process is. You can use these events to create loading bars and progress displays for your game.

Cache

When a file is downloaded by the Loader it nearly always ends up stored in an internal Phaser Cache. There are different caches for different file types. For example, JSON files are stored in the JSON cache, Binary files in the Binary Cache, and so on. These caches are created automatically when the Phaser Game instance first starts up. Files are stored in them using unique string-based keys. If the file has come from the Loader, it will use the same key you used there, to store it in the Cache with.

The Phaser Cache is different to any cache that the browser itself may maintain, in that it only persists for the duration of your game. Once your game has been destroyed, either directly by you, or via a page navigation, the Phaser Cache is cleared. Unlike the browser cache, you are free to add to, and remove items from, any of the Phaser caches at will.

Items stored in a Phaser Cache are global, which means they can be accessed from any Scene in your game. Scene's do not maintain their own set of caches. Instead, they all share the same global set. This is important to understand, because it means that if you load a file in one Scene, it will be available in all other Scenes too.

Mostly, you don't need to worry about interacting with the Phaser Cache. It's primarily an internal system that is used by other systems, such as the Loader, to store and retrieve data. However, there are times when you may want to interact with it directly, and it has a public API for doing exactly this.

Texture Manager

Phaser is a Texture based game framework. This means that it uses textures as the basis for rendering almost everything to the screen. From Sprites to Text, from Tilemaps to Particle Emitters, they all use textures. And the Texture Manager is where they all reside. As with Caches, the Texture Manager is global.

The Phaser Game maintains a single instance of it that is shared across all Scenes in your game. Therefore, adding a Texture from one Scene makes it automatically and instantly available in all other Scenes.

The Texture Manager works in tandem with the Loader. When you load an image file via the Loader, it is automatically passed to the Texture Manager. Phaser uses string-based keys for all of its textures. For example, when loading an image if you give it the key 'player' then it will be stored in the Texture Manager under the same key. When you then need to use this, say for a Sprite, you tell the Sprite to use the texture key 'player'. This string based approach is used through-out Phaser.

Although using the Loader is the most common way to populate the Texture Manager, it has lots of available methods to allow you to create and add textures directly to it. For example, if they need to come from a different source, perhaps as the result of an API call, or from a Canvas element.

The Texture Manager includes what are known as Parsers. A Parser is a function that converts external data in to a format that Phaser can use. The end goal of these functions are to take images and related data and create Texture and Frame instances from them. For example, there are Parsers for loading Texture Atlases,

Unity Atlases, Sprite Sheets and more. Although commonly used as part of the loading progress, you can also call any of the Parsers directly, as needed.

Textures and Frames

The primary role of the Texture Manager is to create and store instances of the Phaser Texture class. The Texture class contains all of the data that Phaser requires in order to use that texture internally. For example, a Sprite contains a reference to both the Texture and Frame it is using. The underlying texture resides in the global Texture Manager. This means that it's very common for multiple Game Objects to all use the same Texture instance.

A Texture is made up from one or more Frames. You can think of a Frame as being a rectangular area within the Texture. By using Frames you can split a single Texture into lots of different sections. When you tell a

Sprite which texture to use, you can also tell it which frame from that texture to use. If you had a texture that contained frames, you could tell a Sprite to use just frame 5 from it.

You may have heard of the term Sprite Sheet or Texture Atlas before. In Phaser, the underlying sprite sheet or atlas would be a single Texture instance that contains as many Frame instances as required to represent the frames in the sheet. The task of the majority of the Texture Manager Parsers is to take image and data files and then create all of the Frames it needs based on that information.

The concept of Frames is also how Phaser handles animations, by 'playing' the Frames in a sequence that you define, at a given frame rate.

There are more advanced types of Texture, such as the Dynamic Texture and the Canvas Texture, which we will cover later. Fundamentally, though, the majority of Phaser Game Objects use a Texture and Frame to render themselves to the screen.

Physics

Phaser has two physics systems built in. The first is called Arcade Physics and the second is Matter JS.

Arcade Physics is, as its name implies, meant for more 'arcade' or 'retro' style games, although is not limited just to those. It's a lightweight physics system that can only handle two different types of physics shapes: rectangles and circles. It's not meant for complex physics simulations, but rather for simple things like platformers, top-down games, or puzzle games. It's very fast and easy to use, with lots of helper functions, but due to its nature it does have its limitations.

Matter JS is an open-source third party physics library and Phaser has its own custom version of it bundled.

The reason for including Matter is that it provides a more advanced 'full body' physics system. If you need to move beyond rectangles and circles, with more complex physics shapes, and features such as constraints, joints and behaviours, then Matter is the system to use.

Both physics systems need to be enabled before they can be used. This can be done via the Game Configuration or on a per-Scene basis. Once enabled, you can then add physics-enabled Game Objects to your game. For example, if you enable Arcade Physics, you can then add a Sprite and enable physics on it. This will allow you to control the Sprite using the built-in physics functions, such as velocity, acceleration, gravity, etc.

By default a Game Object is not enabled for physics. This is because not all Game Objects need to be. For example, a background image or game logo likely doesn't need to be affected by physics, but a player character does. Therefore, you must enable physics on the Game Objects that you specifically want to be affected by it. We will cover this in detail in later chapters.

The two systems are entirely separate. An Arcade Physics sprite, for example, cannot collide with a Matter

Physics sprite. You cannot add the same Sprite to both systems, you need to pick one or the other. However, although it's unusual to do so, both systems can actually run in parallel in the same Scene. This means that you can have a Sprite that uses Arcade Physics and another that uses Matter Physics, and they will both work at the same time, although they will not interact together.

Position, Origin, Scale and Rotation

Game Objects that have the Transform component, which is most of them, have the ability to be positioned within the Game World. Indeed, when you create these Game Objects, you need to specify x and y coordinates for them. This is their placement in the world.

The x coordinate controls their horizontal position, and the y coordinate controls their vertical position. The x coordinate increases as you move to the right, and the y coordinate increases as you move down. This is the same coordinate system as used by the browser.

By default in Phaser Game Objects are centered on their x and y coordinates. This means that if you create a Sprite at the coordinates 300x200, then the center of the Sprite will be placed at 300x200. In some game frameworks the default origin is the top-left, and in others the bottom-left. In Phaser it's the center.

You can change this via the Origin methods of the Game Object. Setting the origin allows you to shift this 'anchor point', so that any point within the Game Object can become the new center.

You can rotate Game Objects by setting either their rotation or angle properties. The reason Phaser has two different properties for the same thing is to allow you to express your values in either radians or degrees.

Methods like `setAngle` expect the value in degrees, where-as `setRotation` expects it in radians.

Phaser uses a right-handed coordinate system, where 0 is East, to the right, and 3.14 (or 180 degrees) is West, to the left. South is 1.57, or 90 degrees and North is -1.57 (or -90 degrees). If you visualise the rotation as a circle, the bottom half is positive and the top-half is negative. This is the same as Adobe Flash, from which the first version of Phaser took its inspiration.

Rotation in Phaser always takes place around the origin of the Game Object. Which means by default Game Objects typically rotate around their center. As you've read, you can adjust the origin. This changes where both the position and rotation occurs. You cannot change the rotation point of a Game Object, only its origin.

Game Objects also have a scale property. This allows you to scale the Game Object horizontally and vertically. By default, a Game Object has a scale of 1, which is 100% of its original size. A value of 2 would be 200% of its original size, and 0.5 would be 50% of its original size.

You can set the scale to any value you like, including negative values. Negative scaling will cause the Game Object to flip on its axis. For example, if you set the scale to -1 on the x-axis, the Game Object will flip horizontally. If you set it to -1 on the y-axis, it will flip vertically. If you set it to -1 on both axis, it will flip both horizontally and vertically.

Scaling in Phaser always takes place from the center of the Game Object and this scale point cannot be changed.

Display List

Phaser uses a Display List to manage the order of Game Objects within the World. Every Scene has its own Display List. When you add a Game Object to a Scene, it is automatically added to the Display List. The Display List is a special type of container that allows you to control the order in which the Game Objects are rendered. By default, Game Objects are rendered in the order in which they were added to the Display List.

The Display List is also responsible for managing the position of Game Objects within the World. When you add a Game Object to the Display List, it is automatically positioned at the bottom of the list. This means that it will be rendered first, and therefore appear behind all other Game Objects.

You can change the position of a Game Object within the Display List by using its helper functions such as `sendToBack`, `sendBackwards`, `bringToTop` and `bringForward`. These allow you to move a Game Object around the Display List, thus influencing the order which things are rendered or checked for input events, as objects "on the top" get input priority.

In Phaser 2 it was possible to add a Game Object as a child of another Game Object. They were, in effect, self-contained Display Lists. This is no longer the case in Phaser 3. The only Game Object in Phaser 3 that can have children is the Container Game Object.

Depth and Visibility

Game Objects have two other properties that impact how and if they are rendered. The first of these is called visible. By default, all Game Objects are visible. This means that they will be rendered. However, if you set the visible property to false , then the Game Object will be skipped by the renderer. It will still exist in the World, and still be updated, but it will not be rendered. This is useful for Game Objects that you may want to hide at certain points in your game, then bring back later.

The second property is known as the Game Objects 'depth'. This is a value that controls the order in which the Game Objects are rendered. By default, Game Objects have a depth of zero. This means that they are rendered in the order in which they were added to the Display List. However, you can change the depth of a

Game Object via its setDepth method. This allows you to explicitly set the order in which Game Objects are rendered, without having to move them around the Display List. Typically, you would use this if you want to programmatically control the rendering order of Game Objects, such as a sprite moving in front or behind other objects in a busy Scene, where moving them all around the Display List would be impractical.

Alpha and Tints

Most Game Objects have the ability to set their 'alpha' value. This is a value between 0 and 1. A value of 1 is fully opaque, where-as a value of 0 is fully transparent. By default, Game Objects have an alpha value of 1.

You can use this property to create effects such as a Game Object 'fading out' over time, or to make a Game Object appear to be semi-transparent. As an internal optimization, Game Objects with an alpha value of 0 will be skipped by the renderer.

For some Game Objects it's possible to set a different alpha value per corner. This is known as a vertex alpha. It allows you to create effects such as a Game Object fading out from one corner to another, or to make a Game Object appear to be semi-transparent at one corner, but not the other. Not all Game Objects support vertex alpha, but those that do will have a setAlpha method that accepts 4 values, one for each corner.

Game Objects also have the ability to set their tint value. This is a color value that is additively blended with the underlying Game Object texture as it is rendered. You can use this property to create effects such as a Game Object 'flashing' a color, or to make a Game Object appear to be tinted a certain color.

You can optionally set a different tint color per corner. This is known as a vertex tint and allows you to create color blended effects across a Game Object. Tinting is an "all or nothing" effect, where the entire Game Object is tinted the same blend of colors. It's not possible to tint just part of a Game Object, or only impact a specific color used by the Game Object texture.

Both vertex alpha and tinting are only available when using the WebGL renderer, they do not have a Canvas equivalent.

Update List

The Update List is an internal system that every Scene has. It works in a similar way to the Display List, except instead of controlling the order of rendering, it controls which Game Objects have their 'preUpdate' methods called. An "update" happens in a Phaser Game every time the browser updates the screen and uses browser based APIs to control it. This is typically 60 times per second, but can vary depending on the device and browser settings.

When an update happens, the Update List is iterated through and each Game Object in it has its preUpdate method called. This is where the Game Object can perform any internal logic it needs to, such as updating its animation system. You can also override this method yourself, adding your own logic to it as needed.

Once all Game Objects in the Update List have been processed, the Scene then has its own update method called. This is where you can perform any Scene-level logic, such as checking for collisions, keyboard input, or updating the position of a Camera.

Not all Game Objects are added to the Update List. Those that require it, are added automatically when created via the Game Object Factory. For example, a Sprite is added to the Update List, where-as a Graphics

Game Object is not. But as with most systems in Phaser, you can manually add and remove entries from the Update List, as needed.

Geometry

Phaser has an extensive set of Geometry classes. These are used internally by the physics and input systems, but are also available for you to use in your own games. The geometry classes on offer include:

Circle, Ellipse, Line, Point, Polygon, Rectangle, Triangle and the Mesh class.

Each of these classes has a set of methods and support functions that allow you to perform geometric operations on them. For example, you can check if a point is contained within a circle, get the bounds of an ellipse, or the nearest point from a line, as well as many other features.

There are also a wide range of intersection functions. You can test for conditions such as a Circle intersecting with a Rectangle, or getting the rays from a point to a polygon.

The Geometry classes are not Game Objects. You cannot add them on to the Display List. Instead, think of them as data structures that you can use to perform geometric operations on, of which most games tend to have quite a few.

Tweens

Tweens are an important part of most games, although it's entirely possible you have never come across the term before. Phaser has a built-in Tween Manager that allows you to create smooth, time-based changes to object properties. For example, you can tween the position of a Sprite from one coordinate to another, over a given duration of time. Or you can tween the alpha value of a Game Object from 1 to 0, making it appear to fade out. The Tween Manager is a Scene-based system, and each Scene has its own instance of it.

Although most often used on Game Objects, tweens can actually adjust any object at all. For example, you can tween the volume of a sound, or the position of a Camera. You can even tween the properties of a JavaScript object, such as an object containing a players score, or health points.

Tweens have a whole raft of features built into them. They can be set to repeat, yoyo, tween multiple objects at once, set multiple properties at once, each with their own custom values, have delays, interpolation, a variety of different smoothing effects and much, much more. They can even be chained together, so that one starts as soon as another finishes. As a result, they are a very powerful system and one that you'll find yourself using a lot in your games.

We will cover tweens in much more depth in a later chapter, but the take-away here is that a 'tween' is when the value of an object is changed over a period of time.

Math

JavaScript itself has a pretty comprehensive Math API, which is of course optimized to run quickly in browser. Phaser extends this with its own set of Math functions, that are primarily geared around common use-cases in games. For example, there are Math functions for working with angles, distances, random numbers, interpolation, and more. Lots of these exist because they are required internally, so we expose them for you to use too. The rest are just functions we've found that we have come to require over the years.

All Phaser Math functions are contained in their own namespace. We do not, and never will, modify or pollute the native JavaScript Math namespace. This means that you can use both Phaser Math functions and native Math functions in your game, without any conflicts.

Animations

The primary means of animation in Phaser is by using 'frame' based animations. As mentioned previously, Phaser maintains a Texture class, which contains as many Frames as may exist on that Texture. The Animation system allows you to play a sequence of these Frames, one after the other, at a given frame rate. This is how you create the illusion of animation on Sprites in your game. To achieve this, you often see texture image files divided into a 'grid' of frames, where each frame is a different animation frame. This is known as a Sprite Sheet or Texture Atlas.

Animations are created via the Animation Manager. Each Scene has its own instance of the Animation

Manager. You can create as many animations as you like, and each animation can have as many frames as you like. You can also create multiple animations that all use the same frames, if you wish. For example, you could have a 'walk' animation that uses frames 1 to 4, and a 'run' animation that uses frames 1 to 8. Both animations would use overlapping frames, but play them at different speeds.

Not all Game Objects can be animated. The main one you'll use is the Sprite Game Object. This carries its own Animation State component with it, allowing you to create and play animations directly on a Sprite instance.

Animations can be either global or local. A global animation is one that is created via the Animation Manager and is available to all Game Objects in your game. A local animation is one that is created directly on a Game

Object, such as a Sprite. Local animations are only available to that Game Object and cannot be used by any other Game Object.

It's worth mentioning that animation can also be achieved by tweening objects, if you just need a blend of motion + subtle changes (like scale or alpha), and that Phaser 3 also has a plugin available for Spine animations, which is a bone-based animation software package published by Esoteric Software.

Renderer

When a Phaser Game first boots, it will create a renderer. Based on the browser and your game configuration, this will be an instance of either the Canvas Renderer or the WebGL Renderer. Canvas is an API that the web browser makes available. In essence, it's a rectangular element that we can draw to. It allows Phaser to create a 'context' upon it and this context is what is used to draw things to the canvas.

WebGL is an API based on top of OpenGL ES that allows us to draw things to the screen via the GPU. Objects being drawn can be batched together, which means that the GPU can often process them extremely quickly. It's a much more powerful system than Canvas. However, it's not supported by all browsers, or all devices. This is why Phaser maintains two renderers.

Phaser will always try to use WebGL if it can, but will fall back to Canvas if it can't. Because Canvas is a much simpler renderer, you don't have access to certain features that Phaser can provide, such as Shaders, special effects, or the ability to use color tints. However, it's still a very capable renderer and can sometimes be a better choice for games that don't require the advanced features of WebGL, or need to operate in hardware constrained environments.

Sound

Web Browsers offer the ability to play audio in two different ways. The first is known as the Audio Tag. This is an HTML tag you can put on a web page that offers UI controls to play and pause/resume audio files. The second is known as the Web Audio API. This is a JavaScript API that allows you to create and control audio files directly from your code.

It's a much more powerful system than the Audio Tag, but is not supported by all browsers.

Phaser has a built-in Sound Manager that allows you to play audio files in your game. It will automatically detect if the browser supports the Web Audio API and if it does, it will use that. If not, it will fall back to the

Audio Tag. This means that you can use the same API to play audio files in all browsers, regardless of their support for the Web Audio API.

As with WebGL vs. Canvas, there are things that only Web Audio can do. Such as positional audio, i.e. having sounds 'follow' a player across the game world. It's also much better suited to playing lots of short duration sound effects in quick succession, i.e. "gunshots" or "explosions".

You can pick which audio system you'd like to use via the Game Configuration, or even disable audio entirely. Not all games need audio, after all.

The Phaser Sound Manager is a global system. This means that it belongs to the Game instance, and if you start to play a sound in one Scene, it won't automatically stop just because you change to another Scene.

This gives you a lot of control, but also means you need to be careful to stop looping sounds when you're done with them, or they'll keep playing.

Tilemaps

A tilemap is a way of storing a level or game world. It's a data structure that contains information about the tiles that make up the level, such as their position, size and type. It's a very common way of creating levels in 2D games, as it allows you to visually design the level in a tile-based editor such as Tiled, then export it as a data file.

Tilemaps are typically orthogonal, which means that the tiles are laid out in a grid, with each tile being the same size. However, Phaser also supports isometric tilemaps, where the tiles are laid out in a staggered grid, and hexagonal tilemaps, where the tiles are laid out in a hexagonal grid.

Phaser has a built-in Tilemap class that allows you to load and render tilemaps in your game. It supports a wide range of tilemap formats, including CSV, Tiled JSON, Tiled XML, and the ability to generate data dynamically at runtime. Because Tiled works on a 'layer' basis, Phaser uses the same principals. You can create a 'TilemapLayer' instance and this will render as a 'layer' in your game. You can have multiple tilemap layers and mix and match regular Game Objects inbetween those.

The Arcade Physics system that is built into Phaser has support for tilemap collision as part of it. You can also convert a tilemap for use in Matter Physics, which gives you more control over things such as sloped tiles.

Plugins

Phaser has a built-in Plugin System that allows you to extend it in an infinite number of ways. Indeed, the majority of the internal systems are implemented as plugins. A plugin can either be global, or Scene-based.

A Global plugin, as the name implies, is available across the whole of Phaser and when you access a global plugin from a Scene, you're accessing one single instance of it.

A Scene-based plugin is created by, and belongs to, the Scene in which it was added. The difference is that you can have several unique instances of Scene Plugins running in multiple Scenes in parallel.

Scenes can be added to your game via the Loader, or you can import them as JavaScript modules. There are a large number of 3rd party Phaser plugins in existence, which add lots of extra functionality that we just cannot include in the core framework.

Curves

A Curve is a mathematical function that allows you to plot a series of points in such a way that they form a line or a curve. Phaser includes support for Cubic Bezier curves, Ellipse Curves, Line Curves, Quadratic Bezier curves and Spline curves.

Phaser also has support for Paths. A Path is a collection of multiple curves, joined into one continuous compound curve.

You can use the curves and paths in a variety of ways. The most common would be to have a Game Object follow the path. For example, a 'space invader' style sprite could follow a path that made it move left and right across the screen, then drop down a bit, then move left and right again, and so on.

Curves are not Game Objects. You do not add them to the display list and they do not render. They're purely a mathematical function with lots of helper utilities available, such as the ability to get the bounds, or tangent, or a specific point from the curve. Phaser does provide the ability to draw a curve to a Graphics Game Object, but this is mostly for debugging purposes.

Scale Manager

The Scale Manager is a global system that handles the scaling, resizing and alignment of the canvas element into which Phaser is rendering your game. When a Phaser game boots it will create a canvas element by default, of the given dimensions set in the game configuration. It's the Scale Managers job, if instructed to do so, to then scale this canvas via CSS to make it fill the available space on the web page.

There are various scaling modes available. The most common is known as 'Scale To Fit'. This will scale the canvas to fill the available space, whilst maintaining the aspect ratio of the game. However, there are other scale modes, including 'resize' which will resize the underlying canvas to fill the available space. There are also modes for 'zooming' a canvas, centering it, or allowing it to enter into fullscreen mode.

Scaling a game is a complex topic. There are lots of different devices, with different screen sizes, pixel densities and aspect ratios. The Scale Manager is designed to help you handle all of this, but it's not a magic bullet. You still need to understand the basics of how it works, and how to configure it to suit your game.

More importantly, the underlying size of the canvas element directly impacts the performance of your game. The larger the canvas, the more pixels it has to render to. This means that a game running at 800x600 will render much faster than one running at 1920x1080. You need to find a balance between the size of the canvas and the performance of your game across the devices that matter most to you.

Game Object Masks

Phaser has the ability to 'mask' Game Objects as they are rendered. A mask allows you to 'hide' areas of the Game Object from rendering. There are two types of mask available: Geometry Masks and Bitmap Masks.

The Geometry Mask works by using geometry data in order to create the mask. For example rectangles, circles, ellipses, polygons and more. This data is used to create a path that forms the mask. Internally, it uses what is known as the stencil buffer in WebGL and the clip path in Canvas.

The Bitmap Mask works by using a texture as the mask. This texture can be any size and shape you like, and can be animated, or even a video. The alpha values of the pixels in the texture control what the mask looks like on-screen. For example, a pixel with an alpha value of 0 will hide the Game Object, where-as a pixel with

an alpha value of 1 will show it. This allows you to create detailed effects, such as feathering, not possible with a Geometry Mask. Bitmap Masks are a WebGL only feature.

Masks in Phaser are slightly unique in that they are drawn and positioned in world space. A Game Object can only have one mask applied to it at any one time. However, you can apply the same mask to multiple Game Objects, if you wish. They are not Game Object specific and if you then move the Game Object, the mask will not 'follow' it. This means they require some careful planning to use effectively.

FX

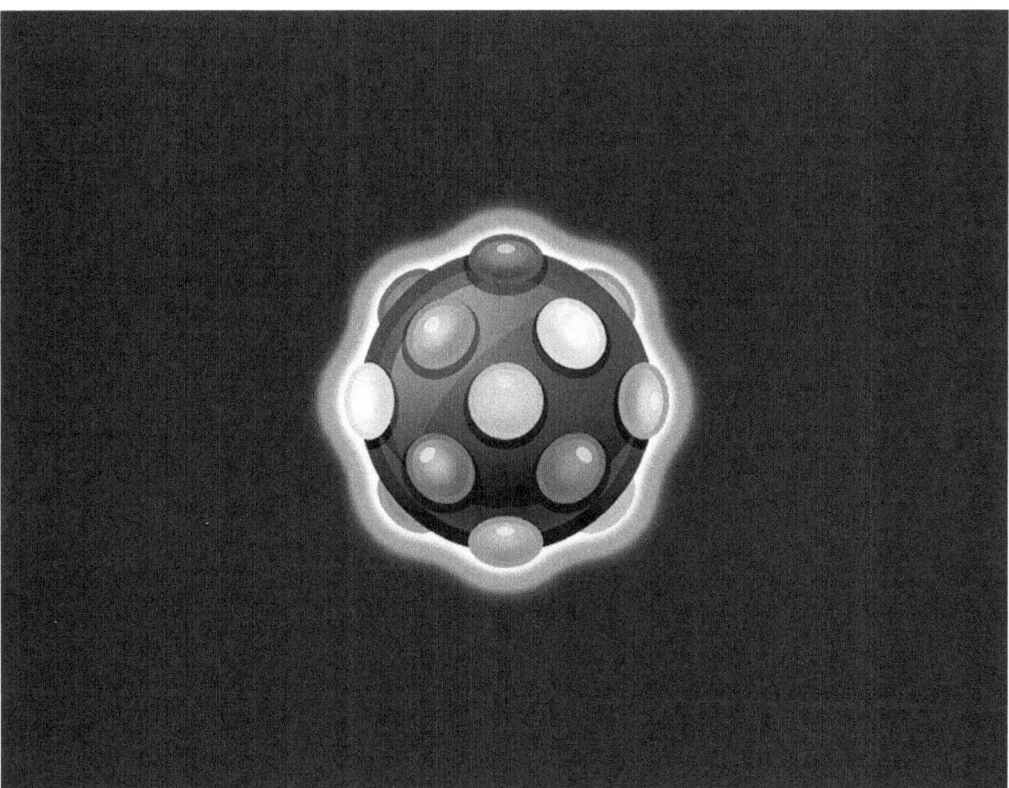

Figure 9.2. FX

As of Phaser v3.60, the framework includes a new FX Pipeline system with lots of built-in effects. This is a powerful and flexible way to apply both pre and post-processing effects to your game. It's a WebGL only feature and is not available in Canvas mode as it relies on shaders.

The built-in FX include: Barrel, Bloom, Blur, Bokeh, Circle, ColorMatrix, Displacement, Glow, Gradient, Pixelate, Shadow, Shine, Vignette and Wipe.

The FX can be enabled on all of the common types of Game Objects and you can stack effects and control the stacking order. For example, you can apply both a glow and vignette effect to a Sprite. Cameras can also have FX applied to them, which impacts everything they render and lets you create effects such as a 'zoom blur' or pixelate.

Time

Every Scene has an instance of the Clock class. It's responsible for keeping track of the elapsed time, delta time, and other time related values. It also allows you to create Timer Events, which are events that fire after a given amount of time has passed. For example, you can create a Timer Event that fires after 5 seconds, or 10 seconds, or 1 minute. You can also create Timer Events that repeat, such as every 5 seconds, or every 10 seconds.

The Clock that belongs to a Scene is used by all Scene systems, such as tweens and sound. It's also used by Game Objects, such as the Sprite animation system. This means that all of these systems are synchronized to the same clock. You have the ability to 'scale' the time of an individual clock, thus slowing down, or speeding-up the systems running within a single Scene.

10. Detailed look into Game Objects

In this chapter, we delve deep into the core of Phaser game development: the game objects. Game objects are the building blocks of any Phaser game, from simple sprites to complex groups that manage multiple sub-objects. Understanding how to effectively create, manipulate, and control these elements is fundamental for any developer looking to create engaging and dynamic games. Let's dive in!

Alpha Component

Figure 10.1 Alpha component

The Alpha Component is responsible for setting the alpha value of a Game Object. This is a value between 0 and 1. A value of 1 is fully opaque, where-as a value of 0 is fully transparent.

By default, Game Objects have an alpha value of 1. The current local alpha value of a Game Object is stored in its alpha property:

```
const alpha = player.alpha;
```

To set the alpha you can use the chainable setAlpha method:

```
player.setAlpha(alpha);
```

By default, Game Objects will have an alpha value of 1. This means they will be fully visible. You can reset the alpha of a Game Object either by setting its alpha property to 1, or by calling the chainable clearAlpha method:

```
player.clearAlpha();
```

You can use this property to create effects such as a Game Object 'fading out' over time, or to make a Game Object appear to be semi-transparent. As an internal optimization, Game Objects with an alpha value of 0 will be skipped by the renderer.

Per Vertex Alpha

For some Game Objects it's possible to set a different alpha value per corner. This is known as vertex alpha. It allows you to create effects such as a Game Object fading out from one corner to another, or to make a Game Object appear to be semi-transparent at one corner, but not the other. Not all Game Objects support vertex alpha, but those that do will have a setAlpha method that accepts 4 values, one for each corner. The corners are given in the order: Top Left, Top Right, Bottom Left and Bottom Right:

```
player.setAlpha(topLeft, topRight, bottomLeft, bottomRight);
```

You can also set the properties directly:

```
player.alphaTopLeft = topLeft;
player.alphaTopRight = topRight;
player.alphaBottomLeft = bottomLeft;
player.alphaBottomRight = bottomRight;
```

The ability to set per-vertex alpha is a WebGL only feature.

Alpha and Parents

When a Game Object has its alpha property set it will multiply its alpha value with that of its parent Container, if it has one. For example, if you have a parent Game Object with an alpha value of 0.5, and a child with an alpha value of 0.5, then the child will be rendered at 0.25 alpha as it's multiplied with the parent's alpha:

```
container.setAlpha(0.5);
child.setAlpha(0.5);
```

Blend Mode Component

The Blend Mode Component allows Game Objects to set a blend mode which is used during rendering. Blend modes allow for different types of combining / blending of the pixels in Game Objects with those of the background.

Figure 10.2 Blend Mode Component.

The current blend mode of a Game Object is stored in its blendMode numeric property:

```
const blendMode = sprite.blendMode;
```

You can set the blend mode of a Game Object using the chainable setBlendMode method:

```
sprite.setBlendMode(mode);
```

The mode value can be one of the BlendModes constants, such as Phaser.BlendModes.SCREEN . It can also be a string, such as SCREEN , or an integer, such as 3 . If you give a string, it must be all upper-case Phaser By Example and match exactly those available in the BlendModes constants list. If you give an integer, it must be a valid Blend Mode constant ID from the list below.

The default value is zero, which is the NORMAL blend mode.

Blend Mode Constants

The available blend modes are:

ID	Constant	Description
0	NORMAL	Normal blend mode. For Canvas and WebGL
1	ADD	Add blend mode. For Canvas and WebGL
2	MULTIPLY	Multiply blend mode. For Canvas and WebGL
3	SCREEN	Screen blend mode. For Canvas and WebGL
4	OVERLAY	Overlay blend mode. For Canvas only
5	DARKEN	Darken blend mode. For Canvas only
6	LIGHTEN	Lighten blend mode. For Canvas only
7	COLOR_DODGE	Color dodge blend mode. For Canvas only
8	COLOR_BURN	Color burn blend mode. For Canvas only
9	HARD_LIGHT	Hard light blend mode. For Canvas only
10	SOFT_LIGHT	Soft light blend mode. For Canvas only
11	DIFFERENCE	Difference blend mode. For Canvas only
12	EXCLUSION	Exclusion blend mode. For Canvas only
13	HUE	Hue blend mode. For Canvas only
14	SATURATION	Saturation blend mode. For Canvas only
15	COLOR	Color blend mode. For Canvas only
16	LUMINOSITY	Luminosity blend mode. For Canvas only
17	ERASE	Erase blend mode. For Canvas and WebGL
18	SOURCE_IN	Source in blend mode. For Canvas only
19	SOURCE_OUT	Source out blend mode. For Canvas only
20	SOURCE_ATOP	Source atop blend mode. For Canvas only
21	DESTINATION_OVER	Destination over blend mode. For Canvas only
22	DESTINATION_IN	Destination in blend mode. For Canvas only

23 DESTINATION_OUT	Destination out blend mode. For Canvas only
24 DESTINATION_ATOP	Destination atop blend mode. For Canvas only
25 LIGHTER	Xor blend mode. For Canvas only
26 COPY	Copy blend mode. For Canvas only
27 XOR	Xor blend mode. For Canvas only

Canvas vs. WebGL

The Canvas Renderer supports all blend modes. However, the WebGL Renderer only supports the following blend modes:

- NORMAL
- ADD
- MULTIPLY
- SCREEN
- ERASE

If you set a blend mode that is not supported by the WebGL Renderer, it will instead use the NORMAL blend mode.

Under WebGL you can create your own custom blend modes.

The Canvas Renderer will use the Canvas globalCompositeOperation feature which is part of the browsers Canvas API. This is why it has so many additional blend modes available.

WebGL Performance Considerations

The Phaser WebGL Renderer will use the built-in GL Blending functions, which are extremely fast. However, they are more limited in scope than the Canvas Renderer, which is why you only have 5 available by default.

Because they use the GL blend functions it means they require a batch flush before they can be set. So, if you have a series of Game Objects that are together in a batch, but one of them has a blend mode set different from the rest, the renderer will stop the batch, draw them all, set the blend mode, draw that one Game Object, then start a new batch again for the rest.

While modern GPUs are designed to handle tasks like this with ease, you should always be mindful of the potential impact this constant batch flushing can have. If you need to change blend modes often, try to organize your Game Objects so that those with shared blend modes are added to the display list consecutively, without breaks, as this will allow them to be rendered in as few batches as possible.

Bounds Component

The Bounds Component is responsible for providing methods you can call that will return various bounds related values from a Game Object.

The 'bounds' of a Game Object can be summed-up as a rectangle that fully encapsulates the visual bounds of the Game Object, taking into account its scale and rotation.

Not all Game Objects have a bounds. For example, the Graphics Game Object does not have an intrinsic bounds because of the way in which it works. However, most texture-based Game Objects, such as Sprites, Text and TileSprites can return their bounds.

If the Game Object has a parent container, then its bounds will be factored based on its influence from the Container.

The bounds of a Game Object can be obtained by calling its getBounds method:

```
const bounds = sprite.getBounds();
```

This will return a Rectangle Shape object, where the x and y values are the top-left of the bounds, and the width and height values are the width and height of the bounds.

You can also pass in a Rectangle object to the getBounds method, and it will set the values based on the bounds of the Game Object:

```
const rect = new Phaser.Geom.Rectangle();
sprite.getBounds(rect);
```

If you don't pass in a Rectangle then a new instance will be created and returned to you. So, if you need to call this method frequently, pass in a Rectangle instance to help ease object creation.

Every time you call this method the bounds are calculated fresh. They are not cached internally, or updated automatically. So be aware of this if you are using bounds in any kind of update loop, or at scale.

Bounds Related Points

As well as the getBounds method, there are also a number of other methods available that return specific points from the bounds of the Game Object. If you don't require the full bounds then getting just the point you do need is more efficient.

These methods are:

- getTopLeft
- getTopCenter
- getTopRight
- getLeftCenter
- getCenter
- getRightCenter
- getBottomLeft
- getBottomCenter
- getBottomRight

They all operate in the same way. You can optionally pass them a Vector2 instance in which to store the resulting point, or they can create one for you. They all also have the includeParent boolean, which allows them to involve a parent container, if the Game Object has one, in the calculations, or not.

For example, here is how to use the getTopLeft method without factoring in a parent:

```
const point = sprite.getTopLeft();
```

And here is how to use it, but factor in a parent:

```
const point = sprite.getTopLeft(null, true);
```

And here is how to use it, but factor in a parent, and store the result in a pre-created Vector2:

```
const point = new Phaser.Math.Vector2();
sprite.getTopLeft(point, true);
```

All of the listed methods can be used in this way.

None of the bounds methods allow you to set the bounds. They are all 'read only' methods.

Crop Component

The Crop Component allows texture-based Game Objects to 'crop' themselves. A crop is a rectangle that limits the area of the texture frame that is visible during rendering.

Cropping a Game Object does not change its size, dimensions, physics body or hit area, it just visually changes what you can see of it during the render-pass.

The current crop state of a Game Object is stored in its isCropped boolean:

```
const isCropped = player.isCropped;
```

To crop a Game Object you can use the chainable setCrop method:

```
player.setCrop(x, y, width, height);
```

It takes four arguments that represent the x/y coordinate to start the crop from, and the width and height of the crop. A crop is always a rectangle and cannot be any other shape.

The coordinates are relative to the Game Object, so 0 x 0 is the top-left of the Game Object texture frame.

Instead of passing in numeric values directly, or you can provide a single Rectangle Geometry object instance as the first and only parameter:

```
const rect = new Phaser.Geom.Rectangle(x, y, width, height);
player.setCrop(rect);
```

Note that this is a Geometry object, not a Rectangle Shape object.

One set, to adjust the crop you can call the setCrop method again with new values, or pass in an updated Rectangle instance.

If you wish to remove the crop from a Game Object, resetting it to show the entire texture again, call the setCrop method with no arguments:

```
player.setCrop();
```

Crop Limitations

Internally, the crop works by adjusting the textures UV coordinates prior to rendering. Therefore the crop can only ever be a rectangle that fits inside the existing texture area.

You cannot crop a Game Object to show more of the texture than originally allowed, or use any other shape than a rectangle.

Because it works by just adjusting the UV coordinates it does provide a way to do super-fast masking, if you need a rectangular mask.

Data Manager

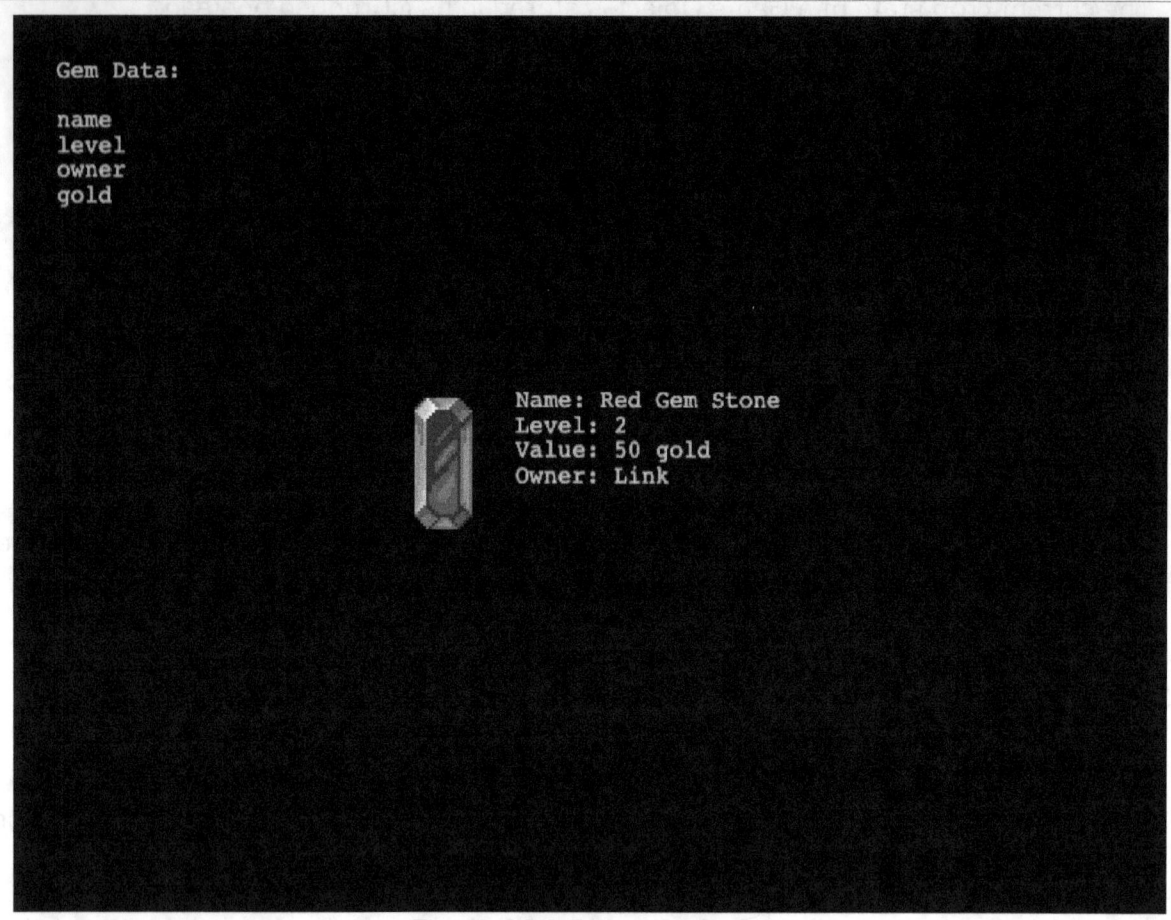

Figure 10.3 Data Manager.

The Data Manager is a component that allows you to store, query and get key/value paired information. This information is isolated to the parent of the Data Manager.

By default in Phaser 3 there is one instance of the Data Manager that belongs to the Game, which is known as the 'registry'. In addition to this, every Scene has a Data Manager instance. And finally, all Game Objects are able to have a Data Manager instance as well. Plus, should you need to, you can create your own instances and manage those.

Data Manager Parents

A Data Manager needs to be bound to a parent. There are four types of parent that a Data Manager can belong to: The Game, a Scene, a Game Object or a custom object.

Game Object Data Manager

All Game Objects have a property called data . This is null by default, but is set to hold an instance of the DataManager class if the method setDataEnabled is called on the Game Object:

```
const sprite = this.add.sprite();
sprite.setDataEnabled();
```

Alternatively, if any of the following data related methods: setData , incData , toggleData or getData are called, they will also trigger the creation of a Data Manager belonging to the Game Object.

Those methods are covered in more detail further in this section.

Once the Data Manager exists it can act as a store for any data you would like to bind to that specific Game Object.

Scene Data Manager Plugin

Every Scene has its own instance of the Data Manager Plugin. This is accessed via the data property from within a Scene, for example:

```
class MyScene extends Phaser.Scene {
  constructor() {
    super("myScene");
  }

  create() {
    this.data.set("lives", 3);
  }
}
```

The Data Manager Plugin is exactly the same as the Data Manager, including all of the same features and methods, but is constructed to function as a Scene Plugin.

Game Data Manager

The Game instance also has a Data Manager, which is accessed via the registry property from within a Scene:

```
class MyScene extends Phaser.Scene {
  constructor() {
    super("myScene");
  }

  create() {
    this.registry.set("lives", 3);
  }
}
```

Unlike the Scene's Data Manager, this one is owned by the Game instance itself. It is created automatically by during the boot process and is then available in all Scenes via the registry property.

This means that any data set into the registry in one Scene is instantly available in all other Scenes in your game. It also means you can use it as a place to store global data, such as highscores, level data, settings and more.

Custom Data Manager Instances

You can create your own instances of a Data Manager. A Data Manager must always have a parent and an Event Emitter it can use. While the parent is typically a Game Object or Scene, it can be any custom object you wish to bind to.

Here's an example of a class that can function as your own Data Manager:

```
class CustomDataManager extends Phaser.Data.DataManager {
  constructor() {
    super(this, new Phaser.Events.EventEmitter());
  }
}

const myData = new CustomDataManager();
```

The first parameter is the parent of the Data Manager, in this case the class itself. The second parameter is the Event Emitter instance it will use. You can use any Event Emitter you like, but it must have an instance of one.

Data Manager Methods

Once a Data Manager has been created or referenced, you're ready to store data within it.

Set Data

The first thing you'll want to do is set some data. You can do this using the set method:

```
// In the Registry
this.registry.set("playerName", "Vasquez");
// From within a Scene
this.data.set("playerName", "Vasquez");
// On a Game Object instance
sprite.setData("playerName", "Vasquez");
// or:
sprite.data.set("playerName", "Vasquez");
```

The set method takes two arguments: A key and a value. The key is a unique string that acts as the identifier for this value, i.e. playerName . As with most things in JavaScript, the key is case-sensitive, so playerName is not the same as PlayerName . It must also be a valid string. Keep this in mind when setting and getting data.

The second argument is the value and this can be anything you like: a string, an integer, an array, an object, or even a reference to another class or function.

If the data is successfully set, a SET_DATA event will be emitted.

Or, if the key already existed in the Data Manager then its previous value will be overwritten with the new one and a CHANGE_DATA event will be emitted instead. Please see the Events section for more details.

Setting Multiple Values

You can set multiple values in one call by passing an object to the set method:

```
// In the Registry
this.registry.set({
  playerName: "Hicks",
  weapon: "M41A Pulse Rifle",
  score: 0,
});
// From within a Scene
this.data.set({ playerName: "Hicks", weapon: "M41A Pulse Rifle", score: 0 });
// On a Game Object instance
sprite.setData({ playerName: "Hicks", weapon: "M41A Pulse Rifle", score: 0 });
// or:
sprite.data.set({ playerName: "Hicks", weapon: "M41A Pulse Rifle", score: 0 });
```

In this case 3 new values will be set into the Data Manager, with the keys playerName , weapon and score . A SET_DATA event will be emitted for each one. If, for example, two of the values were new and one was updating a previous value, then you'd get 2 SET_DATA events and 1 CHANGE_DATA event.

The object passed to the set method is only recursed one-level deep. If you pass a nested object, such as:

```
this.data.set({
  playerName: "Hicks",
  weapon: { name: "M41A Pulse Rifle", ammo: 10 },
  score: 0,
});
```

Then the weapon object will be set as the value of the weapon entry itself, not the individual properties within it.

Merge an existing Object into the Data Manager

You can populate the Data Manager with key/value pairs from an existing object by using the merge method:

```
const weapon = { name: "M41A Pulse Rifle", ammo: 10 };
// In the Registry
this.registry.merge(weapon, true);
// From within a Scene
this.data.merge(weapon, true);
// On a Game Object instance
sprite.data.merge(weapon, true);
```

The first argument is the object to merge into the Data Manager. The second argument is the boolean overwrite . If true it will overwrite any existing values in the Data Manager with the values from the object. If false it will skip any keys that already exist in the Data Manager.

If the key didn't exist in the Data Manager, it will be created and a SET_DATA event will be emitted. If the key did exist and overwrite was true , it will be updated and a CHANGE_DATA event will be emitted.

All of the same rules apply as with the set method, in that the object is only recursed one-level deep, keys are case-sensitive, etc.

Using Objects as Values

While you can use objects as values, you should be careful when doing so. For example:

```
const weapon = { name: "M41A Pulse Rifle", ammo: 10 };
this.data.set({ playerName: "Hicks", weapon });
```

In the above, the weapon value is a reference to the object itself. The Data Manager will not make a copy of it. This means that if you later directly update the weapon object, the value stored in the Data Manager will also be updated. For example:

```
weapon.ammo = 20;
```

However, doing so will not emit any events and you will lose the benefits of using the Data Manager in the first place.

Get Data

Once you've stored some data you can retrieve it again using the get method:

```
// In the Registry
this.registry.get("playerName");
// From within a Scene
this.data.get("playerName");
// On a Game Object instance
sprite.getData("playerName");
// or:
sprite.data.get("playerName");
```

If the key exists in the Data Manager then the value will be returned. If the key doesn't exist, undefined will be returned instead.

To get several values at once, pass an array of keys:

```
// In the Registry
this.registry.get(["playerName", "score"]);
// From within a Scene
this.data.get(["playerName", "score"]);
// On a Game Object instance
sprite.getData(["playerName", "score"]);
// or:
sprite.data.get(["playerName", "score"]);
```

If you pass an array in, then an array of values will be returned, in the same order as the keys given. If a key doesn't exist, undefined will be returned in its place.

This is especially useful for destructuring:

```
const { playerName, score } = this.data.get(["playerName", "score"]);
```

Data Values

When you get data, what you're getting in most cases is a copy of that data. For example, if the data is a string, number or boolean, then calling get will return that value. If you then manipulate the value, the Data Manager will not be aware of this change. For example:

```
const score = this.data.get("score");
score += 10;
```

In this case the score value is a copy of the value stored in the Data Manager. Although you modified it by

adding 10 to it, the Data Manager will not be aware of this change. If you then call get again, the value returned will be the original value, not the updated one.

To avoid this situation, use the values property of the Data Manager:

```
const score = this.data.values.score;
score += 10;
```

Any value set in the Data Manager is available via the values property.

Here, score is a reference to a special value stored in the Data Manager. This time, if you add 10 to it, the Data Manager will be aware of this change and will emit the CHANGE_DATA event, too. If you call get again, the value returned will be the updated one.

You can also modify the values directly, such as:

```
this.data.values.score += 10;
```

Again, this is a 'safe' way to modify the values in the Data Manager, as it will emit the CHANGE_DATA event and the value will be updated.

Increment Data

The inc method will increment a value by the given amount. If the value doesn't already exist in the Data Manager, it will be created and given the value of the amount:

```
// In the Registry
this.registry.inc("score", 10);
// From within a Scene
this.data.inc("score", 10);
```

```
// On a Game Object instance
sprite.incData("score", 10);
// or:
sprite.data.inc("score", 10);
```

In this case, if the score value didn't already exist, it will be created and given the value of 10. If it did exist, it will be incremented by 10. As with other forms of setting data, the relevant events will also be emitted, depending on if the value was created or updated.

To reduce a value, simply pass a negative amount:

```
this.data.inc("score", -10);
```

Note that the inc feature only works if the value is a standard JavaScript number data type. If you try to increment a string, it will append the value onto the end of the string. I.e. a value of "10" will become "1010" . If you try and increment a boolean, it will be converted to a number first, i.e. true becomes 1 and false becomes 0 . Adding numeric values to objects by mistake will actually destroy the original object and replace it with the string [object Object] with your number appended to it! So be sure to only call inc on number data types.

Fundamentally, there's no difference between calling the inc method and just modifying the value via the values property, except that the inc method call is chainable.

Toggle Data

The toggle method will toggle a boolean value between true and false :

```
// In the Registry
this.registry.toggle("musicEnabled");
// From within a Scene
this.data.toggle("musicEnabled");
// On a Game Object instance
sprite.toggleData("musicEnabled");
// or:
sprite.data.toggle("musicEnabled");
```

If the value doesn't already exist in the Data Manager, it will be created and given the value of true . If it did exist, it will be toggled to the opposite boolean value. As with other forms of setting data, the relevant events will also be emitted, depending on if the value was created or updated.

10. Detailed look into Game Objects — Data Manager Methods

Freezing Data

The Data Manager has the ability to be 'frozen'. If you enable this, then no further data can be added or removed from the Data Manager, and values already stored within it cannot be modified. This is useful if you wish to lock-down a Data Manager and make it read-only.

To freeze, or un-freeze a Data Manager, call the chainable setFreeze method:

```
// In the Registry
this.registry.setFreeze(true);
// From within a Scene
this.data.setFreeze(true);
// On a Game Object instance
sprite.data.setFreeze(true);
```

Or, you can modify the freeze property directly:

```
// In the Registry
this.registry.freeze = true;
// From within a Scene
this.data.freeze = true;
// On a Game Object instance
sprite.data.freeze = true;
```

Changing the frozen state of the Data Manager is immediate. For example, if you are adding an object containing several new values, and in the SET_DATA event listener you call setFreeze(true), then the remaining values will never be added.

Removing Data

You can remove a single item of data from the Data Manager using the remove method:

```
// In the Registry
this.registry.remove("playerName");
// From within a Scene
this.data.remove("playerName");
// On a Game Object instance
sprite.data.remove("playerName");
```

If the key exists in the Data Manager it will be removed and a REMOVE_DATA event will be emitted. If the key doesn't exist, nothing happens.

You can remove multiple values at once by passing an array of strings to the remove method:

```
// In the Registry
this.registry.remove(["playerName", "score"]);
// From within a Scene
this.data.remove(["playerName", "score"]);
// On a Game Object instance
sprite.data.remove(["playerName", "score"]);
```

The Data Manager also provides the pop method. This works in the same way as remove , except it returns the value that was removed:

```
// In the Registry
const playerName = this.registry.pop("playerName");
// From within a Scene
const playerName = this.data.pop("playerName");
// On a Game Object instance
const playerName = sprite.data.pop("playerName");
```

If the key doesn't exist in the Data Manager, undefined is returned.

Each key successfully removed, regardless of the method used to remove it, will emit a REMOVE_DATA event.

As with setting data, if the Data Manager has been frozen, no values will be removed.

Reset the Data Manager

You can reset the Data Manager, removing all data it contains, by calling the reset method:

```
// In the Registry
this.registry.reset();
// From within a Scene
this.data.reset();
// On a Game Object instance
sprite.data.reset();
```

This will remove all data from the Data Manager and reset its frozen status to false. No events are emitted by this method. It's just a fast way to clear out a Data Manager entirely, should you wish to do so.

Querying the Data Manager

There are several methods available for querying the Data Manager.

has

The first, and most simple, is the has method. This checks to see if the Data Manager has a key matching the given string:

```
// In the Registry
this.registry.has("playerName");
// From within a Scene
this.data.has("playerName");
// On a Game Object instance
sprite.data.has("playerName");
```

If the key exists in the Data Manager it will return true, otherwise it will return false. As with all uses of keys in JavaScript, please remember this is highly case-sensitive.

count

To return the total number of entries currently being stored in the Data Manager, use the count property:

```
// In the Registry
this.registry.count;
// From within a Scene
this.data.count;
// On a Game Object instance
sprite.data.count;
```

This is a numeric value that represents the total number of entries in the Data Manager.

getAll

To return everything within the Data Manager, use the getAll method:

```
// In the Registry
this.registry.getAll();
// From within a Scene
this.data.getAll();
// On a Game Object instance
sprite.data.getAll();
```

This will return a new object containing all of the data stored in the Data Manager. For example:

```
{
  playerName: 'Hicks',
  weapon: 'M41A Pulse Rifle',
  score: 0
}
```

If the Data Manager is empty, an empty object is returned.

When using getAll you should treat the returned object as read-only. If you modify it directly, the Data Manager will not be aware of the changes.

each

The each method allows you to pass all entries in the Data Manager to a given callback. You pass the callback as the first argument, an optional context as the second and then any further arguments:

```
// In the Registry
this.registry.each((parent, key, value) => {
  console.log(key, value);
});
// From within a Scene
this.data.each((parent, key, value) => {
  console.log(key, value);
});
// On a Game Object instance
sprite.data.each((parent, key, value) => {
  console.log(key, value);
});
```

The callback will be sent three arguments: The parent of the Data Manager, the key and the value. If you specified additional arguments, they will be sent after these three.

The Data Manager does not use, or expect a return value from the callback, so if you wish to modify a value sent to your callback, you must do so via the normal Data Manager methods.

query

The query method allows you to search the Data Manager for keys that match the given Regular Expression. It will then return an object containing any matching key/value pairs.

For example, let's assume we have populated the Data Manager with a number of different weapons:

```
this.data.set({
  "M41A Pulse Rifle": 10,
  "M56 Smartgun": 20,
  "M240 Flamethrower": 30,
  "M42A Scope Rifle": 40,
  "M83 SADAR": 50,
  "M92 Grenade Launcher": 60,
```

We can then use the query method to return all weapons that contain the word 'Rifle':

```
const rifles = this.data.query(/Rifle/);
```

The returned object will contain all matching key/value pairs:

```
{
  'M41A Pulse Rifle': 10,
  'M42A Scope Rifle': 40
}
```

If no matches are found, an empty object is returned.

The list and values properties

The list property is an array containing all of the keys in the Data Manager:

```
// In the Registry
this.registry.list;
// From within a Scene
this.data.list;
// On a Game Object instance
sprite.data.list;
```

The values property is an array containing all of the values in the Data Manager:

```
// In the Registry
this.registry.values;
// From within a Scene
this.data.values;
// On a Game Object instance
sprite.data.values;
```

These objects should be treated as read-only and never modified directly. However, they are made public so that you can use them from any of the regular JavaScript methods, such as destructuring, map, forEach and so on.

Data Manager Events

When the Data Manager is created it has to be given an Event Emitter to use. This means there are a few different ways to listen to the Data Manager events, depending on where you are setting the data. Here are the different ways you can listen for Data Manager events.

The Game Data Manager (the Registry) will emit events from itself:

```
// From within a Scene:
this.registry.events.on("setdata", (parent, key, value) => {
 console.log("Registry set:", key, value);
});
```

A Scene Data Manager will emit events via the Scene Systems, which is mapped to the events property from within a Scene:

```
// From within a Scene:
this.events.on("setdata", (parent, key, value) => {
   console.log("Scene data set:", key, value);
});
```

A Game Object Data Manager will emit events via the Game Object itself:

```
sprite.on("setdata", (parent, key, value) => {
   console.log("Sprite data set:", key, value);
});
```

Finally, if you have created your own instance of the Data Manager, then you would have provided an Event Emitter when you did this. It's this emitter you should listen tgo events from.

Destroying the Data Manager

If the Data Manager belongs to a Game (i.e. the Registry), a Scene, or a Game Object, then it is automatically destroyed when the parent object is destroyed. However, if you created your own Data Manager instance, then you are responsible for destroying it when it is no longer needed.

To do this, call the destroy method:

```
myData.destroy();
```

This will emit a DESTROY event, remove all listeners and clear-up any references it holds to other objects.

Note that if a Scene is shutdown, rather than destroyed, then the Data Manager will persist and retain all data within it. If you want to clear the data from the Data Manager when the Scene is shutdown, then you should listen for the shutdown event and call reset on its Data Manager:

```
class MyScene extends Phaser.Scene {
   constructor() {
     super("myScene");
```

```
    }
    create() {
      this.data.set("lives", 3);
      this.events.once("shutdown", this.shutdown, this);
    }
    shutdown() {
      this.data.reset();
    }
}
```

Depth Component

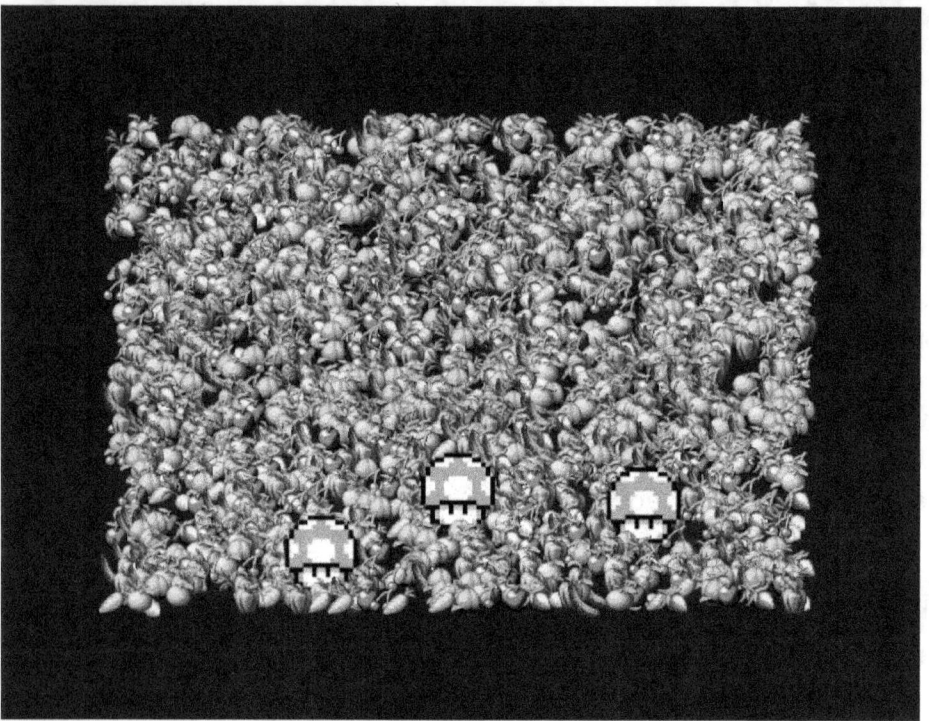

Figure 10.4 Depth Component.

The Depth Component allows Game Objects to be sorted within the Scene based on their 'depth' value, allowing them to move in front or behind other Game Objects. In some game frameworks this is known as the 'z-index'.

When a Scene Camera is preparing to render each frame, it will sort all the renderable Game Objects in the Scene based on their depth value. Those with the lowest depth values are rendered first, with the Game Objects with the highest depth values being rendered last, or 'on top' of the earlier ones.

By default, all Game Objects are given a depth value of zero, meaning they are all sorted based on their creation order, and placement in the Display List. The Depth Component allows you to override this.

The current depth of a Game Object is stored in its depth numeric property:

```
const depth = sprite.depth;
```

You can set the depth of a Game Object using the chainable setDepth method:

```
sprite.setDepth(value);
```

Or, you can modify the depth property directly:

```
sprite.depth = value;
```

The value can be any number, either an integer or a float. The default value is zero.

There is no upper or lower bounds on what the value can be and the numbers do not have to be assigned consecutively. If it's easier for you to give a Game Object a depth of 1000, and another a depth of 500, then you're free to do so.

You can also bind the depth property to a Game Objects position. For example, it's quite common to bind the depth of a Game Object to its y position, so that the higher it is in the Scene, the higher its depth value:

```
update();
{
    sprite.setDepth(sprite.y);
}
```

If one or more Game Objects share the same depth value, then they are sorted based on their index within the Display List. The first one in the list is rendered first, and so on.

Depth Updates

When the depth property of any Game Object is modified, the Depth Component tells the Scene that it needs to run a depth sort on the Display List. This is done by the component calling the

DisplayList.queueDepthSort method and it happens automatically, you don't need to do anything else.

Because sorting the rendering list can be a costly operation if there are a lot of Game Objects, Phaser will queue the depth sort and only execute it at render time. If no Game

Objects have had their depth changed since the last frame, the depth sort is skipped entirely.

Creating new Game Objects, or removing existing ones, will also cause the depth sort to be queued.

Depth and Containers

Container Game Objects can have their depth property set just like any other Game Object and it will influence at which point they are rendered. However, when a child is placed inside a Container, its own depth value is ignored. Instead, the depth of the Container is used by all children and cannot be overridden.

If you wish to adjust the order of children within a Container, there are specific methods available to do this, such as moveUp , moveDown , sendToBack and so on. See the Container documentation for more details.

Game Object Creator

The role of the Game Object Creator is to create Game Objects based on configuration objects. You can also elect to have them automatically added them to the Scene, or not. This makes Creator functions very useful for creating Game Objects in advance, so you can avoid object instantiation during time-critical parts of your game, such as when it is running.

The main difference between the Game Object Creator and the Game Object Factory is that all Creator functions take configuration objects. Where-as the Factory functions take fixed arguments. Which one you use is up to you. The Creator is more flexible and has some powerful features when parsing the config objects, but the Factory functions are easier to understand, remember and parse from languages like TypeScript.

The Creator itself is a very small class, providing just a few properties and hooks. Its power comes from the fact that all Game Objects register themselves with it, dynamically extending the class with new methods. You can even create your own Game Objects that include a creator function, allowing you to extend the Creator to suit your own needs.

10. Detailed look into Game Objects — Game Object Creator

Every Scene has an instance of the GameObjectCreator class. By default, this is mapped to the Scene's make property. For example, here is how to create a Sprite via the Game Object Creator:

```
const sprite = this.make.sprite({
  x: 400,
  y: 300,
  key: "playerAtlas",
  frame: "idle",
});
```

The above example makes some assumptions, such as the texture key and frame name, but you should take it as an example of a simple configuration object, rather than something you can copy and paste.

Internally, there is no actual sprite method in the Game Object Creator itself. If you were to open the class file in an editor, you won't find it. This is because each Game Object is responsible for its own creator function. The Sprite creator code can be found in the src/gameobjects/sprite/SpriteCreator.js file within the Phaser repository. Nearly all Game Objects have similar Creator.js files, which are responsible for registering themselves with the Creator.

All Creator functions call the static GameObjectCreator.register function, and pass it the name of its own creator function, sprite , and a callback. The register function will take this callback and add it to the Creator, under the sprite property.

And it is this callback that is invoked whenever you call this.make.sprite in your game code. In this case, it's responsible for creating the Sprite instance from the config object and adding it to the display list, but any actual logic can take place here.

The callback is invoked using the Game Object Creator as the context, meaning that this within the callback is a reference to the Creator itself.

It's important to understand that while each Scene has its own instance of the Game Object Creator, registration of Game Objects with the Creator is global. This means that once a Game Object has been registered, its creator function is available to use from any Scene in your game.

At the end of the day, the Creator is all about convenience. It allows you to create Game Objects without having to worry about the internal details of how they are created. It also allows you to extend the Creator with your own Game Objects, or even override the existing ones, allowing you to customize the Creator to suit your own needs.

How to set Configuration Properties

As we've seen above, you pass in configuration objects to the Creator functions in order to make the Game Objects. These config objects are parsed by the Creator and the values are used to set the properties of the Game Object being created, such as its position, scale, or rotation.

However, the way in which these properties are parsed is where the real power of the Creator comes in. Most properties are set through a Phaser function called GetAdvancedValue , which allows the properties

to expressed in 5 different ways.

For brevity we'll focus just on creating a Sprite and settings its x/y coordinates. However, you can actually use this approach on nearly all Game Object properties (see the table below).

1. Explicit Value

The first and most obvious way is to simply provide a fixed value:

```
const sprite = this.make.sprite({
  x: 400,
});
```

The Sprite will have an x position of 400.

2. Random Array Value

You can pass in an array of values, in which case a random element from the array will be selected and used:

```
const sprite = this.make.sprite({
  x: [400, 500, 600],
});
```

The Sprite x position will be randomly picked from the given array. So, its x coordinate could be 400, 500 or 600. You can pass in as many values as you like, and the Creator will pick a random one from the array each time.

3. Random Integer Between Min and Max

You can pass in an object with a randInt property. This should be a 2 element array, where the first element is the minimum value and the second is the maximum. A random integer between the two will be selected and used:

```
const sprite = this.make.sprite({
  x: { randInt: [100, 600] },
});
```

The Sprite x position will be a random integer between 100 and 600.

4. Random Float Between Min and Max

You can pass in an object with a randFloat property. This should be a 2 element array, where the first element is the minimum value and the second is the maximum. A random float between the two will be selected and used:

```
const sprite = this.make.sprite({
  x: { randFloat: [100, 600] },
});
```

The Sprite x position will be a random float between 100 and 600.

5. Callback Value

Finally, you can pass in a callback function. This should return a value, which will be used as the property value:

```
const sprite = this.make.sprite({
  x: function (key) {
    return Math.random() * 800;
  },
});
```

The Sprite x position will be a random float between 0 and 800. The callback is sent one parameter, the key of the property being set. In the example above, key would be x .

Game Object Configuration Properties

The following table lists all of the properties you can set on any Game Object. Most Game Objects have additional properties beyond this list, however, the following are common to all Game Objects.

All property values can be expressed via any of the 5 methods outlined above.

10. Detailed look into Game Objects — Game Object Creator

Property	Data Type
x	number
y	number
depth	number
scaleX	number
scaleY	number
rotation	number
angle	number
flipX	boolean
flipY	boolean
visible	boolean
alpha	number
blendMode	number
scrollFactorX	number
scrollFactorY	number
originX	number
originY	number

There are also 3 special properties that act as combinations of the above:

Property	Data Type
scale	number
origin	number
scrollFactor	number

So, rather than specifying scaleX and scaleY separately, you can just specify scale and it will set both values. The same is true for origin and scrollFactor.

Internally in Phaser, setting all of the common properties is handled by the BuildGameObject function, which you can find in the src/gameobjects/BuildGameObject.js file. If you are developing your own Creator function, then you can use this function to handle the common properties for you.

Animation Configuration

If you're creating a Game Object that supports animation, such as a Sprite, then you can also specify the animation details in the config object. For example, to create a Sprite and play an animation on it:

```
const sprite = this.make.sprite({
  x: 400,
  y: 300,
  key: "playerAtlas",
  anims: "idle",
});
```

The anims property is a special property that is parsed by the Sprite Creator function. It tells the Creator that you wish to play an animation on the Sprite. The value of the anims property can be either a string, or an object.

In the example above, we're telling it to play the 'idle' animation, as this is the animation key we have defined.

The Creator function does not create animations, it just plays them. So you have to assume that the animation has already been defined in your game, prior to this call. If it hasn't, the Creator function won't find the animation and will skip setting it.

Rather than pass a string, you can also pass an object, which allows you to specify more details about the animation:

```
const sprite = this.make.sprite({
  x: 400,
  y: 300,
  key: "playerAtlas",
  anims: {
   key: "idle",
   yoyo: true,
   repeat: -1,
  },
});
```

Internally in Phaser, this is handled by the BuildGameObjectAnimation function, which you can find in the src/gameobjects/BuildGameObjectAnimation.js file.

Skipping the Display List

When you call a make function there is a second parameter you can pass, after the configuration object, which is addToScene. This is a boolean value that controls if the Game Object is automatically added to the Scene Display List, or not.

By default, this is true, however you can override in one of two ways. First, by simply passing false as the second parameter:

```
const config = {
  x: 400,
  y: 300,
  key: "playerAtlas",
  frame: "idle",
};
const sprite = this.make.sprite(config, false);
```

Or, by setting the add property in the configuration object itself to false:

```
const sprite = this.make.sprite({
  x: 400,
  y: 300,
  key: "playerAtlas",
  frame: "idle",
  add: false,
});
```

In both cases, the Sprite will be created, but not added to the Scene Display List. This allows you to pregenerate a batch of Sprites in advance, but leave them in a dormant state until you need them.

Also, some Game Objects never need to be added to the Display List. For example, if you create a Graphics Game Object specifically for use as a mask, then you won't need to actually display it, so this allows you to create it without adding it to the Display List.

Removing a Creator Function

If the Game Object Creator already has a function registered with a given name, it will simply skip any further registrations for the same name. Therefore, if you wish to replace one of the internal Phaser Game Objects with your own, you will need to remove the existing entry first before adding yours.

You can do this by calling the remove method:

```
Phaser.GameObjects.GameObjectCreator.remove("sprite");
```

This will remove the sprite method from the Creator, allowing you to then add your own with the same name. This process is immediate.

Game Object Factory

The role of the Game Object Factory is to create Game Objects for you and add them to the Scene, making them immediately ready for use.

The Factory itself is a very small class, providing just a few properties and hooks. Its power comes from the fact that all Game Objects register themselves with it, dynamically extending the class with new methods. You can even create your own Game Objects that include a factory function, allowing you to extend the Factory to suit your own needs.

Every Scene has an instance of the GameObjectFactory class. By default, this is mapped to the Scene's add property. For example, here is how to create a Sprite via the Game Object Factory:

```
const sprite = this.add.sprite(x, y, key);
```

Internally, there is no actual sprite method in the Game Object Factory itself. If you were to open the class file in an editor, you won't find it. This is because each Game Object is responsible for its own factory function. Here is the one for the Sprite:

```
GameObjectFactory.register("sprite", function (x, y, texture, frame) {
  return this.displayList.add(new Sprite(this.scene, x, y, texture, frame));
});
```

This code can be found in the src/gameobjects/sprite/SpriteFactory.js file within the Phaser repository. Nearly all Game Objects have similar Factory.js files, which are responsible for registering themselves with the Factory.

You can see the code is calling the static GameObjectFactory.register function and passing it the name of its own factory function, sprite , and a callback. The register function will take this callback and add it to the Factory, under the sprite property.

And it is this callback that is invoked whenever you call this.add.sprite in your game code. In this case, it's responsible for creating the Sprite instance and adding it to the display list, but any actual logic can take place here.

The callback is invoked using the Game Object Factory as the context, meaning that this within the callback is a reference to the Factory itself. This is why you can see it accessing the this.displayList property. This is a property available in the Game Object Factory class, which is a reference to the Scene Display List.

It's important to understand that while each Scene has its own instance of the Game Object Factory, registration of Game Objects with the Factory is global. This means that once a Game Object has been registered, its factory function is available to use from any Scene in your game.

At the end of the day, the Factory is all about convenience. It allows you to create Game Objects without having to worry about the internal details of how they are created. It also allows you to extend the Factory with your own Game Objects, or even override the existing ones, allowing you to customize the Factory to suit your own needs.

How to bypass the Game Object Factory

If you wish to create a Game Object without using the Factory, you can do so by calling the Game Object constructor directly. For example, to create a Sprite you would do this:

```
const sprite = new Phaser.GameObjects.Sprite(scene, x, y, key);
sprite.addToDisplayList();
```

Removing a Factory Function

If the Game Object Factory already has a function registered with a given name, it will simply skip any further registrations for the same name. Therefore, if you wish to replace one of the internal Phaser Game Objects with your own, you will need to remove the existing entry first before adding yours.

You can do this by calling the remove method:

```
Phaser.GameObjects.GameObjectFactory.remove("sprite");
```

This will remove the sprite method from the Factory, allowing you to then add your own with the same name. This process is immediate.

Adding Custom Game Objects to the Game Object Factory

You can extend the Game Object Factory by adding your own Game Objects to it. This is done by calling the static register method on the Factory itself. This method takes two arguments: The name of the Game Object, and a callback function that will create an instance of it.

10. Detailed look into Game Objects — Game Object Factory

Here is a simple class for our custom Game Object:

```
class Bomb extends Phaser.GameObjects.Sprite {
  constructor(scene, x, y) {
    super(scene, x, y, "bomb");
    this.setScale(0.5);
  }

  preUpdate(time, delta) {
    super.preUpdate(time, delta);
    this.rotation += 0.01;
  }
}
```

This is a very simple Game Object that extends the Sprite class. It's a bomb that spins around on the screen, as managed by the rotation in the preUpdate. We will register this with the Game Object Factory using the bomb key. We'll do this in our Scene init method:

```
class Example extends Phaser.Scene {
  init() {
    Phaser.GameObjects.GameObjectFactory.register("bomb", function (x, y) {
      return this.displayList.add(new Bomb(this.scene, x, y));
    });
  }
}
```

The init method is called first in a Scene. This means we can safely register our custom Game Object here, and it will be available for use in the Scene create method:

```
create();
{
this.add.bomb(200, 200);
this.add.bomb(400, 300);
this.add.bomb(600, 400);
}
```

You can see the full example here: [file: gameobjects/custom-factory.js]

When coding your register functions you have access to the following properties:

Property	Description
this.scene	A reference to the Scene that owns the Game Object Factory.
this.systems	A reference to the Scene Systems.
this.events	A reference to the Scene Event Emitter.
this.displayList	A reference to the Scene Display List.

Property	Description
this.updateList	A reference to the Scene Update List.

In the example above we registered the Game Object in the Scene init method. However, it's also very common to register it in the Game Object file itself in order to keep things tidy and together.

Here is a variation of the Bomb Game Object that registers itself with the Factory:

```js
export class Bomb extends Phaser.GameObjects.Sprite {
  constructor(scene, x, y) {
    super(scene, x, y, "bomb");
    this.setScale(0.5);
  }

  preUpdate(time, delta) {
    super.preUpdate(time, delta);
    this.rotation += 0.01;
  }
}

Phaser.GameObjects.GameObjectFactory.register("bomb", function (x, y) {
  return this.displayList.add(new Bomb(this.scene, x, y));
});
```

We can then import this into our Scene:

```js
import { Bomb } from "./Bomb.js";
```

And call the this.add.bomb method as before.

Game Objects

All Game Objects in Phaser extend from a base class called Phaser.GameObjects.GameObject . On its own, this class can't do much. It cannot render, for example, or be added to the display list. What it does do is provide all of the building blocks and core functionality that Game Objects need.

In this section we will cover the properties and methods that the base Game Object class has. This means, anything you read in this section is also available in every other Game Object within Phaser.

Scene

A Game Object can only belong to one Scene. A reference to the Scene it belongs to is available in the scene property:

```
const scene = sprite.scene;
```

Although it isn't, for internal reasons, you should consider this property as read-only. You cannot change the Scene that a Game Object belongs to once it has been created. The scene property is passed in the constructor of the Game Object and is set immediately.

When a Game Object is destroyed, the reference to the Scene is nulled-out. If you get any errors in your code relating to an 'undefined' Scene, then make sure you are not dealing with a destroyed Game Object.

Game Objects have two callbacks that are invoked when they are added to, or removed from, a Scene:

```
class MySprite extends Phaser.GameObjects.Sprite {
  constructor(scene, x, y, texture, frame) {
    super(scene, x, y, texture, frame);
  }

  addedToScene() {
    super.addedToScene();
    // This Game Object has been added to a Scene
  }

  removedFromScene() {
    super.removedFromScene();
    // This Game Object has been removed from a Scene
  }
}
```

You are free to use these callbacks in your custom Game Objects, in order to set-up any Scene specific data, or to perform any tasks that need to happen when the Game Object is added to, or removed from, a Scene. Be aware that some Game Objects, such as Sprites, use these callbacks, so make sure you always call super when overriding them, as in the example above.

Instead of using the callbacks, you can listen for the ADDED_TO_SCENE and REMOVED_FROM_SCENE events instead:

```
sprite.on(Phaser.GameObjects.Events.ADDED_TO_SCENE, handler);
```

```
sprite.on(Phaser.GameObjects.Events.REMOVED_FROM_SCENE, handler);
```

Both event handlers are sent a reference to the Game Object as the first parameter, and the Scene as the second.

Display List

If the Game Object resides on a Display List, which most do, then this is available via the displayList property:

```
const list = sprite.displayList;
```

A Game Object can either be on a Display List that belongs to its parent Scene, or it can be on a Layer that belongs to the Scene. This property can also be null . As with the scene property, you should consider this property as read-only and never change it directly.

The displayList property is set when the methods addToDisplayList and removeFromDisplayList are called. This happens automatically when you create a Game Object via the Game Object Factory, or add or remove it from a Layer.

A Game Object can only exist on one Display List or Layer at any given time, but may move freely between them. If the Game Object is already on another Display List when this method is called, it will first be removed from it, before being added to the new list.

If a Game Object isn't on any Display List, it will not be rendered. If you just wish to temporary disable it from rendering, consider using the setVisible method, instead of adding and removing it.

The act of adding and removing a Game Object will emit the ADDED_TO_SCENE and REMOVED_FROM_SCENE events respectively.

It's not common to need to call these methods directly, but they are exposed should you require them.

State and Name

The state property is a number or string value that you can use to store the current state of a Game Object. Use this property to track the state of a Game Object during its lifetime. For example, it could change from a state of 'moving', to 'attacking', to 'dead'. The state value should be an integer (ideally mapped to a constant in your game code), or a string. These are recommended to keep it light and simple, with fast comparisons. If you need to store complex data about your Game Object, look at using the Data Component instead.

```
sprite.state = "ALIVE";
```

You can also call the chainable setState method:

```
sprite.setState("ALIVE");
```

The name property is a string-based name that you can use to identify a Game Object. For example, you could use it to store the type of Game Object, such as player or enemy .

```
sprite.name = "player";
```

You can also call the chainable setName method:

```
sprite.setName("player");
```

Neither of these properties are ever used by Phaser directly. They are made available purely for you to take advantage of to help structure your games.

Update List and Active

Every Scene has an Update List. This is a special type of list that is responsible for calling the preUpdate method on all Game Objects on the list, once per game step. Some Game Objects need this, others don't. For example, a Sprite needs to have its Animation component updated every frame, so it adds itself to the Update List. However, a Text object doesn't have any components that require updating, so it doesn't add itself to the Update List. If you create a custom class, then you can choose if it should be added to the Update List, or not. You can do this by calling its addToUpdateList method:

```
sprite.addToUpdateList();
```

As long as the Game Object has a preUpdate method, and doesn't already exist on the Scene Update List, it will be added. You can then use the preUpdate method to run any custom logic that your Game Object requires, i.e.:

```
class Bullet extends Phaser.GameObjects.Image {
  constructor(scene, x, y) {
    super(scene, x, y, "bullet");
    this.addToUpdateList();
  }

  preUpdate(time, delta) {
    this.x += 10;
```

```
    if (this.x > 800) {
      this.setActive(false);
      this.setVisible(false);
    }
  }
}
```

Here we have a custom Game Object called Bullet. It extends from Phaser.GameObjects.Image, which doesn't use the Update List by itself usually. This is why we call addToUpdateList in the constructor. It then uses the preUpdate method to move itself across the screen, and if it goes off the edge, it deactivates itself. This means it will no longer be updated by the Update List, and will be skipped in future game steps.

When preUpdate is called, it is sent two parameters by the Update List. The first is the current timestamp, as generated by the browser. The second is the delta value, which is derived from the timestamp. This is the difference between the current frame and the previous frame. It is a value expressed in milliseconds and is the amount of time that elapsed between frames. This is what you should use to update your Game Object, rather than relying on setTimeout or other methods, because it handles pauses and slowdowns in the browser.

Related to the Update List, the active property is a boolean that controls if the Game Object is processed by the Update List, or not. A Game Object that is active will have its preUpdate method called during the game step, otherwise it will be skipped:

```
sprite.active = false;
```

You can also set the active state of a Game Object by calling the chainable setActive method:

```
sprite.setActive(false);
```

As mentioned, not all Game Objects are added to the Update List. For example, toggling this property on a basic Image Game Object won't actually change anything, because Images are not updated by the Update List. However, if you have a custom Game Object that is on the Update List, this is how you toggle it being processed, or not, without needing to add and remove it from the list.

Parent Containers

A Game Object can only have one parent Container. A reference to the Container it belongs to is available in the parentContainer property:

```
const container = sprite.parentContainer;
```

You should consider this property as read-only. It is set automatically when you add the Game Object to a Container, and nulled when it is removed, or destroyed.

Related to this is the method getIndexList . This will return an array of all the indexes of the Game Objects ancestors, going from its position up to the root of the Display List, via any parent Containers:

```
const indexes = sprite.getIndexList();
```

Internally, this is used by the Input Plugin. But you can call it directly if you need to know the depth of the Game Object within the Display List hierarchy.

Additional Methods

Game Objects also have methods relating to their Data Component and Input Component. Due to the size of these components, they are covered in their own respective sections.

Mask Component

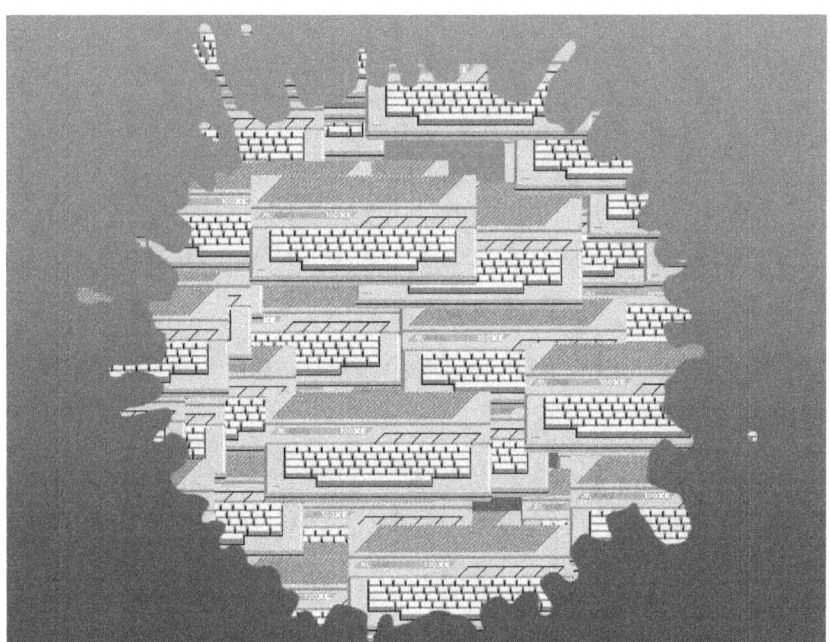

Figure 10.5 Mask Component

The Mask Component allows you to set if a Game Object should be 'masked' during rendering. A mask controls which pixels of the Game Object are visible during rendering.

Anything outside of the mask is not rendered. In Phaser there are two types of mask: a Bitmap Mask and a Geometry Mask.

The current mask of a Game Object is stored in its mask property:

```
const mask = sprite.mask;
```

You can set the mask of a Game Object using the chainable setMask method:

```
sprite.setMask(mask);
```

Or, you can set the mask property directly:

```
sprite.mask = mask;
```

To remove a mask, you can either call the chainable clearMask method:

```
sprite.clearMask();
```

Or, set the mask property to null :

```
sprite.mask = null;
```

When using the clearMask method you also have the option of destroying the mask currently attached to the Gamne Object:

```
sprite.clearMask(true);
```

How Masks Work in Phaser

There are two types of mask in Phaser, which we will cover in the next two sections. Although they offer different features they are both created and applied in the same way.

Masks are global objects. They are not bound to, or belong to any one single Game Object. You can, and often should, use the same mask on as many different Game Objects as you like, at the same time.

Masks are created and positioned in world space only. They are not applied relative to the Game Object they are masking. For example, if you create a mask positioned at world coordinates 200x300, then it will be positioned at 200x300 regardless of where the Game Object it is masking is.

Masks themselves are not Game Objects, they do not live on the display list and cannot be modified like a Game Object, i.e. you cannot set their rotation or scale as you would a Sprite. That does not mean you cannot modify a mask post-creation, it simply means that mask objects do not have a Transform component.

Geometry Mask

A Geometry Mask is a special type of mask that uses the path information from a Graphics Game Object in order to define its shape.

With the Canvas Renderer it uses the 'clipping path' feature of the Canvas API. The WebGL Renderer uses a built-in WebGL feature called the Stencil Buffer.

It's called a Geometry Mask because it uses geometric data in order to create itself. Graphics Game Objects have lots of features available for generating these paths, including lineTo , arc , ellipse and more. Please see the Graphics Game Object documentation for more details.

Because it uses path data for the mask it means you cannot do 'per pixel' masking with this type of mask. It's not suitable for creating a mask from a sprite with a gradient texture, for example. For that you should use a Bitmap Mask instead.

Geometry Masks have the ability to set their invertAlpha boolean properties. This is a WebGL only

feature and allows you to 'invert' which area of the mask is applied, or not.

Bitmap Mask

A Bitmap Mask uses a texture in order to control which pixels will be 'masked out' of the target Game Object during rendering. In order to achieve this it uses a special internal pipeline called the BitmapMask Pipeline. Because of this, it only works with the WebGL Renderer.

As it uses a texture for the shader input it means you can mask things on a per-pixel level, something not possible with the Geometry Mask. The source of the Bitmap Mask can be either a texture-based Game Object, such as a Sprite, or a Dynamic Texture instance.

The Bitmap Mask shader works by taking the alpha level from the mask texture and the alpha level of the masked Game Object and calculating the final resulting alpha level from the two, per pixel. It does not matter what color the mask texture is drawn in, all it looks at is the alpha value of each pixel. For example, if the mask has an alpha value of

0.95 for a specific pixel, and the Game Object texture has an alpha of 0.5 for the same pixel, the final alpha value when rendered will be 0.45. Naturally, the lower the resulting alpha value, the less the Game Object will be visible through it.

Bitmap Masks have the ability to set their invertAlpha boolean properties. This allows you to invert the alpha comparison, so that a low alpha value in the mask texture results in a high alpha value in the masked Game Object, and vice versa.

Note that you cannot set a Bitmap Mask and a Blend Mode on a single Game Object.

Performance Considerations

When using Geometry Masks you should keep in mind the complexity of the path, i.e. how many points it has in it. The more complex the path, the longer it will take both Canvas and WebGL to render the masked Game Objects.

When using Bitmap Masks you should keep in mind the size of the masked texture. The larger it is, the more pixels have to be passed through the mask shader and the more GPU power will be required to render the masked Game Objects.

With both types of mask, the renderer needs to perform a lot of additional calculations to handle the masking. This includes breaking the batch in WebGL, enabling the stencil functions or mask shader and then rendering the masked Game Objects. For this reason you should never apply a mask to a Game Object that doesn't yet require it.

Masks are, however, batched. This means if you have a group of masked Game Objects in sequence in the Display List, all sharing the same mask, then you will only pay the cost of establishing that mask once.

Origin Component

By default most Game Objects are centered on their x and y coordinates. This means that if you create a Sprite at the coordinates 300x200, then the center of the Sprite will be placed at 300x200.

In some game frameworks the default origin is the top-left, and in others the bottom-left. It is also sometimes known as the 'anchor point' or 'pivot point'. However, in Phaser it's called the origin and it defaults to the center. You can change this via the methods available from the Origin Component.

The current origin of a Game Object is stored in its originX and originY numeric properties:

```
const originX = player.originX;
const originY = player.originY;
```

To set the origin of a Game Object you can use the chainable setOrigin method:

```
player.setOrigin(x, y);
```

Or, you can set the originX and originY properties directly:

```
player.originX = 0.5;
player.originY = 0.5;
```

The values are given as a normalized value between 0 and 1. For example, setting the origin to 0.5 means it will be placed exactly in the center of the Game Object, no matter what its dimensions. A value of 0 would be the top-left of the Game Object, and 1 would be the bottom-right.

The origin controls both the placement of the Game Object and also the point around which it rotates. If you wanted to rotate a Game Object around its top-left corner, you would set its origin to be 0x0.

Or, if you wanted to position a Game Object in the bottom-right of the screen, and the screen was 800x600 in size, you could set the origin to be 1x1 and its position to be 800x600.

Game Objects can only have one origin. For example, they do not have a unique origin for rotation and another for position, or scale. If you need to emulate this behavior, you can create use a Container Game Object and then add your other Game Objects to it.

The Display Origin

Phaser also offers what is known as the Display Origin. This is a way to set the origin of a Game Object using pixel values instead of normalized ones. The range of the values is between 0 and the base width or height of the Game Object.

To set the display origin of a Game Object you can use the chainable setDisplayOrigin method:

```
player.setDisplayOrigin(x, y);
```

Or, you can set the displayOriginX and displayOriginY properties directly:

```
player.displayOriginX = 256;
player.displayOriginY = 128;
```

Custom Frame Pivot

Some software, such as Texture Packer, allows you to define a specific 'pivot point' for a texture frame. This is then exported in the JSON data that Texture Packer creates. Phaser will look for these custom pivot points and then set the origin of the Game Object to match it. This is done via the method setOriginFromFrame:

```
player.setOriginFromFrame();
```

This is called automatically if you create a Sprite and provide it with a texture frame that has a custom pivot point in the data. But you can also call it directly, if you need to.

Pipeline Component

The Pipeline Component controls which rendering pipeline the Game Object uses to render with. This is only set if the Phaser Game is using the WebGL Renderer. The Canvas Renderer does not use custom pipelines.

A Pipeline is an internal term and class construct that Phaser uses to handle rendering different types of Game Object. For example, there is the Multi Pipeline, which Sprites use, a Rope Pipeline for the Rope Game Object, and so on. You can also create your own custom pipelines, which can give you a lot of flexibility and power when it comes to rendering. The Pipeline Component is how you set a pipeline on a Game Object.

The current pipeline of a Game Object is stored in its pipeline property:

```
const pipeline = sprite.pipeline;
```

This will be null by default. It is not set until the Game Object is instantiated. As part of that process, all Game Objects call the initPipeline method, which is responsible for setting the default pipeline the Game Object uses. This is an internal method and should not be called directly.

You can set the pipeline of a Game Object using the chainable setPipeline method:

```
sprite.setPipeline(pipeline);
```

Or, you can set the pipeline property directly:

```
sprite.pipeline = pipeline;
```

When using the setPipeline method you can pass either a string, or an instance of a WebGLPipeline to the method. Regardless of which you pass, it will look-up the pipeline in the Pipeline Manager and if found it will be set on the Game Object. If you pass a string that doesn't match any pipeline, it will be ignored. If you pass a pipeline that isn't found in the Pipeline Manager, it will be ignored.

To remove a pipeline, you can either call the chainable resetPipeline method:

```
sprite.resetPipeline();
```

Or, set the pipeline property to match the defaultPipeline property:

```
sprite.pipeline = sprite.defaultPipeline;
```

The defaultPipeline property is set when the Game Object is first created and should be treated as read-only.

If you wish to get the string-based name of the pipeline the Game Object is using, you can call the getPipelineName method:

```
const name = sprite.getPipelineName();
```

Pipeline Data

The Pipeline Component also has a pipelineData property, which is an object that contains data that the pipeline may need during rendering. You can set a key-value object to be used as the pipeline data by passing it to the setPipeline method:

```
sprite.setPipeline(pipeline, { foo: 1, bar: 2 });
```

Or, you can call the setPipelineData method:

```
sprite.setPipelineData("key", value);
```

Pipeline data is not used by any of the default pipelines in Phaser, but is made available for your own custom pipelines. For example, if you wanted to create a pipeline that colored Game Objects in a special way, you could store the color of the Game Object in the pipeline data, ready for it to read prior to rendering.

Creating custom pipelines is an advanced feature of Phaser and requires a good understanding of WebGL and GLSL shaders. It will be covered elsewhere in this guide.

Scroll Factor Component

The Scroll Factor Component allows you to control the scroll factor of a Game Object. The "scroll factor" is how much influence a camera will exert upon a Game Object as the camera scrolls around the game world.

As covered in the Transform section, Game Objects have a position within the world. This position is combined with the Scene camera and used to calculate where the Game Object should be rendered onscreen.

If the camera is moving around the world, the Game Object will appear to move with it, even though its position hasn't changed, simply by virtue of the fact that the camera is now looking at another part of the world.

The scroll factor allows you to modify the relationship between the Game Objects position and how the Camera projects it. Setting a scroll factor never changes the position of the Game Object, or any related physics bodies, it just changes where they are rendered by the camera.

The current scroll factor of a Game Object is stored in its scrollFactorX and scrollFactorY numeric properties:

```
const scrollFactorX = player.scrollFactorX;
const scrollFactorY = player.scrollFactorY;
```

To set the scroll factor of a Game Object you can use the chainable setScrollFactor method:

```
player.setScrollFactor(x, y);
```

Or, you can set the scrollFactorX and scrollFactorY properties directly:

```
player.scrollFactorX = 0.5;
player.scrollFactorY = 0.5;
```

The default value for each axis is 1. This means as the camera scrolls, the Game Object will appear to move at the exact same rate.

A value of zero will stop the Game Object from being influenced by the camera. This will effectively 'lock' it in place on the screen. This can be useful if you wish to create a UI or other interface element that remains in the same place regardless of where the camera is looking.

A value of 0.5 will make the Game Object move at half the rate of the camera. The scroll factor can be any value from zero and above, although realistically you would likely clamp it to a value between 0 and 1.

Sprites and Images

Figure 10.6 Sprites and Images.

Sprites are easily one of the most commonly used Game Objects in the whole of Phaser. On a fundamental level a Sprite isn't much more than a texture mapped quad (a rectangle), but they have a lot of special features and functionality that make them worth using, not least the ability to automatically load and play animations.

The reason this section is covering both Sprite and Image Game Objects is because they are almost identical. The only difference between them is that the Image Game Object does not have the Animation

Component as part of it. So if you don't need frame-based animation, then you can safely use an Image in place of a Sprite. A common example of doing this would be a game logo, or background, or other nonanimated element.

Why does Phaser split them like this? It's because the Animation Component, while relatively compact, still takes up extra space in memory. Also, Sprites have to be added to the Update List, so that their Animation

Components can be updated each game frame. If you don't need animation, then you don't need to add the extra overhead of the Animation Component, or the Update List.

Of course, there are lots of games where it will make no actual difference in terms of performance and it will be safe to use Sprites for everything. But if you're making a game that has a lot of static images in it, or you're at the point where you are trying to optimize everything, then using Images instead of Sprites will help.

The term Sprite has its roots back in the hardware of the computers and arcades of the late 1970s, where it was used to describe a 2D bitmap that was moved around the screen, over the top of a background. These days, use of the term has become more generalized.

Creating an Image

Both images and sprites are created via the Game Object Factory. You access this directly from within a Scene using the add property:

```
var image = this.add.image(x, y, key);
var sprite = this.add.sprite(x, y, key);
```

The first argument is the x coordinate, the second the y coordinate, and the third is the key of the image to use. The key is a reference to an already loaded image that is available in the Texture Manager.

Usually, you create an image or sprite in the create method of a Scene, but you can do it anywhere you like, such as in response to a user input event.

Transform Component

The Transform Component is responsible for managing the position, scale and rotation of a Game Object.

Most Game Objects have this component, but you can test for it programatically by checking if the hasTransformComponent property exists and is true :

```
if (player.hasTransformComponent) {
    // This Game Object has a Transform Component
}
```

Position

The current local position of a Game Object is stored in its x and y properties.

```
const x = player.x;
```

```
const y = player.y;
```

You can set the position using the chainable setPosition , setX and setY methods:

```
player.setPosition(x, y);
player.setX(x);
player.setY(y);
```

Or, you can set the x and y properties directly:

```
player.x = x;
player.y = y;
```

They can be either negative or positive values, and whole numbers or floats.

The position of a Game Object is always relative to its parent Container, if it has one. If it doesn't have a parent, then the position is its location within the Game World.

For example:

```
container.setPosition(300, 200);
child.setPosition(100, 100);
```

In the code above, the Container is positioned at 300 x 200 in the game world. The child of the Container is

positioned at 100 x 100. This means that the child will appear at 400 x 300 in the game world, because its position is relative to the Container.

```
container.setPosition(300, 200);
child.setPosition(-100, -100);
```

In this code, the child will appear at 200 x 100 in the game world, because it has a negative position, relative to its parent.

The position is always set and returned as a number. This allows you to use the position directly in further calculations, or manipulate it as you would any other number:

```
enemy.x = player.x;
enemy.y = player.y - 100;
```

See the Origin Component to learn how Phaser knows which point of the Game Object to use as its x/y anchor.

Phaser also has two additional position related properties: z and w . You can set these optional values when calling setPosition , or they have their own chainable methods setZ and setW. These properties are not typically used internally by Phaser, but are made available should you require them for more advanced position, such as depth sorting.

The copyPosition method allows you to copy a Game Objects position directly to another object:

```
enemy.copyPosition(player);
```

The target object can be any object that has public x and y properties, such as another Game Object, or a Vector2.

You can also set the Game Object to have a random position with the setRandomPosition method:

```
enemy.setRandomPosition();
```

By default, if you don't provide any parameters, the Game Object will be given a position anywhere without the size set by the Scale Manager. However, you can also pass in x, y, width and height parameters to the method, to control a rectangle in which the random position will be set:

```
enemy.setRandomPosition(100, 100, 600, 400);
```

The Geometry classes have a variety of similar methods, for positioning objects within geometric shapes, however this method is handy if you just want to quickly position an object anywhere on-screen.

Scale

The current local scale of a Game Object is stored in its scaleX and scaleY properties.

```
const scaleX = player.scaleX;
const scaleY = player.scaleY;
```

You can set the scale using the chainable setScale method:

```
player.setScale(x, y);
```

Or, you can set the scaleX and scaleY properties directly:

```
player.scaleX = x;
player.scaleY = y;
```

There is also a special property called scale which allows you to set both the x and y scale at the same time, to the same value:

```
player.scale = 2;
```

Scale values can be either negative or positive, and whole numbers or floats.

By default, Game Objects have a scale value of 1, meaning they will be rendered at the same size as their texture frame. By adjusting the scale properties you can make them appear bigger or smaller. The number you give is multiplied by their base size. For example, a scale value of 0.5 would halve the displayed size of the Game Object, where as a value of 2 would double it.

Setting a scale does not change the actual underlying size of the Game Object. If you were to read the width or height of a Game Object after adjusting its scale, the returned values would be the un-scaled original sizes. You can read more about this in the Size Component section.

The scale is always set and returned as a number. This allows you to use the scale directly in further calculations, or manipulate it as you would any other number.

Scaling always takes place around the center of the Game Object, regardless of the Game Objects origin, and cannot be changed.

The scale of a Game Object is always relative to its parent Container, if it has one.

For example:

```
container.setScale(2, 2);
```

In the code above, the Container is scaled by 2 on each axis, meaning and all of its children will be doubled in size.

```
container.setScale(2, 2);
child.setScale(2, 2);
```

In this code, the child will appear at 4x the size of the container, because it has been scaled twice itself and also inherits the double scale from its parent.

If you scale any axis of a Game Object to zero, it will be skipped for rendering. This is because a Game Object with a scale of zero has no dimensions, so it cannot be seen. Therefore, to optimize the rendering pass, Phaser will skip those Game Objects entirely.

If you scale a Game Object negatively, an interesting effect happens. The Game Object will appear flipped.

For example:

```
player.scaleX = -1;
```

This will render the Game Object as if it was flipped horizontally. This is handy for characters that need to face in two directions but you only need to store the textures drawn in one direction, using the negative scale them to render the opposites at run-time. Note that Phaser also has a 'Flip Component' that can be used to flip a Game Object without adjusting its scale.

When you scale a texture based Game Object it's important to understand that the renderer will need to 'guess' at any pixels that are now present because of the increased size of the Game Object. For example, if

you have a 16x16 texture and you scale it by 4, it will appear as 64x64 on screen. All of those extra pixels that didn't exist before in the original texture are created by the GPU during the rendering process. A similar thing happens if you scale a texture down. The GPU has to decide which pixels to not display and tries to create an average that best represents the orignal image.

Lots of art software, like Photoshop, have the ability to apply special filters and effects when resizing images to create more refined results. However, WebGL and Canvas don't have this feature and they tend to favor speed over visual fidelity. After all, unlike Photoshop, they have to do this 60 times a second, or more. If you see a drop in visual quality worse than you were expecting, then you should consider using a smaller, or larger, texture that was pre-scaled in an art package instead.

Rotation

The current local rotation of a Game Object is stored in its rotation property:

```
const rotation = player.rotation;
```

The rotation value is always in radians. If you prefer to work with degrees, you can use the angle property instead:

```
const angle = player.angle;
```

To set the rotation, or angle, you can use the chainable setRotation and setAngle methods:

```
player.setRotation(rotation);
player.setAngle(angle);
```

Or, you can set the rotation and angle properties directly:

```
player.rotation = rotation;
player.angle = angle;
```

Phaser uses a right-handed coordinate system, where 0 is East, to the right, and 3.14 (or 180 degrees) is West, to the left. South is 1.57, or 90 degrees and North is -1.57 (or -90 degrees). If you visualise the rotation as a circle, the bottom half is positive and the top-half is negative. This is the same as Adobe Flash, from which the first version of Phaser took its inspiration.

Rotation in Phaser always takes place around the origin of the Game Object. Which means by default Game Objects typically rotate around their center. As you've read, you can adjust the origin. This changes where both the position and rotation occurs. You cannot change the rotation point of a Game Object, only its origin.

The rotation of a Game Object is always relative to its parent Container, if it has one.

For example:

```
container.setRotation(0.75);
```

In the code above, the Container is rotated by 0.75 radians, meaning all of its children will be rotated by the same amount.

```
container.setRotation(0.75);
child.setRotation(0.75);
```

In this code, the child will be rotated by 1.5 radians in total, because it inherits the rotation from its parent, then adds its own.

The rotation property only contains the local rotation value. If you wish to get the sum rotation of the Game Object taking into account all of its ancestors, you can use the getParentRotation method:

```
const rotation = player.getParentRotation();
```

This will return the total rotation of all parent Containers, in radians. If you need the world rotation, then add the Game Objects rotation to the final value:

```
const rotation = player.getParentRotation() + player.rotation;
```

Local and World Transforms

The Transform Component has a couple of methods that allow you to return a Transform Matrix instance that has been set to be either the local or world transform for the Game Object.

A Transform Matrix is a 3x3 identity matrix use for perform affine transformations. In Phaser, the operations are performed in the order of Translation, Rotation and then Scale, always in that order.

The method getLocalTransformMatrix will return a purely local Transform Matrix:

```
const matrix = player.getLocalTransformMatrix();
```

This matrix will not include any transforms from parent Containers. It will only contain the transforms of the Game Object itself.

The method getWorldTransformMatrix will return a Transform Matrix that contains the Game Objects local transforms, multiplied with those of all of its parent Containers:

```
const matrix = player.getWorldTransformMatrix();
```

Both methods have the option to be passed Transform Matrix instances. If given, the values will be set in those, instead of a new instance being created and returned. If you are calling either of these methods a lot, i.e. in a constant update loop, or en-masse, then you should create some temporary matrices to pass to them, to avoid the constant creation of new objects:

```
const tempMatrix = new Phaser.GameObjects.Components.TransformMatrix();
player.getLocalTransformMatrix(tempMatrix);
```

Or:

```
const tempMatrix = new Phaser.GameObjects.Components.TransformMatrix();
const tempParentMatrix = new Phaser.GameObjects.Components.TransformMatrix();

player.getWorldTransformMatrix(tempMatrix, tempParentMatrix);
```

Visible Component

The Visible Component is responsible for setting the visible state of a Game Object.

A Game Object with a visible state of true is rendered to the display, where-as one with a visible state of false is not. By default, Game Objects have a visible state of true .

The current local visible state of a Game Object is stored in its visible boolean property:

```
const visible = player.visible;
```

To set the visible state you can use the chainable setVisible method:

```
player.setVisible(visible);
```

Or, you can set the visible boolean directly:

```
player.visible = false;
```

By default, Game Objects will have a visible state of true . This means they will be rendered.

Being able to toggle the visibility of a Game Object is very useful for quickly showing or hiding Game Objects, without impacting their positions or other properties.

Hidden Game Objects are skipped by the renderer, saving cycle time, but still retain their internal position and state. This means that you can hide a Game Object, then make it visible again at a later stage, without having to reposition it or set other properties again.

An invisible Game Object is still updated, however. For example, if you had an animated Sprite that was playing through an animation sequence, then setting it to be invisible would not cause the animation to pause as it would still be updating. The same goes for other actions, such as tweens, or physics collisions.

The visible state is purely a rendering toggle.

Parent Visibility

If a Game Object has a parent Container, then the visible state of the parent will control if any of its children are rendered, or not. An invisible parent will skip rendering of all children, regardless of their own visible settings. However, if the parent is visible, then the children visibility will be used instead.

11. Cookbook

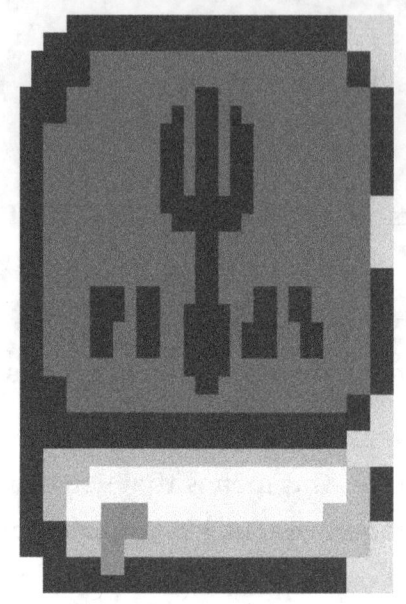

Sometimes you just need examples of very specific use cases. This chapter names some common cases and points you to implementations in games listed at the end.

Same sound with variants

You can play the same sound applying some tweaks through the parameters of the `play` function. This way the sound will be more natural.

Examples: Spooky, Marstranded, WallHammer

Actions on animation events

Sometimes you may need to do something in a specific moment of an animation. There are many examples of this at the end of it, especially for character deaths. But you can also detect a specific frame of an animation to do something. Check out the avocado foe in the game Flatulent World, who shoots his own seed.

Examples: Flatulent World

Mouse right and left click

The use of the mouse as input is shown in many games. You may also need to see how to use the right click (disabling the default behavior) especially considering that you may run your games on a browser. This is also possible with PhaserJS.

Examples: Electron (right click), PushPull, Starshipped

Screen Transitions

Transitions from one screen to another are an art inside the art of games. You should try to pay some attention to this to make your game look more polished.

Examples: Starshipped, **Marstranded**, Raistlin

Lightning effect

If you need to add the effect of a storm with lightning, you can use this trick with just rectangles, tweens and some thunder sounds.

Examples: Spooky, Camp Night, Like Tears in the Rain, Fate

Rain or Snow effect

You just need a sprite (or sprites) representing a raindrop or a snowflake and start a particle emitter. The same can be applied as a trailing effect for any game object.

Examples: Camp Night, Melt Down, Like Tears in the Rain.

Lights in the dark

Lights are just game objects that you can add to your game with different radius and luminosity parameters. These lights can be applied on a dark scene and they add a great effect. They can be randomized and they can represent torches, shots, explosions, gold, etc. Also, lights can be a key part of the game, like in terror games.

Examples: Greedy Willie, Johnny Depth, Get Rich or Die Trying, Camp Night, Shotman, Starshake

Underwater swimming effect

Underwater swimming is really simple, it's just a continuous jump on a screen that lacks ground. To make this swimming more "realistic" you can generate random bubbles and randomized bubble sounds.

Examples: U.F.I.S.H., Johnny Depth, Get Rich or Die Trying

Infinite scrolling background

Find a nice background image or pattern and move it as your character moves.

Examples: Starshake, Make Way

Dynamic map

Instead of creating a predefined map, you can build and render the map as the player moves. Or you can generate some elements randomly.

Examples: Starshipped, Melt Down, Rise Up

Adding/Removing tiles from a tiled map

On a tiled map, it is possible to add/destroy elements dynamically from the code.

Examples: WallHammer, Like Tears in the Rain, Shotman, DrillBill

Map building

If tiled maps can be dynamic, you can let the player design his own level placing/removing tiles.

Example: Platcraft

Composed game objects

Using containers, a player or any other game object can contain more than one element. In the case of Need4Split, we have separated parts.

Examples: LetterChaos, TruckTrack, Need4Split

Find paths and move foes automatically

If you need foes that chase the player inside a dungeon, a labyrinth or in any tiled space, you can apply an implementation of the A* algorithm.

Examples: Marstranded, Shotman, Starshipped, PowerGrid

Enemies shooting at player

How can foes shoot directly at the player? It's easy, the game knows where the player is. We just need the foe and the player position and create a fireball moving in that trajectory. This is shown in many games.

Examples: Raistlin2, Starshipped, Atlantis, Starshake

Detect screen limit

In some cases, it may be interesting to detect when an object touches the limit of the screen, so you can destroy that element and free your game of managing it.

Examples: Starshipped, Starshake

Jump simulation on an isometric view

On a 2D platformer, it's easy to simulate a jump but when the view is not perpendicular to the ground (like Golden Axe or Double Dragon), you have to manage the state of the jump. On the screen there is a jump, but basically, during the jump you have to deactivate some collisions.

Example: Make Way

Parabolic shot

You can throw an element given an angle and speed, to simulate a cannon or any kind of parabolic shot.

Examples: Chat Gasol, WarChat

Bullet hell

Creating these patterns can be achieved using basic functions or making good use of Maths! My examples are not the best, but you can start from here.

Examples: Fate, Starshake

Ships in formation

In space shooters, it's very common to show waves of foes that follow specific paths. The technique for this is relatively easy, then it's up to you to create complex paths.

Examples: Starshake

Life bar

These are little bars that appear next to the player or enemies to tell us the amount of life/energy or whatever they have left. You can change the color of the bar as it goes down (or up).

Examples: TruckTrack, Melt Down, Marstranded

Typing effect

Showing letters one by one is a typical effect that you can use for game intros, or to simulate a computer screen. In this examples the typing effect is done with time-delayed functions.

Examples: Fate, Marstranded, Like Tears in the Rain

Sensors

If you need to trigger some action when a game object touches something you can use overlaps instead of colliders. You can use this in items that the player can pick up or use a sensor for some interesting effect: in the Marstranded game, before you fall into a hole the player touches a sensor around it to play a sound.

Examples: Marstranded

Adding video

Videos are just other assets of the game, very simple to use. They can be interesting for presentations, transitions or even story-building.

Example: Fate

Valid Words

If you need a game where you have to deal with valid words, you need functions to validate those words. Apart from a simple list or dictionary, you could build a Trie to optimize the search. These games are simpler, in some cases, they can deal with multiple languages. They also give points according to letter value, as in the Scrabble game.

Examples: LetterChaos, Chatle, Chat Defense, Wordinary

Keep a scoreboard

Using Firebase free services you can create a DB and read and save score data from your game. In these examples the implementation is not very safe but it's a starting point.

Examples: MakeWay, Goblin Bakery, Keep Rolling, Lucky Shot

Windows build

Do you want to convert your game into a Windows executable? You can do it by installing the nw and nwjs-builder libraries and running some specific build commands.

Examples: TruckTrack

Index of games

This list contains most of the games from my repository mentioned above, with a link to the source code on github.com and another link to a playable version on the itch.io site. Sometimes these games belong to a specific genre, sometimes they are are mix of many things, and sometimes they are just experiments. In your journey, as you build and play other games you will probably grab ideas and mix them your way.

Alfabetica

Simple multiplayer Twitch game, similar to Numerica where we just show a letter of the alphabet and players must enter the next letter.

Source code github.com/pxai/phasergames/tree/master/alfabetica

Play it here pello.itch.io/alfabetica

Atlantis

A platformer game where the hero must reach the exit carefully because every block he jumps on falls after a second. In the meantime, the sea level goes up so time is limited on each stage.

Source code github.com/pxai/phasergames/tree/master/atlantis

Play it here pello.itch.io/pocket-atlantis

Ball Breaker

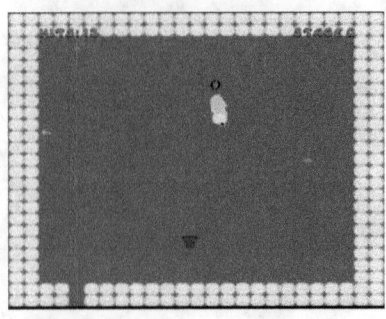

A game where we try to put a bouncing ball in a basket before the ball destroys the stage borders and dies.

Source code
github.com/pxai/phasergames/tree/master/ballbreaker

Play it here pello.itch.io/ballbreaker

BlastEmUp

Proof of concept of multiplayer space shooter using WebSockets built on socket.io library. Covered in the multiplayer chapter.

Source code:
github.com/pxai/phasergames/tree/master/blastemup

BloodHound

A very cheesy Cabal clone, with similar moves and power-ups. I sang the music myself. Built in a single script for a jam with that limitation.

Source code
github.com/pxai/phasergames/tree/master/bloodhound

Play it here pello.itch.io/bloodhound

Brick

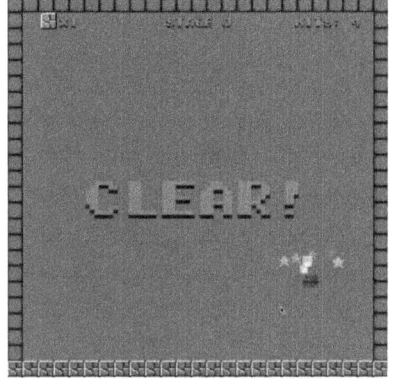

A variation of Ball Breaker but with clouds instead of bricks, and enemies flying around.

Source code github.com/pxai/phasergames/tree/master/brick

Play it here pello.itch.io/brick

Brushkkake

A multiplayer Twitch chat game where we present a canvas and players can paint on it giving coordinates and color.

Source code
github.com/pxai/phasergames/tree/master/brushkkake

Play it here pello.itch.io/brushkkake

Camp Night

A terror game where you try to find a lost child in a dark forest, with symbolic sprites and an eerie atmosphere. As you get close to the child, he calls you louder. A variation of Marstranded.

Source code github.com/pxai/phasergames/tree/master/camping

Play it here pello.itch.io/camp-night

Make Way

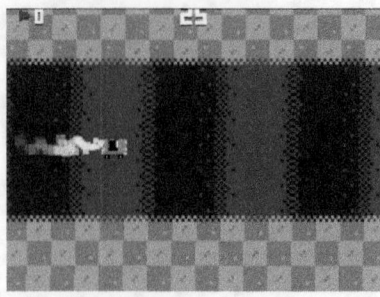

Car game, where you have to endure as much as possible, you can jump if needed and pick up missiles to shot at other cars.

Source code github.com/pxai/phasergames/tree/master/cars

Play it here pello.itch.io/make-way

Chancelord

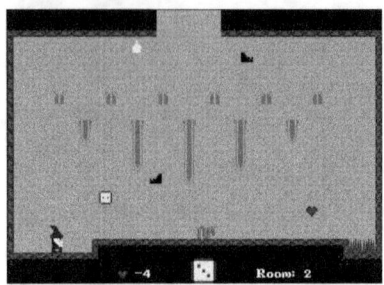

A simple platformer where the player can set custom blocks with different behaviors to reach the exit.

Source code github.com/pxai/phasergames/tree/master/chancelord

Play it here pello.itch.io/chancelord

Chatdefense

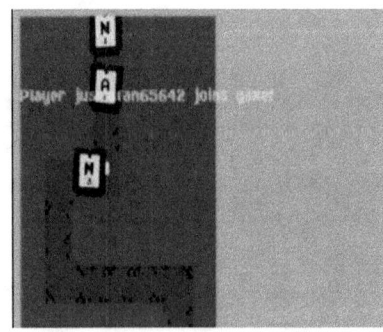

A multiplayer Twitch chat game where we have to defend a castle from incoming letters. If players create valid words with them, those letters are cleared from the path. The points depend on the letters, like in Scrabble.

Source code
github.com/pxai/phasergames/tree/master/chatdefense

Play it here pello.itch.io/chatdefense

Chat Gasol

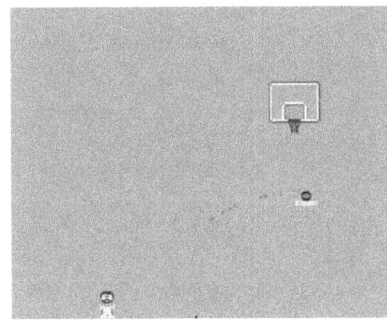

A multiplayer Twitch chat game where players give angle and speed to try basket their ball.

Source code github.com/pxai/phasergames/tree/master/chatgasol

Play it here pello.itch.io/chatgasol

Chatle

A variant of Wordle for Twitch chat games.

Source code github.com/pxai/phasergames/tree/master/chatle

Play it here pello.itch.io/chatle

DrillBill

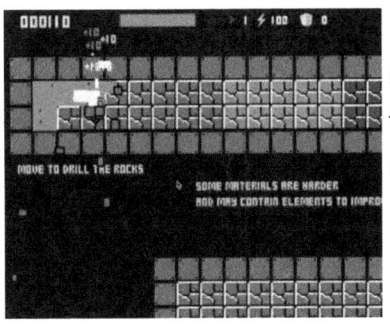

A dungeon crawler where dungeons are blocked by stones and the player must clear them with a drill to find the exit. Stones have different resistances so power-ups can be used to drill harder or move faster.

Source code github.com/pxai/phasergames/tree/master/drill

Play it here pello.itch.io/dril-bill

Dungeon Booble

A roguelike with randomly generated rooms and Matter.js physics that plays homage to Bubble Bobble, covered in this chapter.

Source code github.com/pxai/phasergames/tree/master/dungeon

Play it here pello.itch.io/dungeonbobble

Electron

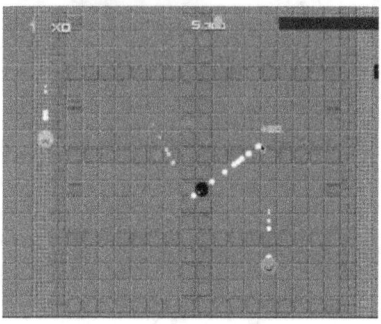

This is an infinite runner where we manipulate an electron and move it applying attraction and repulsion by right-clicking or left-clicking the mouse on the screen.

Source code github.com/pxai/phasergames/tree/master/electron

Play it here pello.itch.io/electron

Flatulent World

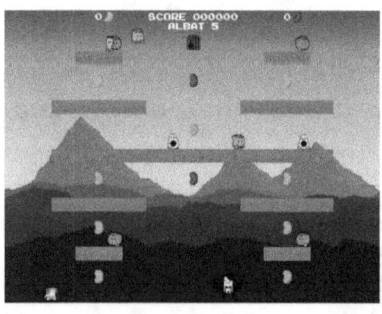

A platformer like Snow Bros or Bubble Booble where we must defeat or push the enemies with farts! Jumping is also done by farting, but we need to get green or red beans to get better farting powers.

Source code github.com/pxai/phasergames/tree/master/fate

Play it here pello.itch.io/fate

Fate

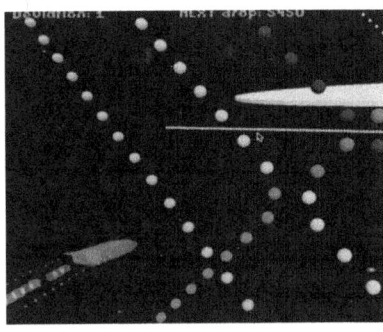

A 3D bullet hell, explained in the 3D chapter.

Source code github.com/pxai/phasergames/tree/master/fate

Play it here pello.itch.io/fate

Puddle Escape

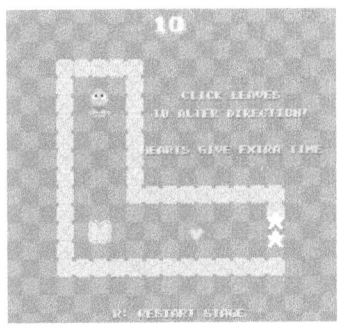

A simple puzzle game where we need to direct a frog out of a maze by putting lily pads on the water.

Source code github.com/pxai/phasergames/tree/master/froggy

Play it here pello.itch.io/puddle-escape

Goblin Bakery

An infinite runner where a Goblin must step on cakes to get them ready, avoiding spikes.

Source code github.com/pxai/phasergames/tree/master/goblin

Play it here pello.itch.io/goblin-bakery

Get Rich or Die Trying

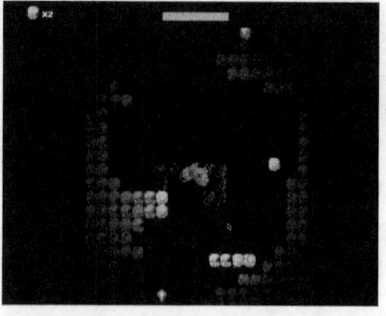

An aquatic adventure where a submarine goes down to get gold, but the more gold it gets the slower it will go while oxygen depletes. Dropping gold gives an extra boost.

Source code github.com/pxai/phasergames/tree/master/goldload

Play it here pello.itch.io/get-rich-or-die-trying

Greedy Willy

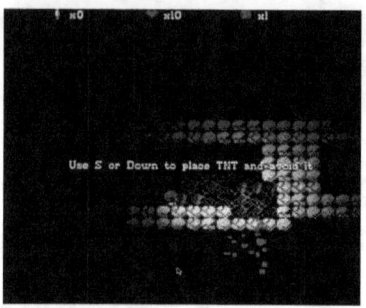

A roguelike in a mine where a greedy grandpa miner explodes his way through using TNT and getting power-ups, while he gets as much gold as he can.

Source code github.com/pxai/phasergames/tree/master/greedy

Play it here pello.itch.io/greedy-willie

Holy Crab

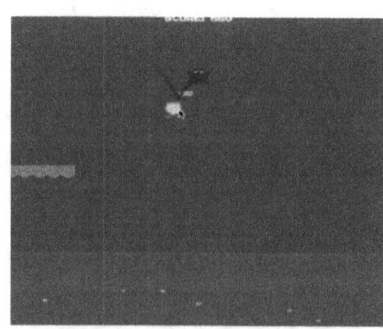

A jumping crab that we move indirectly by placing a platform below him. You have to reach the end of each stage avoiding the seagulls.

Source code github.com/pxai/phasergames/tree/master/holycrab

Play it here pello.itch.io/holy-crab

Johnny Depth

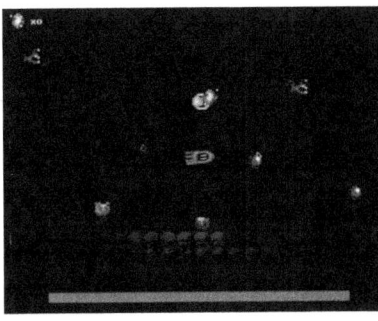

Another submarine adventure where a jelly fish gets jewels while it avoids volcanos, dangerous fish and mines.

Source code
github.com/pxai/phasergames/tree/master/johnny_depth

Play it here pello.itch.io/johnny-depth

Keep Rolling

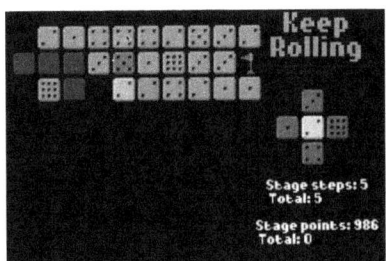

A puzzle game where a rolling dice must move over numbered-tiles. The dice must have a greater or equal number than the tile it wants to move to.

Source code
github.com/pxai/phasergames/tree/master/keeprolling

Play it here pello.itch.io/keep-rolling

LetterChaos

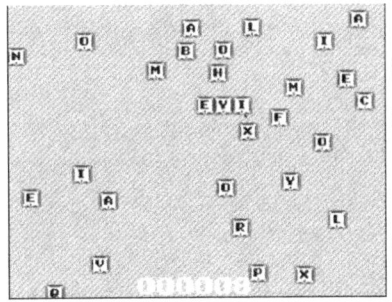

Several letters are spawned on screen continuously and the player needs to create words with them before there are too many.

Source code
github.com/pxai/phasergames/tree/master/letterchaos

Play it here pello.itch.io/word-chaos

Lucky Shot

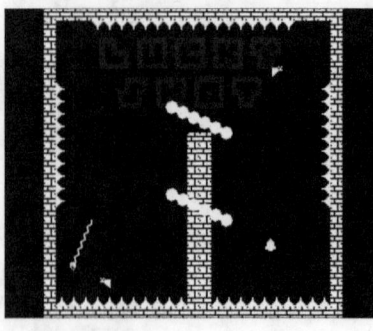

A slingshot that needs to hit a bell avoiding elements in the middle like bats, spikes and spinning platforms. Made with Matter.js physics.

Source code github.com/pxai/phasergames/tree/master/luckyshot

Play it here pello.itch.io/lucky-shot

Marstranded

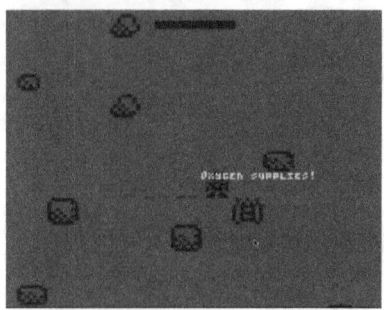

A story game already covered in its chapter. Inspired by Cold Scream.

Source code github.com/pxai/phasergames/tree/master/mars

Play it here pello.itch.io/marstranded

Metabolik

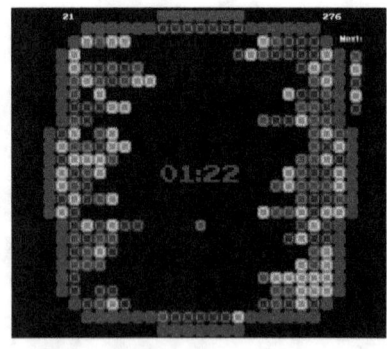

A circular Tetris-like game where we try to join blocks of the same color to clear them.

Source code github.com/pxai/phasergames/tree/master/metabolik

Play it here pello.itch.io/metabolik

Moriarty

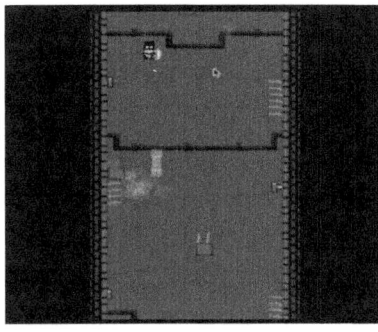

A game that uses Matter.js physics where we need to direct a guy up and then down through a pipe full of deadly traps.

Source code github.com/pxai/phasergames/tree/master/moriarty

Play it here pello.itch.io/moriarty

Need 4 Split

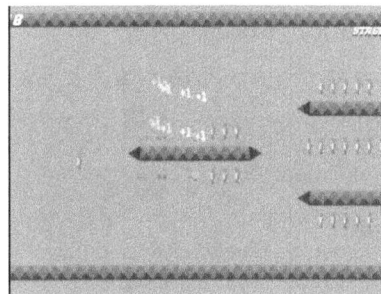

A similar game to Geometry Dash where we also get coins. The player block can be split into different distances to pick up more coins or to avoid spikes.

Source code github.com/pxai/phasergames/tree/master/need4split

Play it here pello.itch.io/needforsplit

Nightmare

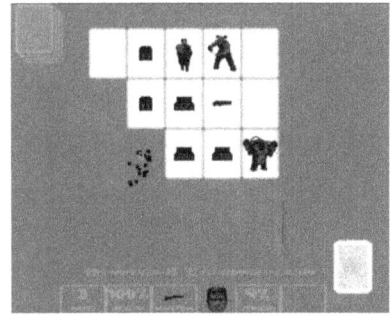

A card game that works like a dungeon crawler based on the Doom game lore.

Source code github.com/pxai/phasergames/tree/master/nightmare

Play it here pello.itch.io/nightmare

Shogun Killer

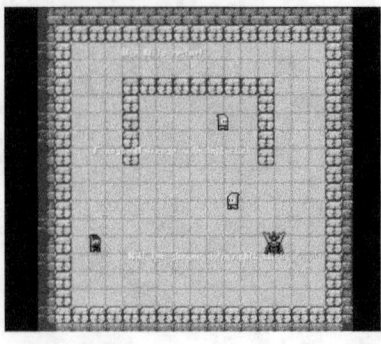

A puzzle-like shooter where we need to freeze some ninjas to use them as bouncing points to hit the Shogun with a shaken.

Source code github.com/pxai/phasergames/tree/master/ninjagolf

Play it here pello.itch.io/shogun-killer

Melt Down

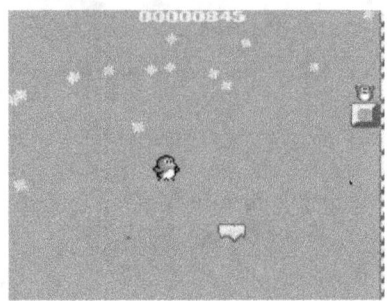

An infinite runner where a penguin must jump up on dynamic blocks to escape from the growing water level. All blocks are slippery and the penguin can jump and flap to reach higher.

Source code github.com/pxai/phasergames/tree/master/penguin

Play it here https://pello.itch.io/meltdown

Platcraft

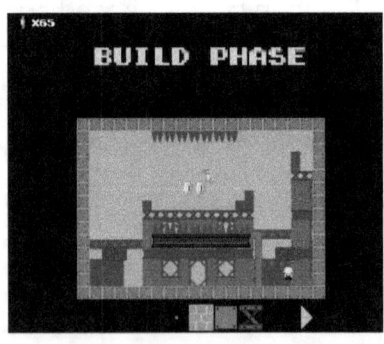

A platformer where before you start the stage you get a budget and it lets you customize the stage with blocks that have different prices depending on their value to solve the stage.

Source code github.com/pxai/phasergames/tree/master/platcraft

Play it here pello.itch.io/platcraft

Powergrid

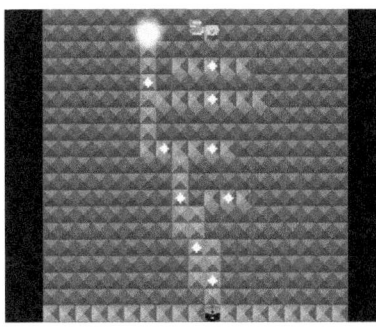

A puzzle game where you have to turn switches on and off to create circuits and turn on all the bulbs of each stage. It uses the A* algorithm to check that the circuits are correct.

Source code github.com/pxai/phasergames/tree/master/powergrid

Play it here pello.itch.io/power-grid

Spooky

A creepy dungeon-like little horror game where the player must get a key and reach to door to get to the next room, avoiding ghosts and the devil himself.

Source code github.com/pxai/phasergames/tree/master/pumpkin

Play it here pello.itch.io/spooky

Push Pull

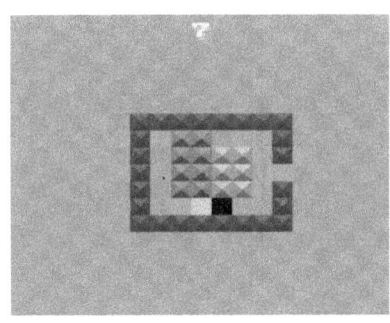

Puzzle game of blocks similar to Rush Hour, where you need to make a way out for a little block by moving other blocks. Covered in this chapter.

Source code github.com/pxai/phasergames/tree/master/pushpull

Play it here pello.itch.io/pushpull

Raistlin

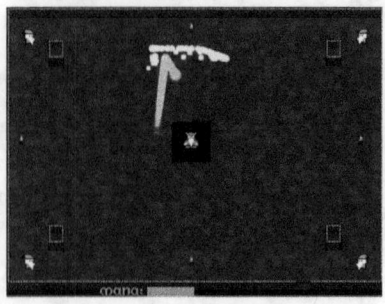

A game where a wizard creates shields (by painting with the mouse) to make the fireballs bounce and send them out of the stage.

Source code github.com/pxai/phasergames/tree/master/raistlin

Play it here pello.itch.io/raistlin

Raistlin2

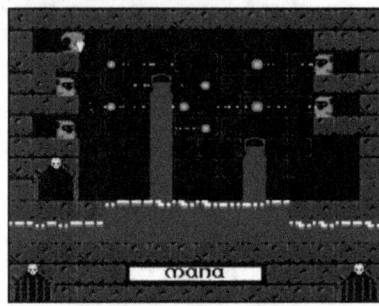

A platformer where a wizard has to reach the exit by creating platforms (by painting with the mouse), creating shields against attacks or even throwing fireballs at enemies. The player has limited mana so he must choose wisely how to use it.

Source code github.com/pxai/phasergames/tree/master/raistlin2

Play it here pello.itch.io/raistlin2

Rise Up

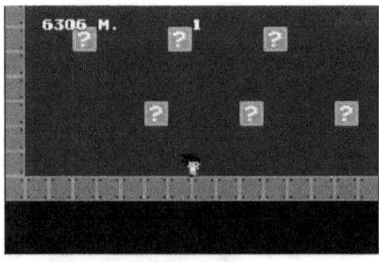

A platformer where single blocks appear on the stage that the player must use to climb up to the top. Each block has different effects and they change on every run.

Play it here pello.itch.io/rise-up

Romanica

Another multiplayer Twitch game, similar to Numerica, here with Roman numerals.

Source code github.com/pxai/phasergames/tree/master/romanica

Play it here pello.itch.io/romanica

Runner

Very minimalistic infinite runner, already covered in the first chapter.

Source code github.com/pxai/phasergames/tree/master/runner

Play it here pello.itch.io/runner

Shotman

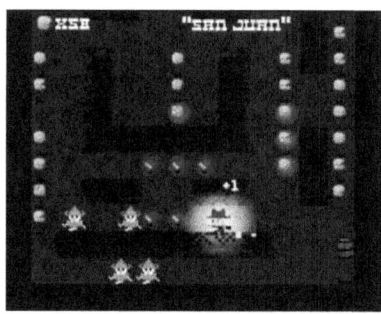

A Pacman-like game but with a shotgun. Shots can open ways through the walls and they will kill ghosts for a few moments. To kill the ghosts for good, you must shoot at TNT barrels when they are close to them. Shots are limited in each stage.

Source code github.com/pxai/phasergames/tree/master/shotman

Play it here pello.itch.io/shotman

Slotgeon

Another multiplayer Twitch game. It's a dungeon crawler where each room elements are shown as a slot machine result. Players chose the action to do (fight, run,...). Very experimental, it needs improvement.

Source code github.com/pxai/phasergames/tree/master/slotgeon

Play it here pello.itch.io/slotgeon

Sonsofbitches

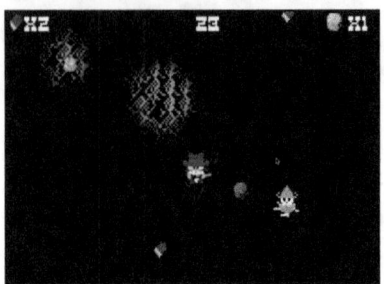

A variant of Shotman but without walls, so instead of stages you just need to survive as much as you can.

Source code
github.com/pxai/phasergames/tree/master/sonsofbitches

Play it here pello.itch.io/sonsobitches

Squiz

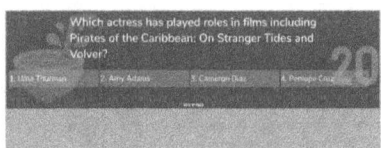

A multiplayer Twitch game that offers a quiz game for chat users. You can define the number of questions for the round, the topic and then player must chose the right answer from A, B, C and D. Questions are taken from a wonderful free API.

Source code github.com/pxai/phasergames/tree/master/squiz

Play it here pello.itch.io/squiz

Starhshake

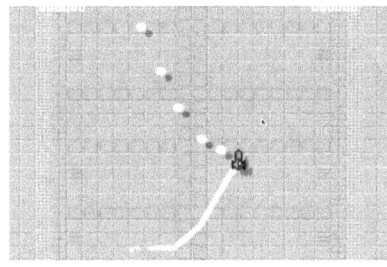

A space shooter already covered in its chapter.

Source code github.com/pxai/phasergames/tree/master/starshake

Play it here pello.itch.io/starshake

Starshipped

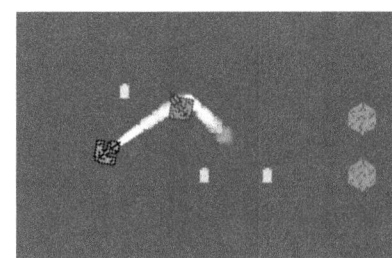

A space shooter where the player must fight against another ship. The enemy ship hunts down the player automatically using the A* algorithm. The stage is generated on the fly with random asteroids and ammo capsules. The camera zooms in and if any ship gets out of screen bounds it gets destroyed. That mechanic and general idea is based on Alva Majo's Shipped game.

Source code
github.com/pxai/phasergames/tree/master/starshipped

Play it here pello.itch.io/starshipped

Like Tears in the Rain

A platformer where the player can place blocks on the stage just by typing. The block position will depend on the relative position of the key on your keyboard, and the blocks will be on the screen for a few seconds.

Source code github.com/pxai/phasergames/tree/master/tears

Play it here pello.itch.io/like-tears-in-the-rain

Tetris

An implementation of the Tetris game, with unit tests.

Source code github.com/pxai/phasergames/tree/master/tetris

TrackTruck

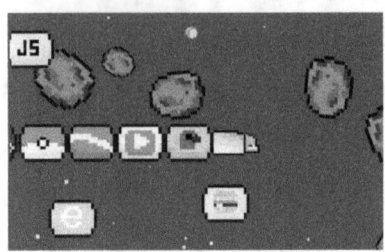

A space truck picks up containers while it prevents asteroids from hitting its long growing body.

Source code github.com/pxai/phasergames/tree/master/tracktruck

Play it here pello.itch.io/truck-track

U.F.I.S.H.

A UFO falls to the sea and swims its way out while fighting hostile submarines and fish. It can use a tracking beam to catch coins and shoot them.

Source code github.com/pxai/phasergames/tree/master/ufish

Play it here pello.itch.io/ufish

WallHammer

A platformer already covered in its chapter.

Source code
github.com/pxai/phasergames/tree/master/wallhammer

Play it here pello.itch.io/wallhammer

WarChat

A Worms-like game for Twitch chats, but with fireball-throwing wizards instead of worms.

Source code github.com/pxai/phasergames/tree/master/warchat

Play it here pello.itch.io/warchat

Weezard

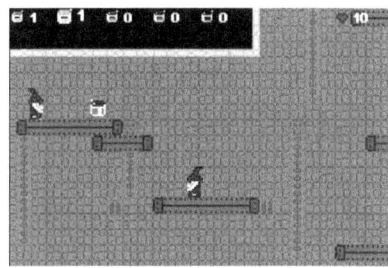

A platformer where a wizard can pick up different types of potions with different effects to clear his way through a single long stage. One of the potions turns the screen inside up, Inception style.

Source code github.com/pxai/phasergames/tree/master/weezard

Play it here pello.itch.io/weezard

Wordinary

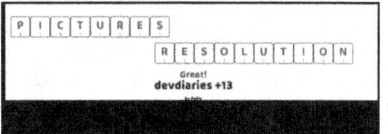

Another Twitch chat game where a word is shown and players must try to suggest a word that can be chained to it. Points are given depending on the word complexity, as in Scrabble.

Source code github.com/pxai/phasergames/tree/master/wordinary

Play it here pello.itch.io/wordinary

Wordle

An implementation of Wordle, but it allows to enter invalid words (which can be easily changed).

Source code github.com/pxai/phasergames/tree/master/wordle

Zenbaki

Yet another multiplayer Twitch game, similar to Numerica, here with arithmetic operations. Covered in the multiplayer chapter.

Source code github.com/pxai/phasergames/tree/master/zenbaki

Play it here pello.itch.io/zenbaki

Zombies

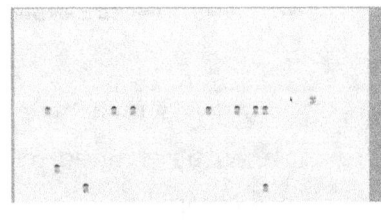

And last but not least, another multiplayer Twitch game where players are split between humans and zombies. The positions are invisible until somebody uses a command (like the Marco Polo game) or random lightning hits the screen. Everybody needs to enter coordinates to move, some to reach the chopper, others to touch the humans. Touched humans become zombies and keep playing.

Source code github.com/pxai/phasergames/tree/master/zombies

Play it here pello.itch.io/zombie-night

12. Assets

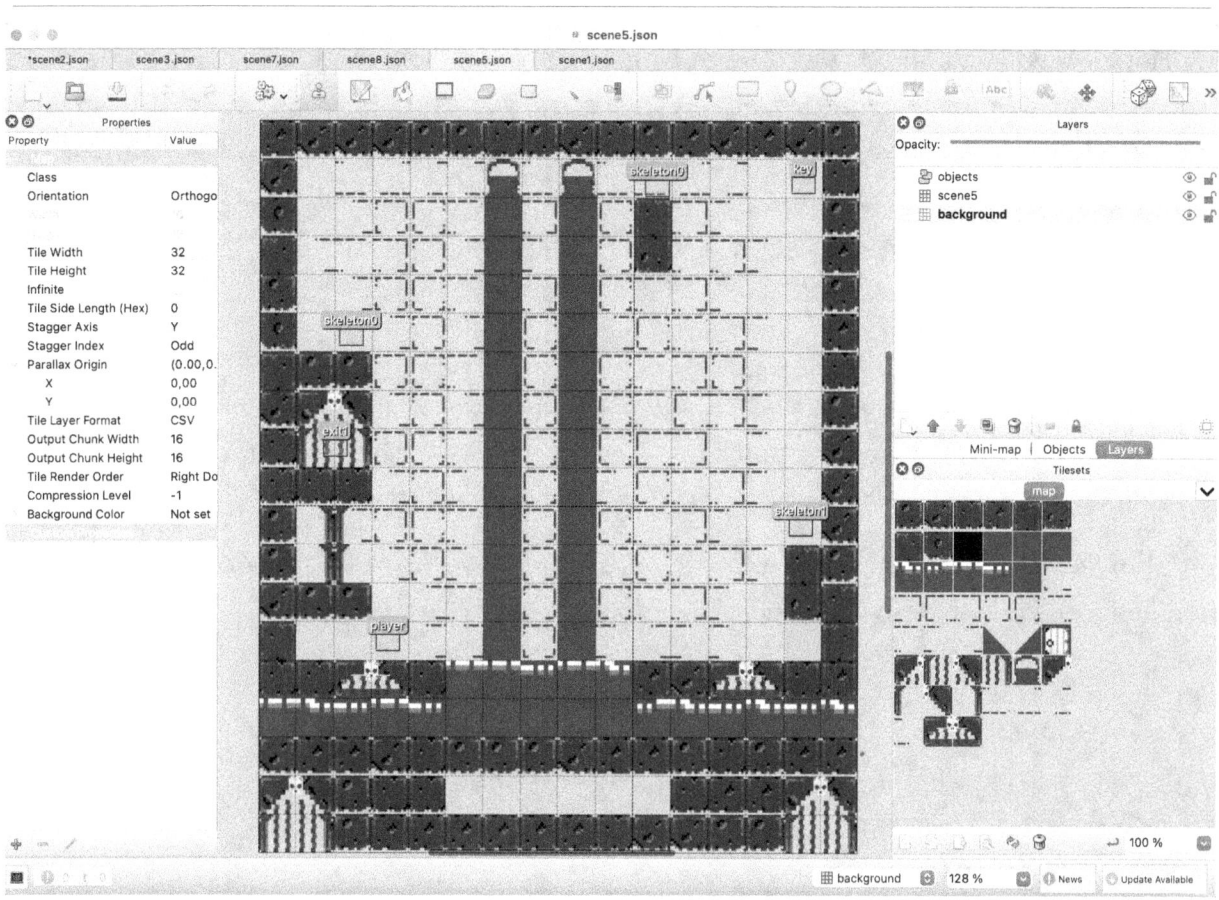

If you are not an artist, or a composer, or a sound designer and you need to use art assets, you can find a lot of free assets on the internet. You can use them for free, but you should always check the license of the asset.

Here we will talk about the different types of assets you can use in your game. Just keep one thing in mind: whatever style you choose, you should be consistent. This means that if you choose a pixel art style, you should use pixel art for all the assets and 8-bit styler sounds. If you choose a realistic style, you should use realistic assets for all the assets, and so on.

Fonts

Please, don't use system default fonts in your game. Adding a nice font to your game is a simple way to make it look way better, and it requires little effort.

Showing text with Phaser is relatively easy, but if we want to show customized text, we need to use a custom font. This is a simple process.

Practically you can choose any font you want from sources like:

- dafont.com
- fonts.google.com
- fontsquirrel.com
- 1001fonts.com

Then, you have to turn this font into a bitmap font. This type of font is used in all the examples of this book. This is a process that is done with a tool like: https://snowb.org/

You just need to upload the font there and then:

- You can name the font in the tab.
- You change the font color to white, so later you can tint to another color.
- You can change the size of the font if you want to show it bigger or smaller without losing quality.
- Finally, you can download it in xml format that Phaser will load perfectly.

12. Assets

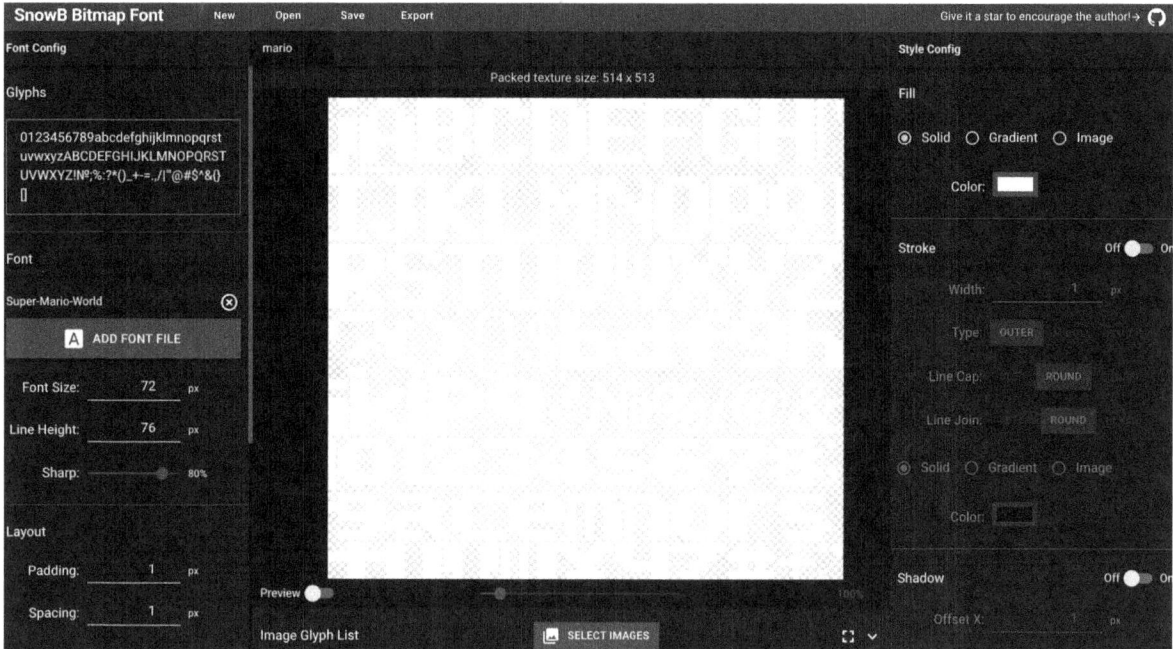

Figure 12.1 Snowb bitmap font generator.

Graphic assets and Pixel Art

Well, unless you want to develop a text-based game (that is cool too), you will need some graphics. You have two options, download assets or build your own art. Or both.

Downloading assets

Not everybody is an artist, and not everybody has the time or skills to create pixel art or nice SVG graphics. These are some of the best sources to find free assets:

- Itch.io Apart from hosting games Itch.io is a great place to find all kind of assets. Many of them are free.

- Kenney Probably one of the most famous asset creators. He has a lot of free assets and also some paid ones. The only issue is that this site is already well known, so you will find his assets in many games.

- **OpenGameArt** Another great place to find assets. You can find a lot of free assets here.

Building your own pixel art

Figure 12.2 Piskel in action.

If you want to create your own pixel art, you can use tools like:

- Aseprite (license)
- Piskel (free)

Another option is to create scalar vector graphics instead of Pixel Art. You can use tools like:

- Inkscape (free)
- Illustrator (license)

If you want to manipulate images, you can use tools like:

- Gimp (free)
- Photoshop (license)

Optimizing your visual assets

You should always optimize your assets. This means that you should try to make them as small as possible without losing quality. This is important because the smaller the assets, the faster the game will load. This is especially important for web games.

Another obvious optimization is to use sprite sheets whenever possible. This means that you should put all the images in a single file and then use them as frames of an animation.

On top of that, you should definitely use texture packers. Texture packers are tools that take all the images and create a single file with all the images. This is important because on a browser it reduces the number of requests to the server, and it also reduces the size of the images.

You can download texture packers or just use online tools like:

- Free Text Packer
- Leshy SpriteSheet Tool

Ideally, you should include this packing inside the automated building process of your game.

Audio assets

You have read this many times, but I must insist: add sounds to your game. The effort investment/result relation is very high. It's the most basic form of feedback and it's very important for the player to feel the game.

As it happens with graphics, you also can find many audio assets out there. These are some of the best sources to find free sounds:

- itch.io Itch.io also contains a lot of free sounds and music.
- OpenGameArt Also contains a lot of free sounds and music.
- Freesound A great place to find all kind of sounds, not just for games.
- Zapsplat Another great place to find all kind of sounds, not just for games.

- Youtube Why not? You can find a lot of music here, including 8-bit versions of any song.

Generating your own sounds

If you want to create your own sounds, you can use tools like:

- https://sfxr.me/ A simple tool to create 8bit-like sounds.

Converting/Editing your audio assets

Probably the best command line tool to convert and transform sounds is ffmpeg. It's a very powerful tool that can do a lot of things with sounds. The most basic one is to change file formats. For example, the command to convert a file from wav to mp3 would be:

```
ffmpeg -i input.wav myoutput.mp3
```

Audacity

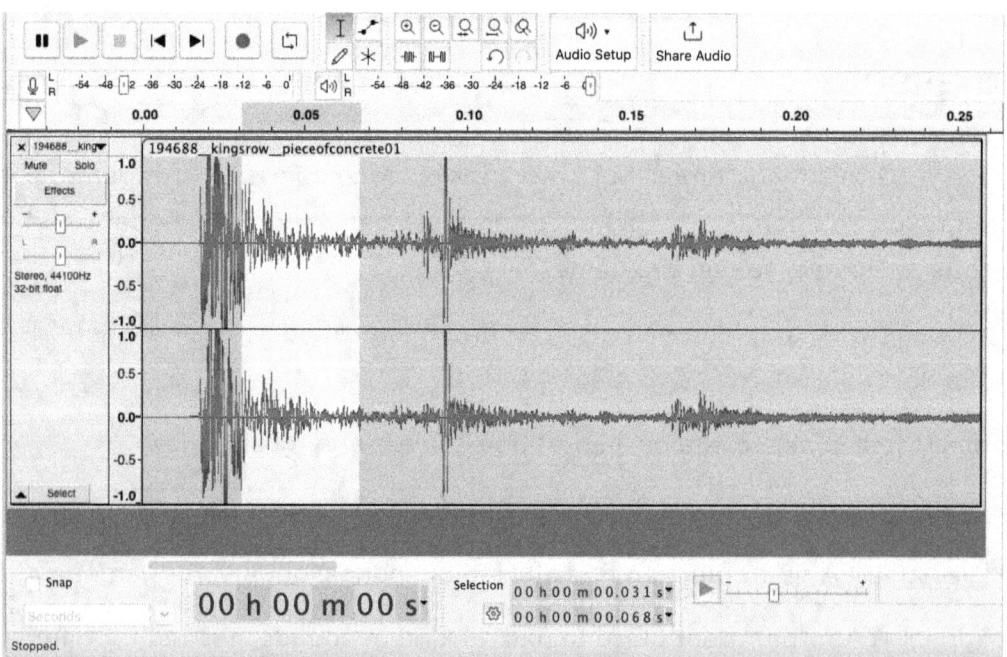

Figure 12.3 Audacity audio editor in action.

How can you edit your sounds or convert them in a more visual way? For this case I would go for Audacity. You can use it to edit sounds, to convert them, to add effects, etc.

Optimizing your audio assets

You should optimize your audio assets in the same way you optimize your visual assets. Obviously, you should use the right format for the right sound. For example, you should use ogg/mp3 for music and mp3 for sound effects.

As well as you can use texture packers for images, you can also use audio packers for sounds. This is important because it reduces the number of requests to the server, and it also reduces the size of the sounds.

You can download audio packers or just use online tools like:

- [Audiosprite](#) it is a ffmpeg wrapper that will take a folder of sounds and create a single file with all the sounds.

Maps

Maps are assets that define the layout of the levels. Usually, maps are created with a map editor that build scenes with different tiles, and then they are loaded into the game. By adding layers to the maps, you can define the background, the solid parts, the enemies' position, the items, etc.

Using tiled maps is a great way to create levels, for several reasons:

- It simplifies the process of creating levels.

- It separates the logic from the design. This means that you can create the levels without having to write code.

- It allows you to program one generic scene and then you can just load different levels.

- With a simple group of assets and some *savoir faire*, you can create a lot of good-looking different levels.

12. Assets

Tiled

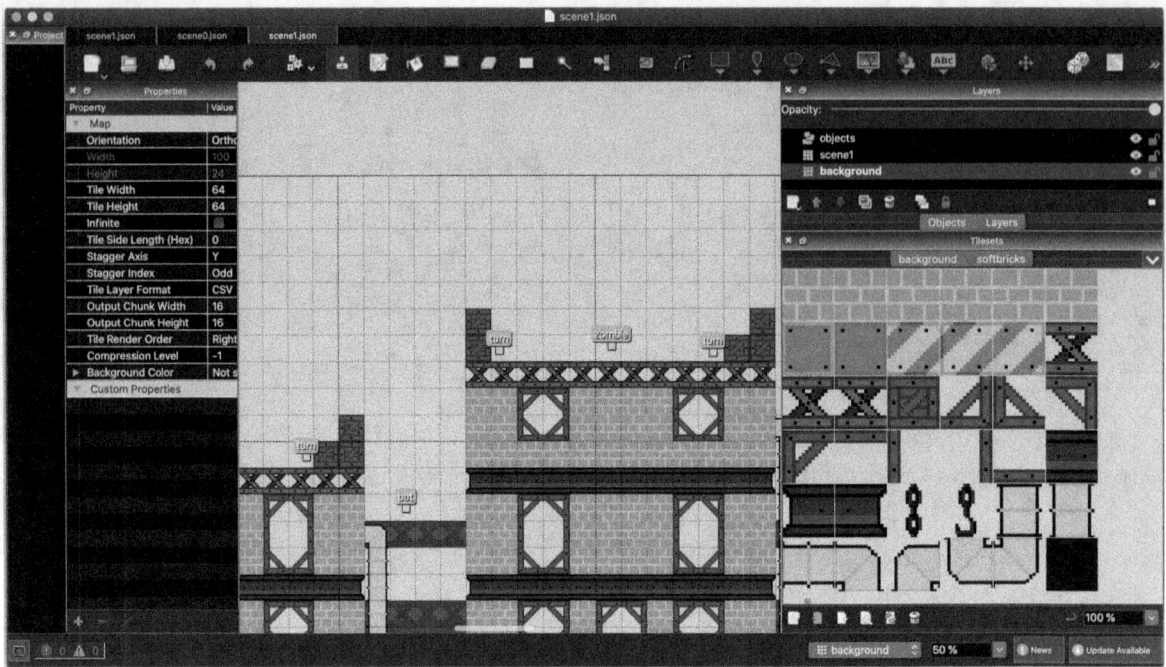

Figure 12.4 Scene design with Tiled.

You can use Tiled to create your maps. Tiled is a free and open-source map editor. It supports orthogonal, isometric and hexagonal maps. It also supports multiple layers, and it can export to JSON, XML, and CSV.

All the games in this book use Tiled to create the maps. You can download it from: https://www.mapeditor.org/

Steps to create a map with Tiled

The first thing once you open Tiled is in the menu `File > New > New map...` There you will choose the type of map, the size of tiles and size of the map, the tile size:

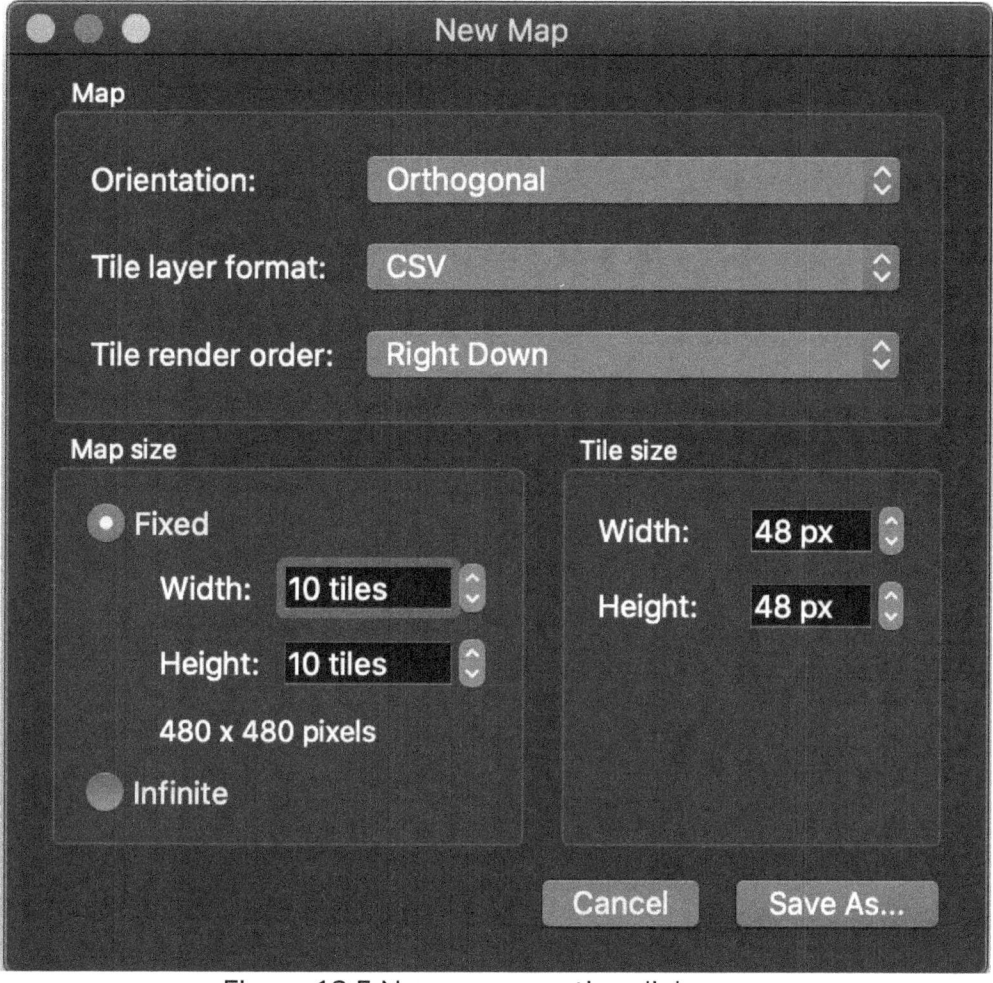

Figure 12.5 New map creation dialog.

Then you add the tileset (`New Tileset...` in the editor) this is an image that contains all the tiles you want to use, and obviously the size of each tile must match the size of the tiles you have chosen before.

Then you can start drawing the map. But be careful. You should go to the layers section and set proper layers like:

- Scene layer: a layer that contains the solid parts of the map.
- Background layer: a layer that contains the background of the map.
- Object layer: a layer that may contains enemies, items or any other object that you can place when you load the scene.

Then you can start drawing the map. You can use the tileset that comes with the examples of this book. You can also create your own tileset.

12. Assets

Ideally, you should name each map and the scene layer with a sequential name (scene0, scene1,...) so you simplify the loading as the game progresses.

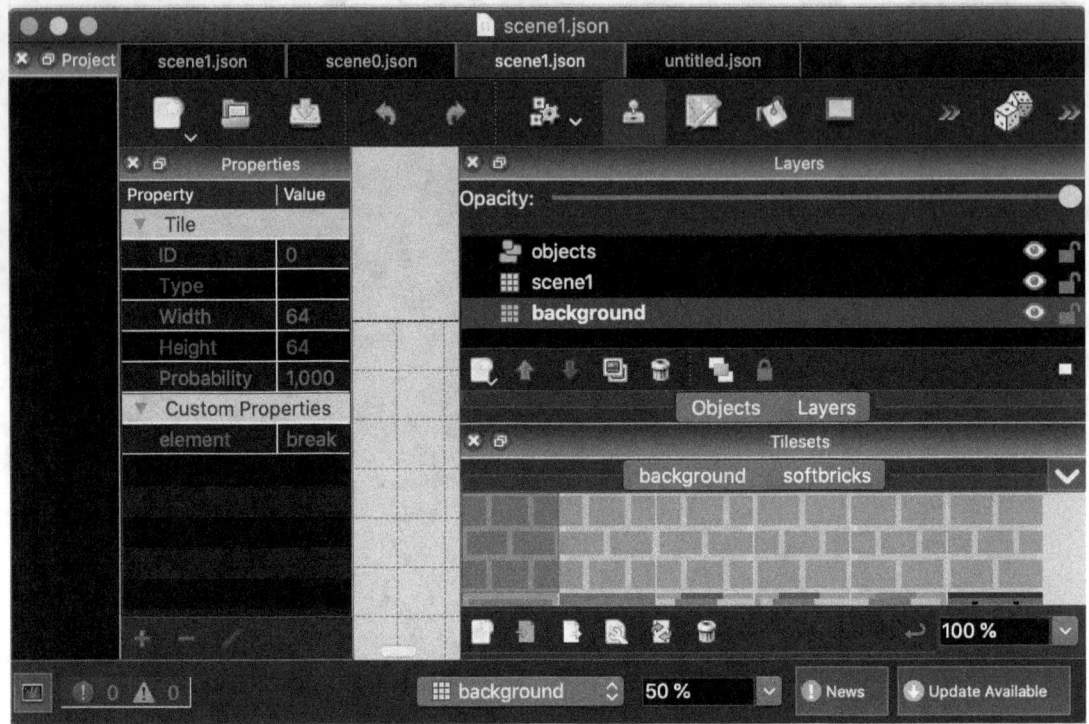

Figure 12.6 FigureSetting custom properties to tiles.

In some games like WallHammer, there are bricks that can be destroyed but others are solid. To do this, you can set custom properties to tiles. You just need to select the tile (or tiles) and click on the little wrench icon below. You will then see the properties of the tiles, and there you can add custom properties. As you can see in the image, the tile has a custom property called `element` that is set to `break`.

Anything you add to the properties of the tile will be available when you load the map in Phaser. In the scene code you can then add the behavior you want to the tiles.

Setting custom properties to objects

On the object layer you can place anything and then you need to set a name to it. This name will be used to identify the object when you load the map in Phaser. You can also set the type property or add custom properties to the objects, and then you can use these properties in the scene code.

That way you could, for example, set an enemy type and also some property like speed, level, initial direction or whatever you need.

Loading the map

The simplest way to work with Phaser is to generate a JSON file and load it. We will need to load the game as well as the tileset assets. This is something that is shown in the examples of this several times.

13. Build & Delivery

Examples here: https://github.com/pxai/phasergames/tree/master/project_templates

There are several setups available to run and build PhaserJS-based games. Being a JavaScript framework, most of them are just the same as any other web project, including tools like Gulp, Webpack, Vite, etc. We can also use online environments so we don't need to install anything locally. In this chapter, we'll see some of them, starting from the simplest setup.

Static HTML

PhaserJS runs on the browser, so we can just open an HTML file, include the Phaser library and start coding right there.

index.html

This is how the static HTML file would look like.

```html
<!DOCTYPE html>
<html lang="en">
<head>
    <meta charset="UTF-8">
    <meta name="author" content="Pello Xabier Altadill Izura">
    <meta name="viewport" content="width=device-width, initial-scale=1.0">
    <title>Phaser Basic template</title>
    <script src="https://cdnjs.cloudflare.com/ajax/libs/phaser/3.60.0/phaser.min.js" integrity="sha512-YQL0GVx/Too3vZjBl9plePRIYsRnd1s8N6QOvXPdZ+JMH2mtRTLQXGUDGjNW6zr1HUgcOIury67IvWe91oeEwQ==" crossorigin="anonymous" referrerpolicy="no-referrer"></script>
</head>
<body>
    <div id="container"></div>
    <script src="./GameScene.js"></script>
    <script src="./init.js"></script>
</body>
</html>
```

Once we include the PhaserJS library, we also include our own JavaScript files. We could directly write JavaScript code in the HTML file, but that would end up being too messy.

init.js

This is the file that creates the game with a basic config.

```
const config = {
    width: 400,
    height: 300,
    parent: "container",
    type: Phaser.CANVAS,
    scene: [GameScene]
};

new Phaser.Game(config);
```

This configuration holds a reference to a game scene that we can put in another file.

GameScene.js

This is just a simple Game Scene:

```
class GameScene extends Phaser.Scene {
    constructor () {
        super({ key: "GameScene"});
    }

    preload () {
        console.log("Preload");
    }

    create () {
        console.log("Create");
    }

    update (time, delta) {
        //console.log("Update", time, delta);
    }
}
```

Running it

To Run this, we can just open the HTML file on the browser and reload on each change. If you use tools like Visual Studio code, you can install extensions to automate that simple task.

NodeJS + Local phaser library

If you're familiar with the NodeJS environment, then you should try starting the project with NPM. NodeJS provides a local environment to run JavaScript code and combined

13. Build & Delivery — NodeJS + Local phaser library

with the npm package manager, we can deal with project setup and package dependencies.

Setup

With npm, it's very easy to start a NodeJS project. We just need to run this inside the project directory:

`npm init`

That will create the package.json file, that contains the basic configuration of the project and it will hold the list of dependencies or libraries that we install using npm itself.

Then we install the phaser package:

`npm i --save phaser`

This command will download the Phaser library and it will put it inside the `node_modules` directory.

index.html

This would be the HTML file, where we will change the reference to the PhaserJS library. We will use the file inside the local `node_modules/phaser` directory.

```html
<!DOCTYPE html>
<html lang="en">
<head>
    <meta charset="UTF-8">
    <meta name="author" content="Pello Xabier Altadill Izura">
    <meta name="viewport" content="width=device-width, initial-scale=1.0">
    <title>Phaser NPM template</title>
</head>
<body>
    <div id="container"></div>
    <script src="./node_modules/phaser/dist/phaser.js"></script>
    <script src="./src/GameScene.js"></script>
    <script src="./src/init.js"></script>
</body>
</html>
```

src/init.js

The init file does not change:

```
const config = {
    width: 400,
    height: 300,
    parent: "container",
    type: Phaser.CANVAS,
    scene: [GameScene]
};
new Phaser.Game(config);
```

src/GameScene.js

Same as before.

NodeJS + Local Phaser with modules

This is just the same setup as before, but it only changes the way we import the source files.

Setup

The setup is the same as before:

```
npm init
```

Then we install phaser:

```
npm i --save phaser
```

index.html

Now pay attention. This is how we can change the way we refer to source code:

```
<!DOCTYPE html>
<html lang="en">
<head>
    <meta charset="UTF-8">
    <meta name="keywords" content="game, phaser, platform, Pello">
    <meta name="description" content="game built with phaser">
    <meta name="author" content="Pello Xabier Altadill Izura">
    <meta name="viewport" content="width=device-width, initial-scale=1.0">
    <title>Phaser NPM template</title>
</head>
<body>
    <div id="container"></div>
```

```html
        <script src="./node_modules/phaser/dist/phaser.js"></script>
        <script src="./src/init.js" type="module"></script>
</body>
</html>
```

src/init.js

This is how the init looks like in this case:

```js
import GameScene from "./GameScene.js";

const config = {
    width: 400,
    height: 300,
    parent: "container",
    type: Phaser.CANVAS,
    scene: [GameScene]
};

new Phaser.Game(config);
```

Next is the `Scene` class, but it will look the same as before.

Gulp

Gulp is a project management tool that lets us run and build web-based projects: https://gulpjs.com/

Setup

We must install Gulp as part of our NodeJS project:

```
npm init
```

Then we install the Gulp command globally, which will allow us to run the `gulp` command and run gulp scripts:

```
npm install --global gulp-cli
```

After that, we need to add the `gulp` package as a dev dependency. That means that this will be used just during the development and build process, but it won't go into the final build code of our game.

```
npm install --save-dev gulp
```

Then we install PhaserJS as before:

13. Build & Delivery

```
npm i --save phaser
```

gulpfile.js

Now, here comes the gulpfile. It contains a list of tasks that we can chain to build the game and include the assets (images, sounds, etc) in the build directory.

```javascript
const { src, dest, watch, pipe, series, parallel, lastRun } = require('gulp');
const del = require('del');
const babel = require('gulp-babel');
const uglify = require('gulp-uglify');
const rename = require('gulp-rename');
const browsersync = require('browser-sync').create();
const open = require('gulp-open');
const browserify = require("browserify");
const source = require("vinyl-source-stream");
const sourcemaps = require('gulp-sourcemaps');
const terser = require('gulp-terser-js');
const buffer = require('vinyl-buffer');

const PHASERLIB = "node_modules/phaser/dist/phaser.min.js";

function clean () {
    return del(["dist"]);
}

function html(param) {
    return src("./assets/html/*.html")
        .pipe(dest("./dist"))
        .pipe(browsersync.stream());
}

function assets () {
    return src(["./assets/**.*/","!./assets/html/*.html"])
        .pipe(dest("./dist/assets", {force:true}))
        .pipe(browsersync.stream());
}

function vendor() {
  return src([`${PHASERLIB}`])
      .pipe(dest("./dist"))
}


function build() {
  return browserify({
        entries: ["src/init.js"],
        debug: true,
    })
    .transform('babelify', {
        presets: ['@babel/preset-env'],
```

```
        plugins: ['@babel/plugin-transform-runtime']
    })
    .bundle()
    .pipe(source('index.min.js'))
    .pipe(buffer())
    .pipe(sourcemaps.init({loadMaps: true}))
    .pipe(terser())
    .pipe(sourcemaps.write('.'))
    .pipe(dest("dist"))
    .pipe(browsersync.stream());
}

function buildProd() {
    return browserify({
        entries: ["src/init.js"],
        debug: false,
    })
    .transform('babelify', {
        presets: ['@babel/preset-env'],
        plugins: ['@babel/plugin-transform-runtime']
    })
    .bundle()
    .pipe(source('index.min.js'))
    .pipe(buffer())
    .pipe(terser())
    .pipe(dest("dist"));
}

function browserSync(done) {
    browsersync.init({
      server: {
        baseDir: "dist"
      },
      port: 3000
    });
    done();
}

function watchIt(done) {
    watch(["./assets/**.*/","./src/**/*.js","gulpfile.js"], parallel(html, vendor,
assets, build));
    done();
}

exports.build = build;
exports.production = series(clean, html, vendor, assets, buildProd);
exports.default = series(clean, parallel(html, vendor, assets, build),
parallel(browserSync, watchIt));
```

With this Gulp file, we can just run the project or create a build. While we run the project, it will detect any change in source code or the assets and it will rebuild and reload the game on the browser.

assets/html/index.html

Our index will be placed inside the `assets/html` directory:

```html
<!DOCTYPE html>
<html>
    <head>
        <meta charset="UTF-8" />
        <title>Phaser Game template</title>
        <meta name="keywords" content="game, phaser, platform, Pello">
        <meta name="description" content="game built with phaser">
        <meta name="author" content="Pello Xabier Altadill Izura">
        <script src="phaser.min.js"></script>
        <script src="index.min.js"></script>
        <link rel="stylesheet" href="assets/css/styles.css" />
    </head>
    <body>
    </body>
</html>
```

This will just contain a reference to the `init.js` file. Gulp will take care of putting all the code together.

src/init.js

The init just contains references to the scene and that imported code will be available to it thanks to gulp.

```js
import Game from "./game";

const config = {
    type: Phaser.AUTO,
    scale: {
        mode: Phaser.Scale.FIT,
        parent: "phaser-example",
        autoCenter: Phaser.Scale.CENTER_BOTH,
        width: 800,
        height: 600
    },
    physics: {
        default: "arcade",
        arcade: {
            gravity: { y: 300 },
            debug: false
        }
    },
    scene: [Game]
};
```

```
new Phaser.Game(config);
```

src/game.js

Same as before.

Webpack

Same as Gulp, Webpack is another project management system for building and running web-based projects.

Setup

`npm init`

We can install both the Webpack command line interface and Webpack library as dev dependencies:

`npm install webpack webpack-cli --save-dev`

Then, we have to install Phaser as we did before.

`npm i --save phaser`

webpack.common.js

Webpack looks more like a configuration rather than code. It allows us to group some functions in a file and then add others in other files. This is what we do here. Some common building operations go to this file:

```js
const webpack = require("webpack");
const path = require("path");
const htmlWebpackPlugin = require("html-webpack-plugin");
const { CleanWebpackPlugin } = require("clean-webpack-plugin");
const CopyWebpackPlugin = require("copy-webpack-plugin");

module.exports = {
  entry: {
    bundle: path.join(__dirname, "src/init.js")
  },
  output: {
    path: path.resolve(__dirname, "dist"),
    filename: "[name].[chunkhash].js"
  },
```

```
  module: {
    rules: [
      {
        use: "babel-loader",
        test: /\.js$/,
        exclude: /node_modules/
      }
    ]
  },
  plugins: [
    new htmlWebpackPlugin({
      template: "assets/html/index.html",
      filename: "index.html"
    }),
    new CleanWebpackPlugin({options: "dist/*.*"}),
    new CopyWebpackPlugin({ patterns: [{ from: './assets', to: './assets' }] }),
  ],
  stats: {
    colors: true
  }
}
```

Now, depending on the type of task we need (dev run or production build), we add other features in different files.

webpack.dev.js

This is the Webpack configuration for development. It will include the common part and also it will open a browser to show the project with hot reloading on changes.

```
const { merge } = require('webpack-merge');
const path = require("path");
const common = require('./webpack.common.js');

module.exports = merge(common, {
  mode: 'development',
  devtool: 'inline-source-map',
  devServer: {
    contentBase: path.join(__dirname, 'dist'),
    port: 8080,
    open: true,
    writeToDisk: true
  }
});
```

To run this mode, we just need to run:

```
npm start
```

webpack.prod.js

If we want to run a build for production, we use this file. It reuses common config but instead of opening the browser, it just optimizes the code.

```js
const { merge } = require('webpack-merge');
const common = require('./webpack.common.js');

module.exports = merge(common, {
  mode: 'production',
});
```

To create the build, we run this and it will leave the production build inside the dist directory.

```
npm run build
```
We can zip that directory to publish it on itch.io.

assets/html/index.html

The HTML is also located in the assets directory.

```html
<!DOCTYPE html>
<html>
    <head>
        <meta charset="UTF-8" />
        <title>Phaser Game template</title>
        <meta name="keywords" content="game, phaser, platform, Pello">
        <meta name="description" content="game built with phaser">
        <meta name="author" content="Pello Xabier Altadill Izura">
        <link rel="stylesheet" href="assets/css/styles.css" />
    </head>
    <body>
    </body>
</html>
```

src/init.js

The source code does not change. Webpack will get this file and include any other source code referenced here (including PhaserJS itself and the scene files).

src/game.js

Same as before

Parcel

Parcel is another more modern project management tool that lets us run and build web-based projects: https://parceljs.org/

Setup

As with the others, we must install Parcel as part of our NodeJS project

```
npm init
```
Then we install the Parcel command: it's just one development dependency:

```
npm install --save-dev parcel
```
With that, we are ready to use Parcel in our project. Then we install PhaserJS as before:

```
npm i --save phaser
```

package.json

For Parcel, we can set the whole configuration in the `package.json` file

```json
{
  "name": "phaser_parcel_template",
  "version": "1.0.0",
  "description": "Project template for phaser using parcel",
  "main": "index.js",
  "scripts": {
    "start": "parcel src/index.html -p 8000",
            "build": "parcel build src/index.html --out-dir dist",
            "test": "echo \"Error: no test specified\" && exit 1"
  },
  "parcelCleanPaths": [
            "dist"
        ],
        "staticFiles": {
            "staticPath": "assets",
            "watcherGlob": "**"
        },
  "devDependencies": {
    "@babel/core": "^7.10.5",
    "@babel/plugin-proposal-class-properties": "^7.10.4",
    "babel-eslint": "^10.1.0",
    "eslint": "^6.8.0",
    "minimist": ">=1.2.2",
    "parcel-plugin-clean-easy": "^1.0.2",
    "parcel-plugin-static-files-copy": "^2.4.3"
```

13. Build & Delivery Parcel

```json
    },
    "author": "Pello Xabier Altadill Izura",
    "license": "ISC",
    "dependencies": {
        "phaser": "^3.60.0"
    }
}
```

Parcel will take care of the rest automatically.

jsconfig.json

This is a config file that we need for this project.

```json
{
        "compilerOptions": {
                "target": "es6",
                "moduleResolution": "node",
                "checkJs": true,
                "esModuleInterop": true
        }
}
```

assets/html/index.html

Our index will be placed inside the assets/html directory:

```html
<!DOCTYPE html>
<html>
    <head>
        <meta charset="UTF-8" />
        <title>Phaser Game template</title>
        <meta name="keywords" content="game, phaser, platform, Pello">
        <meta name="description" content="game built with phaser">
        <meta name="author" content="Pello Xabier Altadill Izura">
        <link rel="stylesheet" href="css/styles.css" />
    </head>
    <body>
    </body>
</html>
```

The rest will remain the same.

Vite

Vite is another project management, well-known for its speed https://vitejs.dev/

Setup

We must install Vite as part of our NodeJS project:

```
npm init
```
And then we just install Vite as a dev dependency:

```
npm install --save-dev vite
```
In the case of Vite, it has its way of creating projects. You can check them out on Vite's website.

Then we install PhaserJS as before:

```
npm i --save phaser
```

vite.config.js

This is the basic Vite config file that we use for this project.

```js
import { defineConfig } from 'vite'

export default defineConfig({
        plugins: [],
        server: { host: '0.0.0.0', port: 8000 },
        clearScreen: false,
    build: {
      assetsDir: 'assets',
    },
})
```

Just with those few lines, we get the same result that we got with many lines of `gulpfile.js`.

assets/html/index.html

Our index will be placed inside the `assets/html` directory:

```html
<!DOCTYPE html>
<html>
    <head>
```

```
        <meta charset="UTF-8" />
        <title>Phaser Game template</title>
        <meta name="keywords" content="game, phaser, platform, Pello">
        <meta name="description" content="game built with phaser">
        <meta name="author" content="Pello Xabier Altadill Izura">
        <link rel="stylesheet" href="assets/css/styles.css" />
    </head>
    <body>
    </body>
</html>
```

The rest of them will work the same way.

Online: phasereditor2d

Another way to run and build PhaserJS-based games is by using online environments. This one was created specifically for PhaserJS.

https://www.phasereditor2d.com/

Online: repl.it

Replit is a great site where we can run almost any kind of project. Web-based projects are no exception, so it's pretty easy to have an environment ready to run Phaser games.

You can use this one as an example.

https://replit.com/@pello/Phaserjs-3-template?v=1

The Replit community is huge and you may find many other templates by others. Anyway, it's relatively easy to create your own.

Online: codesandbox

Codesandbox is another powerful environment. It's almost like owning a development laptop on your browser.

As it happens with Replit, Codesandbox is full of templates built by the community. This is one example using vite:

https://codesandbox.io/p/sandbox/phaser-js-3-vite-template-ntz4xr

Converting to Windows app

It is possible to turn our PhaserJS game into a Windows executable. We just need to install some dependencies:

```
npm i --save-dev nw nwjs-builder nwjs-builder-phoenix
```
We will also need to add some config in package.json. Check out the TruckTrack project as an example.

Automating itch.io upload

Another interesting tool for fast publishing and updating our game in itch.io is Butler. https://itch.io/docs/butler/

This is a command line tool that will allow us to automatically update the published game.

So once installed, we can just build and upload the game from the command line:

```
cd dist && rm -f assets/html/index.html && butler push . pello/zenbaki:html --userversion 0.0.1 && cd .. && butler status pello/zenbaki:html
```

Netlify publish

https://netlify.com

Another simple and fast option to publish our game is using a service like Netlify. The most convenient is first managing our code in a repository like GitHub.

Every time we push changes, we can fire an update in Netlify and run a build. Then we can just tell Netlify to publish the build directory.

14. Juice

14. Juice

Juice is all the polishing work that you do to make your game look and feel nice. Juice does not add anything to the mechanics or the core of the game, it's all about the presentation and the feedback of the game in all aspects: graphics, sound, music, transitions, and general effects.

The most basic juice is the feedback that you get when you press a button. If you press a button and nothing happens, you don't get any feedback. But if you press a button and you get a sound, a visual effect, a vibration, etc. you get feedback and you feel that you are doing something. And that's the most basic juice. But there are many other things that you can add that will turn feedback into dopamine shots.

The possibilities are endless and you can add as much juice as you want. But you should be careful because too much juice can be overwhelming and it can make the game feel slow. So you should add juice to the point where it feels nice but not too much. When it's too much? It can be a matter of personal taste, but as long as it does not interfere with the gameplay and allows you to know what is going on, it's fine to add as much as possible.

Ideas

So... what kind of feedback can you add to your game? Well, there are many things that you can add. Let's see some of them.

Sound effects

Sound effects have the best cost/benefit ratio. They are easy to add and they can make a huge difference. Sounds are a great way to give feedback to the player and they should be almost mandatory in any game, and the bare minimum that you should add to your game.

You can add sound effects to almost everything: when you press a button, when you move, when you jump, shoot, hit an enemy, die, win, lose, get a power-up, get a coin, get a bonus, get a new weapon, get a new level, new life, get a new enemy, get a new boss, when you get a new world or when you get a new anything!

Visual feedback

The cheapest way to add visual effects is tweens and we have seen a great deal of them in the examples. You can tween positions to simulate shakes, you can tween alpha to simulate flashes,... You can tween scale up/down an object to make it funnier. Also, you should add ease properties to your tweens for better effects.

Blinking is another great effect that you can add to any object. You can make it blink when it's hit, when it's destroyed, when it's picked up, etc. Sometimes, a blinking player means that it is invulnerable.

Trailing is quite easy to add to any moving object of the game. You can add a particle generator or just create simple sprites or squares in the position of the object and make them fade out. This will give the impression of movement and speed.

When a character jumps you can add some smoke on the ground and the same on landing. The smoke can be just squares or circles with a fading alpha, or sprites with a simple animation.

When something shoots, you can add a shooting explosion, an animated or tweened bullet with a trail, an explosion when the bullet hits something, etc.

Whenever you pick something up you can add an effect (along with a sound). Also, if it's something that alters a player's life, score or coin count, there you can add an extra effect.

Points! When you kill an enemy or you get a coin, you can add a points counter that goes up and vanishes. That will give you a nice feedback of what you are doing. Points can also move from the player to the scoreboard to visualize how they are added.

Move feedback

This refers to effects that you can add to elements for more realistic and satisfying feedback. If you hit or get hit, you can move the character a bit in the opposite direction. When you shoot a big weapon you can add some recoil to the player or ship. Also, when you shoot something big you can shake before you do it.

Furthermore, you can alter the physics so an overlap can be a soft collide and create objects that feel more resistant.

Light

Even in simple 2D games, you can add great light effects. It can add a nice effect on shots, explosions, deaths, etc. Also, in any game where you want to add some atmosphere, you can add a light source and make it flicker, change color, change intensity, change position, etc. In some cases, it can even be part of the mechanics of the game itself.

Screen effects

You can also make good use of the whole screen for feedback. The most common screen effect is the shake. You can shake the screen when you get hit or when you destroy a lot of enemies in one go. Shaking the screen is just one line of code and the effect is great and recognizable by all players.

Shining and blinking is another common effect. You can make the screen shine when you get a power-up or when you get a new weapon. It can be also a lightning effect to simulate storms. But use it carefully or show a warning because it can be annoying or damaging for sensible audiences.

Not all games must show a clear conventional view of the game. You can give some retro style by adding tv-like lines, a combed effect, a pixelated effect, a sepia effect, a black and white effect, or a negative effect. There's even a genre of games that exploits the "found footage" concept where you show scenes as if they were video recordings.

References

I recommend you to watch the following videos about juice. The first one is great, it shows you how to add juice to a game like Arkanoid or Breakout. The game looks very simple and dull, and as they move forward adding juice, the game becomes more and more fun. The second one is a talk about the juice in general and it's also very interesting.

Juice it or lose it - a talk by Martin Jonasson & Petri Purho:

https://www.youtube.com/watch?v=Fy0aCDmgnxg

How Game Juice Made My Game Come to Life:

https://www.youtube.com/watch?v=OsFc1f5ghRU

14. Juice

Screen shake

https://www.youtube.com/watch?v=AJdEqssNZ-U

15. Jams

Game Jams are game development competitions where you have to build a game in a limited amount of time. The time can range from hours to months, and normally there's a theme and/or limitation that you have to follow. Once the game is completed, people can play and rate the games in different categories: fun, graphics, sound, etc.

In these jams they normally let you use any tool you want, but some jams are more restrictive and force you to use a specific tool or framework. They also let you develop your project with other people or do it solo. Anyway... why should you care?

Why you should participate in a jam

The best way to learn is by doing. This is a great truth also in programming. And the best way to learn game development is by building games. So, if you want to learn game development, you should build games. And that's what jams are good for.

Game Jams add an extra layer of difficulty to the game development process. You have to build a game in a limited amount of time, so you have to focus on the core of the game and leave the rest aside. You have to be creative and find solutions to problems that you wouldn't have in a normal development process. As you are running against the clock, you'll spend a few days (or hours) in a very intense and focused process. And at the end, you'll have a completed game. Maybe it's not perfect, maybe it does not have all the features that you dreamed of, but it's a completed project. And that's a great feeling. Would you be able to finish a game if you didn't have time constraints? How many side-projects have you abandoned?

As you take part in different jams, you will learn new techniques and you'll improve your skills: you will add what you learn from previous jams and you will avoid the mistakes you made. Besides, you will have to take care of all the aspects of building a game, not just graphics, art or programming, but also logos, game page design, demo videos, etc.

Winning? Forget about it. It's really hard to get everything right: the theme, the idea, the execution, the art, the music, the sound, the gameplay, the fun, the polish... Don't worry about being the winner. Quite often what you think is a great idea won't be understood or considered fun by others. But also, ideas that you may consider simple or even stupid may have great success. In the end, what matters is what you learn by taking part in several jams. And by the way, you'll be building a portfolio of games that you can show to others.

No Leg Lenny
by Robin Six
Ranked **6th** with 70 ratings (Score: 4.329)
View submission page →

Criteria	Rank	Score*	Raw Score
Theme	#4	4.371	4.371
Overall	#6	4.329	4.329
Fun	#10	4.186	4.186
Visuals	#10	4.429	4.429
Juice	#14	4.157	4.157
Audio	#21	3.857	3.857

Figure 15.1 Criteria scores in a ranked game jam.

Feedback

Trying other games in jams is not just polite, it's necessary to improve yourself. You'll have to review other projects and believe me, you will learn a lot in that process: discovering ideas, art, effects, transitions, etc. that you didn't know before. And you'll also learn what not to do. You'll see many games that are not fun, that have a bad design, that are not polished. And you'll learn from that too.

Besides, in a Jam you can present your idea and see if it's good or not. You can ask other people to play it and see what they think. Depending on the reviews you can decide to continue with the project or not. And if you decide to continue, you'll have a lot of feedback to improve it. Worst case scenario, you'll have a prototype that you can use in the future but you won't waste more time on it.

The game idea

Believe me, developing a good idea is as hard as building the game itself. First, it must be something that fits the limitation. Second, it must be fun, and ideally, it must be something new. And there are so many games out there that it's becoming harder and harder to bring something different to the table.

It is often said that you should automatically discard your first idea because probably it's the most obvious one. An indirect approach or twisting an apparently unrelated concept may turn into something original and it will be highly appreciated.

But whatever it is, it must be something that you can quickly generate a prototype of. That will give you the assurance that the idea may work well.

You should definitely not get into something too complicated, especially for weekend jams.

Jam types

Nowadays there are many jams, but the most popular are the online ones. They are normally hosted on a website like www.itch.io or www.gamejolt.com.

Next, we'll see some of the most popular jams. And you should consider participating in one of them. It's a great way to learn and meet people.

Little short jams

There are several types of jams, but the most common are the short ones. They are normally online and last from 48 to 72 hours.

TriJam

https://trijam.itch.io/

Figure 15.2 TriJam logo.

Trijam is the three-hour game jam that takes place every weekend. The jam is not very restrictive with the time and it has a weekend schedule from Friday afternoon to Sunday afternoon. The theme/limitation is announced on Friday and you have to submit your game before Sunday evening. So in theory you have to build something in three hours.

It takes place in itch.io and it comes with an extra. Every Wednesday, before the winner is announced you can join a Twitch stream to see some of the games and even ask for yours to be tested. The streamers are patient and nice, and they will play your game if you ask them to.

Games developed for Trijam are not super polished but it's a good chance to build a quick prototype and test an idea.

Minijam

https://minijamofficial.com/

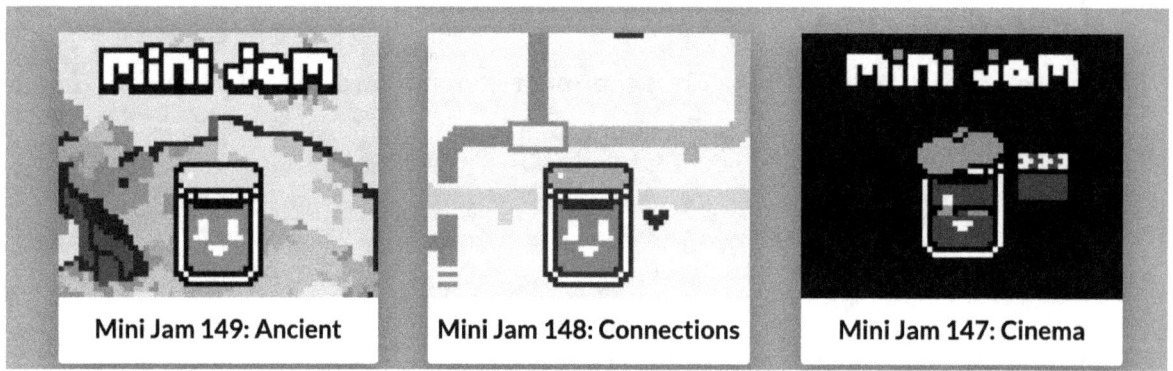

Figure 15.3 Different editions of Minijam.

Minijam is a 72-hour game jam that takes place every two weeks on itch.io. The limitation is announced on Friday and you have to submit your game before Sunday midnight. Apart from the limitation, every Minijam has a theme that you can follow or not because it is just for inspiration.

Minijam is quite popular and it's a perfect jam to build something playable and nice looking. Sometimes the limitations are really hard but it's amazing to see the ideas that people come up with. If you can implement a good idea and you have enough time to polish it, you can get a very nice game. Compared to Trijam, the games are more polished and complete and you can go deeper.

Big Jams

Big jams are longer and they have massive participation. They are normally online and last from one week to one month. Again, you should not aim to win, but to be part of them, to build something and to learn from others.

Here are some of them:

Ludum Dare

https://ludumdare.com/

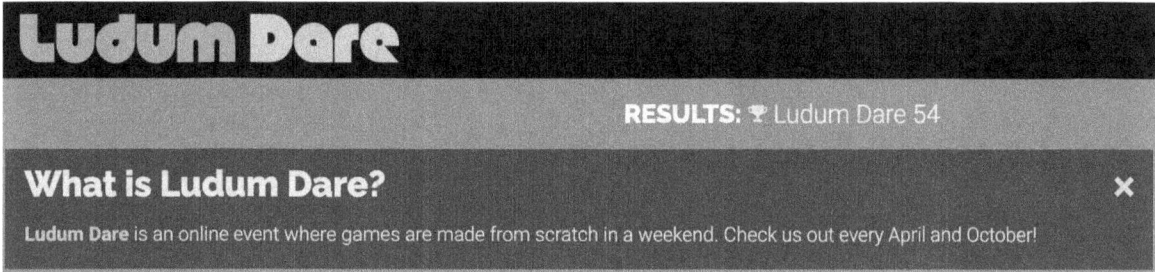

Figure 15.4 Ludum Dare site.

Ludum Dare is one of the oldest and most popular jams. It takes place twice a year: the Compo and the Jam. The Compo is the solo modality and you have to build everything from scratch. The Jam is the team modality and you can use any asset that you want. The theme is announced on Friday and you have to submit your game before Monday midnight.

Ludum Dare is a massive jam with thousands of participants. It's a great chance to build a game and get feedback from other developers. The games are normally quite polished and complete. Some of the games developed for this jam are quite popular and have been published on Steam.

GMTK Jam

https://gmtk.itch.io/

Figure 15.5 GMTK Jam logo.

This is not as old as Ludum Dare but it is one of the biggest on itch.io. It is held once per year and participants must complete a game in 48 hours. The theme is announced on Friday and you have to submit your game before Sunday midnight.

It's organized by the Game Maker's Toolkit YouTube channel and being so popular and massive it's a good chance to get a lot of feedback and learn from others.

Technical jams

Apart from the previous jams, some jams are more focused on the technical side of game development. These jams can be interesting if you want to learn a new framework or tool, or if you want to improve your skills in a specific area.

The best place to find these jams is itch.io: https://itch.io/jams. You can search for jams and filter them by type.

You can also search for jams on other sites like www.gamejolt.com or even on Google.

Frameworks

General Jams are not restrictive about the tools you use. However, some of them are focused on a specific framework or tool. For example, there are jams for Unity, Unreal, Godot, Pico8, and even PyGame.

From Pico8 jams you can learn a lot about pixel art, how to optimize your code and assets and a lot of juicy pixel art tricks. Check them out!

Art jams

There is a whole branch of jams focused on art. In these jams you don't have to build a game but just create art. It can be pixel art, or 3D art, or music, or sound effects, or anything related to art.

Juicy jams

Oh my! Juicy jams are the best! They are focused on the juice of the game. Even if you don't take part in them you should check the entries: it's a great way to learn how to make your games look and feel nice.

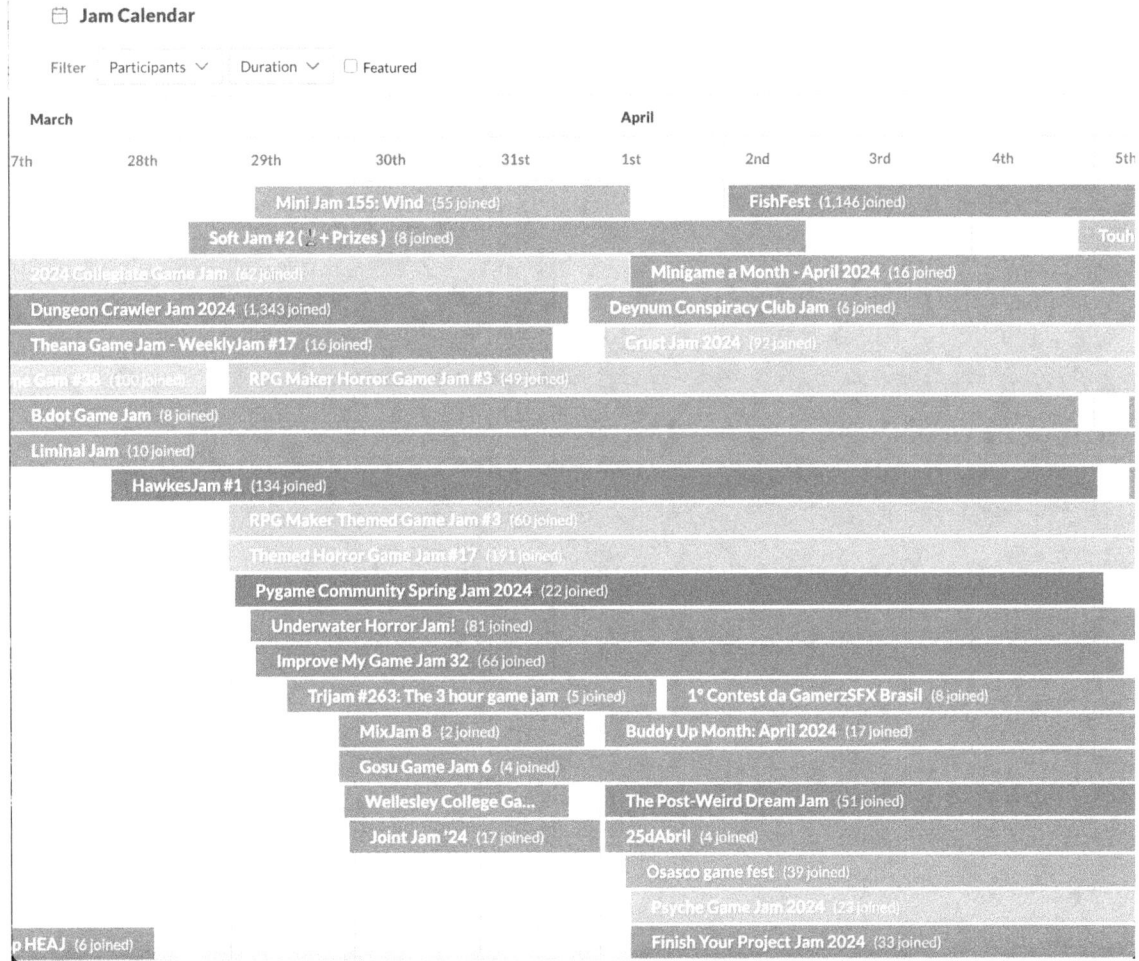

Figure 15.6 View of ongoing jams calendar on itch.io.

Rule of thumb

Probably the most important rule of thumb when you build a game for a Jam is to keep it simple. You have a limited amount of time, so you have to focus on the core of the game and leave the rest aside. Don't try to add too many features, don't try to make it perfect, and don't try to make it too big. Just focus on the core and make it as fun and polished as possible. We'll cover this in more detail in the next chapter.

16. 4:44 Rule

16. 4:44 Rule

This rule is especially good for solo developers, who must try to maximize the effort to create a good game. Many casual and simple games are based on a simple mechanic, so once you have that working it's time to put all your efforts into making it look and feel good. That is what the 4:44 rule is all about.

The name of 4:44 rule comes from the supposition that you have 48 hours to make a game. And 4:44 means 4 hours and 44 hours. So you have 4 hours to make a game and 44 hours to polish it. And that's the rule that you should keep in mind.

How is it applied?

The first 4 hours

Even if you had 48 hours to make a game, if you follow this rule you should be able to make your game in 4 hours! So, how is it possible? Well, the idea is that you should focus on the core of the game and leave the rest aside. You should focus on the core mechanic and make it as fun and polished as possible later. And that's what you should do in the first 4 hours.

At the end of those 4 hours, you need to figure out whether it's good or whether you're happy with it. Ask yourself, is really it a good game? Is it worth spending more time on it? If the answer is no, then you should stop and start a new game.

If the answer is yes, then you should keep going and spend the rest of the time polishing it. How do you really know if what you have is good? Probably if you feel it's good, it's good. But you can also ask other people to play it and see what they think. If they like it, then it's good. If they don't like it, or they don't understand it easily, then it's not good. But you should be able to tell if it's good or not. If you are not sure, probably it's not good enough.

You could also start asking yourself and compare with other ideas: What is the interesting thing? What's the thing that made you continue the game? This is good, is it the movement? Is it the jump? Is the interaction? Is it a new type of mechanic? Is it something you've never seen before?

A good idea and design isn't when you can't add things anymore. A good design is when you can't take anything away anymore without breaking the idea. Also, adding more stuff to a game doesn't make it better. It's the other way around! We'll go deeper into design in the next chapter.

Once you decide to go on, it is important that you just **DON'T ADD** anything new, any feature, any mechanic,... just don't introduce new stuff. Commit to the idea and move forward to the next step.

The next 44 hours

So you already have a good idea in a working game but it doesn't look and feel nice. No worries, because now you have 44 hours ahead of polishing, polishing and re-polishing. And believe me, it feels super good to see a game that you like and that you can polish. It's like a diamond that you can polish and make it shine.

Polishing makes:

- Make it look better.
- Make it sound nice.
- Feel nicer when you play it.

In other words: improve the game feel and MAKE IT JUICY!!

The good news is that you can rely on a multidisciplinary team to help you with the polishing. You can ask for help to a designer, an artist, a musician, a sound designer, etc. And you can also ask for help from other developers. But you should be able to do it yourself. And that's why you should keep it simple. Even if you don't have people helping you, you can probably use all types of assets from the internet.

You should be at a point where adding things to your game is just to make it better, without changing the core. But remember that you should not add new features. You should not add new mechanics, levels, enemies or new weapons. You should not add anything new. You should just add polishing stuff.

There are several elements that you can add to your game to make it more complete as a product:

- A set of characters, a story, a little universe.
- A nice splash.
- Settings or menu screen.

- Scoreboards.
- Tutorial screen.

But never work on them unless you already have a good idea ready. When you are constrained by time, these secondary items should go to a *nice-to-have* list of things.

Figure 16.1 Flappy Birds could be a perfect example of this rule.

Just for jams?

Where do you apply the 4:44 rule? In Game jams obviously. Obviously, it is also a good rule to follow when you are building a game as a solo developer, as you don't have the resources to build a full game. But it's also a good rule to follow when you are building a game with a team. Meaning that a game should have a core mechanic that is fun and that you can build a game around it. And that's what you should focus on.

Think of a classic like SuperMario. The mechanic is that you run and jump. That's it. But with those mechanics, you move forward, you jump over enemies, you jump over holes, you jump over blocks, etc… The rest is a world built around that mechanic. And that's what you should do. Build a game around a core mechanic. Because that is one of the main rules that we will cover next: good level design.

17 Level design

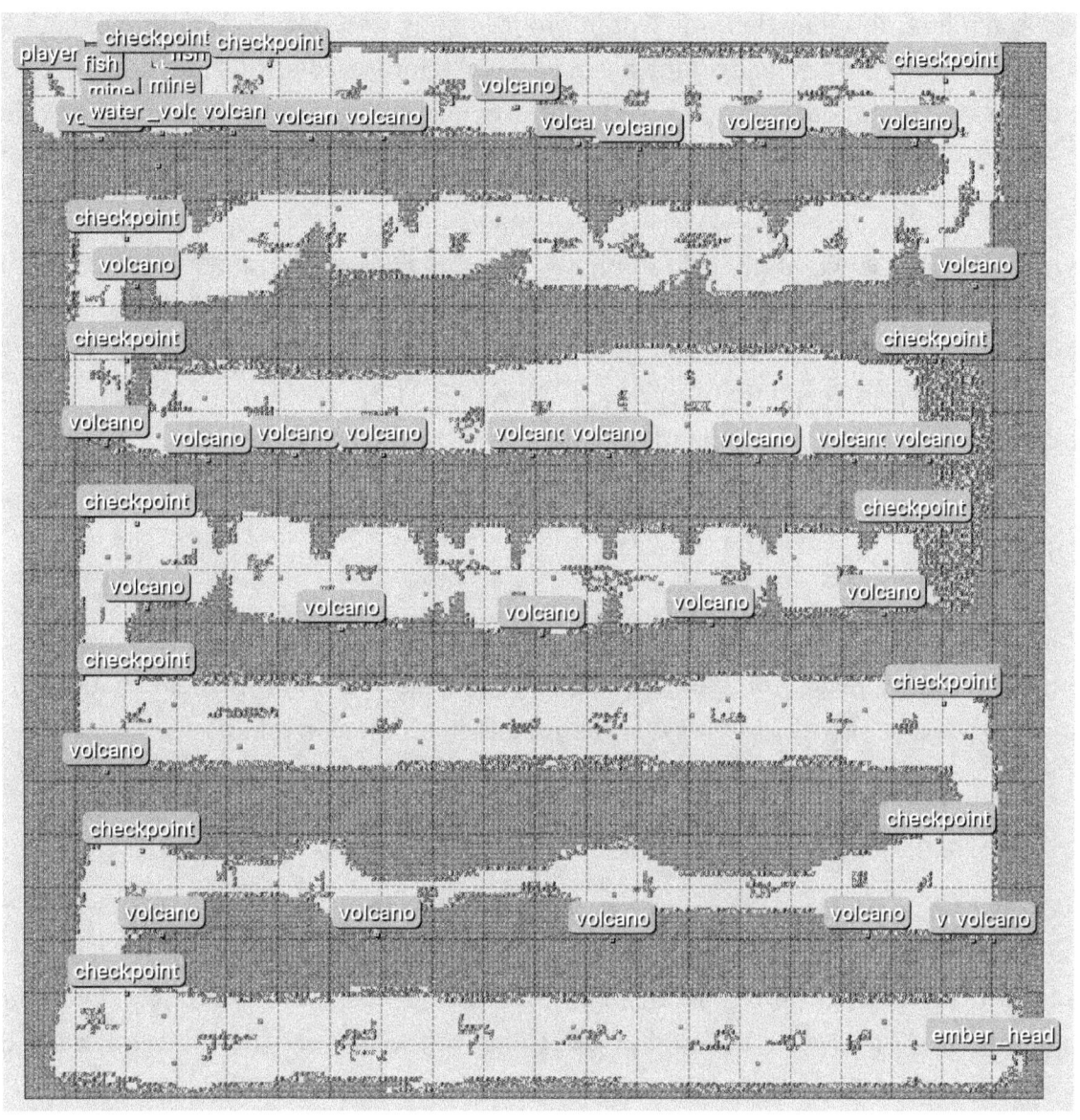

Well, this book just pretends to introduce game development using Phaser, but I would like to add something about design. I don't pretend to say anything revolutionary just some principles that are well-known and you should take into account when you develop a game. You may be proficient in programming and putting together assets and code, but there are other important aspects to take into account. Ok, let's say that you are perfectly able to load a scene with a platform using Phaser and tiled maps. But... can you create a level that is actually right? The next ideas explain what is right and what is not.

Level design is a huge topic and there are many books and resources about it. But it is not easy to just choose one because this is not exactly a science. This humble book is intended to be a mere introduction to a framework and game building in general. So I can't and I won't go deep into level design. However, I'll try to summarize the key points in this chapter that I think you could consider even if you are building your little games.

Some tips

Most of this tips are taken from GDC. I don't like to call them rules, but tips. Most of them are common sense, some of them seem to overlap and some of them should not be applied in specific genres... but it's always good to keep them in mind.

Levels should look good

Without being an expert in art or design, let me say that you should try to make your levels look good. Yeah right, but how? Well, that's not just about the art, it's also about the layout, the colors, the transitions, the effects, the music, the sound, etc. Everything should be in HARMONY and should be appealing to the player. And that's not easy. But you should try to make it look good.

If you suck at art and mixing, just try not to mix styles. Don't put a realistic player in a pixel art world or vice versa. Don't use default fonts. Don't mix colors that don't match. Don't add music that sounds out of place. Don't mix realistic sound effects with chiptune effects.

- Use assets from somebody else and try to get the whole bundle of assets so all elements share the same style.

17 Level design Some tips

- Create or use a color palette. You can try to base it on your assets.

- Use a font that matches the style of the game, there are infinite ones on sites like dafont.com.

- Use music that matches the style of the game. You can find free music on sites like freemusicarchive.org.

- Create or use sounds that match the style of the game. You can find free sounds on sites like freesound.org or create them with generators like sfxr.me.

Pico8 games look great because they are constrained to a limited palette of colors a limited resolution, and sound effects. But they are also great because they are consistent. Everything looks like it belongs to the same world.

Modular levels

Figure 17.1 Groups of tiles to build entire worlds.

This is another basic tip, that should be applied to any game. Building games is a hard task to do. Building levels is even harder. So you should try to make your levels modular. That means that you should be able to reuse elements of the levels in other levels, and also combine them to create new elements in your game. Even the simplest level building tools like tiled allow to reuse of elements. It's part of the tile artists to create a set of assets that can be combined in different ways to create different elements. In platform games, tiles can be like our Lego pieces. Also if we can add some variations to these elements (like color to simulate dark ambiance or underwater stages), the efficiency will be even higher. Variation it's also necessary to avoid repetition and make every new level look different. But not too different, as we need to keep the harmony of

17 Level design — Some tips

the game and the certain familiarity of the player; like blocks that are unbreakable and other elements that are breakable.

You can even make the level reusable by making the player go through it several times (as you would do in a racing game) or making him go back and forth (as you would do in climbing a mountain and going back down).

Fun above all

Wow! Captain Obvious to the rescue! Well, this is what games are all about right? But who decides what is fun? Well this could be a very subjective topic.

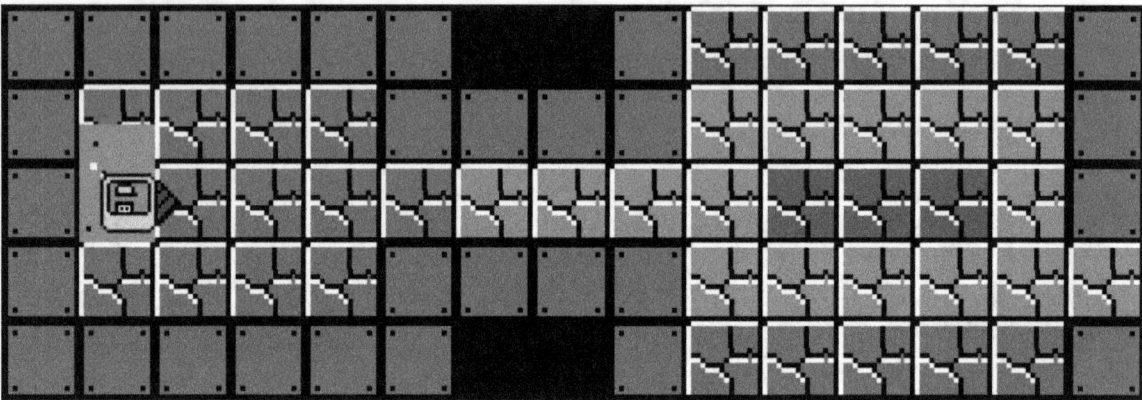

Figure 17.2 Drilling through dungeons can be surprisingly fun: Drill Bill.

There are some things that you can do to make your levels fun, but... there are some pitfalls that you should avoid that anybody could agree on.

The first thing that you should do is to make your levels playable. Unless you want to create an *ultrahard* game for hardcore players, you should make your levels beatable, ideally in different levels. That means that you should be able to complete them. If you can't complete your own levels, then you are doing it wrong. You should be able to complete them without dying, or at least you should be able to complete them. If you can't, then you should make them easier. You can make them harder later, but you should be able to complete them.

You can also let the player learn that by using certain skills he can reach or get special places and rewards. So you don't just create an intuitive level, but also a chance to explore different ways to complete it and try it again to get more rewards. That's good *replayability*!

There is something deeper than simple fun that is harder to get right: **game feel**. As happens with any feeling, it's hard to give a definition, but it could be how good the interactive experience is for the player's senses: audio and visual experience and more specifically control response. This is a topic that anybody interested in being a good game developer should invest some time in. There are specific books about this but you can read a nice introduction to this topic in this document:

https://puccjogos.github.io/balanceamento-2017-1s/materiais/GameFeel_Chap1.pdf

Don't make them too opened

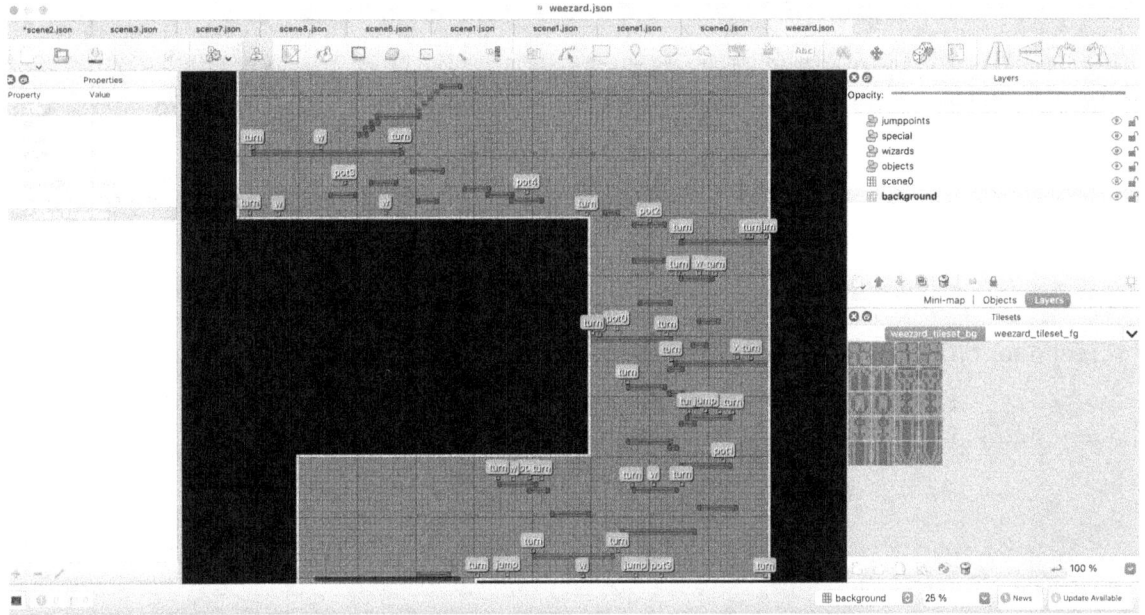

Figure 17.3 This scene has misleading gaps.

This is probably the most common mistake in a level design, especially in platformers. When you show the layout of a level to a player, it should be obvious the way he must follow. If you show a level with many paths, the player will get lost and he will probably get frustrated. If you don't add certain boundaries the player may end up in a place where there's no way out or it's just a dead-end. If you make the player go back and forth too many times, he will get bored. Walking your way back is not fun.

What about open worlds? Well, open worlds are not exactly open. They are just big and they give you the impression that you can go anywhere. But in fact, you can't. You can only go where the designer wants you to go. And that's the key. You should give the player the impression that he can go anywhere, but you should guide him to where you want him to go. Even open worlds have special places that you can only access when you have certain skills or items. And that's the way to go.

Another key point is to make your levels clear. Players should be able to recognize immediately what to do or where to go. Somehow you have to guide the player through the level but keeping the illusion that he is free to go anywhere. For example, you can disable going back. You can disable some paths until some condition is true.

Levels designed for the mechanics

This was the conclusion of 4:44 rule chapter. This should be obvious too, and as crucial as fun. Games, normally, offer the player some mechanics to play with, so your levels should be built in a way that you can apply the mechanics of your game. So if your game is about jumping, you should build levels where you can jump. If your game is about shooting, you should build levels where you can shoot. If your game is about going fast, don't slow the player down.

You can get creative and add levels where the player has to use the same mechanics to achieve a different effect. But your levels have to require the player to use the mechanics of the game. Otherwise, you are not building a game, you are building a movie where the player just walks through and watches.

Show don't tell

One of the first rules in literature is "Show, don't Tell". It means that instead of using words to describe something, you should show it. And that's the same in level design. You should not use words to tell the player what to do, you should show it and make it obvious.

The first place where you should apply this rule is in the tutorial. You should not explain the player what to do, you should show it using a really simple and straightforward level. The player should be able to play the tutorial without reading anything. If the first thing that you do in your game is to show a wall of text, you are, again, doing it wrong.

It's not easy to give instructions without words, but you can use the layout of the level to guide the player. You can use blinking arrows, signs, color patterns, or anything that makes it obvious like carrot and stick motivation: showing prizes or dangers to guide the player.

You can also build the story by just showing elements in the environment in the game. This is also used in movies, where you can show a clock, a sunset, a newspaper or other less obvious clues.

But don't get it wrong. There are genres, games and situations where text is part of the game if needed, like in RPGs, adventure games, or puzzle games. You may use an introduction, as sometimes they do in movies, to set the scene. But even in those cases, you should try to make it as simple as possible.

Tell What but not How

Figure 17.4 The infamous Golden Axe trick.

This is similar to the previous tips or it is a consequence of them. Any game should have an objective. Even a sandbox-like open-world game like Minecraft can be played with a final objective. So players should know what the objective of the stage or level is, but you should never tell them how to do it. On top of that, players should have different choices to complete the level. They should be able to choose different paths, different weapons, different skills, different strategies, etc.

Players can get also creative and use the elements of the game in a way that it was not designed. Instead of punishing the player for "cheating" that should be rewarded. A classic example was in Golden Axe, where you could hit enemies close to the cliffs and they would fall. Maybe that wasn't the way the game was designed, but it was fun to clear the path of annoying thralls.

Your game can also offer secondary missions or objectives that can lead to power-ups or make completion easier. But you should never force the player to complete them. They should be optional. Once again you give some free will in a constrained environment.

Tutorialesque levels

Making levels obvious does not mean that they must remain easy. Levels should be challenging and they should teach the player new skills and strategies. As the player moves forward, he should learn new skills (or use new tools) and use them to complete the level. Educating the user should also be done incrementally, starting with a simple case and then adding complexity.

In other words, you should not have just an obvious tutorial at the beginning. Ideally, all the levels should be tutorials. Learning skills also make games super fun and memorable for the player. It's like learning a new skill in real life. It's fun and rewarding.

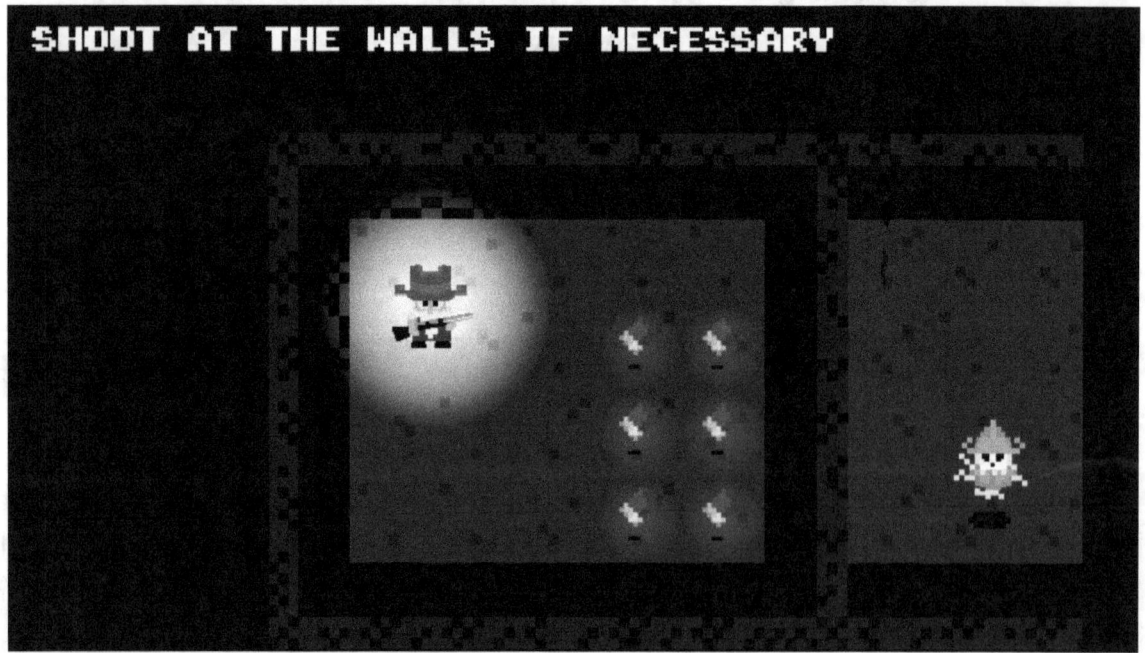

Figure 17.5 Easy stage to learn a new skill.

With this added skills, the player should be able to complete the level, but it should be challenging. If the player can complete the level without any effort, then it's too easy.

17 Level design — Some tips

If the player can't complete the level, then it's too hard. To keep the balance between easy and hard, you have to help the player not just giving extra lives, but providing him with new skills. The player will then feel that he can beat the levels because he is learning new skills, not because the level gave him some magic potion.

If you need to add some text or description for the players, probably you are not doing it right. As early as possible, let somebody try your game or levels and see how it goes. You'll be surprised when you discover that what is obvious for you may be not for others. And those outsiders are your future players!

Let the player dream

Figure 17.6 Games can also let the player be evil too.

This is not just about level design. Why do people play games? Because they want to feel that they can do things that they can't do in real life: kill nazis, kick Vegetta's ass, climb with pickaxes or even find the princess in the last castle. Yeah, there are casual games, but even if a simple resources managing game, an ordinary player can build and rule entire civilizations.

Would you imagine Mario just walking through a green field to a pink castle? That wouldn't be very "super". Instead, he can break bricks and smash the enemies. So let the player be something great and let him do memorable deeds. The player should feel that he is in control of the game. He should feel that he is the one who is making the decisions and that he is the one who is moving forward. Or at least he should feel that his actions have good or bad consequences in the game. Good books let you imagine the most extraordinary stories. Movies let you see extraordinary things. But games, my friend, should let you do extraordinary things. So your levels should be the scenarios where you let the player do those extraordinary things.

Expect the unexpected

This sounds like a total contradiction to previous tips but it's just as necessary as the rest. While you create levels with increasing difficulty and enemies, you may end up repeating the same patterns over and over. And so the player gets bored. You should try to add some unexpected elements to the levels to keep the player engaged: surprise!

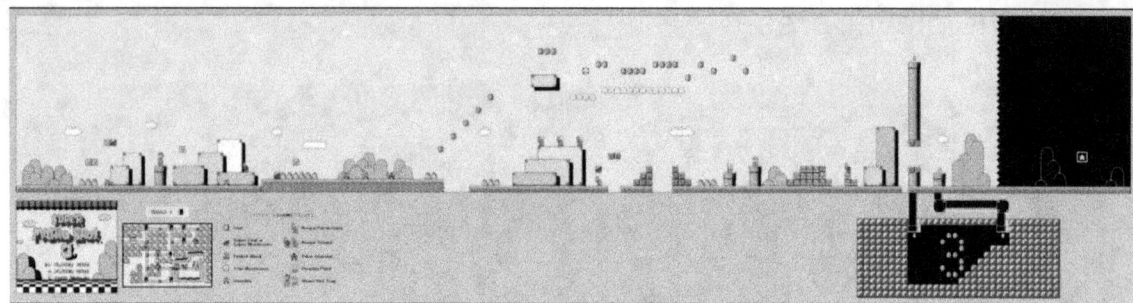

Figure 17.7 This level has some surprises if you fly too high.

The unexpected can come in different forms. It's not just a big enemy that comes from nowhere. You can break a pattern of the game, like falling into a pit and showing an underground level. Going too high and finding a flying level. Going to the past or the future. Changing the gravity. Changing the rules of the game. Changing the perspective. Changing day for night. But not all the time, just once in a while.

Anyway, adding unexpected elements or surprises is a double-edged sword: it can make a detail of the game memorable or it can make the game feel broken. So you should be careful and test it specially.

About difficulty levels

Old games used to have a choice at the beginning of the game where the player was able to choose the difficulty level of it. But ideally, the game should provide different levels of difficulty in a natural way, giving the player the choice to choose the difficulty level of the game. Using a risk reward pattern, players who want to try a hard path will be rewarded (allowing them to complete the game in a harder way) and players who want to try easy paths will be rewarded too (allowing them to complete the game more efficiently).

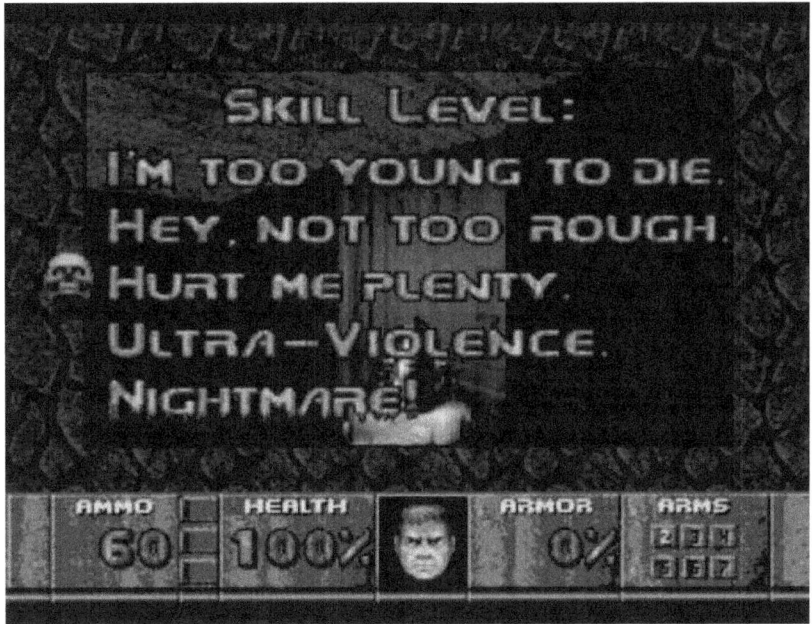

Figure 17.8 Classic difficulty level choice.

Adding these options to the levels, you won't be just making the game accessible to all profiles of players, but also adding *replayability* to the game. Players will be able to play the game again and try different paths.

Create emotions

So games must be fun, but another way to make them memorable is to trigger emotions in the player. And that's not just about fun. You can make the player feel chased, trapped, free, satisfied etc. One of the most common emotions in games is fear and there's a whole bunch of games that are based on fear. But there are many other emotions that you can trigger in the player and they can change through the game.

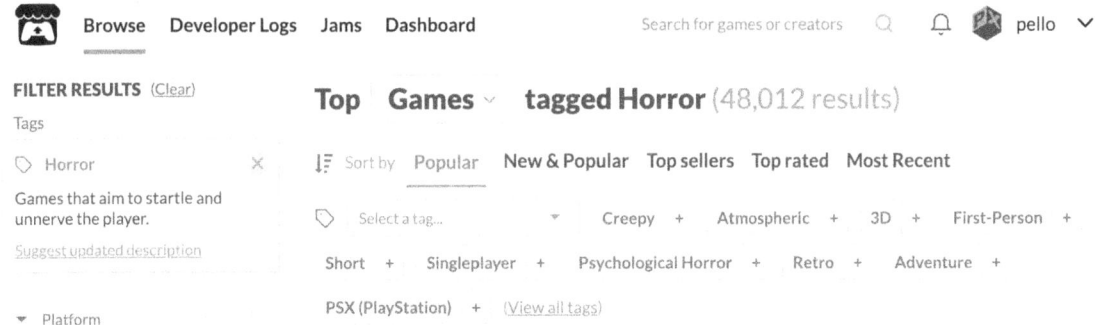

Figure 17.9 Horror is one of the most popular genres on itch.io.

Your level, whether they are two-dimensional platformers or 3D scenarios, can make use of the space to create those emotions. You can make the player go through a pipe

17 Level design — Some tips

system and feel cornered all the time. You can use big scenarios to make the player feel epic situations or freedom. You can use darkness for fear, red light for danger, brightness for safety. Or you can also make him run against the clock, but not with a countdown on screen, but with a scenario that drowns or is falling apart.

Also, if we consider a game a piece of art, then it should be able to create a reaction or an emotion. If you cam make the player feel something, you'll bring the game experience to the next level.

References

Probably one of the best resources to learn level design is this YouTube list by GDC.

https://www.youtube.com/watch?v=iNEe3KhMvXM&list=PLqXVQbXBZAKLJeQvD7MlaW-GHNkitBcGZ

Also it's worth checking out the videos from the Extra Credits channel about level design. It's a great resource to learn about level design and game design in general.

https://www.youtube.com/watch?v=qA6etEmM2o0&list=PLz82K2iAqtV55t0bAFgrgDuqqNixT1p9w

18 Further reading

This book is just a mere introduction to building games using a very specific framework. However, many of the concepts covered throughout the pages like game loop, assets, colliders, physics and maps, are common in game development. So, if you move to another environment you should have all the key concepts clear.

Either way, game development is not just a branch of computer programming. It's a whole industry with many aspects. So there are many things that you (and me too xD) have to learn.

Other environments

Unity

https://unity.com/

A proprietary game development environment that provides everything you need in a single program. One of the most popular environments (for Windows and macOS) for companies and until recently for indie devs too. A great cataclysm came in the summer of 2023 when the company decided to change the license conditions, which resulted on a massive developer migration to other alternatives.

Unreal

https://www.unrealengine.com/

Another engine that became an all-mighty and well-known proprietary environment.

Godot

https://godotengine.org/

An open-source environment for game design. Probably the most important after the proprietary ones. After the changes in Unity policies, many indie developers started the exodus to Godot.

Pico8

https://www.lexaloffle.com/pico-8.php

This is an open-source virtual machine with its own tools for code, pixel edition, music, etc. Pico8, as opposed to other environments, has the rare virtue of adding constraints to what you can do: from size limitations to colors. That forces developers to focus on simplicity and optimize the resources. The programming language is LUA. You can check out infinite Pico8 games in itch.io and if you like pixel art you'll find them gorgeous!

Sites

- https://www.phaser.io Phaser site.
- https://discord.gg/phaser Phaser discord
- https://rexrainbow.github.io/phaser3-rex-notes A great reference
- https://itch.io The place to be for any indie dev.
- https://hacknplan.com/ Task organizer for game devs.

Youtube

- https://www.youtube.com/@Gdconf Game design conference
- https://www.youtube.com/@RichardDavey Rich from Phaser
- https://www.youtube.com/@WClarkson Phaser games
- HTML5 Game Development Mini-Degree
- https://www.youtube.com/c/SebastianLague
- https://www.youtube.com/@GMTK
- https://www.youtube.com/playlist?list=PLhyKYa0YJ_5BkTruCmaBBZ8z6cP9KzPiX Game design